INTERNATIONAL MACRO

INTERNATIONAL MACROECONOMICS

Emmanuel Pikoulakis

with contributions from
Frederick van der Ploeg
and
Ronald MacDonald

First published 1995 by
MACMILLAN PRESS LTD
Houndmills, Basingstoke, Hampshire RG21 2XS
and London
Companies and representatives
throughout the world

ISBN 0–333–59895–4 hardcover
ISBN 0–333–59896–2 paperback

A catalogue record for this book is available
from the British Library.

10   9   8   7   6   5   4   3   2   1
04   03 02 01 00 99 98 97 96 95

Printed in Great Britain by
Mackays of Chatham PLC
Chatham, Kent

To the memory of my parents

Contents

List of Tables and Figures		x
Acknowledgements		xiii

Introduction   **1**

1 Approaches to the Balance of Payments and the Exchange Rate: The Case of Capital Immobility   **5**
1.1 Introduction   5
1.2 The accounting framework of the balance of payments   6
1.3 The elasticities approach to the balance of payments and the exchange rate   9
1.4 The absorption approach to the balance of payments and the exchange rate   13
1.5 The monetary approach to the balance of payments and the exchange rate   24

2 The Asset Approach to the Exchange Rate: Monetary Models of the Exchange Rate   **32**
2.1 Introduction   32
2.2 Monetary models of the exchange rate: the case of flexible prices   33
2.3 Monetary models of the exchange rate: full employment and sticky prices   39
2.4 Monetary models of the exchange rate: demand-determined outputs and sticky prices   49
2.5 Concluding remarks   58

3 The Asset Approach to the Exchange Rate: Portfolio Balance Models of the Exchange Rate and the Current Account   **60**
3.1 Introduction   60
3.2 A mean-variance analysis of portfolio choice   61
3.3 Monetary policy, expectations and the exchange rate   63
3.4 Monetary policy and the degree of asset substitution   71

3.5 The exchange rate, the current account and expectations   73
3.6 Responses of the exchange rate and the current account to sterilised and non-sterilised, unanticipated, open-market operations   76
3.7 Concluding remarks   83

4 Exchange Rates, Expectations and the Current Account   85
4.1 Introduction   85
4.2 A description of the model: setting the agenda   87
4.3 Short-run equilibrium responses under exogenous expectations   89
4.4 Impact, dynamic and steady-state adjustments under static expectations   94
4.5 The nominal exchange rate and the current account under perfect foresight   100
4.6 Concluding remarks   109

5 The Cost of Disinflation in a Floating Exchange Rate Regime   111
5.1 Introduction   111
5.2 The basic Buiter–Miller model   112
5.3 The cost of disinflation when non-sterilised intervention takes place   121
5.4 Conclusion   124

6 The Exchange Rate and the Current Account when Prices Evolve Sluggishly: A Simplification of the Dynamics and a Reconciliation with the Absorption Approach   126
6.1 Introduction   126
6.2 An extended version of a Mundell–Fleming model and the current account   128
6.3 A reconciliation with the absorption approach   135
6.4 A phase diagram analysis of the saddle path: an illustration   138
6.5 Concluding remarks   142

7 Growth and the Balance of Payments under Alternative Exchange Rate Regimes: The Case of a Small Economy   144
7.1 Introduction   144
7.2 A growth model of an open economy with capital immobility and fixed exchange rates   146
7.3 A growth model of an open economy with perfect capital mobility and fixed exchange rates   152
7.4 A growth model of an open economy with perfect capital mobility and flexible exchange rates   156
7.5 Secular and cyclical movements in the balance of payments   158

	7.6 Seigniorage and the foreign exchange regime	158
8	**Economic Stability under Fixed, Flexible and Managed Exchange Rates**	**160**
	8.1 Introduction	160
	8.2 A symmetric two-country model	161
	8.3 The solution of the exchange rate under pure floating	170
	8.4 Solving the model under alternative exchange rate regimes	172
	8.5 Reporting and commenting on results	176
	8.6 Concluding remarks	181
9	**International Interdependence and Macroeconomic Policy Coordination** (*by Frederick van der Ploeg*)	**183**
	9.1 Introduction	183
	9.2 Monetary interdependence under floating exchange rates	187
	9.3 International policy coordination under floating exchange rates	191
	9.4 Managed exchange rates	195
	9.5 Interpretation of results and comparison with monetary union	198
	9.6 Can international policy coordination be counterproductive?	200
	9.7 Rational expectations and wage-price dynamics	205
	9.8 Idiosyncratic supply shocks and the case for monetary union	208
	9.9 Concluding remarks	213
10	**Monetary and Portfolio Balance Models: Which does the Empirical Evidence Support?** (*by Ronald MacDonald*)	**217**
	10.1 Introduction	217
	10.2 Uncovered and risk-adjusted uncovered interest rate parity	219
	10.3 Evidence for a risk premium from the literature on the optimality of the forward rate as a predictor of the future exchange rate	222
	10.4 Reduced-form exchange rate modelling: some in-sample and out-of-sample evidence	228
	10.5 The out-of-sample forecasting performance of asset approach reduced forms	232
	10.6 Explanations for the poor performance of asset approach reduced forms	233
	10.7 Tests of forward looking monetary and portfolio balance models	235
	10.8 Purchasing power parity: a review of the recent evidence	238
	10.9 Concluding remarks	242
Mathematical Appendix		245
Bibliography		254
Index		264

List of Tables and Figures

Tables

8.1 Asymptotic variances under fixed exchange rates 177
8.2 Asymptotic variances under pure float 177–8
8.3 Asymptotic variances under managed floating: insulating aggregate demand from the real exchange rate without requiring a fixed real exchange rate 179–80
8.4 Asymptotic variances under managed floating: the Miller–Williamson proposals of fixing the real exchange rate 181
9.1 Policy responses to a common adverse supply shock under alternative exchange-rate regimes 207
9.2 Effects of an idiosyncratic adverse supply shock under alternative exchange-rate regimes 210
9.3 Policy responses to an idiosyncratic adverse supply shock under alternative exchange-rate regimes 212

Figures

1.1a A stable foreign exchange market 12
1.1b A stable foreign exchange market 12
1.1c An unstable foreign exchange market 12
1.2 Balance of payments adjustments to a devaluation when resources are underemployed: the absorption approach 17
1.3 Adjustments to a devaluation at full employment 18
1.4 Policies for internal and external balance 19
1.5 Internal balance, external balance and the real exchange rate 22
1.6 The path of output, of domestic prices and of the nominal exchange rate 23
1.7 Balance of payments adjustments to a devaluation: the monetary approach 27

2.1a   A permanent and unanticipated increase in m_d 37
2.1b   A permanent and unanticipated increase in $(\pi - \pi^*)$ 38
2.2   Deriving the perfect foresight path   41
2.3   Adjustments in the real exchange rate and in relative liquidity to
       monetary disturbances   45
2.4a   A permanent and unanticipated increase in m_d: adjustments in e
       and in p_d when prices are sticky and when prices are flexible   47
2.4b   An unanticipated increase in $(\pi - \pi^*)$: adjustments in e and in p_d
       when prices are sticky and when prices are flexible   48
2.5   Adjustments to unanticipated monetary disturbances   51
2.6   Adjustments to monetary disturbances: a case of undershooting   53
2.7a   Exchange rate adjustments in a sticky-price, underemployment
       model – a case of overshooting: $k\delta + \psi\gamma - 1 < 0$ 56
2.7b   Exchange rate adjustments in a sticky-price, underemployment
       model – a case of undershooting: $k\delta + \psi\gamma - 1 > 0$ 57
3.1a   Portfolio balance loci in $((r_b)^*, E)$ space   65
3.1b   Portfolio balance responses to a rise in F 66
3.1c   Portfolio balance responses to a rise in M 67
3.1d   Portfolio balance responses to a rise in B: the case where foreign
       and domestic bonds are (relatively) close substitutes   68
3.1e   Portfolio balance responses to an open-market increase in M in
       exchange for B $(dM + dB = 0)$ 69
3.1f   Portfolio balance responses to an open-market increase in F in
       exchange for B $(dB + EdF = 0)$ 70
3.1g   Portfolio balance responses to an increase in the expected rate of
       depreciation of the exchange rate when bonds are 'close' substitutes   72
3.2   Portfolio balance and the exchange rate in a single-bond world   73
3.3   The current account and the exchange rate under rational
       expectations: deriving the saddle path   77
3.4   The current account and the exchange rate under rational
       expectations: responses to an unanticipated open-market purchase of
       domestic bonds for money   80
3.5a   Current account and exchange rate responses (under rational
       expectations) to an unanticipated open-market purchase of domestic
       bonds for foreign bonds: the 'close' substitutes case   82
3.5b   Current account and exchange rate responses (under rational
       expectations) to an unanticipated open-market purchase of domestic
       bonds for foreign bonds: the 'poor' substitutes case   83
4.1   Short-run equilibrium in the markets for goods and assets   91
4.2–6 Impact, dynamic and steady-state adjustments under static
       expectations: the current account and the real exchange rate   95–6
4.7a   The nominal exchange rate and the current account under static
       expectations: adjustments to an open-market operation   98
4.7b   The nominal exchange rate and the current account under static
       expectations: adjustments to an increase in export demand   99

xii   *List of Tables and Figures*

4.8a The nominal exchange rate and the current account under rational
      expectations: deriving the saddle path   102
4.8b The nominal exchange rate and the level of foreign assets:
      steady-state adjustments to open-market operations   105
4.8c The nominal exchange rate and the level of foreign assets:
      steady-state adjustments to an increase in export demand   106
4.8d The nominal exchange rate and the level of foreign assets: impact
      and dynamic adjustments to open-market operations under perfect
      foresight   107
4.8e The nominal exchange rate and the level of foreign assets: impact
      and dynamic adjustments to an increase in export demand under
      perfect foresight   108
5.1   *IS-LM* adjustments in (i,y) space: the stable cases considered   114
5.2   Phase diagrams in (c, ℓ) space   118
5.3   Adjustments in competitiveness and liquidity to an unanticipated
      reduction in μ 119
5.4a The paths of money and prices   121
5.4b The path of output   122
5.5a The paths of money and prices in a model of non-sterilised
      intervention   125
5.5b The path of output in a model of non-sterilised intervention   125
6.1   The joint determination of F and c across steady states: adjustments
      to a reduction in μ when $\lambda\mu > 1$, and to an increase in ϕ 134
6.2   The joint determination of F and c across steady states: adjustments
      to an increase in foreign income when $\sigma/f = v/\delta$ 136
6.3   Adjustments across steady states to a shift in preferences towards
      the foreign good at the expence of the domestic good   137
6.4. The characteristics of the stable path of ℓ, F and c associated with
      an unanticipated pure fiscal expansion   141
6.5a The path of inflation   141
6.5b The path of output   141
6.6a The time path of the real exchange rate   142
6.6b The time path of the real interest rate   142
7.1   Growth, the balance of payments and capital immobility   152
7.2   Growth, the balance of payments and capital mobility   154
9.1   The two-country Mundell–Fleming model   189
9.2   Reaction functions under managed exchange rates   197

Acknowledgements

Emmanuel Pikoulakis wishes to express his gratitude for the invaluable support provided by his publisher, Mr Stephen Rutt, throughout this project, and also to Mr Keith Povey for the high quality and promptness of his editorial services.

The author and publishers are grateful to the following for permission to reproduce extracts from: *Private Behaviour and Government Policy in Interdependent Economics* (1990), by permission of Oxford University Press and the *Greek Economic Review*; *Problems of International Finance* (1984) ed. J. Black and G.S. Dorrance, by permission of Macmillan Publishers; *Exchange Rates and Open Economy Economics* (1989) ed. M. Taylor and Ronald MacDonald, by permission of Blackwell Publishers; Papers from Proceedings volumes by permission of Tagung Geld, Banker and Versicherungen. Every effort has been made to trace all the copyright-holders, but if any have been inadvertently overlooked the publishers will be pleased to make the necessary arrangement at the first opportunity.

Introduction

Since the 1950s we have been witnessing a process of increasing integration in world capital markets and, as a result, capital movements have come to play an increasingly prominent role in balance of payments adjustments. With the advent of flexible exchange rates in the early 1970s, after the collapse of the Bretton Woods system, capital mobility was seen to contribute to enhanced exchange rate volatility and this, in turn, was thought to contribute to the volatility of other macroeconomic variables. The subject of macroeconomic adjustments under flexible exchange rates and capital mobility became a fertile area for theoretical and empirical research and this trend will probably continue in the near future as institutions evolve to deal with issues arising from increasing economic interdependence. Against the background of these developments we have endeavoured to bring together in this book, for the purpose of a systematic and rather in depth treatment, the core elements of the current theory of open economy macroeconomics, not neglecting the major issues confronting policy makers or the empirical evidence, to date, on the major strands of theory. We hope that final year undergraduate students with a good background in macroeconomics and some elementary background in calculus and matrix algebra, and first year postgraduate students attending a course on international macroeconomics will find this book of benefit. It is hoped that practitioners in this field may also benefit from reading this book.

Although the present book is intended as a textbook its contents and its style set it apart from other textbooks where, for instance, growth and the balance of payments are rarely treated. Nor do other textbooks deal with the stochastic properties of exchange rate regimes. As far as style goes, our main preoccupation has been not only to derive and confirm existing results but also, occasionally, to challenge these results. We hope that we have provided the interested reader with an adequate toolkit to pursue further his or her interests in the field of international macroeconomics. What follows gives an outline of the contents of the book.

Chapter 1 is an introductory chapter which deals exclusively with the macroeconomics of open economies without capital mobility. It conveniently introduces the three traditional approaches to the balance of payments and the exchange rate to model the balance of payments and the exchange rate in a world characterised by capital immobility. In our exposition we endeavour to bring out the process of evolution from one approach to another and to offer a synthesis. Most of the balance of payments analysis in this chapter centres around adjustments to a devaluation, a theme so dear to earlier writers. When exchange rates are taken to be flexible and capital is immobile internationally exchange rate adjustments serve to maintain current account balance at all times. This flow theory of the exchange rate is in contrast with asset views of the exchange rate which emerge as soon as capital mobility is introduced. Policy issues are discussed and, in particular, the appropriate mix of policies to achieve internal and external balance is analysed in some detail.

Chapter 2 provides a comprehensive and systematic account of the class of exchange rate models that came to be known as monetary models of the exchange rate. The analysis in this chapter comprises all the varieties of monetary models, namely flexible price models, sticky price models with fixed outputs, and sticky price models with demand-determined outputs. The analysis, cast in a two-country framework for the purpose of injecting more generality into the model, compares and contrasts adjustments to changes in the stock of money with adjustments to changes in the growth rate of money to compare and contrast 'liquidity' with 'inflationary' effects on the exchange rate. In the case where output in each country is taken to be demand-determined the possibility of undershooting is examined and responses of output to undershooting and to overshooting are compared to disprove the mistaken but widely held belief that exchange rate volatility is necessarily associated with and contributes to output volatility.

Chapter 3 provides a comprehensive and systematic account of the class of exchange rate models that came to be known as portfolio balance models of the exchange rate. In this class of models, interest-bearing assets denominated in different currencies are taken to be less than perfect substitutes and, thus, relative returns and the exchange rate are jointly determined by portfolio balance considerations. To bring into sharper focus the features that distinguish portfolio balance models from monetary models we pay considerable attention to the analysis of adjustments to a sterilised intervention; that is, the type of intervention that changes the composition of bonds in portfolios without changing the money supply. At a point in time portfolio balance considerations determine the exchange rate; over time the exchange rate is driven by the evolution of expectations and the current account.

The theme of expectations, the exchange rate and the current account under perfect capital mobility is further pursued and developed in Chapter 4 which extends previous analyses to allow domestic and foreign consumption goods to be imperfect substitutes. This chapter brings into sharper focus the role of expectations by comparing adjustments in the exchange rate and the current account under static expectations with adjustments under perfect foresight. Perfect foresight is shown to play an integrating role: unlike static expectations, where it is possible to insulate the spot exchange rate from some types of shocks, this possibility no longer exists under perfect foresight.

Chapter 5 builds on the class of monetary models with sticky prices and demand-determined outputs developed in Chapter 2 to offer an analysis of macroeconomic adjustments to a policy of disinflation similar to that pursued in the UK in the late 1970s, and early 1980s, and to compare the stabilisation properties of managed floating with pure floating. In this chapter, as in Chapter 2, we show how the essentially static IS–LM apparatus can be suitably adapted to illustrate dynamic adjustments in an open economy under perfect capital mobility, perfect substitutability, perfect foresight and flexible exchange rates.

Chapter 6 extends the analysis of sticky-price monetary models with demand-determined outputs to include the current account and to provide an analysis of macroeconomic adjustments to a pure fiscal expansion. The chapter introduces and develops a technique that allows for a qualitative analysis of the path of adjustment when this path is driven by two predetermined variables – foreign assets and the price level – and a forward-looking variable, the exchange rate. In this case, as we show, one can draw phase diagrams in the two-dimensional space defined by the two predetermined variables to analyse the path of the economy without recourse to simulation exercises.

Growth and the balance of payments under fixed and flexible exchange rates are examined in Chapter 7. In a growing economy it is no longer necessary for each account in the balance of payments to be zero at the steady state. If population is growing, for instance, saving and investment will both be positive at the steady state and, therefore, the current account will not be zero except by chance or by policy design. Whether the capital account registers a secular deficit or surplus depends on whether the domestic economy is a net creditor or a net debtor, which in turn depends on productivity, thrift and the world market rate of return on capital. Observed balance of payments accounts consist of the sum of a cyclical and a secular component and it may be important to distinguish one from another. In any event we can no longer neglect the dynamics of capital accumulation.

In all previous chapters the analysis was carried out in a non-stochastic framework. In a stochastic world, the real world, we employ stochastic measures to evaluate policies. We employ conditional or unconditional variances to compare the relative efficiency of alternative policies. How does the asymptotic variance of output and of prices, for instance, compare between a regime of fixed real exchange rates, similar to the regime proposed by Miller and Williamson, a regime of fixed nominal exchange rates and a regime of purely floating exchange rates? How important are foreign shocks relative to domestic shocks? How do shocks in demand, supply or velocity transmit themselves to output, prices, interest rates and so on? In short, what are the stabilisation properties of exchange rate regimes? These are the main questions that Chapter 8 attempts to answer. Any attempt to rank exchange rate regimes in a welfare sense must first address the questions posed in this chapter. And although, in the final analysis, the answers must come from empirical analysis the empirical analysis must be guided by theory.

In Chapter 9 Rick van der Ploeg examines the issues that arise from international interdependence and considers the merits of macroeconomic policy coordination across various types of exchange rate regimes, focusing particular attention on issues relating to European monetary union. Finally, in Chapter 10, Ronald MacDonald offers an authoritative survey of the empirical evidence on exchange rate determination. This extensive survey pays particular attention to the empirical evidence on the two main classes of exchange rate models, namely monetary models and portfolio balance models.

In this book we have chosen to provide a rather systematic and in depth analysis. The trade-off, unfortunately, is that several topics, especially those which address institutional arrangements, have had to be left out. The considerable amount of mathematical treatment offered is almost always supplemented by detailed diagrammatic illustrations. The mathematical tools necessary for a formal analysis are no more than some elements of calculus and matrix algebra. A refresher mathematical appendix deals, in a few pages, with precisely the main analytic tools needed to appreciate the formal analysis.

I acknowledge, with gratitude, the moral support offered to me by Mr. Stephen Rutt throughout the time it took to write this book.

Finally, I wish to dedicate this book to the memory of my parents.

CHAPTER 1

Approaches to the Balance of Payments and the Exchange Rate: the Case of Capital Immobility

1.1 Introduction

During the last three decades we have seen an increasingly prominent role being assigned to the study of macroeconomic adjustments in open economies. Partly this reflects parallel developments in the field of macroeconomics; new tools developed to deal with macroeconomic adjustments in a closed economy lend themselves naturally to the study of the open economy. More importantly, though, this reflects the fact that economies are becoming increasingly more interdependent. As a result, the need to coordinate economic policy at the international level is increasing and partly as a response to this need new institutional arrangements are evolving. Academics and practitioners alike focus increasing attention on issues relating to the management of open economies. And while more openness to trade has undoubtedly played an important role, it is the increasing mobility of capital internationally that distinguishes the last three decades and that is primarily responsible for macroeconomic interdependence. In this chapter we present a brief review of developments in the theory of the balance of payments and the exchange rate which span the three decades ending with the beginning of the 1960s and which are characterised by a relative immobility of capital internationally. The rest of the book presents developments during the last three decades.

During the period under review the balance of payments was, by and large, identified with the balance of trade in goods and services and it was natural,

5

therefore, for economists working in the early 1930s to seek to apply price theory to explain the aggregate of exports and imports and to view the exchange rate primarily as the relative price of commodities exchanged internationally. Their writings led to the development of what later became known as the 'elasticities approach' to the balance of payments and the exchange rate. The earlier versions of this approach made no attempt to integrate the foreign sector of the economy with the domestic sector. However, with the advent of the development of national accounts, it became natural to view the trade balance as a component of the national accounts and to seek to apply macroeconomic principles, popularised by Keynes's writings, to explain the balance of payments without eschewing earlier developments. National accounting identified the surplus (deficit) in the current account of the balance of payments with the excess (shortfall) of income over absorption, where the term 'absorption' was used to define aggregative spending by residents on currently produced goods and services. Explaining movements in absorption relative to income was seen as the key to explaining movements in the current account of the balance of payments and, not suprisingly, this approach was labelled the 'absorption approach' to the balance of payments (and the exchange rate).

Financial flow accounting identifies the overall balance of payments with the flow changes in the stock of international reserve assets in the custody of the monetary authorities. In the absence of any changes in the stock of domestic assets in the custody of these authorities the overall balance of payments surplus (deficit) becomes exactly identified with the flow accumulation (decumulation) of high-powered money in the portfolios of wealth holders. The balance of payments becomes an integral part of the theory that explains the dynamics of adjustment in the stock of (high-powered) money. This approach of modelling the balance of payments is labelled the 'monetary approach'. In the case where the exchange rate is perfectly flexible and the balance of payments always balances the monetary approach to the exchange rate takes the view that the exchange rate is first and foremost the relative price of monies and applies the tools of monetary theory to model the exchange rate.

A brief review of these three approaches to the balance of payments and the exchange rate for the case where capital is immobile internationally is presented in Sections 1.3, 1.4 and 1.5. In our exposition we endeavour to underline the common elements and to stress the process of evolution that lies behind the development of these approaches. No attempt is made at this stage to extend the methodology adopted by each approach to the case where capital is mobile internationally. In Section 1.2 we present the accounting framework that links the balance of payments with the national accounts and with financial flow accounts.

1.2   The accounting framework of the balance of payments

Notation

GDP = gross domestic product in real terms.
GNP = gross national product in real terms.

Y = gross national disposable income in real terms.
A = gross absorption in real terms.
C = consumption expenditures by private residents in real terms.
I = gross investment expenditures by private residents in real terms.
C_g = consumption expenditures by the domestic government in real terms.
I_g = gross investment expenditures by the domestic government in real terms.
G = $C_g + I_g$.
X = exports of goods and non-factor services in real terms.
M = imports of goods and non-factor services in real terms.
NFI = income accruing to domestically owned factors employed abroad less income accruing to foreign-owned factors employed domestically in real terms.
$NTRA$ = net transfers, including taxes, from (to) abroad in real terms.
T_x = taxes net of transfers paid by residents to the domestic government in real terms.
S = gross private saving in real terms.
S_n = gross national saving in real terms.
I_n = gross national investment in real terms.
E = the price of foreign currency in units of domestic currency identified with the nominal exchange rate.
FA = net foreign assets; asset claims abroad by residents less claims on domestic assets by non-residents measured in foreign currency.
FR = (net) foreign reserves measured in foreign currency and held by the monetary authorities.
H = high-powered money measured in domestic currency.
DA = domestic assets held by the monetary authorities measured in domestic currency.
CU = the surplus in the current account of the balance of payments in real terms.
K = the surplus in the capital account of the balance of payments in real terms.
P = the price of the domestic good in units of domestic currency.
$P*$ = the price of the foreign good in units of foreign currency.
$Y*$ = foreign income in units of the foreign good.

National accounts, financial flows and the balance of payments

In this section we will show how to link components of the balance of payments and the overall balance of payments with the national accounts and with financial flows. To this effect consider, first, the following identities:

$$GDP \equiv C + I + G + X - M \tag{1.1}$$

$$GNP \equiv GDP + NFI \tag{1.2}$$

$$GNP + NTRA \equiv C + I + G + \{(X - M) + NFI + NTRA\} \tag{1.3}$$

$$CU \equiv X - M + NFI + NTRA \tag{1.4}$$

$$A \equiv C + I + G \tag{1.5}$$

$$Y \equiv GNP + NTRA \tag{1.6}$$

$$Y \equiv A + CU = C + I + G + CU \tag{1.7}$$

Equation (1.7) expresses a fundamental relation that states that the surplus (deficit) in the current account of the balance of payments is identical with the excess (shortfall) of gross national disposable income over gross absorption. The same equation gives rise to an alternative fundamental identity which links the current account of the balance of payments with national saving and national investment. To show this we will subtract T_x and C from both sides of (1.7) and write:

$$(Y - T_x) - C = I + (G - T_x) + CU, \text{or} \tag{1.8}$$

$$S = I + (G - T_x) + CU = I + I_g + (C_g - T_x) + CU, \text{or} \tag{1.9}$$

$$S + (T_x - C_g) = I + I_g + CU, \text{or} \tag{1.9*}$$

$$S_n = I_n + CU \tag{1.10}$$

Equation (1.10) identifies the surplus (deficit) in the current account of the balance of payments with the excess (shortfall) of gross national saving over gross national investment. Consider, next, how the same equation gives rise to an alternative specification of the surplus in the current account of the balance of payments which links this account with financial flows. To show this we first link saving with the accumulation of assets which absorb saving and write:

$$S_n = [E\Delta(FA)/P] + I_n \tag{1.11}$$

That is, gross national saving can be used either to accumulate net financial claims abroad $[E\Delta(FA)/P]$ or to accumulate physical capital, gross of depreciation, I_n. Accordingly,

$$CU = [E\Delta(FA)/P] \tag{1.12}$$

That is, a surplus (deficit) in the current account of the balance of payments measures the rate at which residents accumulate (run down) their net claims abroad. Consider, next, that when a nation accumulates net financial claims abroad these claims can be lodged either in private portfolios or in the custody of the monetary authorities which are the sole custodians of international reserves. Hence,

$$[E\Delta(FA)/P] = -K + [E\Delta(FR)/P] \tag{1.13}$$

where K is the net sale of claims abroad by all sectors other than the monetary authorities and has been identified with the surplus in the capital account in real terms. The above expression says that the net accumulation of claims abroad can be used either to build the monetary authorities' reserves or to augment the portfolios of all the other sectors of the domestic economy. Finally, equations (1.12) and (1.13) suggest that the surplus in the current account of the balance of payments plus the surplus in the capital account of the balance of payments equals the surplus in the overall balance of payments:

$$CU + K = [E\Delta(FR)/P] \tag{1.14}$$

To conclude, consider the monetary authorities' balance sheet constraint and notice that an expansion (contraction) of high-powered money derives either from an expansion (contraction) of domestic assets (credit) or from the purchase (sale) of international reserves by the monetary authorities:

$$E\Delta(FR) + \Delta(DA) = \Delta H \tag{1.15}$$

When the authorities do not intervene in the foreign exchange market the exchange rate adjusts, instantly, to clear the foreign exchange market and the overall balance of payments always balances; that is, $\Delta(FR) = 0$, $CU = -K$ and $\Delta H = \Delta(DA)$. Accordingly, when the exchange rate is perfectly flexible and domestic credit is constant, the stock of high powered money is also constant. When the authorities intervene in the foreign exchange market in order to peg the exchange rate, and in the absence of domestic credit expansions or contractions, variations in the stock of foreign reserves are reflected one to one in variations in the stock of high-powered money; that is, $\Delta H = E\Delta(FR)$.

1.3 The elasticities approach to the balance of payments and the exchange rate

The pegged exchange rate case: the Marshall–Lerner–Robinson condition for a successful devaluation

Can a devaluation improve the balance of payments? If so, what are the precise conditions that determine whether such a policy will prove successful? These were some of the fundamental questions that preoccupied some theorists in the 1930s and which led to the development of an approach that came to be known as the elasticities approach to the balance of payments. To set the stage for our discussion of the elasticities approach, we begin by assuming that capital is completely immobile internationally and we further assume, without much loss in generality, that *NFI* and *NTRA* are each equal to zero, so that $X - M = CU = [E\Delta(FR)/P]$.

Let M^* measure imports of goods and non-factor services in units of the foreign good and let EP^*/P measure the price of the foreign good in units of the domestic good. Accordingly, $M \equiv [(EP^*/P)]M^*$ will measure imports in units of the domestic good and $T \equiv X - M$ will measure the trade balance in units of the domestic good. Elementary consumer price theory would suggest that the demand for the domestic good abroad and the demand for the foreign good domestically, to be denoted by X_d and M^*_d respectively, are determined by:

$$X_d = X[(EP^*/P), Y^*], \quad \partial X_d/\partial(EP^*/P) > 0, \quad \partial X_d/\partial Y^* > 0, \qquad (1.16a)$$

$$M^*_d = M^*[(EP^*/P), Y], \quad \partial M^*_d/\partial(EP^*/P) < 0, \quad \partial M^*_d/\partial Y > 0 \qquad (1.16b)$$

To simplify matters further we take X and M^* to be demand-determined and write:

$$X = X_d = X[(EP^*/P), Y^*], \text{ and} \qquad (1.16a^*)$$

$$M^* = M^*_d = M^*[(EP^*/P), Y] \qquad (1.16b^*)$$

Now let $T^* \equiv (PX/E) - P^*M^*$ define the trade balance (which in this model is exactly equal to the overall balance of payments) in units of foreign currency and consider the effect of a devaluation on this balance of payments. That is, consider whether $\partial T^*/\partial E$ is positive, zero or negative. Notice that devaluation is defined as a policy-induced rise in E. That is, we are examining the case where the authorities decide to peg the level of E at a higher value. Differentiating T^* with respect to E we get:

$$\partial T^*/\partial E = -(P/E^2)X + (P/E)(\partial X/\partial E) - P^*(\partial M^*/\partial E) =$$
$$-(P/E^2)X + (P/E)(\partial X_d/\partial E) - P^*(\partial M^*_d/\partial E) \qquad (1.17)$$

To evaluate this expression the use of the chain rule will prove handy.
First: $\partial(X_d)/\partial P = [\partial(X_d)/\partial(EP^*/P)][\partial(EP^*/P)/\partial(P)] = -[\partial(X_d)/\partial(EP^*/P)](EP^*/P^2)$.
Second: $\partial(X_d)/\partial E = [\partial(X_d)/\partial(EP^*/P)][\partial(EP^*/P)/\partial E] = [(\partial X_d)/\partial(EP^*/P)](P^*/P)$.
Hence: $[\partial(X_d)/\partial E](E/X_d) = -[(\partial X_d)/\partial P](P/X_d) \equiv \eta_f$, where η_f is the own price elasticity of export demand and, therefore, $\partial X/\partial E = \partial X_d/\partial E = \eta_f(X_d/E) = \eta_f(X/E)$. In the same fashion one can show that $-[\partial(M^*_d)/\partial P^*](P^*/M^*_d) \equiv \eta_h = -[\partial(M^*_d)/\partial E](E/M^*_d)$, where η_h is the own price elasticity of import demand. Accordingly $-\partial(M^*_d)/\partial E = -\partial(M^*)/\partial E = \eta_h(M^*_d/E) = \eta_h(M^*/E)$. Substituting these results in the expression given by equation (1.17) we get:

$$\partial T^*/\partial E = -(P/E^2)X + (P/E)(\partial X/\partial E) - P^*(\partial M^*/\partial E) =$$
$$-(P/E^2)X + \eta_f(PX/E^2) + (P^*M^*/E)\eta_h \qquad (1.17^*)$$

Next assume that devaluation takes place from a position of equilibrium, that is from a position where $P^*M^* = PX/E$. Using this condition in the expression given immediately above to substitute out P^*M^* we find that a devaluation will improve, leave unchanged, or cause a deterioration in the balance of payments, depending on whether

$$PX/E^2[\eta_f + \eta_h - 1] \gtreqless 0 \tag{1.18}$$

This is the elasticities condition, also known as the Marshall–Lerner–Robinson condition, which asserts that a devaluation will improve, leave unchanged or cause a deterioration in the balance of payments, depending on whether the sum of the own price elasticities of export and import demands exceeds, is equal to or falls short of unity.

Why is the outcome of a devaluation an empirical matter? Well, consider first that a devaluation, other things equal, will raise the volume of X and will reduce the volume of M^*. For a given P^* and P, payments in foreign currency reduce, whereas receipts in domestic currency rise. However, with a higher E, receipts in foreign currency may actually fall. So there is some ambiguity as to the outcome of net receipts in foreign currency. The elasticities formula underlines, precisely, the conditions that need to be met to resolve this ambiguity. The intuition becomes clearer when one notices that the higher η_h and η_f are the higher the volume effects of a devaluation and therefore the higher the likelihood that net receipts in foreign currency rise as a result of a devaluation.

The elasticities condition and the stability in the market for foreign exchange

One often encounters demand and supply curves drawn against a vertical axis measuring the (nominal) price of foreign exchange E and a horizontal axis measuring the quantity of foreign exchange. In terms of this 'foreign exchange market' representation two obvious questions spring to mind. First, how are such demand and supply curves derived and second, what determines whether this market for foreign exchange is stable?

In the absence of any capital flows the demand curve for foreign exchange reflects the transactions demand for foreign currency to make good import payments, whereas the supply curve reflects foreign currency receipts from exports. That is, P^*M^* is the demand for foreign exchange, whereas PX/E is the supply of foreign exchange. While the demand for foreign exchange is unambiguously downward-sloping, the supply curve, for reasons explained above, may be either upward-or downward-sloping. Moreover a downward-sloping supply curve may cut the demand curve either from below or from above. In the former case a rise (fall) in E creates an excess demand (excess supply) and this market is unstable. As it turns out, this market for foreign exchange will be stable if and only if the Marshall-Lerner-Robinson condition for a successful devaluation is satisfied. To see this consider, first, that the slope of the supply curve, drawn against a vertical axis measuring E, is shown to be equal to $1/[(PX/E^2)(\eta_f-1)]$ and that the slope of the demand curve is shown to be equal to $1/[-\eta_h(P^*M^*/E)]$. When the supply curve is upward-sloping the market for foreign exchange is obviously stable and the Marshall–Lerner–Robinson condition is obviously satisfied. When the supply curve is downward-sloping stability can still be satisfied provided that, in the neighbourhood of equilibrium, the supply curve is steeper than the demand curve, that is, provided that $-1/[(PX/E^2)(\eta_f - 1)] > 1/[\eta_h(P^*M^*/E)]$ in the neighbourhood of equilibrium. But this turns out to yield precisely the Marshall–Lerner–Robinson condition for a successfull devaluation! Figures 1.1a–1.1c illustrate.

In these figures, *QFE* stands for the quantity of foreign exchange. Figures 1.1a and 1.1b depict two cases of a stable foreign exchange market; they correspond to the situation where $\eta_h + \eta_f > 1$ in the neighbourhood of equilibrium. In Figure 1.1c we depict an unstable market for foreign exchange; it corresponds to the case where $\eta_h + \eta_f < 1$ in the neighbourhood of equilibrium. Figures 1a and 1b make it clear that, if the authorities were to raise the price of foreign exchange above E_0,

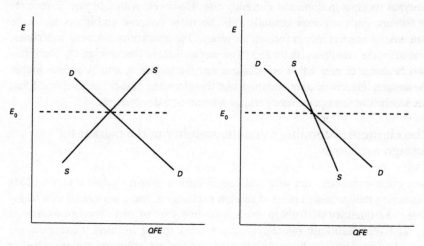

Figure 1.1a   A stable foreign   Figure 1.1b   A stable foreign
        exchange market   exchange market

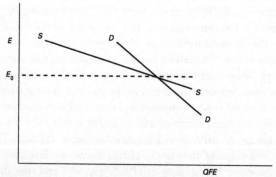

Figure 1.1c   An unstable foreign exchange market

the trade balance would register a surplus. In Figure 1.1c the same policy will induce a trade balance deficit. Notice that one could use these figures to study the response of the trade balance to a variety of disturbances. For instance, a rise in Y^* will cause the supply schedule for foreign exchange to shift to the right and this will induce an improvement in the trade balance at the initial E.

To conclude our exposition of the elasticities approach to the balance of payments we must underline the fact that this approach is essentially static; it has very little to say about the forces at work that eliminate balance of payments disequilibria and whether these forces are *dynamically stable*. All it does is to indicate the initial trade balance response to a change in the exchange rate.

The elasticities approach to the exchange rate

Now suppose that E is market-determined and thus perfectly flexible. In all other respects the model is the same as above except, of course, that H is now policy-controlled. One can no longer ask about the effects of a devaluation. Rather one can ask if a rise in Y^*, for instance, will cause the domestic currency to depreciate (that is, cause a rise in E) or appreciate (that is, cause a fall in E). Now notice that a rise in Y^* will shift the supply of foreign currency to the right. Assuming that the market for foreign exchange is stable, that is assuming that the sum of the own price elasticities of import and export demands exceeds one, there will be an incipient balance of payments surplus which will cause the domestic currency to appreciate. The market for foreign exchange will instantly settle to a new equilibrium at a lower price. The elasticities condition can be used to provide the answer!

1.4   The absorption approach to the balance of payments and the exchange rate

The pegged exchange rate case

The absorption approach to the balance of payments focuses on the current account of the balance of payments and stresses the fact that a surplus (deficit) in this account must reflect either an excess (shortfall) of income over absorption or an excess (shortfall) of saving over investment. Initial developments of this approach were, essentially, exercises in static equilibrium analysis; focus was directed on the short-run relationship between components of the national accounts and the current account of the balance of payments and little attempt was made to pursue the dynamics of asset accumulation. However later developments brought into play the role of the stock of assets in the process of adjustment to a balance of payments equilibrium. To appreciate the relevance of dynamics in the process of adjustment, consider, for instance, balance of payments adjustments in an economy without growth. In such an economy steady-state income is constant and equal to steady-state absorption; at the steady state agents neither save nor dissave and any accumulation of assets ceases. Accordingly at the steady state the current account must balance. Outside the steady state income may exceed (fall short of) absorption or saving may exceed (fall short of) investment and the current account may register a surplus (deficit). To trace the evolution of the current account over time we need to trace the evolution of wealth and its components in the process of adjustment from short-run equilibrium to the steady state. In our rendition of this approach we will attempt to bring into the discussion some elements of dynamic analysis.

To capture the essential features of the absorption approach and in line with the spirit of this chapter we will continue to identify the current account balance with the overall balance of payments and, ignoring transfers, with the trade balance as well. Our analysis will focus around adjustments to a devaluation in a small country. To begin with we assume that resources are less than fully employed and that, as a result, prices are given.

Consider now the following model:

$$A = A(Y, r), \qquad \partial A/\partial Y > 0, \ \partial A/\partial r < 0 \qquad (1.19)$$

$$X = X[(EP^*/P), Y^*] \qquad (1.20)$$

$$M^* = M^*[(EP^*/P), Y] \qquad (1.21)$$

$$T \equiv X - [(EP^*)/P]M^* \qquad \partial T/\partial E > 0, \ -1 < \partial T/\partial Y < 0,$$

$$= T(E, Y; Y^*), \qquad \partial T/\partial Y^* > 0 \qquad (1.22)$$

$$H/P = L(Y, r), \qquad \partial L/\partial Y > 0, \ \partial L/\partial r < 0 \qquad (1.23)$$

Equation (1.19) models absorption as a function of income and of the interest rate. A rise in income is shown to raise absorption but a rise in the interest rate is shown to reduce absorption since investment and, possibly, consumption are inversely related to the interest rate. Equations (1.20), (1.21) and (1.22) model exports, imports and the trade balance, respectively. The model employed to describe equations (1.20)–(1.22) is the exact same model employed to illustrate the workings of the elasticities approach. Assuming that the Marshall–Lerner–Robinson condition for a successful devaluation is satisfied, the trade balance is shown to improve with a depreciation. An increase in foreign income is shown to improve the trade balance since this increase will serve to raise demand for the domestic good abroad. Similarly, an increase in domestic income is shown to deteriorate the trade balance since part of this increase will be used to finance additional imports. Equation (1.23) models money market equilibrium. Money demand is modelled along the lines of an inventory-theoretic approach similar to the Baumol–Tobin model and popularised in macroeconomic textbooks. Other things equal, an increase in domestic income raises the volume of transactions requirements which serves to raise the demand for money whereas, other things equal, an increase in the rate of interest serves to reduce money demand since it raises the opportunity cost of holding money. In what follows it will prove convenient to remodel money market equilibrium as follows:

$$r = r(Y, H/P), \qquad \partial r/\partial Y \equiv (-\partial L/\partial Y)[\partial L/\partial r]^{-1} > 0,$$

$$\partial r/\partial (H/P) \equiv (\partial L/\partial r)^{-1} < 0 \qquad (1.23^*)$$

Equation (1.23^*) models interest rate adjustments required for money market clearing. Other things equal, a rise in income requires an increase in the interest rate to restore portfolio balance at the given money supply whereas, other things equal, an increase in the money supply requires a reduction in the interest rate in order to raise money demand sufficiently and restore portfolio balance at the increased money supply. Assuming that the money market clears at all times we may substitute (1.23^*) into the absorption schedule to arrive at a model of absorption that is adjusted for money market clearing:

$$A = A[Y, r(Y, H/P)] = \tilde{A}(Y, H/P),$$

$$\partial \tilde{A}/\partial Y \equiv \partial A/\partial Y + (\partial A/\partial r)(\partial r/\partial Y)?$$

$$\partial \tilde{A}/(\partial H/P) \equiv (\partial A/\partial r)(\partial r/\partial (H/P)) > 0 \qquad (1.24)$$

In the above $\tilde{A}(Y, H/P)$ is a semi-reduced form expression for absorption that takes account of equilibrium in the money market. The expression $\partial \tilde{A}/\partial Y$ measures the *total* short-run equilibrium effect of a change in income on absorption. This total effect is the sum of the *direct* income effect $\partial A/\partial Y$ identified with the marginal propensity to spend out of income at a given interest rate and the *indirect* income effect $(\partial A/\partial r)(\partial r/\partial Y)$ which measures the reduction in absorption induced by an increase in the interest rate brought about by an increase in the level of income. Evaluating $\partial \tilde{A}/\partial Y$ in the neighbourhood of the steady state to get a better idea about the likely magnitude of this effect we obtain $\partial \tilde{A}/\partial Y = \alpha_Y - (\alpha_r/\mu_r)\mu_Y$, where α_Y is the partial elasticity of absorption with respect to income identified with the direct effect, α_r is the elasticity of absorption with respect to the interest rate and μ_Y and μ_r are the income and the interest elasticity of money demand, respectively. In what follows we will be assuming that $1 - \partial \tilde{A}/\partial Y > 0$; a most plausible and not so restrictive assumption. The expression $\partial \tilde{A}/\partial (H/P)$ reflects the indirect effect of real balances on absorption; an increase in real balances requires a reduction in the interest rate to restore portfolio balance and this, in turn, boosts absorption. Equation (1.25) below expresses short-run equilibrium in the market for the domestic good *and* in the money market.

$$Y = \tilde{A}(Y, H/P) + T(E, Y, Y^*) = \tilde{D}(Y, E, H/P, Y^*),$$

where

$$\partial \tilde{D}/\partial Y \equiv \partial \tilde{A}/\partial Y + \partial T/\partial Y, \quad \partial \tilde{D}/\partial E \equiv \partial T/\partial E,$$

$$\partial \tilde{D}/\partial (H/P) \equiv \partial \tilde{A}/\partial (H/P), \quad \partial \tilde{D}/\partial Y^* \equiv \partial T/\partial Y^* \qquad (1.25)$$

The sign of $\partial \tilde{D}/\partial Y$ is still ambiguous but as long as $1 - \partial \tilde{D}/\partial Y > 0$ (which is obviously satisfied, by assumption) the model will be shown to be stable and the qualitative results of the analysis will not be affected by this ambiguity.

How is the steady-state level of income determined? That is, what is the level of Y at which $Y = A$? To answer this all we have to do is to set $T = 0$ and solve for Y to obtain the steady-state level of income. To this effect set

$$T(E, Y, Y^*) = 0 \tag{1.26}$$

and solve for Y to get:

$$Y = \bar{Y} = \bar{Y}(E, Y^*), \tag{1.27}$$

where

$$\partial \bar{Y}/\partial E = - (\partial T/\partial E)[(\partial T/\partial Y)]^{-1} > 0, \quad \partial \bar{Y}/\partial Y^* = -(\partial T/\partial Y^*)[(\partial T/\partial Y)]^{-1} > 0$$

In the above, $\bar{Y}$ is the reduced-form solution for steady-state output obtained by setting $T = 0$. As equation (1.27) makes clear, steady-state output increases as a result of a devaluation and it also increases with a rise in foreign income.

What about the short-run effect of a devaluation on output? How does it compare with the steady-state effect? To answer this we must turn to equation (1.25). Using this equation to derive the short-run reduced solution for Y, to be expressed by $\tilde{Y}(Y^*, E, H/P)$, we may write:

$$Y = \tilde{Y}(Y^*, E, H/P), \tag{1.28}$$

where

$$\partial \tilde{Y} / \partial Y^* = (\partial \tilde{D} / \partial Y^*) / [1 - (\partial \tilde{D} / \partial Y)] > 0, \partial \tilde{Y} / \partial E = (\partial \tilde{D} / \partial E) / [1 - (\partial \tilde{D} / \partial Y)] > 0,$$

$$\partial \tilde{Y} / \partial (H / P) = \partial \tilde{D} / \partial (H / P) / [1 - (\partial \tilde{D} / \partial Y)] > 0$$

Since $\partial \tilde{Y}/\partial E = [(\partial \tilde{D}/\partial E) / [1 - (\partial \tilde{D}/\partial Y)] = [(\partial T/\partial E) / [1 - \partial \tilde{A} / \partial Y - \partial T/\partial Y] < \partial \bar{Y}/\partial E.$ *the short run increase in output induced by a devaluation is smaller than the long-run increase; in the short run real balances are predetermined and this serves to put upward pressure on the interest rate which dampens the expansionary effect of a devaluation, whereas over time the rise in real balances through the foreign exchanges relieves this pressure.* To appreciate the intrinsic dynamic nature of this approach and its close resemblance to the modern version of the monetary approach we use Figure 1.2 to illustrate balance of payments adjustments to a devaluation.

On the vertical axis of Figure 1.2 we will measure absorption adjusted for money market clearing $\tilde{A}$ and the trade surplus T, whereas on the horizontal axis we will measure income which in this model is identified with GDP. Thus all variables are measured in units of the domestic good. The 45° line is a locus of *potential* steady-state or long-run equilibria points since the condition $\tilde{A} = Y$ must be met on this locus. Taking Y^* to be constant, setting $E = E_1$, for instance, and evaluating $T(E_1, Y, Y^*) = 0$ we solve for the steady-state value of output associated with E_1 and given by, say, $\bar{Y}_1$. Setting $E = E_3 > E_1$, for instance, and evaluating $T(E_3, Y, Y^*) = 0$ we find that the steady-state value of output associated with E_3 is given by, say, $\bar{Y}_3 > \bar{Y}_1$. In particular

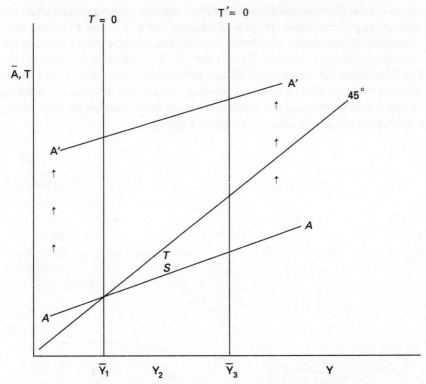

Figure 1.2   Balance of payments adjustments to a devaluation when resources are underemployed: the absorption approach

$$\bar{Y}_3 - \bar{Y}_1 = -(E_3 - E_1)\,(\partial T/\partial E)[(\partial T/\partial Y)]^{-1}$$

The AA and the $A'A'$ loci graph two absorption schedules adjusted for money market equilibrium; they model the relation $A = \tilde{A}(Y, H/P)$. The $A'A'$ locus corresponds to a higher H/P. The $T = 0$ and $T' = 0$ loci help to identify the steady-state value of output associated with a particular exchange rate level.

To begin with let us assume that before devaluation takes place the initial position is at the intersection of the AA locus with the 45° locus and that immediately after a devaluation equal to $(E_3 - E_1)$ takes place output rises to, say, $Y_2 < \bar{Y}_3$ (we will show shortly how to locate the short-run output response precisely). Accordingly, in the short run the trade balance registers a surplus equal to the distance TS defined by the gap between the 45° locus and the AA locus at Y_2. This surplus, in turn, raises H/P through the foreign exchanges and this serves to shift the absorption schedule upwards. This process of adjustment continues until the absorption schedule intersects the 45° locus directly above $\bar{Y}_3$.

Now suppose the economy is fully employed. Can a devaluation succeed in creating a trade surplus? The answer is yes. To illustrate, assume that when resources are fully employed P becomes perfectly flexible. Assume, for instance, that a rise in E by creating an excess demand for the domestic good serves to raise P proportionally so that EP^*/P remains unchanged throughout the adjustment process. However such an induced rise in P serves to reduce H/P. Consequently absorption falls below the full employment output creating the necessary room for a positive T to fill the gap. The inflow of foreign reserves that follows and the monetisation of such an inflow serves to raise H until H/P is restored to its previous equilibrium position. Thus as real balances are building up absorption keeps rising and continues to do so until it reaches the level of full employment output. To illustrate, consider Figure 1.3

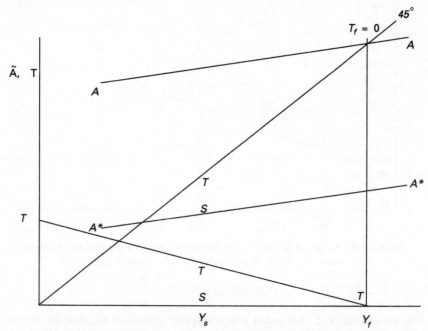

Figure 1.3   Adjustments to a devaluation at full employement

Figure 1.3 is essentially the same as Figure 1.2, except for one important difference. In Figure 1.3 we draw a TT locus which, given EP^*/P and Y^*, measures the trade surplus for any value of Y. This will prove useful in determining the short-run equilibrium without resorting to algebra. Let us start from a position of long-run equilibrium at the full employment level of output Y_f. That is, let us assume that $A = \tilde{A}(Y_f, H/P) = Y_f$ and that $T = T(EP^*/P, Y_f, Y^*) = T_f = 0$. Now consider a rise in E which is followed by an equiproportionate rise in P, leaving the real exchange rate, EP^*/P, unchanged. Accordingly the TT and the $T_f = 0$ loci remain undisturbed. The absorption schedule adjusted for money market clearing, though, shifts down to the position occupied by, say, the A^*A^* locus. As explained above, the downward shift of this locus is due to the 'real balance' effect caused by the rise in P induced by a devaluation taking place at the full employment level. With the help of the TT locus we can ascertain that short-run output is equal to Y_s; at Y_s the surplus recorded by the *TT* schedule at the rate of *TS* matches the excess of income over absorption. Over time, trade balance surpluses help restore H/P to its pre-devaluation level; over time the absorption schedule shifts upwards until it intersects, once more, the 45° locus at Y_f.

Policies for internal and external balance: the absorption approach

We revert to the less than full employment case and we continue with our assumption of complete capital immobilty. Let the objective of policy be to achieve internal and external balance at the full employment level without risking the prospect of accelerating inflation. We will consider three types of policy: an exchange rate policy, a fiscal policy and a monetary policy. By exchange rate policy we mean variations in E to achieve the policy objective. By fiscal policy we mean variations in fiscal parameters (tax rates, subsidies, transfers, government spending on goods and services, and so on) to achieve the policy objective. By monetary policy we mean variations in domestic credit to achieve the same objective. With the help of Figure 1.4 we will illustrate some of the policy issues raised by the model and how to resolve them.

A locus such as *EB EB* can serve to describe the combinations of E and Y required to maintain the trade account constant. Such a locus must slope

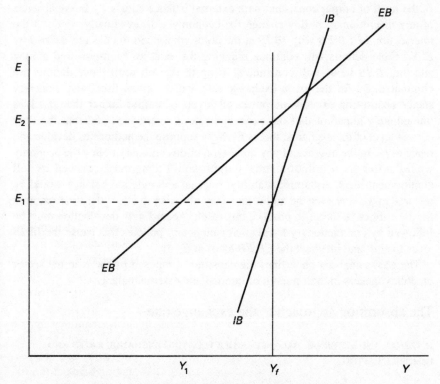

Figure 1.4   Policies for internal and external balance

upwards: higher values of E serve to improve the trade account whereas higher values of Y serve to deteriorate this account, and to keep the trade account constant a depreciation of the exchange rate must be associated with an increase in output. One may label the *EB EB* locus an 'iso-trade account locus'. Conceptually there is a family of such loci. Here we draw the single member of that family defined by $T(E, Y, Y^*) = 0$. Thus the *EB EB* locus depicted is intended to model external balance. The *IB IB* locus is a locus of combinations of E and Y that can serve to describe internal balance. It reflects the condition that the markets for money and goods clear at all times and it is defined by $Y = A + T = \tilde{D}(Y, E, H/P, Y^*)$. Since $1 - \partial\tilde{D}/\partial Y > 0$, a rise in Y creates an excess supply and to wipe out this excess supply we require higher values of E. This explains why this locus is also upward-sloping. At any point in time the economy is on the *IB IB* locus but not necessarily on the *EB EB* locus; under fixed exchange rates the two loci intersect only when absorption equals income. Notice that the *IB IB* locus is steeper than the *EB EB* locus. This is because the excess supply in output generated by a given increase in output exceeds the deterioration in the trade balance and this requires a bigger depreciation to restore internal balance than to restore external balance. Formally $[1 - \partial\tilde{A}/\partial Y - (\partial T/\partial Y)/(\partial T/\partial E) > - (\partial T/\partial Y)/(\partial T/\partial E)$.

Now suppose that the authorities peg E at E_1. Given the fiscal stance of the authorities and given the stock of domestic assets, the economy is shown to achieve internal balance at the full employment level of output, Y_f. However at E_1 the level of output consistent with external balance equals Y_1. In the absence of any discretionary policy change the economy will, eventually, settle at the intersection of *EB EB* with *IB IB* at the point whose coordinates are defined by E_1, Y_1; trade deficits will continue reducing the stock of high-powered money and the *IB IB* locus will continue shifting to the left until these deficits are eliminated. So for the given exchange rate and the given fiscal and monetary stance absorption exceeds output at all levels of output higher than Y_1. It is immediately apparent that the exchange rate is overvalued and that the only correct level of the exchange rate is E_2. Now suppose the authorities devalue and repeg at E_2. In the absence of any other type of discretionary policy the economy would suffer from inflation since output would temporarily exceed its full employment level. Assuming stability, internal and external balance would be restored at Y_f. However the authorities may not wish to allow the time required for the corrective forces to produce this result. Accordingly devaluation must be followed by contractionary fiscal and/or monetary policies that cause the *IB IB* locus to shift and intersect the *EB EB* locus at E_2, Y_f.

The above analysis underlines the constraints imposed by the external sector on policy makers in their pursuit of internal and external balance.

The absorption approach to the exchange rate

INTERNAL AND EXTERNAL BALANCE UNDER FLOATING EXCHANGE RATES AND IMMOBILE CAPITAL

Consider now an economy model which is identical to the model we employed immediately above, with one crucial exception: E is now allowed to vary freely, subject to market forces. With the exchange rate taken to be perfectly flexible the overall balance of payments balances at all times and the stock of high-powered money becomes exogenously determined. Since overall balance of payments equilibrium prevails at all times and since capital is completely immobile the current account must also balance at all times.Can such a model embody any interesting dynamics worth pursuing?

As long as we were dealing with a fixed exchange rate model we could justifiably eschew any price dynamics in order to highlight the dynamics of variations in high-powered money through the foreign exchanges. In the context of a flexible exchange rate model this practice is less justifiable; we are no longer justified in ignoring price changes. Of course we could always take the extreme position that wages and prices in domestic currency adjust infinitely fast to ensure full employment at all times. And while this assumption will be pursued when we come to discuss models with capital mobility, in the present context this is a very unpalatable assumption to make since it would deprive the model of any dynamic considerations. The time has come to consider, at an elementary level, the workings of a Phillips-type relation avoiding, for the moment, any complications arising from the dynamics of expectations. Accordingly we will come to consider the possibility that the domestic price level is falling (rising) as long as current output remains below (above) its full employment level.

To shed some light onto the workings of such a model and to understand the policy issues raised by it, let us employ a very similar diagrammatic apparatus to that employed immediately above. For convenience and for reasons to become clear shortly we let the vertical axis in Figure 1.5 measure the real exchange rate denoted by λ and identified with the relative price of the foreign good EP^*/P so that $\lambda \equiv EP^*/P$. The EB EB and IB IB loci in Figure 1.5 are constructed on the exact same principles as the EB EB and IB IB loci in Figure 1.4. In this model E is purely endogenous (and hence the stock of H is purely exogenous), P^* and Y^* are determined abroad (by the small country assumption) and P will be taken to be short run-predetermined (temporarily fixed) allowing Y to be demand-determined. *The EB EB and IB IB loci will always intersect; at any short run-predetermined P and for any set of parameters and exogenous variables,instantaneous adjustments in E and Y suffice to ensure that the balance of payments always balances. Moreover the long-run (full employment) equilibrium real exchange rate is uniquely defined by the intersection of the EB EB locus with the full employment locus Y_f.*

Let the EB EB and IB IB loci intersect at λ_1, Y_u. Of course, the economy will not be locked into this position indefinitely even in the absence of discretionary policy. A Phillips curve-type relationship along the lines outlined above may come into play to propel the economy towards full employment. However this process of adjustment may take too long for the authorities to contemplate no intervention. In order for the authorities to achieve their objective faster they would have to cause the IB IB locus to intersect the EB EB locus at Y_f. To this effect an expansionary monetary and/or fiscal policy is required. Such a policy will cause absorption to exceed income at the initial exchange rate. Incipient balance of payments deficits will cause a depreciation of the exchange rate and, in turn, this depreciation will serve to elimininate these incipient deficits and to further boost demand to full employment equilibrium attained at λ_2, Y_f.

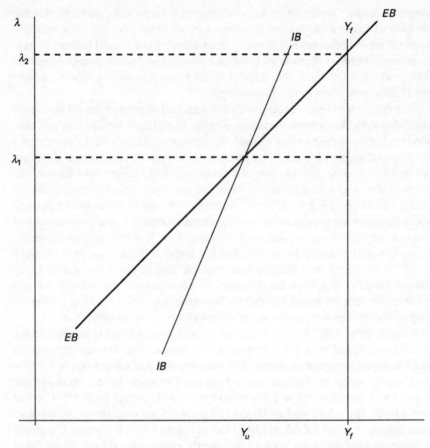

Figure 1.5   *Internal balance, external balance and the real exchange rate*

THE REAL EXCHANGE RATE, THE NOMINAL EXCHANGE RATE AND THE PHILLIPS
CURVE: THE ABSORPTION APPROACH

What if the authorities are happy to let market forces take their course? What
would the economy's path towards full employment look like? In particular,
what is the behaviour of *the real and the nominal* exchange rate along this path?
To start with let us assume, as suggested above, that the price of the domestic
good in domestic currency P is falling (rising) whenever output is below (above)
its full employment level. Starting from a point such as (Y_u, λ_1) we are on a path
along which P is falling and, therefore, H/P is rising. In turn, a rising H/P boosts
absorption and output. Since the current account always balances, a rising output
must be associated with a depreciating real exchange rate in order to eliminate
incipient current account deficits. In terms of Figure 1.5 the *IB IB* locus is
shifting up along a stationary *EB EB* locus. In (Y, λ) space *the adjustment path is
along the EB EB locus. Along this path domestic prices are falling, output is*

rising, the real exchange rate is depreciating and the balance of payments balances.

To ascertain the characteristics of the joint path of the nominal exchange rate E and of the price level P we argue as follows: firstly, since at any point in time $T = T(EP^*/P, Y, Y^*) = 0$ and $Y = \tilde{Y}(EP^*/P, H/P, Y^*)$ it follows that $T = T[EP^*/P, \tilde{Y}(EP^*/P, H/P, Y^*), Y^*] = 0$ can serve to determine the relation between E and P at any point in time, given H, P^*, Y^*. Linearising this expression around the steady state and solving for the joint path of E and P we find:

$$E - \overline{E} = v(P - \overline{P})$$

(1.29)

where $v \equiv (\overline{E}/\overline{P})[1 + [(T_Y/T_\lambda)(\overline{Y}/\overline{\lambda})(\alpha_r/\mu_r)][1 - \tilde{A}_Y]^{-1}], \quad T_Y \equiv \partial T/\partial Y$

$T_\lambda \equiv \partial T/\partial \lambda, 1 - \tilde{A}_Y \equiv (1 - \alpha_Y) + (\alpha_r/\mu_r)\mu_Y$, and where $\overline{E}, \overline{P}, \overline{Y}, \overline{\lambda}$ denote the steady-state values of E, P, Y and λ.

Obviously the sign of v is an empirical matter. Not surprisingly, a falling P and a rising EP^*/P can allow for either a rising E or for an E that falls less than in proportion to the fall in P. There is an intuitive and informative way to illustrate the forces at work that determine the path of the nominal exchange rate. For this purpose consider Figure 1.6.

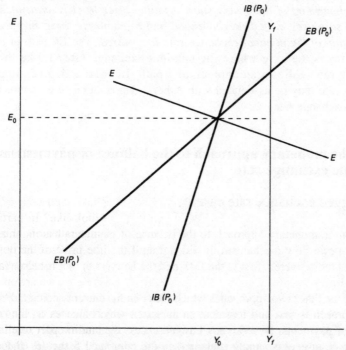

Figure 1.6   The path of output, of domestic prices and of the nominal exchange rate

In Figure 1.6 we revert to the practice of measuring the nominal exchange rate on the vertical axis. However, since prices are changing over time, the position of the *EB EB* and *IB IB* loci in (E, Y) space depends on the level of the short run-predetermined P. Letting $P = P_0$, for instance, serves to determine (Y_0, E_0). At (Y_0, E_0) P is falling since $Y_0 < Y_f$ and the *EB EB* and *IB IB* loci are both shifting to the right. The relative magnitude of these shifts in the horizontal direction will determine whether E is falling or rising along the adjustment path. To ascertain the joint path of (E, Y) we may reason as follows: the price elasticity of output required to maintain equilibrium in the current account of the balance of payments is given by $-(T_N/T_Y)(\bar{\lambda}/\bar{Y})$; this provides a measure of the horizontal shift of the *EB EB* locus due to a change in P. It can also provide a measure of the price elasticity of output in the neighbourhood of the steady state. The price elasticity of output required to maintain equilibrium in the markets for money and goods and in the current account of the balance of payments is given by $(\alpha_r/\mu_r)(1 - \tilde{A}_Y)^{-1}$; this provides a measure of the horizontal shift of the *IB IB* locus due to a change in P. It can also provide a measure of the price elasticity of absorption adjusted for money market clearing in the neighbourhood of the steady state. These observations, together with equation (1.29) and the definition of v lead us to the following conclusion. *If the price elasticity of absorption adjusted for money market clearing is less than the price elasticity of output in the neighbourhood of the steady state, a falling price level is associated with incipient surpluses in that neigbourhood and to eliminate these surpluses an appreciation of the nominal exchange rate is required.* The *EE* path in Figure 1.6 illustrates the case where the nominal exchange rate, unlike the real exchange rate, follows an appreciating path. In short a depreciating real exchange rate may be associated with either a depreciating or an appreciating nominal exchange rate.

1.5   The monetary approach to the balance of payments and the exchange rate

The pegged exchange rate case

Although the monetary approach to the balance of payments has its origins in Hume's specie flow mechanism, it was not until the late 1950s to early 1960s that it was rediscovered, first at the IMF and the University of Chicago and later at the LSE.

Unlike the other two approaches which focus on the current account, the monetary approach is first and foremost an approach which focuses on the overall balance of payments. By Walras's Law an excess demand (supply) for money must reflect an excess supply (demand) in the combined securities and goods markets. In turn, if the combined securities and goods markets register an excess supply then the overall balance of payments must register a surplus and the monetisation of this surplus serves, over time, to eliminate money excess demand. Hence the determinants of the balance of payments surplus (deficit) are the same determinants that define an excess demand (supply) for money; the money market becomes the central focus of attention. And whereas the other two approaches focus, primarily, on flow variables to explain another flow variable – namely the balance of payments – the monetary approach focuses on flow adjustments to the *stock* of money to explain variations in the stock of foreign reserves and the stock of money. However one could argue that the modern version of the monetary approach has evolved from the absorption approach and that it extends the absorption approach in two directions: the first extension embraces the capital account in addition to the current account to 'explain' the overall balance of payments, while the second extension simply formalises the dynamics of adjustment in the money market. In what follows we will eschew the former extension and focus exclusively on the latter.

To illustrate the workings of the monetary approach and to underline the claim that the modern version of this approach evolved from the absorption approach we will maintain the exact same basic model we employed to illustrate the workings of the absorption approach. Our main aim here is to formalise the dynamics of adjustment in the money market in a most simple way. Of course, to ignore the capital account of the balance of payments is to rob the monetary approach of one of its distinctive characteristics. Nevertheless we will maintain the same framework of analysis for all three approaches; once more the balance of payments will be identified with the current account balance.

Consider, once more, the short-run equilibrium (reduced form) solution for output presented in equation (1.28), above, and reproduced, for convenience, here:

$$Y = \tilde{Y}(Y^*, E, H/P) \qquad (1.28)$$

Next consider the short-run equilibrium solution for T, that is, the value of the trade balance consistent with short-run equilibrium in the goods market and in the money market. This is simply the solution for T obtained by substituting $\tilde{Y}(Y^*, E, H/P)$ for Y in the $T(E, Y, Y^*)$ function, as equation (1.30) illustrates:

$$T = T[\tilde{Y}(Y^*, E, H/P), E, Y^*] = \tilde{T}(Y^*, E, H/P), \qquad (1.30)$$
where

$$\partial\tilde{T}/\partial Y^* = (\partial T/\partial Y)(\partial\tilde{Y}/\partial Y^*) + \partial T/\partial Y^* > 0,$$

$$\partial\tilde{T}/\partial E = (\partial T/\partial Y)(\partial\tilde{Y}/\partial E) + (\partial T/\partial E) > 0,$$

$$\partial\tilde{T}/\partial(H/P) = (\partial T/\partial Y)[\partial\tilde{Y}/\partial(H/P)] < 0$$

To interpret the results in (1.30) above, we argue as follows: starting from a position of steady-state equilibrium with underemployed resources, an increase in Y^* and/or an increase in E will deliver, momentarily, a short-run equilibrium at which the current account is in suplus, whereas an increase in H/P will, momentarily, cause the current account to register a deficit. For the moment we will content ourselves with this interpretation; a fuller explanation of these results will be forthcoming shortly.

Next consider that $E(\partial FR/\partial t)(1/P) = \tilde{T}(Y^*, E, H/P)$: In the absence of capital flows, the trade surplus (deficit) that emerges from the short-run equilibrium solution reflects the rate of accumulation (decumulation) of foreign reserves by the monetary authorities. Furthermore, assuming that domestic credit is constant, $E(\partial FR/\partial t)(1/P) = (\partial H/\partial t)(1/P)$ and, as a result:

$$(\partial H/\partial t)(1/P) = \tilde{T}(Y^*, E, H/P) \tag{1.31}$$

In the absence of capital flows and of domestic credit expansion, the trade surplus that emerges from the short-run equilibrium solution measures the rate at which high-powered money accumulates (decumulates). Since Y^* and E are both exogenously determined and since H/P is endogenous one may assume that for a given set of values for Y^* and E there corresponds a unique steady-state value of H/P consistent with neither accumulation nor decumulation of H. Setting $\tilde{T}(Y^*, E, H/P) = 0$ and solving for H/P we obtain the steady-state solution for real high-powered money. To show, explicitly, the dependence of steady-state real high-powered money on the levels of the exogenous variables consider, for instance, setting $Y^* = Y^*_1$, $E = E_1$ and $\tilde{T}(Y^*_1, E_1, H/P) = 0$ to obtain, say, $H/P = m_1$. Setting $E = E_2 > E_1$ and repeating the same procedure we find, say, that $H/P = m_2 > m_1$. That is, steady-state real high-powered money increases as a result of a devaluation. The reasoning for this result runs as follows. When resources are underemployed steady-state domestic output increases with a devaluation and this requires an increase in the stock of real high-powered money to meet the increased transactions requirements at the steady state. The balance of payments surpluses that accompany a devaluation and the monetisation of these surpluses provide the mechanism via which residents acquire the necessary amount of real balances. The reader can easily confirm that an increase in Y^*, like a devaluation, also serves to raise steady-state high-powered money and, thereby, create the necessary balance of payments surpluses to accommodate the increased money demand. There is one more question to be asked about the nature of the steady state and that is a question about stability. If the steady state is displaced, will the forces generated by such a displacement bring the economy back to a position of rest? Fortunately the answer is yes; since $\partial \tilde{T}/\partial (H/P) < 0$ we can rest assured that whenever H/P exceeds (falls short of) its steady-state value balance of payments deficits (surpluses) will bring H/P back to its steady-state value. Figure 1.7 illustrates the dynamics of balance of payments adjustments to a devaluation.

In Figure 1.7 the vertical axis measures the balance of payments in units of the domestic good which, in the absence of domestic credit creation, is identified with the expansion of high-powered money measured in the same units. The horizontal axis measures real high-powered money, H/P. Loci such as the *HH* or

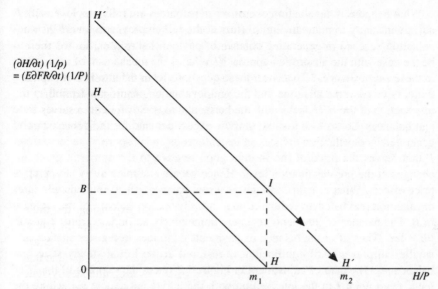

$(\partial H/\partial t)\,(1/p)$
$= (E\partial FR/\partial t)\,(1/P)$

Figure 1.7   Balance of payments adjustments to a devaluation: the monetary approach

the $H'H'$ loci can serve to measure the balance of payments associated with any level of H/P at a given set of exogenous variables; these loci simply graph the relation $T = \tilde{T}(Y^*, E, H/P)$ for a given set of values for Y^* and E. The slope of such loci is equal to $\partial \tilde{T}/\partial\,(H/P) < 0$. Assuming Y^* to be constant throughout our analysis the position of these loci simply depends on the level of the exchange rate. For instance, the position of the HH locus is defined by $E = E_1$ and the position of the $H'H'$ locus is defined by $E = E_2 > E_1$. The intersection of the HH locus with the horizontal axis determines steady-state real balances at, say, m_1. Similarly the intersection of the $H'H'$ locus with the horizontal axis determines steady-state real balances at, say, $m_2 > m_1$. Formally, evaluating $\tilde{T}(Y^*, E_1, H/P) = 0$ we obtain $H/P = m_1$, whereas evaluating $\tilde{T}(Y^*, E_2, H/P) = 0$ we obtain $H/P = m_2$. Suppose that the initial exchange rate is set at E_1 and observe that for values of real balances less (more) than m_1 the economy is running balance of payments surpluses (deficits). Similarly suppose that the exchange rate is pegged at E_2 and observe that for values of real balances less (more) than m_2 the economy is running balance of payments surpluses (deficits).

Suppose now that initial $E = E_1$ and that the economy is at its steady state when the authorities devalue to $E = E_2$. Then it is simple to ascertain that the HH locus will shift up to the position occupied by the $H'H'$ locus. This is because a devaluation, by raising domestic income, raises the steady-state demand for money to a level equal to $m_2 > m_1$ and this in turn generates a series of flow adjustments in the money stock designed to achieve the rise in H/P to m_2. The initial money inflow is equal to OB, equal to the initial balance of payments surplus. Thereafter the path of the economy traces the portion of the $H'H'$ locus from I to H'.

What happens if devaluation occurs when resources are fully employed and P adjusts instantly to maintain equilibrium at the full employment level? Will devaluation succeed in generating balance of payments surpluses, as was seen to be the case with the absorption approach? What is the mechanism of adjustment in these circumstances? To answer these questions let us refer to Figure 1.7 once more. Let us assume this time that the pre-devaluation position is defined by the intersection of the $H'H'$ locus with the horizontal axis. So m_2 defines steady state real balances. Let us also assume that the excess demand for the domestic good generated by devaluation induces an instantaneous and proportionate increase in P that leaves the price of the foreign good relative to the domestic good unchanged at the pre-devaluation level. Hence we are assuming away any relative price effects. What remains, though, is a real balance effect: immediately after devaluation real balances reduce from m_2 to, say, m_1, on account of the increase in P. The balance of payments registers immediately an initial surplus equal to $OB = Im_1$. Thereafter the balance of payments continues to register smaller and smaller surpluses until equilibrium is restored at the initial steady-state real balance m_2. The path of adjustment in Figure 1.7 traces the segment of the $H'H'$ locus from point I to the intersection with the horizontal axis at m_2. Along the adjustment path output is at its full employment level and the relative price of goods is constant. This serves to illustrate that what matters for dynamic stability is the operation of a real balance effect; the elasticities condition serves only to determine the initial balance of payments flow.

Some early attempts at empirical verification of the monetary approach to the balance of payments

Early attempts to verify empirically the monetary approach to the balance of payments focused on the money markets of individual countries and were designed to show that balance of payments surpluses (deficits) reflected excess money demands (supplies) and that these surpluses (deficits) served the purpose of bringing these markets to equilibrium. To appreciate the findings of these early attempts consider a stylised version of the methodology of such research. Using the balance sheet constraint of the monetary authorities and ignoring any complications that might arise from capital gains (losses) due to exchange rate changes we may write:

$$\Delta H/H = \Delta D/H + E\Delta FR/H \tag{1.32}$$

Letting H_d denote the demand for high-powered money we may, for instance, assume the following functional form for H_d:

$$H_d = P(Y)^\alpha (r)^{-\beta}, \alpha > 0, \beta > 0 \tag{1.33}$$

Assuming that the market for high-powered money always clears we can set $H = H_d$. Taking logarithms and diferentiating with respect to time we get:

$$\partial(\log H)/\partial t = \partial(\log P)/\partial t + \alpha \, \partial(\log Y)/\partial t - \beta \partial(\log r)/\partial t \qquad (1.34)$$

By the use of the chain rule we verify that for any variable, say x, $\partial \log x/\partial t = (\partial x/\partial t)\,(1/x)$ which is the proportional rate of change of x per unit time. In discrete time this can be approximated by $\Delta x/x$. Accordingly we can write:

$$\Delta H/H = \Delta P/P + \alpha \, (\Delta Y/Y) - \beta(\Delta r/r) \qquad (1.35)$$

So a researcher interested in estimating the parameters α and β and who is further interested in testing the hypothesis that the elasticity of the demand for nominal high-powered money with respect to the price level equals unity could run a regression equation of the above form. Moreover, if the same researcher wishes to test a most simple version of the monetary approach to the balance of payments, he or she could run the following regression:

$$E\Delta FR/H = \Delta P/P + a(\Delta Y/Y) - b(\Delta r/r) - \Delta D/H \qquad (1.36)$$

and test whether the regression coefficients a and b are significantly different from α and β, respectively, in a statistical sense. In addition he or she would be testing whether the regression coefficients of $\Delta P/P$ and of $-\Delta D/H$ are, statistically, significantly different from unity. If no significant difference is to be found, in a statistical sense, then one would not reject the monetary approach to the balance of payments.

Notice the strong predictions of this approach. For instance, a rise (fall) in income is seen to improve (deteriorate) the balance of payments, unlike what one may be led to predict using competing approaches. Notice also that a rise (fall) in the interest rate is seen to deteriorate (improve) the balance of payments unlike, again, what one may be led to predict using competing approaches. Since a balance of payments surplus (deficit) is seen as a flow adjustment to the stock of high-powered money designed to keep this market in equilibrium, it is easy to understand why an excess demand (supply) for high-powered money gives rise to, and is eliminated through, foreign exchange surpluses (deficits).

A most simple version of the monetary approach to the exchange rate

In its most simple version the monetary approach to the exchange rate focuses exclusive attention on money markets domestically and abroad since in the first instance the exchange rate is thought to be a monetary phenomenon: in the first instance, the exchange rate is taken to be the relative price of monies rather than the relative price of goods.

In its most simple version this approach also relies on the law of one price, otherwise known as purchasing power parity (*PPP*). Purchasing power parity asserts that arbitrage ensures that identical goods produced domestically and abroad must sell at equal prices when prices are expressed in the same currency. For instance, let the jth commodity be produced domestically and abroad and let P_j denote the price of commodity j in domestic currency and P^*_j denote the price of the same commodity in foreign currency. Ignoring transportation costs we may assert that:

$$P_j = EP^*_j \tag{1.37}$$

for all j.

If all commodities were to be produced both domestically and abroad, and if the weight of identical commodities in consumers' baskets were to be the same domestically and abroad then national price indices would be linked with the following condition:

$$P = EP^* \tag{1.38}$$

This is the condition for *PPP* in its absolute version. In this version the condition ignores complications that arise from non-traded commodities. However, if all relative commodity prices were to be constant, including the relative prices of non-traded commodities, then one could still use the relative version of *PPP* given by:

$$\Delta \log P = \Delta \log E + \Delta \log P^* \tag{1.39}$$

Let us now assume that money markets, domestically and abroad, always clear and that equilibrium in these markets can be adequately captured by the following expressions:

$$m = p + ky = \lambda r, \tag{1.40a}$$

$$m^* = p^* + ky^* - \lambda r^* \tag{1.40b}$$

where m,p,y stand for the logarithms of the stock of domestic money, of the domestic price level, and of the domestic output, respectively, and where m^*,p^*,y^* stand for the logarithms of the foreign stock of money, of the foreign price level, and of the foreign output, respectively. Furthermore we will define $e \equiv \log E$ and use the absolute version of *PPP* to write:

$$e = p - p^* = m - m^* - k(y - y^*) + \lambda(r - r^*) \tag{1.41}$$

It must be stated at the outset that equation (1.41) expresses a long-run or steady-state theory of the exchange rate. Only if one were to assume that P and P^* are perfectly flexible and that outputs are determined by the full employment of the given resources could one use (1.41) as a short-run theory of the exchange rate. However, even if we were to take outputs as exogenous, we would still have to explain the interest rate differential $r - r^*$ in order to close the model. Under capital immobility the domestic interest rate is not related to the foreign interest rate and this points to the fact that we would have to explain these two interest rates individually. Setting aside any complications that may arise from considerations about the formation of expectations we could, for instance, hypothesise that r measures the marginal product of capital domestically and that r^* measures the marginal product of capital abroad and take each interest rate to be exogenous by virtue of the assumption that the physical stock of capital domestically and abroad is fixed. At any rate this practice would run against the spirit of the modern version of the monetary approach to the exchange rate which builds on capital mobility and takes the interest rate differential to be endogenously determined. But this is the subject matter of the chapters to follow.

To conclude our discussion let us focus on the theory of the exchange rate embedded in equation (1.41) on the assumption that money differentials, output differentials and interest rate differentials are exogenous. According to this equation a rise in the stock of domestic money relative to foreign money is seen to depreciate the domestic currency, whereas a rise in the domestic output relative to foreign output is seen to appreciate the domestic currency. Also a rise in the domestic interest rate relative to the foreign interest rate serves to depreciate the domestic currency. In short, an excess supply of domestic money relative to foreign money serves to depreciate the price of domestic money relative to the price of foreign money, whereas an excess demand for the domestic money relative to foreign money serves to appreciate its relative price. Notice that the coefficients of $m - m^*$ and of $y - y^*$ have the dimensions of an elasticity whereas the coefficient of $r - r^*$ has the dimensions of a semi-elasticity. Finally the attention of the reader is drawn to the strong predictions of this approach which are at variance with predictions about the behaviour of the exchange rate that stem from approaches which emphasise 'flow' variables and which take the exchange rate to reflect, primarily, the relative price of commodities. Equation (1.41) and several versions of it have been used to test, empirically, the monetary approach to the exchange rate. We will return to this issue in Chapters 2 and 10.

CHAPTER 2

The Asset Approach to the Exchange Rate: Monetary Models of the Exchange Rate

2.1 Introduction

The exchange rate can play a dual role: on the one hand, it can help to determine the relative price of commodities and, on the other, it can help to determine the relative price of assets denominated in different currencies. A general equilibrium theory of the exchange rate would have to bring into the analysis the markets for assets and the markets for goods. In the first instance the asset approach to the exchange rate builds on the assumption that purchasing power parity (PPP) prevails in the long run which, effectively, rules out variations in relative commodity prices across steady states. Thus attention focuses on assets denominated in different currencies to develop a long run equilibrium theory of the relative price of these assets; *in the first instance the long-run equilibrium exchange rate is an asset phenomenon.* If one were to further assume that PPP rules in the short run as well then one would effectively have a single-commodity world and, thus, one could effectively assert that the exchange rate is purely an asset phenomenon.

When interest-bearing assets denominated in domestic and in foreign currency are taken to be perfect substitutes variations in their relative supply cannot help to explain variations in their relative price unless, of course, such variations induce a change in expectations. In effect we have a single-bond world. In that case the asset approach focuses attention on the relative supply and demand of domestic and foreign monies to develop a theory of the exchange rate. This approach of modelling the exchange rate has led to the development of monetary models of the exchange rate.

When interest-bearing assets denominated in domestic and in foreign currency are imperfect substitutes relative supplies and demands in these assets play a crucial role in determining their relative price. This approach of modelling the exchange rate focuses on portfolio balance considerations and has led to the development of portfolio balance models of the exchange rate. The present chapter reviews monetary models of the exchange rate, while Chapter 3 reviews portfolio balance models of the exchange rate. By bringing together in two consecutive chapters the various strands of the asset approach to the exchange rate we hope to accomplish two purposes. Firstly, we hope to present a brief and very selective review of recent developments in exchange rate theory and, secondly, we hope to make the material presented in other chapters easier to follow.

Models of the exchange rate can be single-country models or two-country models. Monetary models of the exchange rate, in particular, extend themselves to two-country models very naturally and easily. In the present chapter we exploit this feature of monetary models and, therefore, we cast our entire analysis around two-country models.

Frankel (1979), in particular, has drawn our attention to the important distinction between 'liquidity' effects and 'inflationary' effects on exchange rates. Broadly speaking, liquidity effects are associated with variations in the stock of monies whereas inflationary effects are associated with variations in the (relative) *growth rate* of monies. To allow for the modelling of both these effects one would have to build into monetary models the possibility of secular rates of growth in monies. The monetary models presented in the present chapter allow for such a possibility. In fact, most of our analysis in the present chapter centres upon a comparison between adjustments to liquidity changes and adjustments to changes in the secular rates of inflation.

The outline of Chapter 2 is as follows: Section 2.2 reviews monetary models with flexible prices. Section 2.3 reviews monetary models with sticky prices and full employment. It is this class of models which is particularly associated with the phenomenon of overshooting. Section 2.4 reviews monetary models with sticky prices and less than full employment outputs. In this class of models 'overshooting' is not a foregone conclusion; rather it is an empirical matter. To assess the likely empirical importance of this issue we simulate initial responses in a model with undershooting and in a model with overshooting under plausible, albeit hypothetical, parameter values. Section 2.5 concludes the chapter.

2.2 Monetary models of the exchange rate: the case of flexible prices

Introduction

As we have explained already, monetary models of the exchange rate develop a theory of the exchange rate under perfect capital mobility and perfect asset substitutability. To define a simple and workable notion of the degree of asset substitutability we will need to define and explain the notion of (international) interest rate parity conditions. In particular the notion of uncovered interest rate parity (UIP) will provide one of the building-blocks to monetary models of the exchange rate. The other building-block we are already familiar with from Chapter 1; this is the notion of purchasing power parity (PPP). In effect PPP assumes a single good traded internationally. To start with we will reproduce the exchange rate model developed and explained in Chapter 1 which is built on PPP. We will then introduce and incorporate UIP to provide a complete asset theory of the exchange rate under perfect capital mobility, perfect asset substitutability, flexible prices, full employment and rational expectations. In Sections 2.3 and 2.4 we will relax the assuption that PPP rules at all times by introducing short-run price stickiness to develop a rational expectations model of the exchange rate with full employment and without full employment to explain exchange rate adjustments when prices are sticky.

Purchasing power parity and the monetary model

We have already explained that under the absolute version of PPP national price levels are linked by:

$$P = EP^* \tag{2.1}$$

where P and P^* denote the domestic and the foreign price levels expressed in domestic and foreign currency, respectively, and where E denotes the price of foreign currency in units of domestic currency. Taking logarithms we write:

$$p = e + p^*, \text{ or } e = p - p^* = p_d \tag{2.2}$$

where
p = the logarithm of P.
p^* = the logarithm of P^*.
e = the logarithm of E.
p_d = the price differential $p - p^*$.

In what follows we will be assuming that money markets domestically and abroad always clear and we write:

$$m = p + ky - \lambda r, \quad m^* = p^* + ky^* - \lambda r^*, \quad k > 0, \lambda > 0 \tag{2.3}$$

where
m, m^* = the logarithm of the stock of the domestic and the foreign money, respectively.
y, y^* = the logarithm of the domestic and the foreign product, respectively.
r, r^* = the domestic and the foreign nominal interest rate, respectively.

Money market equilibria and price flexibility suggest that the price differential is endogenously defined as follows:

$$p_d = m - m^* - k(y - y^*) + \lambda(r - r^*) = m_d - k(y_d) + \lambda(r_d) \tag{2.4}$$

where
$m_d \equiv m - m^*$: the (nominal) money differential.
$y_d \equiv y - y^*$: the output differential.
$r_d \equiv r - r^*$: the nominal interest rate differential.
　　Accordingly the PPP path of the exchange rate is defined as follows:

$$e = p_d = m_d - k(y_d) + \lambda(r_d) \tag{2.5}$$

For the moment we will continue to assume that p and p^* are perfectly flexible and we will take y and y^* to be at their full employment level and, hence, effectively exogenous. There remains to explain how the interest rate differential r_d is determined. For this purpose we will digress to present a brief description of interest rate parity conditions. In particular, UIP will constitute the other major building-block for monetary models.

Uncovered interest rate parity and the monetary model

Let us suppose that in addition to a spot market for foreign exchange there exists a forward market; let F denote the forward price of foreign currency. A resident who invests one unit of domestic currency in interest-bearing assets denominated in foreign currency with one-period maturity will receive $(1/E)(1+r^*)$ in foreign currency at maturity. If this investor wishes cover from exchange risks he or she may convert the proceeds from this investment into domestic currency at the (one-period) forward rate and receive $(F/E)(1+r^*)$. Alternatively the investor may invest in interest-bearing assets denominated in domestic currency with one period maturity and receive $(1+r)$. Arbitrage will ensure that $(1+r) = (1+r^*)(F/E)$ provided that domestic and foreign assets are identical in all respects except, of course, the currency in which they are denominated. This condition is known as covered interest parity (CIP).

　　Now suppose that the investor is risk-neutral: that is he or she is choosing a portfolio that offers the highest expected return regardless of risk. Let us also continue to assume that domestic and foreign interest-bearing assets differ only in terms of the currency they are denominated. In this case arbitrage will ensure that $(1+r) = (1+r^*)(1+\Delta e^{\epsilon})$, where Δe^{ϵ} is the expected rate of depreciation of the exchange rate conditional on an information set available at t. This condition is known as uncovered interest parity (UIP). Noting that $\log(1+r) \simeq r$ and that $\log[(1+r^*)(1+\Delta e^{\epsilon})] \simeq r^* + \Delta e^{\epsilon}$, for sufficiently small r, r^* and Δe^{ϵ}, we can approximate the two interest rate parity conditions as follows:

$$r = r^* + f - e \qquad \text{CIP (covered interest parity)} \tag{2.6}$$

$$r = r^* + \Delta e^{\epsilon} \qquad \text{UIP (uncovered interest parity)} \tag{2.7}$$

where
$f \equiv \log F$, $e \equiv \log E$, $\Delta e^\epsilon \equiv {}_t E(e_{t+1}) - e_t$,
${}_t E \equiv$ the expectations operator conditional on an information set that includes all variables observable at time t.

From the standpoint of a domestic investor the return on foreign currency-denominated assets is uncertain. In particular capital gains or losses on foreign currency denominated assets are uncertain since they reflect variations in the exchange rate which are random. An investor with an uncovered position expects, with uncertainty, a return on foreign currency denominated assets equal to $(r^* + \Delta e^\epsilon)$. However our investor can insure against the uncertainty attached to capital gains (losses) by taking a covered position which will yield a certain return on foreign currency-denominated assets equal to $(r^* + f - e)$. Such an investor is prepared to pay an insurance premium equal to $(r^* + \Delta e^\epsilon) - (r^* + f - e)$. Since this insurance premium is a premium to cover risk, economists call it a risk premium. Hence the risk premium, to be denoted by rp, is defined by:

$$rp = \Delta e^\epsilon - (f - e) = {}_t E(e_{t+1}) - f \tag{2.8}$$

Clearly, for risk neutral investors $r_p = 0$. In what follows in this chapter we will be assuming risk neutrality so that $rp = 0$ and so that

$$r_d = \Delta e^\epsilon = (f - e) \quad \text{and} \tag{2.9}$$

$$_t E(e_{t+1}) = f \tag{2.10}$$

Using UIP to substitute out r_d in equation (2.5) we have:

$$e = p_d = m_d - k(y_d) + \lambda(\Delta e^\epsilon) \tag{2.5*}$$

The task now is to solve for the rational expectations path of Δe^ϵ under flexible prices. This is the subject matter of the next sub-section.

Rational expectations and flexible prices

To inject some generality into the model consider that m grows at the constant rate π and that m^* grows at the constant rate π^*. One may also wish to consider the possibility of purely white noise random shocks causing monetary growth rates and full employment levels to deviate from their constant mean paths. Under rational expectations the solution to Δe^ϵ is $\pi - \pi^*$. To see this define, for simplicity, $d_t \equiv e_{t+1} - e_t$, and note that (2.5*) can lead to :

$$d_t = \pi - \pi^* + \lambda[{}_{t+1}E(d_{t+1}) - {}_t E(d_t)] + v, \quad v \text{ (white noise)} \tag{2.11}$$

Applying the expectations operator $_tE$ on both sides and rearranging we get:

$$_tE(d_t) = (\pi - \pi^*)/(1 + \lambda) + [(\lambda)/(1 + \lambda)]_t E(d_{t+1}), \tag{2.12}$$

which, upon forward substitution, yields $_tE(d_t) = \pi - \pi^*$. Hence,

$$e = p_d = m_d - k(y_d) + \lambda(\pi - \pi^*) \tag{2.5**}$$

Equation (2.5**) provides a complete theory of the exchange rate on the assumption that outputs are defined by full employment, that prices are perfectly flexible, that UIP and PPP rule at all times and that expectations are rational. Apart from white noise shocks, when prices are perfectly flexible the current path of the economy coincides with the steady-state path; ignoring white noise shocks we have $e = \bar{e}$, $p_d = \bar{p}_d$ and $r_d = \bar{r}_d = \pi - \pi^*$, where a bar over a variable is used to denote its steady-state value. We wish to underline the fact that in this model the interest rate differential reflects purely the growth differential in monies. Along its path the nominal exchange rate is depreciating at the rate $\pi - \pi^*$. To complete our analysis of the monetary model with flexible prices we will illustrate adjustments to a once-and-for-all unanticipated increase in m_d and in $(\pi - \pi^*)$.

Adjustments to monetary disturbances

Figure 2.1a illustrates adjustments to a once-and-for-all, permanent and unanticipated increase in the domestic money relative to foreign money m_d.

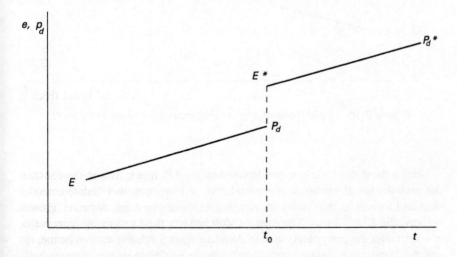

Figure 2.1a   A permanent and unanticipated Increase in m_d

Figure 2.1a graphs the time paths of e and of p_d. Along the EP_d locus $e = p_d = \bar{e} = \bar{p}_d$. The slope of the EP_d locus is equal to $\pi - \pi^*$ which, without loss in generality, is assumed to be positive. Let the authorities announce and implement a permanent increase in the *level* of m_d at time t_0. At t_0 both e and p_d 'jump' onto their new path depicted by the the $E^*P^*_d$ locus whose slope is also equal to $\pi - \pi^*$. Thus a once-and-for-all unanticipated increase in the level of domestic money relative to foreign money induces an instantaneous and equiproportionate increase in p_d to bring money markets back to equilibrium and it induces an equiproportionate depreciation of the exchange rate to preserve PPP.

Figure 2.1b illustrates a once-and-for-all, permanent and previously unanticipated increase in the relative monetary growth rate $(\pi - \pi^*)$.

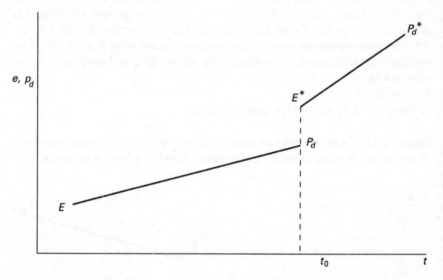

Figure 2.1b   A permanent and unanticipated increase in $(\pi - \pi^*)$

Until t_0 the path of e and p_d are depicted by the EP_d locus. At t_0 the increase in the growth rate of domestic money relative to foreign money induces both a shift and a pivot to this locus; for $t \geq t_0$ the new path for e and for p_d is defined by, say, the $E^*P^*_d$ locus. The upward shift reflects the fact that an increase in $\pi - \pi^*$ raises the opportunity cost of domestic money relative to foreign money and this requires an instant increase in p_d and in e to bring money markets back to equilibrium and to preserve PPP. The steeper slope reflects the fact that along the new path p_d and e rise at a higher rate to accommodate the higher growth rate in domestic money relative to foreign money.

2.3 Monetary models of the exchange rate: full employment and sticky prices

The model

We will continue to assume that the domestic and the foreign money grow exponentially at the rate π and π^*, respectively and that the domestic and the foreign output are constant at full employment (for simplicity we will ignore random shocks in the paths of monies and outputs). We will continue also to assume that PPP rules in the long run. However, in the short run prices may be allowed to deviate from their trend path. *When prices are sticky in the short run the exchange rate e may deviate from the price differential p_d in the short run; the exchange rate may deviate from PPP outside states.* Bearing in mind these remarks we go back to equation (2.4) and rewrite it as follows:

$$r_d = [m_d - k(y_d) - p_d](-\lambda)^{-1} \tag{2.13}$$

The short-run predetermined (sticky) price differential p_d (together with m_d and y_d) serves to determine the current interest rate differential r_d. Taking deviations from the steady state and introducing the concept of relative liquidity ℓ_d defined by $\ell_d \equiv (m_d - p_d)$ we write:

$$[r_d - \bar{r}_d] = [r_d - (\pi - \pi^*)] = -(\ell_d - \bar{\ell}_d)(1/\lambda) = [p_d - \bar{p}_d](1/\lambda) \tag{2.14}$$

In the short-run the path of relative liquidity ℓ_d may deviate from its long-run path $\bar{\ell}_d$ because the path of the short-run sticky price differential p_d may deviate from its long-run path $\bar{p}_d$; hence the current interest rate differential may deviate from its long-run value defined by the growth rate in relative money supplies $\pi - \pi^*$. In the short-run the gap of the current nominal interest rate differential from its steady state is proportional to the gap between the current and the steady-state price differential. Whenever p_d exceeds (falls short of) $\bar{p}_d$ liquidity effects dictate that the current interest rate differential exceeds (falls short of) the steady-state interest rate differential. *Given the secular growth rates of monies, variations of the nominal interest rate differential from the steady-state inflation differential reflect liquidity effects.*

In the absence of stochastic shocks the dynamics of monetary models are usually cast in terms of differential rather than difference equations; we will follow this practice. In this respect note that according to UIP the perfect foresight path of the expected rate of depreciation of the exchange rate is defined by $r_d = De$, where D is the differential operator so that, for instance, $De \equiv \partial e/\partial t$. Notice also that the perfect foresight path of the expected rate of depreciation of the exchange rate along the steady-state path is defined by $\pi - \pi^* = D\bar{e} = D(\bar{p}_d)$. Making these substitutions in equation (2.14) above we will write:

$$D(e - \bar{e}) = (p_d - \bar{p}_d)(1/\lambda) \tag{2.15}$$

Equation (2.15), which applies UIP and perfect foresight to money markets, provides one of the two equations of motion under sticky prices; it states that the deviation of the current rate of depreciation of the exchange rate from its trend rate is proportional to the gap between the current and the steady-state path of the price differential. As we have seen, liquidity considerations dictate that whenever the current price differential p_d exceeds (falls short of) its steady-state value $\bar{p}_d$ the current interest rate differential r_d exceeds (falls short of) its steady-state value $\bar{r}_d$, as well. In turn the UIP condition dictates that an interest rate differential that exceeds (falls short of) its trend is associated with a perfect foresight path along which the current rate of depreciation of the exchange rate De exceeds (falls short of) its trend rate $D\bar{e}$.

The other crucial dynamic relationship will determine the rate of change of the price differential $D(p_d)$. One may reasonably postulate that a rise in the demand for the domestic good relative to the foreign good, given relative supplies, raises $D(p_d)$. Other things equal, a rise in the real interest rate differential $r_d - D(p_d)$ reduces the demand for the domestic good relative to the foreign good whereas a rise in the gap between the current exchange rate e and the current price differential p_d, $(e - p_d)$, by raising the price of the foreign good relative to the domestic good, raises the demand for the domestic good relative to the foreign good. Hence we may take $D(p_d)$ to be a decreasing function of $r_d - D(p_d)$ and an increasing function of $(e - p_d)$ and we may write:

$$D(p_d) = \xi_1(e - p_d) - \xi_2[r_d - D(p_d)] = \xi_1(e - p_d) - \xi_2(r_d) + \xi_2 D(p_d) \qquad (2.16)$$

or

$$(1 - \xi_2)D(p_d) = \xi_1(e - p_d) - \xi_2(r_d) = \xi_1(e - p_d) - \xi_2(De), \quad \xi_1 > 0, \xi_2 > 0 \qquad (2.16')$$

Notice that (2.16′) makes use of UIP (to substitute out r_d) and of perfect foresight. To preclude indeterminancy we will have to exclude the possibility that $(1 - \xi_2) = 0$ and, as we will argue shortly, to preclude instability we must rule out the possibility that $(1 - \xi_2) < 0$; hence, the existence of a uniquely stable saddle path will be predicated on the assumption that $(1 - \xi_2) > 0$. But this is a most reasonable assumption to make because it simply requires that the inflation differential rises whenever the real exchange rate depreciates and it falls whenever the nominal interest rate differential rises. Taking deviations from the steady state we may write:

$$D(p_d - \bar{p}_d) = \varphi(e - \bar{e}) - \varphi(p_d - \bar{p}_d) - vD(e - \bar{e}),$$
$$\varphi \equiv \xi_1/(1 - \xi_2), v \equiv \xi_2/(1 - \xi_2) \qquad (2.16^*)$$

Putting (2.15) and (2.16*) in matrix form we now have:

$$\begin{bmatrix} 1 & v \\ 0 & 1 \end{bmatrix}\begin{bmatrix} D(p_d - \bar{p}_d) \\ D(e - \bar{e}) \end{bmatrix} = \begin{bmatrix} -\varphi & \varphi \\ 1/\lambda & 0 \end{bmatrix}\begin{bmatrix} (p_d - \bar{p}_d) \\ (e - \bar{e}) \end{bmatrix}$$

(2.17)

whose solution is given by:

$$\begin{bmatrix} D(p_d - \bar{p}_d) \\ D(e - \bar{e}) \end{bmatrix} = \begin{bmatrix} -[\varphi + v/\lambda] & \varphi \\ 1/\lambda & 0 \end{bmatrix}\begin{bmatrix} p_d - \bar{p}_d \\ e - \bar{e} \end{bmatrix}$$

(2.17′)

As we will confirm shortly, the determinant of the coefficient matrix in (2.17′) equals the product of the two roots that govern the path of the solution. On the assumption that $(1 - \xi_2) > 0$, this determinant is negative and we can immediately see that one root is stable and the other unstable. But this is just as well because in the case of global stability an infinite number of initial conditions for the 'jump' variable e would satisfy stability; in short the path of the exchange rate would not be uniquely defined. Needless to say that global instability is also undesirable and for obvious reasons. Figure 2.2 illustrates how the perfect foresight path may be located and what are its characteristics.

The horizontal axis of Figure 2.2 measures the deviation of the exchange rate from its trend $(e - \bar{e})$ and the vertical axis measures the deviation of the price

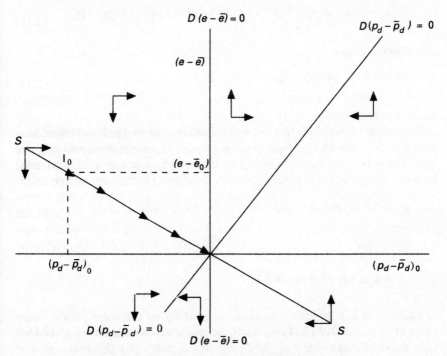

Figure 2.2 *Deriving the perfect foresight path*

differential from its trend $(p_d - \bar{p}_d)$. Along the $D(p_d - \bar{p}_d) = 0$ locus the current inflation differential equals the relative growth rate of monies defined by $D(m - m^*) = \pi - \pi^*$. Other things equal, a rise in $(p_d - \bar{p}_d)$ creates a relative excess supply of the domestic good because it raises its relative price and because it raises the nominal interest rate differential whereas, other things equal, a rise in $(e - \bar{e})$ creates a relative excess demand because it reduces the relative price of the domestic good. A higher price differential must be associated, therefore, with a higher nominal exchange rate to preserve equality between the current and the steady-state inflation differential; this explains why the $D(p_d - \bar{p}_d) = 0$ locus is upward-sloping. Above (below) this locus there is a relative excess demand (supply) for the domestic good and the price differential is rising at a rate above (below) its trend rate. Along the $D(e - \bar{e}) = 0$ locus the current rate of depreciation of the exchange rate equals its trend rate and the current nomimal interest rate differential equals its trend rate as well. To the right (left) of this locus the current level of relative liquidity is below (above) its steady state and, therefore, the current interest rate differential exceeds (falls short of) the steady-state interest rate differential and the exchange rate depreciates at a rate above (below) its trend rate. The arrows in Figure 2.2 suggest that the only stable path is the *SS* path which is identified with the perfect foresight path otherwise known as the saddle path. To derive formally the slope of the saddle path consider, first, that the stable path is driven by one stable root – call it ρ. Hence,

$$D(p_d - \bar{p}_d) = \rho(p_d - \bar{p}_d), \quad D(e - \bar{e}) = \rho(e - \bar{e}) = (1/\lambda)(p_d - \bar{p}_d) \quad (2.18)$$

and hence we have:

$$(e - \bar{e}) = (1/\rho\lambda)(p_d - \bar{p}_d) \quad (2.19)$$

along the saddle path.

To evaluate, analytically, the slope of the saddle path we need to evaluate, analytically, the stable root ρ. Since $D(p_d - \bar{p}_d) = \rho(p_d - \bar{p}_d)$ along the saddle path and since $D(p_d - \bar{p}_d) = -[\varphi + (\upsilon/\lambda)](p_d - \bar{p}_d) + \varphi(e - \bar{e})$ by equation (2.17'), we must have $(e - \bar{e}) = [\rho + \varphi + (\upsilon/\lambda)](1/\varphi)(p_d - \bar{p}_d)$. Combining with (2.19) we get:

$$(e - \bar{e}) = (1/\rho\lambda)(p_d - \bar{p}_d) = [\varphi + (\upsilon/\lambda) + \rho](1/\varphi)(p_d - \bar{p}_d) \quad (2.20)$$

and, hence:

$$\rho^2 + \rho[\varphi + (\upsilon/\lambda)] - \varphi/\lambda = 0 \quad (2.21)$$

In equation (2.21) we have a quadratic in ρ which we can solve for the stable value of ρ. Notice that (2.21) is simply the characteristic equation in ρ obtained from the coefficient matrix of (2.17') and this explains why the determinant of this coefficient matrix can be taken to measure the product of the roots of the solution to the differential equations described by (2.17').

Adjustments to monetary disturbances: liquidity effects and inflationary effects

Let us assume that the economy is on its steady-state path when at time t_0 the authorities announce and implement an increase in the *level* of domestic money which raises m_d. For $t \geqslant t_0$, $(p_d - \bar{p}_d) < 0$, where $(p_d - \bar{p}_d)$ can serve to denote the gap between the path of the current price differential and the *new and higher* steady-state path of this differential. In Figure 2.2 the economy is instantaneously placed at a point such as I_0 on the saddle path; the nominal exchange rate instantly 'overshoots' its *new and higher* steady-state path and the real exchange rate $(e - p_d)$ depreciates instantly above its zero PPP trend. To understand this instant adjustment notice, first, that the rise in liquidity above its trend reduces the interest rate differential below its trend and, as a result, incipient capital outflows induce a 'jump' depreciation that places the nominal exchange rate above its *new and higher* path. *At $t = t_0$ there emerges an incipient capital outflow that raises the price of foreign currency denominated assets to the point where $r_d = (r_d)_0 = (De)_0 < (D\bar{e})_0 = \pi - \pi^*$; the nominal exchange rate must instantly overshoot its new and higher steady-state path to induce a rate of appreciation relative to trend sufficient to preserve UIP and eliminate incipient capital outflows.* Having explained the initial (instant) adjustment of the nominal and the real exchange rate let us also explain the nature of the initial (instant) adjustment of other variables. The first obvious point to make is that at I_0 we have a real exchange rate $(e - p_d)$ which is above its zero long-run PPP trend and a nominal interest rate differential which is below its trend and these facts combined suffice to explain the inflationary pressures exerted on the economy which induce a current inflation differential in excess of its trend rate; at the initial point of adjustment the real interest rate differential $r_d - D(p_d)$ is negative and the real exchange rate is appreciating, that is $D(e - p_d) < 0$. Along the stable adjustment path the price differential is rising at a rate above its trend rate and, therefore, relative liquidity is falling monotonically to its initial steady state; steady-state relative liquidity is invariant to once-and-for-all changes in the level of monies. In turn, as relative liquidity is falling to its steady state the nominal interest rate differential is rising to its steady state, and the rate of depreciation of the nominal exchange rate is approaching its trend rate. Also along the stable path the real exchange rate is appreciating towards its zero trend and the real interest rate differential is rising to zero. In short, this confirms and explains why the *SS* locus can serve to illustrate the stable path and that the adjustment path is from point I_0 to the point of origin.

Let us now conduct a different experiment. Consider an economy on its steady-state path when at time t_0 the domestic authorities announce and implement a previously unanticipated increase in the growth rate of domestic money (relative to foreign money). As we have seen, this causes an upward shift in the time path of $\bar{p}_d$ $(= \bar{e})$ and it also causes this path to be steeper. At t_0, and until steady-state equilibrium is re-established, we have $p_d < \bar{p}_d$. For the sake of illustration we may assume that the economy is instantly placed at I_0, in Figure

2.2 above, thereafter tracing the saddle path to the new steady state. Both types of policy change examined hitherto would seem to induce similar qualitative adjustments: (1) in both cases the nominal and the real exchange rate overshoot their respective steady-state paths, (2) in both cases there is an instant depreciation of the nominal and the real exchange rate relative to their respective steady state paths, (3) in both cases the current nominal interest rate differential falls short of its steady-state value initially, (4) in both cases the real interest rate differential is negative initially, and (5) in both cases relative liquidity is falling along the saddle path since along this path the current inflation differential exceeds its trend rate. There are three crucial differences, though, which cannot be readily established from Figure 2.2. Firstly, a previously unanticipated increase in the growth rate of domestic money relative to foreign money serves to raise the steady-state nominal interest rate differential $\bar{r}_d$; across steady states the nominal interest rate differential rises by the full amount of the increase in the secular inflation differential $D\bar{p}_d$. Secondly, and as a result, a previously unanticipated increase in the core rate of growth of domestic money relative to foreign money reduces domestic liquidity relative to foreign liquidity across steady states. Thirdly, since outputs are fixed and monies cannot jump, a previously unanticipated increase in the core rate of growth of domestic money relative to foreign money leaves the initial nominal interest rate differential unaffected.

The comments in the paragraph above indicate that Figure 2.2 has its limitations: it cannot adequately distinguish and contrast liquidity effects from secular inflationary effects. For this purpose we use Figure 2.3 to illustrate and explain, again, adjustments to the same two policy changes examined above.

The horizontal axis in Figure 2.3 measures relative liquidity $\ell_d \equiv m_d - p_d$ and the vertical axis measures the real exchange rate $(e - p_d)$. The assumption of long-run PPP means that the steady-state real exchange rate $(\bar{e} - \bar{p}_d)$ is zero. Let (initial) steady-state relative liquidity be defined by $(\ell_d)^*$ and consider a previously unanticipated increase in the level of domestic money occurring at t_0 that raises m_d. Since prices are short-run sticky relative liquidity instantly rises above steady-state liquidity to, say, $(\ell_d)_0$. As a result of the increase in the current level of relative liquidity the current nominal interest rate differential must instantly fall to restore (relative) money market equilibria. *At t_0 there emerges an incipient capital outflow that raises the price of foreign currency-denominated assets to the point where $r_d = (r_d)_0 = (De)_0 < (D\bar{e})_0$; the nominal exchange rate must instantly overshoot its new and higher steady-state path to induce a rate of appreciation relative to its trend rate sufficient to preserve UIP.* A once-and-for-all permanent and unanticipated increase in the level of relative nominal money induces an instant depreciation of the real exchange rate when prices are short-run sticky. In Figure 2.3 point I_0 can serve to define the instantaneous adjustment in the real exchange rate and in relative liquidity.

At I_0 there is a state of excess demand in the goods market which translates into a current rate of the inflation differential in excess of its trend rate; at t_0, $D(p_d - \bar{p}_d)_0 > 0$. Along the stable adjustment path the current price differential p_d must be approaching its steady-state path $\bar{p}_d$ from below and the current nominal

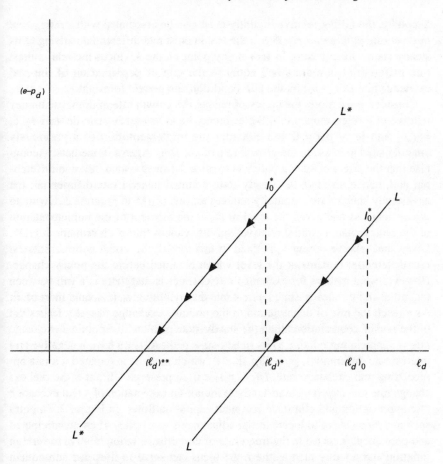

Figure 2.3 *Adjustments in the real exchange rate and in relative liquidity to monetary disturbances*

exchange rate e must be approaching its steady-state path defined by $\bar{e} = \bar{p}_d$ from above; along the stable path the real exchange rate is appreciating to restore PPP. It is also clear that along the stable path relative liquidity is falling since the current rate of inflation differentials exceeds the trend rate; relative liquidity must fall back to its initial steady-state since steady-state liquidity is invariant to a once-and-for-all change in the level of nominal monies. A locus such as the LL locus in Figure 2.3 can serve to illustrate short-run, dynamic and steady-state adjustments in relative liquidity and in the real exchange rate induced by an unanticipated increase in the stock of domestic money relative to foreign money.

Having established that the LL locus can serve as the locus of adjustments in liquidity and in the real exchange we can extract more information from such a locus. Firstly, the falling relative liquidity ℓ_d must be associated with a rising nominal interest rate differential r_d to maintain continuous market clearing.

Secondly, the falling relative liquidity must also be associated with a *rising real interest rate differential* $r_d - D(p_d)$; the real interest rate differential is rising to its steady-state value of zero. In fact at any point on the *LL* locus the real interest rate differential is maintained equal to the rate of depreciation of the real exchange rate $D(e - p_d)$ by the UIP condition and perfect foresight.

Consider, once more, the policy of raising the growth rate of domestic money relative to foreign money. Let the economy be at its steady state defined by $\ell_d = (\ell_d)^*$ and $(e - p_d) = 0$ and consider the implementation of a previously unanticipated increase in the growth rate of m_d, Dm_d. Agents immediately recognise that the effect of such a policy is to raise the steady-state inflation differential and, hence, to raise the steady state nominal interest rate differential; the new steady-state relative liquidity reduces to, say, $(\ell_d)^{**}$ in Figure 2.3. Owing to price stickiness and given the level of m_d at the moment of the implementation of the policy change, initial relative liquidity cannot 'jump'; it remains at $(\ell_d)^*$. Given that relative output y_d is fixed in this model, the initial nominal interest rate differential remains at the level which obtained before the policy change. However what matters for exchange rate changes is that there is a gap between the initial and the steady-state interest rate differential; at t_0, $(r_d)_0$ falls short of $\bar{r}_d$. As a result the rate of depreciation of the nominal exchange rate at t_0 falls short of the rate of depreciation along the steady-state path and the nominal exchange rate is appreciating relative to its steady-state path. At t_0 we have a negative real interest rate differential, $[r_d - D(p_d)]_0 < 0$, which must be associated with an appreciating real exchange rate, $D(e - p_d)_0 < 0$, to preserve UIP; at t_0 the real exchange rate must depreciate instantly to induce an expectation of a real exchange rate appreciation and eliminate incipient capital outflows. In Figure 2.3 a point such as I_0^* can serve to locate initial adjustments to a policy of an unanticipated and permanent increase in the trend rate of domestic inflation relative to foreign inflation and a locus such as the L^*L^* locus can serve to illustrate subsequent adjustments. Along the adjustment path relative liquidity is falling and, therefore, the nominal interest rate differential is rising to maintain money markets in equilibrium, the negative real interest rate differential is rising to zero and the real exchange rate is approaching its PPP value.

To conclude our analysis of the present model we will illustrate the time paths of the nominal exchange rate and of the price differential associated with an unanticipated increase in m_d, first, and with an unanticipated increase in $D(m_d)$, second, and compare with the corresponding time paths in a flexible price model. In Figure 2.4a, let the EP_d locus describe the path of the price differential and of the nominal exchange rate before the authorities announce and implement an increase in the stock of domestic money relative to foreign money. Let the authorities announce and implement such an increase at t_0. Had prices been flexible the exchange rate and the price differential would jump, immediately, onto the path described by the $E^*P^*_d$ locus. Instead, owing to price stickiness, the exchange rate jumps to e_0 and follows the path along the e_0e locus. The path of the price differential is described by the P_dP_d locus.

Qualitatively very similar adjustments occur when the policy change involves an increase in $D(m_d)$. Figure 2.4b illustrates.

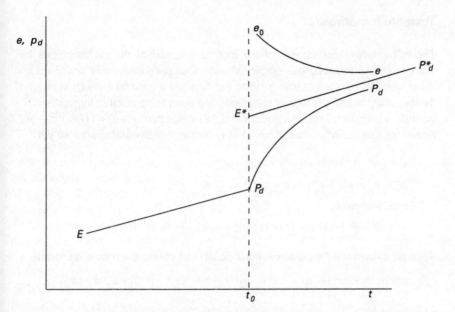

Figure 2.4a   A permanent and unanticipated increase in m_d: adjustments in e and in p_d when prices are sticky and when prices are flexible

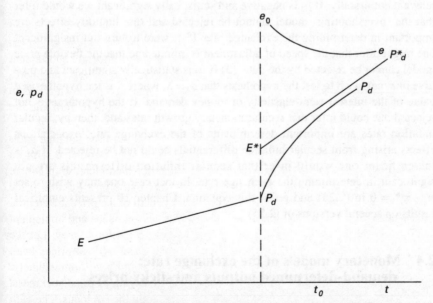

Figure 2.4b   An unanticipated increase in $(\pi - \pi^*)$: adjustments in e and in p_d when prices are sticky and when prices are flexible

Testable hypotheses

The full employment version of the monetary model of the exchange rate has been subjected to numerous empirical tests. Our purpose here is not to review the empirical literature; rather it is to put forward a general enough version of the monetary model capable of encompassing competing testable hypotheses. To this effect consider, first, that equation (2.19) states that $(e - \bar{e}) = (1/\rho\lambda)(p_d - \bar{p}_d)$. Assuming that m, m^*, y and y^* are always on their steady-state paths we get:

$$\bar{e} = (m - m^*) - k(y - y^*) + \lambda(\pi - \pi^*),$$

$$p_d - \bar{p}_d = \lambda[r - r^*) - (\pi - \pi^*)],$$

and, therefore,

$$e = (m - m^*) - k(y - y^*) + (1/\rho)[(r - \pi) - (r^* - \pi^*)] + \lambda(\pi - \pi^*)$$

Suppose a researcher were to estimate (2.24) and obtain the following results:

$$e = a_0(m - m^*) + a_1(y - y^*) + a_2[(r - \pi) - (r^* - \pi^*)] + a_3(\pi - \pi^*) \tag{2.25}$$

We may then observe the following (1) Assuming that the coefficients a_0 and a_1 are statistically significant and have the correct signs, the first hypothesis to test is that $a_0 = 1$ and that $a_1 = -k$, where k is the hypothesised value of the income elasticity of money demand. (2) If the above hypothesis is not rejected then we may proceed to test whether the sticky price or the flexible price version is most relevant empirically. If a_2 is negative and statistically significant we would infer that the 'overshooting' model cannot be rejected and that liquidity effects are important in determining the exchange rate. If a_2 were to turn out insignificant one might infer that the speed of adjustment is infinite and that the flexible price model cannot be rejected by the data. (3) If a_3 is statistically significant and positive one may wish to test the hypothesis that $a_3 = \lambda$, where λ is the hypothesised value of the interest semi-elasticity of money demand. If the hypothesis is not rejected one could infer that secular monetary growth rates and, thereby, secular inflation rates are important determinants of the exchange rate; expectations effects arising from secular inflation differentials could not be rejected. If a_3 is insignificant one would infer that secular inflation differentials are not significant in determining the exchange rate. In that case one may wish to set $\pi - \pi^* = 0$ in (2.25) and retest this equation. Chapter 10 presents empirical results on several versions of (2.25).

2.4 Monetary models of the exchange rate: demand-determined outputs and sticky prices

The model

We now relax the assumption that full employment rules at all times to allow outputs to be demand-determined in the short run. This is a very considerable step towards generality. The relative output supply y_d will be modelled as a decreasing function of the real interest rate differential measured by $r_d - D(p_d)$ and as an increasing function of the real exchange rate measured by $(e - p_d)$:

$$y_d = -\gamma [r_d - D(p_d)] + \delta (e - p_d), \quad \gamma > 0, \ \delta > 0 \tag{2.26}$$

Notice that (2.26) incorporates the assumption of perfect foresight since the currently observed inflation differential is replacing its currently expected value. One could say that this equation describes an open economy two-country *IS* relation. The modelling of relative liquidity ℓ_d remains unchanged from our earlier analysis:

$$\ell_d = ky_d - \lambda r_d \tag{2.27}$$

One could describe (2.27) as an open economy two-country *LM* relation. To model the inflation differential we will postulate a Phillips-type relationship to relate relative excess demand to the inflation differential. Such a relation may be captured by:

$$D(p_d - \bar{p}_d) = \psi (y_d - \bar{y}_d) \qquad \psi > 0 \tag{2.28}$$

According to (2.28) the excess (shortfall) of the current inflation differential from its trend is proportional to the gap of the current output differential from its trend. Equation (2.28) can be described as an open economy two-country Phillips curve relation. To close the model we will append the UIP condition (under perfect foresight) to model the real interest rate differential:

$$i_d \equiv r_d - D(p_d) = D(e - p_d) \tag{2.29}$$

In the above equation, i_d is used to denote the real interest rate differential. As the model stands, long-run PPP combined with UIP and perfect foresight imply a long-run output differential $\bar{y}_d$, and a long-run interest rate differential $\bar{i}_d$, equal to zero. Using this new notation to rewrite the equilibrium condition in the goods markets and in the money markets we have:

$$y_d = -\gamma (i_d) + \delta (e - p_d) \quad \text{and} \tag{2.26'}$$

$$\ell_d = ky_d - \lambda [(i_d + D(p_d)] = ky_d - \lambda (i_d) - \lambda D(p_d) \tag{2.27'}$$

For some purposes it will prove convenient to substitute out the current inflation differential from money markets by incorporating the Phillips curve into these markets to obtain:

$$\ell_d = ky_d - \lambda (i_d) - \lambda [\psi y_d + D(\bar{p}_d)] = (k - \lambda \psi) y_d - \lambda (i_d) - \lambda D(\bar{p}_d) \tag{2.27*}$$

Equation (2.27*) can be interpreted as an *LM* relation adjusted for inflation. Notice that the coefficient $(k - \lambda \psi)$ measures the total effect of relative income on the demand for relative liquidity given the current real interest rate differential and given the secular inflation differential. To interpret this coefficient, observe the following: (1) other things equal, a unit rise in relative income raises the demand for relative liquidity by k units to accommodate the relative increase in transactions requirements; (2) other things equal, a unit rise in relative income raises the inflation differential by ψ units (by the Phillips curve) and, at a given real interest rate differential, it causes the nominal interest rate to rise by ψ units and the demand for relative liquidity to fall by $\lambda\psi$ units; (3) hence $(k - \lambda\psi)$ can measure the total effect of relative income on the demand for relative liquidity given the real interest rate differential and the secular inflation differential. In principle this total effect can be of either sign and, as we show below, the model can be stable provided that $\gamma(k - \lambda\psi) + \lambda > 0$. This stability requirement corresponds to the intuitively appealing requirement that an increase in relative aggregate demand raises relative output at a given real exchange rate. Since a more general treatment of the model is provided elsewhere we are justified here in simplifying our exposition and considering only the case where $(k - \lambda\psi) > 0$ to illustrate adjustments.

For some purposes it will prove convenient to substitute out the inflation differential from goods markets by adjusting aggregate demand for inflation to obtain

$$
\begin{aligned}
(1 - \gamma\psi)y_d &= -\gamma r_d + \delta(e - p_d) + \gamma D(\bar{p}_d) \\
&= -\gamma(r_d - \bar{r}_d) + \delta(e - p_d), \quad (\bar{y}_d = 0)
\end{aligned}
\tag{2.26*}
$$

Equation (2.26*) can be thought of as an *IS* relation adjusted for inflation; adjusted for inflation, a unit rise in relative output raises the demand for the domestic good relative to the foreign good by $\gamma\psi$ units and generates a (relative) excess supply of $(1 - \gamma\psi)$ units. Armed with the structure of the model given above we now turn our attention to the analysis of adjustments to monetary disturbances.

Adjustments to monetary shocks: liquidity effects and secular inflation effects

Consider once more adjustments to a previously unanticipated increase in the level of relative monies m_d and in the secular inflation differential $D(\bar{p}_d) = D(m_d)$. To start with we will assume the existence of a stable saddle path to illustrate such adjustments. At the end of this section we will prove the existence of a uniquely stable saddle path. Our present analysis will build upon equations (2.26'), (2.27*) and (2.29). Figure 2.5 will provide a helpful illustration.

The vertical axis in Figure 2.5 measures the real interest rate differential i_d which can also serve to measure the rate of depreciation of the real exchange rate since, by the UIP condition, $i_d = D(e - p_d)$. At the steady state the real interest rate differential is zero in this model and, thus, i_d can also measure

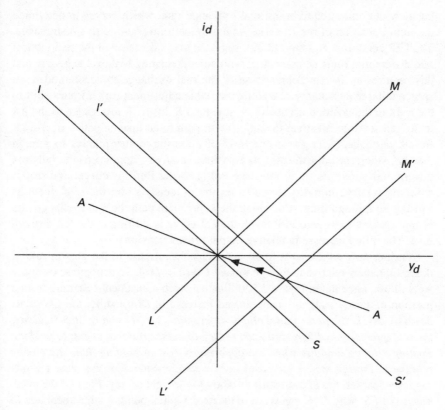

Figure 2.5   Adjustments to unanticipated monetary disturbances

deviations from the steady state. The horizontal axis in this figure measures the relative output differential y_d which can also serve to provide a measure of the gap between the current and the steady-state inflation differential since $D(p_d - \bar{p}_d)$ $= \psi(y_d - \bar{y}_d) = \psi y_d$ by the Phillips curve. At the steady state the real output differential is zero in this model and, thus, y_d can also measure deviations from the steady state. Assuming that we start from a position of steady state we construct an *IS* locus (equation (2.26′)) and an *LM* locus adjusted for inflation (equation (2.27*)) passing through the origin. The slope of the *IS* locus is $-1/\gamma < 0$ and the slope of the *LM* locus is $(k - \lambda\psi)/\lambda$ which, for the purpose of illustration, and without much loss in generality, is taken to be positive. Thus the model meets the stability condition asserted. (in Chapter 5 we examine the possibility of a negatively sloping *LM*.)

Consider now a previously unanticipated increase in m_d occurring, say, at time t_0. As a result the *LM* locus shifts down to the position occupied by, say, the *L′M′* locus. The intersection of the *L′M′* locus with the *IS* locus indicates an instant reduction in the real interest rate differential and an instant increase in relative output. However this intersection cannot serve to locate the initial position; the initial equilibrium real exchange rate, which serves to determine the initial position of the *IS* curve, cannot remain invariant to this disturbance. The UIP condition, equation (2.29), suggests that a decrease in the real interest rate differential must be associated with an appreciating real exchange rate and this requires an instant depreciation of the real exchange to accommodate an appreciating real exchange rate along the stable adjustment path. *IS* must shift to the right to the position occupied by, say, the *I'S'* locus. A locus such as the *AA* locus can serve to illustrate the adjustment path to an unanticipated, once-and-for-all, permanent increase in the level of domestic money relative to foreign money. Along the adjustment path a positive relative output keeps the inflation differential above its trend rate, according to the Phillips curve, and this is reducing relative liquidity down to its initial steady state; the *L'M'* locus is shifting up through time. Also along the adjustment path the real exchange rate is appreciating to its zero PPP level; the *I'S'* curve is shifting to the left through time. The initial increase in relative output proves transitory.

Consider now adjustments to an unanticipated increase in the growth rate of domestic money relative to foreign money $D(m_d)$ $(= D\bar{p}_d)$. To economise on space we will use, once more, Figure 2.5 to illustrate such adjustments. Starting from a position of steady state an unanticipated increase in $D(m_d)$ shifts the *LM* locus down to, say, *L'M'*; *at the initial output differential ($y_d = 0$) and relative liquidity, the real interest rate differential must reduce to induce rational agents to hold the existing relative liquidity when the opportunity cost of holding domestic money relative to foreign money increases across steady states.* For the same reasons suggested earlier, the *IS* must shift instantly to the right to, say, *I'S'* and the intersection of *I'S'* with *L'M'* can serve to locate the initial point of adjustment and to define the entire stable adjustment path in (y_d, i_d) space. Again a locus such as the *AA* locus can serve to illustrate adjustments in (y_d, i_d) space; again the initial increase in relative ouput is seen to be transitory. However there are differences between adjustments to an increase in the level of *m* and adjustments to an increase in $D(m_d)$. In the latter case the nominal interest rate differential increases across steady states and, as result, relative liquidity reduces across steady states.

The phenomenon of undershooting

In the present model the phenomenon of overshooting is not a foregone conclusion, rather it is an empirical matter. Since output responds to policy changes, an expansionary monetary policy, for instance, may induce a short-run increase in output which may require an increase in the nominal interest rate differential to restore short-run equilibrium at the initial equilibrium exchange rate. In these circumstances the nominal exchange rate will undershoot its path; the instant depreciation of the nominal exchange rate associated with such an expansionary monetary policy will place the exchange rate below its long-run equilibrium path. In these circumstances the nominal exchange rate will be depreciating at a rate above its trend rate in order to preserve UIP. In Figure 2.6 we use the *IS–LM* apparatus to illustrate a case of undershooting.

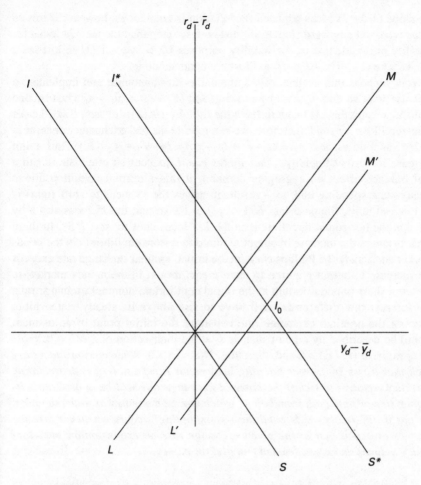

Figure 2.6   Adjustments to monetary disturbances: a case of undershooting

In Figure 2.6 the vertical axis measures the gap between the current and the steady state nominal interest rate differential $r_d - \bar{r}_d$ and the horizontal axis measures the gap between the current and the steady-state output differential $y_d - \bar{y}_d \,(= y_d)$. The *IS* locus through the origin plots the combinations of $(r_d - \bar{r}_d)$ and $(y_d - \bar{y}_d)$ required to clear the goods market, to satisfy the Phillips curve and maintain equality between the current and the steady-state real exchange rate; it plots the member of the family of loci defined by equation (2.26*) for which $(e - p_d) = (\bar{e} - \bar{p}d) = 0$. The slope of such loci is measured by $(1 - \gamma\psi)(-1/\gamma)$. Similarly the *LM* locus through the origin plots the combinations of $(r_d - \bar{r}_d)$ and $(y_d - \bar{y}_d)$ required to maintain equality between the current and the steady-state relative liquidity; it plots the member of the family of loci defined by equation (2.27) for which $\ell_d = \bar{\ell}_d$. The slope of such loci is measured by (k/λ). The sign of the slope of the *IS* locus adjusted for inflation is ambiguous; however if this *IS* locus were to be upward sloping it must be less steep than the the *LM* locus for stability purposes; that is, for stability purposes $k/\lambda > (\gamma\psi - 1)(1/\gamma)$. In Figure 2.6 we take $(1 - \gamma\psi)(-1/\gamma) < 0$ to illustrate undershooting.

Now suppose that at time, say, t_0 the authorities announce and implement a unit rise in m so that m_d rises by one unit and $(\ell_d - \bar{\ell}_d) = (\bar{p}_d - p_d)$ rises by one unit. As a result the *LM* locus shifts to the right by $1/k$ units to, say, $L'M'$. Under long-run PPP $\bar{e} = \bar{p}_d$ and, therefore, we can rewrite the real exchange rate term in (2.26*) as follows: $(e - p_d) = (e - \bar{e}) + (\bar{p}_d - p_d) = (e - \bar{e}) + (\ell_d - \bar{\ell}_d)$. Thus a unit increase in current liquidity, *other things equal*, induces an effect similar to a real balance effect on aggregate demand; it raises current spending above steady-state spending and, as a result, it causes the *IS* locus to shift right by $\delta/(1 - \gamma\psi)$ units. Suppose that $\delta/(1 - \gamma\psi) > 1/k$ so that the *IS* locus shifts by more, in the horizontal direction, than the *LM* locus does to, say, I^*S^*. In these circumstances the increase in output required to restore equilibrium in the goods market and satisfy the Phillips curve at the initial nominal exchange rate exceeds the increase in output required to restore equilibrium in the money market; to preserve short-run equilibrium at the initial equilibrium nominal exchange rate, the interest rate differential will have to rise above its steady-state value: keeping the nominal exchange rate constant, the initial point of adjustment would be described by a point such as I_0 at the intersection of $L'M'$ with I^*S^*. At I_0 we have $(r_d - \bar{r}_d) > 0$ and, therefore, $D(e - \bar{e}) > 0$. *When circumstances are such that a rise in current liquidity induces an expectation of a depreciating currency (relative to trend) the nominal exchange rate will be approaching its higher steady state path from below, which can be described as undershooting. To put it differently, undershooting (overshooting) occurs whenever circumstances are such that at the given exchange rate an expansionary monetary policy induces an excess demand (supply) for money.*

A formal solution of the model

To conclude this section we offer a more formal analysis to confirm our findings. Combining the *IS* relation, equation (2.26′), with the Phillips curve and the UIP condition to substitute out the output differential and the real interest rate differential from this relation, and using the condition of long-run PPP, we arrive at the following differential equation:

$$(1 - \psi\gamma)D(p_d - \bar{p}_d) + \psi\gamma D(e - \bar{e}) = \psi\delta(e - \bar{e}) - \psi\delta(p_d - \bar{p}_d) \tag{2.30}$$

Combining the *LM* relation given by equation (2.27) with the Phillips curve and the UIP condition to substitute out the output differential and the nominal interest rate differential from this relation, and taking deviations from the steady state we arrive at the following differential equation:

$$(k/\psi)D(p_d - \bar{p}_d) - \lambda D(e - \bar{e}) = -(p_d - \bar{p}_d) \tag{2.31}$$

The simultaneous differential equations (2.30) and (2.31) yield the following reduced-form solution in matrix representation:

$$\begin{bmatrix} D(p_d - \bar{p}_d) \\ D(e - \bar{e}) \end{bmatrix} = \begin{bmatrix} \alpha_{11} & \alpha_{12} \\ \alpha_{21} & \alpha_{22} \end{bmatrix} \begin{bmatrix} (p_d - \bar{p}_d) \\ (e - \bar{e}) \end{bmatrix} \tag{2.32}$$

$$\alpha_{11} = \psi(\lambda\delta + \gamma)(1/\Delta) < 0, \quad \alpha_{12} = (-\lambda\psi\delta)(1/\Delta) > 0,$$

$$\alpha_{21} = (k\delta + \psi\gamma - 1)(1/\Delta) \gtrless 0, \quad \alpha_{22} = (-k\delta)(1/\Delta) > 0,$$

$$\Delta = -[\gamma(k - \lambda\psi) + \lambda] < 0$$

The first thing to confirm is that the existence of a unique saddle path, which rests upon the assumption that the determinant of the coefficient matrix in (2.32) is negative, requires Δ to be negative. As we remarked earlier, this is a most plausible and appealing condition since it corresponds to the assumption that an increase in the demand for the domestic good relative to the foreign good, given the real exchange rate, increases the supply of the domestic good relative to the foreign good y_d. The second thing to note is that the slope of the $D(p_d - \bar{p}_d) = 0$ locus is unambiguously positive: around the steady state a rise in the price differential reduces aggregate demand for the domestic good relative to the foreign good because of relative price effects and because of relative liquidity effects and this requires a depreciation of the nominal exchange of sufficient magnitude to restore equality between relative demand and relative supply. The third thing to note from (2.32) is that the slope of the $D(e - \bar{e}) = 0$ locus depends on the sign of $[k\delta + \psi\gamma - 1]$. In turn, as Figures 2.7a and 2.7b indicate, the characteristics of the saddle path crucially depend upon the slope of the $D(e - \bar{e}) = 0$ locus and, therefore, crucially depend upon the sign of $[k\delta + \psi\gamma - 1]$. When $k\delta + \psi\gamma - 1 > 0$ the $D(e - \bar{e}) = 0$ locus and the saddle path are upward-sloping and undershooting occurs. When $k\delta + \psi\gamma - 1 < 0$ the exact opposite occurs. This confirms our earlier finding. One final remark: if the $D(e - \bar{e}) = 0$ locus were to be upward-sloping it must be less steep than the $D(p_d - \bar{p}_d) = 0$ locus to satisfy stability. Figures 2.7a and 2.7b can help to illustrate adjustments in a model with overshooting and in a model with undershooting. The construction and the workings of these two diagrams should be self-explanatory by now and therefore we will not attach any further comments to them.

Initial responses to undershooting and to overshooting: a numerical example

Overshooting is very often thought to be associated with and to contribute to large and persistent departures of output from natural rates. In principle, however, this cannot be correct. When output, the exchange rate and the interest rate are all endogenous variables, overshooting may or may not be associated with larger departures of output from natural rates than undershooting is. It is simply an empirical matter. To underline the empirical nature of this issue and to enable us to contrast and compare inital responses to overshooting with responses to undershooting we have constructed four models. Model A is a

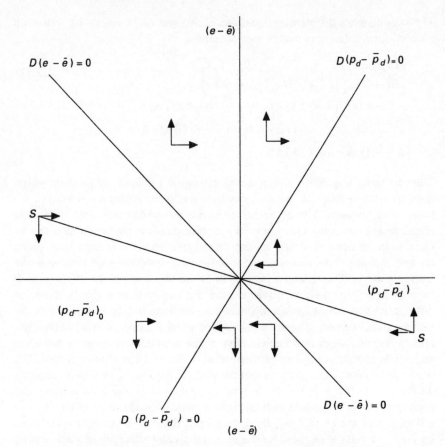

Figure 2.7a   Exchange rate adjustments in a sticky-price,
underemployment model – a case of overshooting: $k\delta + \psi\gamma - 1 < 0$

model where overshooting occurs, in contrast to model B where undershooting occurs. In model A deviations of output from its natural rate are larger than in model B. Model C is a model where overshooting occurs, in contrast to model D where undershooting occurs. In model C deviations of output from its natural rate are smaller than in model D.

MODELS A AND B

To facilitate comparison we have allowed all parameters except one to be identical in both models: In model A we have taken the income elasticity of money demand k to be equal to one, while in model B this elasticity is set equal to two. The other parameters are set as follows: $\gamma = \delta = \psi = 0.5$, $\lambda = 4$. As a result, the stable root that governs the speed of adjustment, call it ρ, turns out as follows: model A, $\rho = -0.395$; model B, $\rho = -0.283$. In model A, a 1 per cent increase in liquidity depreciates the real exchange rate by 1.133 per cent

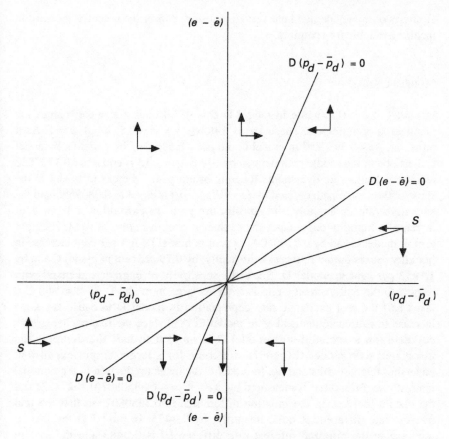

Figure 2.7b   Exchange rate adjustments in a sticky-price,
underemployment model – a case of undershooting: $k\delta + \psi\,\gamma - 1 > 0$

instantly, whereas in model B the real exchange rate depreciates, instantly, by 0.882 per cent. Since along the stable path $D(p_d - \bar{p}_d) = \rho(p_d - \bar{p}_d)$ and since, by the Phillips curve $(1/\psi)\rho(p_d - \bar{p}_d) = y_d$, a 1 per cent increase in liquidity causes output to increase, instantly, by 0.79 per cent in model A and by 0.57 per cent in model B. It is easy to establish that in model A the nominal interest rate falls, initially, and that it rises in model B, initially. It is also easy to establish that in both models the real interest rate falls, initially, and that the fall in the real interest rate is more pronounced in model A than in model B. Undoubtedly a bigger real exchange rate depreciation in model A is associated with a bigger output increase and a smaller real exchange rate depreciation in model B is associated with a smaller output increase. Undoubtedly the real interest rate falls by more in model A than it does in model B. Is it the bigger real exchange rate depreciation or is it the bigger fall in the real interest rate that is responsible for the larger increase in output in model A? This should warn us that it is not so trivially simple to translate observed associations between endogenous variables into cause and effect. What one can say is that in model B the higher income elasticity of money demand has served to absorb part of the potential increase in income available for spending.

MODELS C AND D

In model C $\delta = 0.5$, while in model D $\delta = 1$. All other parameter values are identical in both models. These are as follows: $\gamma = \psi = 0.5$, $\lambda = 4$, $k = 1$. As it turns out, $\rho = -0.3950802$ in model C and $\rho = -0.5965965$ in model D. In model C the slope of the saddle path defined by $(e - \bar{e})/(p_d - \bar{p}_d)$ is equal to -0.1327822 and the exhange rate overshoots its equilibrium path, whereas in model D the slope of the saddle path defined by $(e - \bar{e})/(p_d - \bar{p}_d)$ is equal to 0.0809595 and the exchange rate undershoots its equilibrium path. In particular, a 1 per cent increase in liquidity depreciates the exchange rate, instantly, by 1.1327822 per cent in model C and by 0.9190404 per cent in model D. A 1 per cent increase in liquidity causes output to increase, instantly, by 0.79 per cent in model C and by 1.1932 per cent in model D. Since the sensitivity of aggregate demand with respect to the real exchange rate is twice as large in model D as in model C it takes half the real exchange rate depreciation in model D to cause the same increase in aggregate demand as in model C. And since the real exchange rate depreciation associated with model D is more than half the depreciation associated with model C there is still room for a larger output expansion, undershooting notwithstanding. In model C the instant reduction in the nominal interest rate differential is measured by $\rho(e - \bar{e}) = -0.3950802(0.1327822)$ and the instant increase in the inflation differential is 0.3950802, so that the real interest rate differential falls, instantly, by 0.4475. In model D the instant increase in the nominal interest rate differential is 0.0483 and the instant increase in the inflation differential is 0.5965965, so that the instant reduction in the real interest rate differential is 0.5483. Thus, one could say, the larger reduction in the real interest rate differential in model D can explain the larger increase in output, undershooting notwithstanding.

2.5 Concluding remarks

In this chapter we have covered all the major varieties of monetary models encountered in the literature. We have attempted to inject more generality than one usually finds in textbook expositions of monetary models. Firstly, we have cast our framework of analysis in terms of two-country models; secondly, we have allowed for the possibility of secular monetary growth; and thirdly, we have allowed for the possibility of undershooting.

All these varieties of models have one common feature; they all observe the UIP condition associated with perfect substitutability of bonds; they all observe the implications following from a world with a single bond. Let this world consist of a bond denominated in domestic currency, call it B, and a bond denominated in foreign currency, call it F. Then, the single bond can be measured by $B + EF$ and the single, common, return on this bond can be measured by, say, $r^* + tE(e_{t+1}) - e_t$. Our entire analysis could have been centred, alternatively, around this single-bond market rather than the money market. In this chapter we have decided not to break with tradition.

CHAPTER 3

The Asset Approach to the Exchange Rate: Portfolio Balance Models of the Exchange Rate and the Current Account

3.1 Introduction

We will now relax the assumption that interest-bearing assets denominated in different currencies are perfect substitutes in portfolios and that agents are risk-neutral. In this chapter we will consider the more general setting in which agents are risk-averse and assets are imperfect substitutes. As a result the UIP condition will no longer hold and, therefore, the risk premium need not be zero. At any point in time the nominal exchange rate will be determined by portfolio balance considerations; over time the exchange rate will be driven by the current account and by the evolution of expectations. Since the current account adds an additional relation to the dynamics of exchange rate determination, and in order to focus attention on the role of the current account and of expectations in the evolution of the exchange rate, we will eschew any consideration of sluggish adjustment in prices. In fact, and throughout this chapter, we will maintain the assumption that wages and prices adjust instantly to ensure that full employment output prevails and that PPP holds at all times. The outline of this chapter is as follows. In Section 3.2 we employ a mean-variance analysis to build the asset sector of the model. In Section 3.3 we consider the short-run response of the exchange rate to monetary policy changes and to changes in expectations. In Section 3.4 we look briefly at the properties of portfolio balance when domestic and foreign bonds are perfect substitutes in order to bring into sharper focus some of the issues arising from considerations about the degree of asset substitution. In Section 3.5 we consider the dynamic structure of the model with the view to deriving the saddle path characteristics of the exchange rate and the current account under rational expectations. In Section 3.6 we consider impact, dynamic and steady-state adjustments to open-market operations between the domestic bond and money and between the domestic bond and the foreign bond. Notice that the latter type of (sterilised) open-market operation can only be meaningful if interest-bearing assets denominated in different currencies are imperfect substitutes, unless, of course, expectations can alter as a result of such operations. Section 3.7 concludes the chapter.

3.2 A mean-variance analysis of portfolio choice

Most of the microfoundations of modern portfolio analysis build on mean-variance analysis. Basically there are two routes one can take along the path of mean-variance analysis: one assumes either that the utility of wealth is a quadratic function or that asset returns are joint normally distributed. The preferred route is to assume joint normality in the distribution of asset returns and to assume that the utility of wealth is characterised either by constant absolute risk aversion or by constant relative risk aversion. In the latter case asset demands are homogeneous of degree one in wealth and asset shares are linear in expected returns provided that time runs continuously or that the holding period is 'sufficiently small' in discrete time (Friedman and Roley, 1987; Pikoulakis, 1991). In what follows we will take asset demands to be homogeneous of degree one in wealth and we will model, accordingly, the portfolio sector of a small open economy in which agents hold domestic money M, domestic currency-denominated bonds B, which are not traded internationally, and foreign currency-denominated bonds F, which are traded internationally. We will identify the expected return on M by r_m, the expected return on B by r_b and the expected return on F by r_f. We will take W to denote the market value of current wealth in domestic currency and define $W \equiv M + B + EF$, where E is the price of foreign currency in units of domestic currency. Thus, under our assumptions, asset market equilibrium can be conveniently characterised as follows:

$$(B/W) = b(r_b, r_f, r_m), \quad \partial b/\partial(r_b) > 0, \quad \partial b/\partial(r_f) < 0, \partial b/\partial(r_m) < 0 \tag{3.1a}$$

$$(FE/W) = f(r_b, r_f, r_m), \quad \partial f/\partial(r_b) < 0, \quad \partial f/\partial(r_f) > 0, \partial f/\partial(r_m) < 0 \tag{3.1b}$$

$$(M/W) = m(r_b, r_f, r_m), \quad \partial m/\partial(r_b) < 0, \quad \partial m/\partial(r_f) < 0, \partial m/\partial(r_m) > 0 \tag{3.1c}$$

Assets are taken to be (strong) gross substitutes: a rise in the own expected rate of return on any asset increases the demand for that asset and diminishes the demand for each other asset. At any point in time, and for *any* vector of asset prices and returns, asset demands must fully exhaust the market value of wealth defined by the same vector of prices and returns. This is a Walras's Law-type constraint operating in the assets market which renders one of the equilibrium conditions in that market redundant. One very simple way to express this constraint is the following: $b(\;) + f(\;) + m(\;) \equiv 1$. This suggests that one asset market equilibrium condition, say the money market equilibrium condition, can be obtained residually since $m(\;) \equiv 1 - [b(\;) + f(\;)]$. In particular this wealth constraint imposes adding up restrictions. Letting r_j, for instance, denote the expected return on the jth asset and using the notation introduced above to describe portfolio shares, we have the following restrictions: $\partial b/\partial r_j + \partial f/\partial r_j + \partial m/\partial r_j \equiv 0$, for all $j = 1, 2, 3$; summing the responses of asset demands to a change in any of the expected returns amounts to zero. The general implications of our analysis hitherto can be summed up as follows: in a world of N asset markets, the $N - 1$ independent asset-market equilibria can determine at most $N - 1$ yields; one yield can serve as numeraire. Taking r_m, for instance, as our numeraire and dropping the money market equilibrium condition we can rewrite our asset market representation as follows:

$$(B/W) \;= \tilde{b}[(r_b - r_m), (r_f - r_m)] \tag{3.2a}$$

$$(EF/W) = \tilde{f}[(r_b - r_m), (r_f - r_m)] \tag{3.2b}$$

$$W \equiv M + B + EF \tag{3.2c}$$

The system of equations defined by (3.2a) – (3.2c) must be supplemented by equations which define, precisely, the expected asset returns. Taking r_b, r_m and r_f to be expected *real* returns we append the following definitions:

$$r_b \;= (r_b)^* - \pi^\epsilon \tag{3.2d}$$

$$r_m \;= (r_m)^* - \pi^\epsilon \tag{3.2e}$$

$$r_f \;= r^* + x - \pi^\epsilon \tag{3.2f}$$

where $(r_b)^*$, $(r_m)^*$ and r^* are expected nominal returns, π^ϵ is the expected rate of domestic inflation and where x is the expected rate of depreciation of the nominal exchange rate E. As is the customary practice $(r_m)^*$ will be taken to be institutionally determined and, without loss in generality, we will set $(r_m)^* = 0$. Making the necessary substitutions, the model to consider will be defined as follows:

$$(B/W) \;= \tilde{b}[(r_b)^*, (r^* + x)], \qquad \partial\tilde{b}/\partial(r_b)^* > 0, \partial\tilde{b}/\partial(r^* + x) < 0 \tag{3.3a}$$

$$(EF/W) = \tilde{f}[(r_b)^*, (r^* + x)], \qquad \partial\tilde{f}/\partial(r_b)^* < 0, \partial\tilde{f}/\partial(r^* + x) > 0 \tag{3.3b}$$

$$W \equiv M + B + EF \tag{3.3c}$$

By the small country assumption we will take r^* to be exogenously given. It will also prove convenient, for illustration purposes mainly, to follow the practice of some writers and treat x as short-run predetermined and to model the evolution of expectations through time separately. In addition M is exogenous by virtue of the fact that the authorities do not systematically intervene in the market for foreign exchange to peg the exchange rate and B will be taken to be exogenous by virtue of the assumption that domestic bonds are not traded internationally and that government budgets are kept continuously in balance. Of course, at any point in time the authorities may engage in open-market operations to alter the outstanding amounts of M, B and F. Finally F will be taken to be short-run predetermined; at any point in time the number of foreign bond holdings domestically is predetermined by past acquisitions through saving or through open-market operations.

In (3.3a)–(3.3c) we have three equations to determine $(r_b)^*$, W and E in terms of M, B, F, r^* and x. This is the short-run solution of the model. Of course, when we come to model expectations we will abandon the fiction that x is short-run predetermined. The section that follows is intended to illustrate the short-run equilibrium properties of E and of $(r_b)^*$

3.3   Monetary policy, expectations and the exchange rate

The characteristics of portfolio balance in $((r_b)^*, E)$ space: setting the stage for a short-run analysis of portfolio balance

The exogenously given stocks of money and bonds can vary, and by discrete changes, only through open-market operations. However it will prove instructive to employ, occasionally, the proverbial helicopter to bring about changes in M and in B outside the open market. There are three kinds of open-market operations to distinguish: an open-market exchange between the domestic bond and money defined by $dM + dB = 0$, an open-market exchange between the foreign bond and money defined by $dM + EdF = 0$ and an open-market exchange between the domestic bond and the foreign bond defined by $dB + EdF = 0$. In Chapter 4 we consider, in detail, an open-market exchange of the second type, so we confine our attention here to the other two types of open-market operations. As we have remarked earlier in the introduction, an open-market exchange between the domestic and the foreign bond can only be meaningful if these two types of bonds are imperfect substitutes. We will elaborate on this important point later. Since bonds cannot exchange for bonds directly but only through the medium of money, an exchange operation between the two bonds involves, in practice, two transactions: an open-market purchase of B in exchange for M, say, and an open-market sale of F in exchange for M designed to sterilise the effects of the first operation on money and leave domestic money holdings unchanged. In addition to changes brought about by monetary policy, the short-run predetermined stock of F can change *over time* through purchases from abroad or sales to abroad that reflect saving or dissaving, as the case may be. As the stock of F cumulates or decumulates the asset market has to adjust to variations in this stock. Therefore we will need to examine the short-run equilibrium effect of discrete changes in F in order to be able to trace the effect of changes in F through the current (capital) account. Finally we will need to examine the effects of changes in the expected rate of depreciation on the short-run characteristics of portfolio balance to enable us to appreciate better the joint evolution of expectations and of the stock of foreign assets through time when we come to discuss the dynamics of the model. Most of our analysis in this section will be conducted by means of a diagrammatic exposition designed to illustrate the short-run equilibrium characteristics of the joint determination of the exchange rate E and of the market rate on bonds $(r_b)^*$. Using (3.3c) to substitute out the expression for W we write:

$$B = \tilde{b}[(r_b)^*, (r^*+x)](M + B + EF) \tag{3.4a}$$

$$EF = \tilde{f}[(r_b)^*, (r^*+x)](M + B + EF) \tag{3.4b}$$

Equations (3.4a) and (3.4b) suffice to determine $(r_b)^*$ and E in terms of the exogenous and the short-run predetermined variables. In Figure 3.1a below the BB locus traces the combinations of the nominal exchange rate E and the interest rate $(r_b)^*$ that preserve equilibrium in the domestic bond market; it is a graphic representation of (3.4a) drawn in $((r_b)^*, E)$ space. Similarly, the FF locus traces the combinations of the same two variables that are consistent with equilibrium in the foreign bond market; it is a graphic representation of (3.4b) drawn in $((r_b)^*, E)$ space. Starting from a position of equilibrium, a 1 per cent depreciation of the nominal exchange rate, say, raises the market value of the existing number of foreign bonds proportionately and it raises nominal wealth by (EF/W) per cent: at the existing $(r_b)^*$, the domestic bond market turns into a state of excess demand and the foreign bond market turns into a state of excess supply. To restore equilibrium in the domestic bond market $(r_b)^*$ must fall to reduce demand for the domestic bond down to the level of the existing supply. Similarly to restore equilibrium in the foreign bond market $(r_b)^*$ must fall as well to raise the demand for foreign bonds to the higher market value of these bonds. This explains why both loci are negatively sloping. However the FF locus must be less steep: (1) At the initial interest rate, a depreciation by dE creates an excess demand for domestic bonds equal to $F(B/W)dE$ and an excess supply of foreign bonds equal to $F[(M + B)/W]dE$. (2) Hence, other things equal, we require a bigger reduction in $(r_b)^*$ to equilibrate the foreign bond market than to equilibrate the domestic bond market when E depreciates by dE. (3) This is *a fortiori* true since the own interest rate derivative in the domestic bond market is bigger, in absolute size, than the cross-derivative in the foreign bond market; that is, $\partial(B/W)/\partial(r_b)^* > - \partial(FE/W)/\partial(r_b)^*$. In the same figure the MM locus traces the combinations of $(r_b)^*$ and E which clear the money market. A depreciation of the exchange rate raises the demand for money since it raises the market value of wealth and to restore equilibrium in the money market the interest rate $(r_b)^*$ has to rise to eliminate excess demand and bring money demand down to the given level of money supply. Since all three loci intersect at the same point, the point of intersection between any two loci and the slope of the remaining locus suffice to determine the position of this remaining locus. In

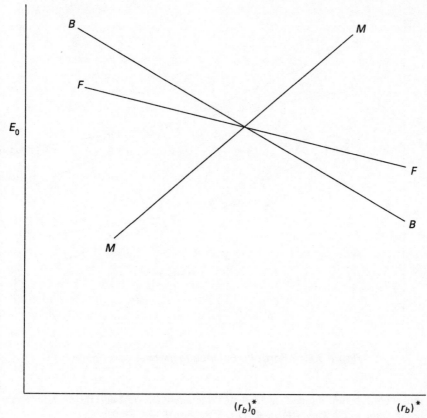

Figure 3.1a Portfolio balance loci in ((r_b),E) space*

our analysis we will be using whichever two of the three loci are most convenient to illustrate the problem at hand.

Portfolio balance responses to disturbances: a short-run analysis

PORTFOLIO BALANCE RESPONSES TO AN INCREASE IN F

It is easy to confirm that an increase in the number of foreign bond holdings F that is associated with an equiproportionate appreciation of the exchange rate E would leave wealth unchanged and it would also leave the distribution of wealth unchanged. This observation points to the following conclusion: to restore portfolio balance at the initial equilibrium interest rate, an increase in F would require the BB and FF loci (and the MM locus) to shift down by the same distance, thus leaving the interest rate unchanged and causing an appreciation of the exchange rate equiproportionate to the said increase in F. In Figure 3.1b the BB locus shifts to B*B* and the FF locus shifts to F*F* and, as a result, the

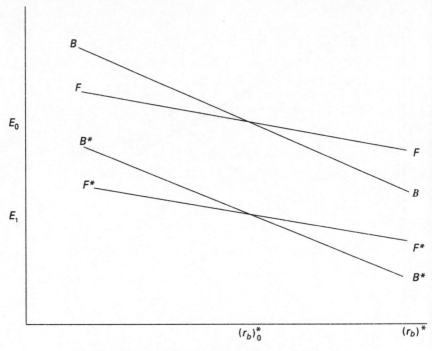

Figure 3.1b   Portfolio balance responses to a rise in F

initial equilibrium interest rate remains unchanged at $(r_b)_0^*$ and the exchange rate appreciates to E_1. Thus $\partial E/\partial F = -(E/F)$, $\partial (r_b)^*/\partial F = 0$.

<small>PORTFOLIO BALANCE RESPONSES TO AN (HELICOPTER) INCREASE IN M</small>

Suppose that a helicopter distributes, randomly, additional money. At the (pre)existing asset prices and returns the money market turns into a state of excess supply, whereas each of the two bond markets turns into a state of excess demand. To restore equilibrium in the money market at the initial (equilibrium) exchange rate the interest rate $(r_b)^*$ must fall to raise money demand to the level of the increased supply; in Figure 3.1c the *MM* locus shifts left to, say, the *M*M** position. To restore equilibrium, say, in the domestic bond market at the initial (equilibrium) exchange rate the interest rate $(r_b)^*$ must (also) fall to reduce the demand for the domestic bond down to the level of the existing bond supply *B*; in Figure 3.1c the *BB* locus shifts left to, say, the *B*B** position. However, comparing the relative magnitude of shifts in the horizontal direction it must be the case that the shift in the *MM* locus exceeds the shift in the *BB* locus. Firstly, at the initial exchange rate and interest rate(s) the money market registers an excess supply equal to $[(B + FE)(1/W)]dM$; that is, equal to the *sum* of excess demands in the other two markets. Secondly, the sensitivity of the

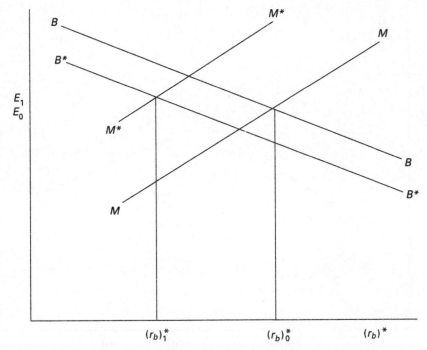

Figure 3.1c   Portfolio balance responses to a rise in M

share of wealth allocated to money (M/W) with respect to changes in $(r_b)^*$ is less than the sensitivity of the share of wealth allocated to domestic bonds (B/W) with respect to changes in $(r_b)^*$; that is, $-[\partial(M/W)/\partial(r_b)^*] < [\partial(B/W)//\partial(r_b)^*]$. Hence the decrease in $(r_b)^*$ required to restore equilibrium in the money market at the *initial* exchange rate must exceed the decrease in $(r_b)^*$ required to restore equilibrium in the domestic bond market. As a result, the exchange rate must depreciate to accommodate portfolio balance. In Figure 3.1c the exchange rate depreciates from E_0 to E_1 and the interest rate decreases from $(r_b)_0^*$ to $(r_b)_1^*$. To summarise: $\partial E/\partial M > 0$, $\partial(r_b)^*/\partial M < 0$. (See also p. 79.)

PORTFOLIO BALANCE RESPONSES TO AN (HELICOPTER) INCREASE IN B

Suppose that a helicopter distributes, randomly, additional domestic bonds. At the (pre)existing asset prices and expected returns the domestic bond market turns into a state of excess supply, whereas each of the other two markets turns into a state of excess demand. To restore equilibrium in the domestic bond market at the initial (equilibrium) exchange rate the interest rate $(r_b)^*$ must rise to raise the demand for domestic bonds to the level of the increased supply; in Figure 3.1d the *BB* locus shifts right to, say, the B^*B^* position. To restore equilibrium in the money market at the initial (equilibrium) exchange rate the

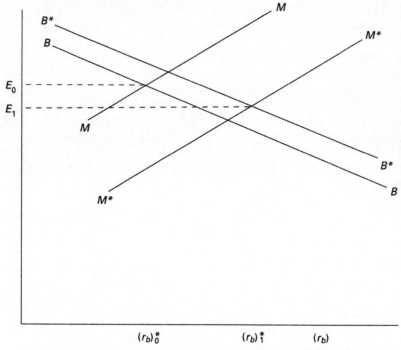

Figure 3.1d *Portfolio balance responses to a rise in B: the case where foreign and domestic bonds are (relatively) close substitutes*

interest rate $(r_b)^*$ must also rise to reduce money demand down to the level of the given supply; in Figure 3.1d the MM locus shifts right, to say, the M^*M^* position. The figure also illustrates the case where an increase in the bond supply B requires an appreciation of the exchange rate E to restore portfolio balance. This is the *particular* case where the foreign bond is a closer substitute for the domestic bond than money is; that is the case, where $- [\partial(FE/W/\partial(r_b)^*] (W/FE) > - [\partial(M/W)/\partial(r_b)^*] (W/M)$. In these circumstances a given increase in the interest rate $(r_b)^*$ would reduce the desired share of wealth allocated to foreign bonds (FE/W) proportionately more than it would reduce the desired share of wealth allocated to money (M/W); at unchanged supplies of F and M portfolio balance would require an appreciation of the exchange rate. To conclude, whether an autonomous increase in B requires an appreciation or a depreciation of the exchange rate to restore portfolio balance depends on the relative degree of substitution of bonds and money. To summarise: $\partial(r_b)^*/\partial B > 0$ and $\partial E/\partial B \lessgtr 0$ as $- [\partial(FE/W)/\partial(r_b)^*] (W/FE) \gtrless - [\partial(M/W)/\partial(r_b)^*](W/M)$. In Figure 3.1d, below, the exchange rate appreciates, by assumption, from E_0 to E_1 and the interest rate increases from $(r_b)_0^*$ to $(r_b)_1^*$. (See also p. 79.)

PORTFOLIO BALANCE RESPONSES TO AN OPEN MARKET EXCHANGE OF MONEY FOR
DOMESTIC BONDS: $dM + dB = 0$ $(dM > 0)$

Suppose that the monetary authorities conduct an open-market purchase of
domestic bonds in exchange for money. Valued at the initial equilibrium exchange
rate the market value of foreign asset holdings and of wealth remain unchanged
and, hence, the market for the foreign bond can remain in equilibrium at the initial
interest rate; in short, the *FF* locus does not shift. However, the *BB* locus must
shift to the left: to restore equilibrium at the initial exchange rate the interest rate
must fall to bring demand for the domestic bond down to the reduced supply level.
In Figure 3.1e the *BB* locus shifts to $B'B'$ and, as a result, the equilibrium interest
rate falls to $(r_b)_1{}^*$ and the equilibrium exchange rate depreciates to E_1. Thus

$$\partial E/\partial M \mid_{(dM + dB = 0)} > 0, \; \partial(r_b)^*/\partial M \mid_{(dM + dB = 0)} < 0.$$

Qualitatively, a helicopter money increase and a money increase through the
open market bring about similar responses. To accommodate the increase in M
and the the decrease in B $(r_b)^*$ must fall and to accommodate the decrease in
$(r_b)^*$ the exchange rate must depreciate.

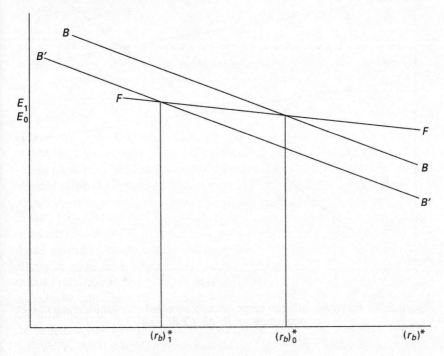

Figure 3.1e   *Portfolio balance responses to an open-market increase in M
in exchange for B (dM + dB = 0)*

PORTFOLIO BALANCE RESPONSES TO AN OPEN-MARKET EXCHANGE OF DOMESTIC
BONDS FOR FOREIGN BONDS: dB + EdF = 0 (dB < 0)

The literature on sterilised intervention is particularly rich. This is not surprising
since it is desirable to know to what extent and on what terms the authorities can
intervene in the market for foreign exchange to achieve the desired outcome on
the price of foreign exchange without having to change the stock of money.
Clearly this question can only arise in the context where domestic and foreign
bonds are less than perfect substitutes. To shed light on this issue, consider the
following transactions taking place in immediate succession. Firstly, let the
authorities conduct an open-market purchase of domestic bonds for money; that
is, let $dB < 0$, $dM + dB = 0$. Secondly, let the authorities restore the money
supply to its previous level by an open-market sale of foreign bonds in exchange
for money; that is, let $dM + EdF = 0$ such that $EdF + dB = 0$, $(dB < 0, dM = 0)$.
Figure 3.1f will help to illustrate short-run equilibrium adjustments.

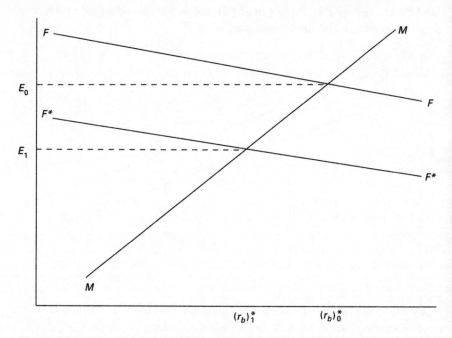

*Figure 3.1f   Portfolio balance responses to an open-market increase in F in
exchange for B (dB + EdF = 0)*

In Figure 3.1f we use the *MM* and *FF* loci to illustrate portfolio balance
responses to this type of open-market operation. To restore equilibrium in the
market for the foreign bond at the initial exchange rate the interest rate $(r_b)^*$
must reduce sufficiently to raise the demand for foreign bonds to the level of the

increased market value of these bonds; the *FF* locus must shift left to, say, the *F*F** position. At the initial exchange rate the money market can remain in equilibrium at an unchanged $(r_b)^*$; the *MM* locus does not shift. As a result the exchange rate appreciates from E_0 to E_1 and the interest rate falls from $(r_b)^*_0$ to $(r_b)^*_1$. To summarise: $(\partial E/\partial B)\,|_{(dB + EdF = 0)} > 0$, $\partial(r_b)^*/\partial B\,|_{(dB + EdF = 0)} > 0$.

To explain these results we may argue as follows. When domestic and foreign bonds are imperfect substitutes, an increase in the market value of foreign bonds relative to domestic bonds must be associated with an increase in the relative yield on foreign bonds to induce agents to accommodate this change in the composition of their portfolios. At a given E, r^* and x, an increase in the stock of F relative to B must be associated with a reduction in the interest rate on the domestic bond $(r_b)^*$. This, in turn, raises the demand for money and since money supply is given the exchange rate must appreciate to reduce wealth and, thereby, reduce money demand to the level of the given money supply. The appreciation of the exchange rate helps to moderate the reduction in the interest rate on the domestic bond and this, in turn, helps to moderate the appreciation necessary for portfolio balance, thus ensuring the stability of these forces.

ASSET MARKET RESPONSES TO AN INCREASE IN THE EXPECTED RATE OF
DEPRECIATION OF THE EXCHANGE RATE

An increase in the expected rate of depreciation of the nominal exchange rate x raises the return on the foreign bond and, as a result, it raises the demand for the foreign bond and reduces the demand for the domestic bond and for money. In Figure 3.1g, below, both the *MM* and *BB* loci shift up; to restore equilibrium in the money market and in the domestic bond market the exchange rate must depreciate to raise the market value of wealth sufficiently and, thus, reduce the share of wealth allocated to money and to the domestic bond in order to accommodate an increase in the share of wealth allocated to the foreign bond. If foreign and domestic bonds are 'sufficiently' close substitutes the interest rate on the domestic bonds will have to rise since the closer substitutes these bonds are the smaller the absolute size of the risk premium required to accommodate a shift in the share of these bonds in portfolios. In Figure 3.1g the vertical shift of the *BB* locus to B^*B^*, by assumption, exceeds the vertical shift of the *MM* locus to M^*M^*; as a result, the interest rate rises from $(r_b)^*_0$ to $(r_b)^*_1$, and the exchange rate depreciates from E_0 to E_1 To summarise: $\partial E/\partial x > 0$, and $\partial(r_b)^*/\partial x \gtrless 0$ as $-[\partial(B/W)/\partial x](W/B) \gtrless -[\partial(M/W)/\partial x](W/M)$.

3.4 Monetary policy and the degree of asset substition

Our aim here is, firstly, to show that under some circumstances monetary models of the exchange rate can be treated as a special case of portfolio balance models and, secondly, to show that sterilised intervention is impotent in this context. If,

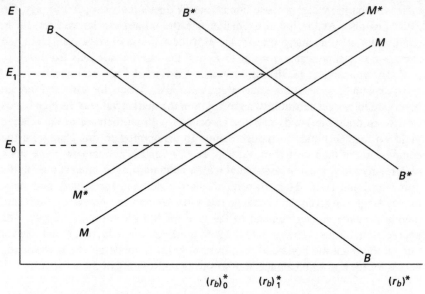

Figure 3.1g   Portfolio balance responses to an increase in the expected rate of depreciation of the exchange rate when bonds are 'close' substitutes

for instance, the returns on the foreign and the domestic bond were to be positively and perfectly correlated then these two assets would, in effect, be perfect substitutes in portfolios: the BB and the FF loci would collapse into a single-bond locus, call it SB, and we would have a single-bond world. Moreover, in a two-dimensional diagram with horizontal axis measuring risk premium r_p and a vertical axis measuring the exchange rate E this SB locus would be vertically located at the point where $r_p \equiv (r_b)^* - (r^* + x) = 0$. For any given $r^* + x$, the MM locus could be drawn positively sloping: higher values of E would serve to raise wealth and, thus, raise money demand requiring a rise in $(r_b)^*$; that is, a rise in r_p, to restore equilibrium. The MM locus would serve to determine the exchange rate. In this sense the exchange rate would be purely a monetary phenomenon. Figure 3.2 illustrates.

In the figure the M^*M^* locus serves to determine E at E_1 Other things equal, an increase in the expected rate of depreciation x would mean that $(r_b)^*$ would have to rise to preserve any given r_p and hence money demand would have to fall. To restore money market equilibrium the exchange rate would have to depreciate in order to increase the market value of nominal wealth and, thereby, raise money demand to the given level of money supply; the M^*M^* locus would shift to MM and the exchange rate would depreciate to E_0. Finally notice that sterilised intervention would be wholly ineffective unless it were to induce a change in expectations: the SB locus cannot shift and, under sterilised intervention, the MM locus would only shift as the result of a change in x.

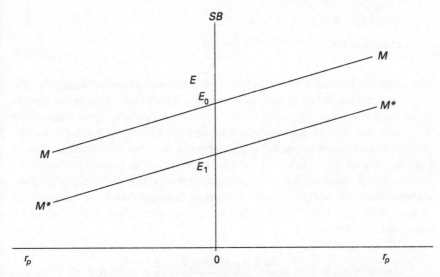

Figure 3.2 Portfolio balance and the exchange rate in a single-bond world

3.5 The exchange rate, the current account and expectations

Our purpose here is to derive the association between the current account and the exchange rate along the adjustment path defined by rational expectations. To do so we will have to employ local stability analysis since the model is non-linear and this will involve the linearisation of two equations of motion: one equation of motion will define the evolution of foreign asset holdings through the current account and the other will define the evolution of expectations along a perfect foresight path. To begin with we will look into the evolution of the current account given expectations and then we will define the rational expectations path.

Assuming perfect flexibility in wages and in prices, output is always maintained at its full employment level. Employing the small-country assumption and the assumption that prices abroad are stable we can choose units to set the foreign currency price $P* = 1$. Thus, under the assumption that PPP holds at all times, $E = P$. Let us observe now that, when markets clear, the excess of realised national saving over national investment records the current account. In the absence of government saving and investment and in the absence of private investment in physical capital, private saving suffices to define the current account (and the capital account). Following Dornbusch and Fischer (1980) and in line with our analysis in Chapter 4, we will model saving along the lines of a life-cycle hypothesis and, thus, we will take saving to be a decreasing function of real wealth defined by W/P (= W/E). Thus the current account is modelled as follows:

$$(E/P)(\dot{F}) = \dot{F} = S(w), \quad (\partial S/\partial w) < 0,;$$

where $w \equiv (W/P) = (W/E), \quad \partial F / \partial t \equiv \dot{F}$

$$(3.5)$$

According to (3.5), saving is entirely used to finance purchases of foreign bonds; saving records the deficit in the capital account which is identical to the surplus in the current account. Equation (3.5) gives rise to a reduced-form relationship that links the rate of accumulation of foreign bonds with the (short-run predetermined) stock of these bonds and with the (short-run predetermined) expected rate of depreciation of the exchange rate: at any point in time these predetermined variables serve to determine real wealth w and thereby the flow accumulation of foreign bonds. To derive this reduced-form relationship observe, first, the reduced-form relationship that defines real wealth given by equation (3.6a) below:

$$w \equiv (W/P) = (W/E) \quad = \frac{M + B + E(M,B,F,x)F}{E(M,B,F,x)} = w(M,B,F,x)$$

$$= \frac{M+B}{E(M,B,F,x)} + F$$

$$(3.6a)$$

For the purposes of stability analysis we need to linearise $w(\ )$ with respect to F and to x. From Section 3.3 we know that, other things equal, an increase (decrease) in F decreases (increases) the nominal exchange rate E proportionally, leaving nominal wealth unchanged. Since $P = E$ by PPP it follows that real wealth rises with F. From Section 3.3 we also know that an increase (decrease) in the expected rate of depreciation serves to depreciate (appreciate) the exchange rate and since the price level P is identified with E by PPP, an expectation of depreciation reduces real wealth; $(\partial w/\partial x) < 0$. In particular:

$$w = w(M,B,F,x); \quad \partial w/\partial F = W/FE > 0,$$

$$\partial w / \partial x = -(M+B)(1/E^2)(\partial E/\partial x) < 0$$

$$(3.6b)$$

Linearising w around steady-state F, to be denoted by $\bar{F}$, and steady-state x given by $\bar{x} = 0$ (on the assumption that there is no secular domestic inflation) we write:

$$w = \bar{w} + (\partial w/\partial F)(F - \bar{F}) + (\partial w/\partial x)x$$

$$(3.7)$$

Finally, using (3.5) and (3.7) we can express the current account (in the neighbourhood of the steady state) as follows:

$$\dot{F} = \Psi_F(F - \bar{F}) + \Psi_x(x)$$

$$(3.8)$$

where: $\Psi_F \equiv (\partial S/\partial w)(\partial w/\partial F) < 0$, $\Psi_x \equiv (\partial S/\partial w)(\partial w/\partial x) > 0$, and where Ψ_F and Ψ_x will be taken to measure responses around the steady state.

Linearising $E = E(M, B, F, x)$ around $\bar{F}$ and $\bar{x}$ $(= 0)$ and solving for x we obtain the evolution of expectations around the steady state. This is given by (3.9) below:

$$x = \frac{(E - \bar{E}) - (\partial E/\partial F)(F - \bar{F})}{(\partial E/\partial x)} = \Phi_E(E - \bar{E}) + \Phi_F(F - \bar{F})$$

where $\Phi_E \equiv 1/(\partial E/\partial x) > 0$, $\Phi_F \equiv -(\partial E / \partial F)/(\partial E / \partial x) > 0$.

$$(3.9)$$

We have already explained why it is that the association between the exchange rate and the expected rate of depreciation of the exchange rate is positive. To explain the also positive association between the stock of foreign asset holdings and expectations we may argue as follows. Other things equal, an increase in the supply of foreign assets induces a reduction (appreciation) in the price of these assets, whereas an increase in the expected rate of increase in this price (an expectation of a *depreciating* exchange rate) induces an increase (depreciation) in this price. Hence, to maintain a constant price for foreign assets, an increase in the supply of these assets must be associated with an expectation of a depreciating exchange rate.

For notational convenience let us define $e \equiv \log E$. Setting the expected rate of depreciation x equal to the actual rate $\dot{e} \equiv \partial e/\partial t$ in (3.8) and (3.9) we obtain the perfect foresight path. In matrix form the dynamics is defined as follows:

$$\begin{bmatrix} 1 & -\Psi_x \\ 0 & 1 \end{bmatrix} \begin{bmatrix} \dot{F} \\ \dot{e} \end{bmatrix} = \begin{bmatrix} \Psi_F & 0 \\ \Phi_F & \Phi_E \end{bmatrix} \begin{bmatrix} F - \bar{F} \\ E - \bar{E} \end{bmatrix}$$

$$(3.10a)$$

$$\begin{bmatrix} \dot{F} \\ \dot{e} \end{bmatrix} = \begin{bmatrix} \Psi_F + \Psi_x \Phi_F & \Psi_x \Phi_E \\ \Phi_F & \Phi_E \end{bmatrix} \begin{bmatrix} F - \bar{F} \\ E - \bar{E} \end{bmatrix}$$

$$(3.10b)$$

At first glance the sign of the term $\Psi_F + \Psi_x \Phi_F$ would seem ambiguous. However taking a closer look at this term with the view to interpreting its meaning will also serve to resolve this ambiguity. Notice, first, that a unit increase in F raises real wealth directly by W/FE units given expectations. This is the 'direct' wealth effect of foreign assets on wealth. Notice, second, that in the neighbourhood of the steady-state exchange rate $\bar{E}$ a unit increase in F induces an expectation of a depreciating exchange rate at the rate of $\Phi_F = (E/F)[(\partial E/\partial x)]^{-1}$ units. As a result, in the neighbourhood of $\bar{E}$ a unit increase in F induces a reduction of wealth by $(M + B)/(FE)$ units. This is the 'indirect' wealth effect of foreign assets on wealth working through expectations; it is entirely due to the endogenous nature of expectations. Combining the direct with the indirect effect we arrive at the total wealth effect of F, which is simply $(W/FE) - [(M + B)/(FE)] = 1$. Hence the term given by $\Psi_F + \Psi_x\Phi_F$ is equal to $\partial S/\partial w < 0$. The sign of the other terms in the coefficient matrix of (3.10b) is unambiguous and so is their interpretation. Before proceeding to establish the characteristics of the saddle path it is comforting to know that the existence and uniqueness of a stable path is quaranteed by virtue of that fact that the determinant of the coefficient matrix of (3.10b) is negative since $\Psi_F\Phi_E < 0$.

Figure 3.3 below will help to establish the characteristic of the saddle path. Setting $\dot{e} = 0$ in (3.10b) we obtain a locus of combinations of the exchange rate and the stock of foreign bonds which is compatible with a zero rate of depreciation of the exchange rate. From our short-run portfolio analysis we know that an increase (decrease) in the stock of foreign bonds requires an appreciation (depreciation) of the exchange rate proportional to the increase (decrease) in the stock of foreign bonds to restore portfolio balance at *unchanged returns*. Hence starting from a position of steady state defined by a zero rate of depreciation, an increase in F associated with a proportional decrease in E will maintain $x = 0$. This explains why the $\dot{e} = 0$ locus is downward-sloping. Setting $\dot{F} = 0$ in (3.10b) we obtain a locus of combinations of the exchange rate and the stock of foreign bonds which is compatible with a current account balance. From our short-run analysis we know that real wealth increases with an increase in the stock of foreign bonds and that real wealth reduces with an expectation of a depreciating exchange rate. Since a depreciation of the exchange rate is associated with an expectation of a depreciating exchange rate it follows that an increase in F must be associated with an increase in E to maintain wealth constant and to preserve current account (and capital account) balance. This explains why the $\dot{F} = 0$ locus is upward-sloping. Above (below) the $\dot{e} = 0$ locus the exchange rate is depreciating (appreciating) and $\dot{e} > 0$ ($\dot{e} < 0$). Above (below) the $\dot{F} = 0$ locus the current account is in surplus (deficit) and $\dot{F} > 0$ ($\dot{F} < 0$). The direction of the arrows in Figure 3.3 shows the direction of motion of E and F. The only stable path is the locus labelled SS and identified with the saddle path. Along the saddle path a current account surplus (deficit) is associated with an appreciating (depreciating) exchange rate; current account surpluses (deficits) raise (reduce) the stock of foreign bonds and this requires an appreciating (depreciating) exchange rate to preserve portfolio balance.

3.6 Responses of the exchange rate and the current account to sterilised and non-sterilised, unanticipated, open-market operations

Introduction

In this section we will illustrate impact, dynamic and steady-state responses of the exchange rate and the current account to two types of open-market operations: an open-market exchange of money for domestic bonds and an open-market exchange of domestic bonds for foreign bonds.Since any shock will,

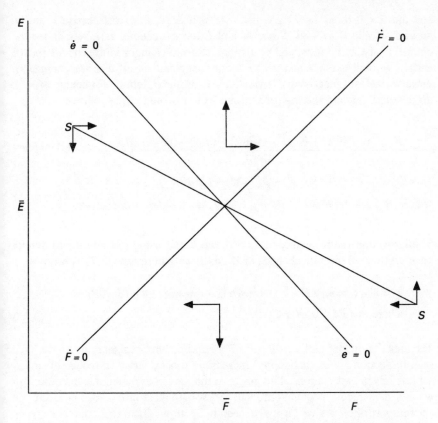

*Figure 3.3 The current account and the exchange rate under rational
expectations: deriving the saddle path*

normally, shift the position of the $\dot{F} = 0$ locus and the $\dot{e} = 0$ locus we will have to
be able to allow for such shifts. The *new* steady state will be defined by the
intersection of the *new* $\dot{F} = 0$ locus and the *new* $\dot{e} = 0$ locus. Through this
intersection we can draw a saddle path locus with the properties described in
Section 3.5. If the shock under consideration does not involve any change in the
predetermined stock of foreign bonds F the initial position is fully defined by the
initial steady-state $\bar{F}$ and the saddle path. In the case of the open-market
operations in foreign bonds the initial position is fully defined by the stock of
these bonds immediately after these operations and the position of the (new)
saddle path locus.

How to allow for shifts in the $\dot{F} = 0$ and the $\dot{e} = 0$ loci

Hitherto we have linearised the exchange rate and real wealth in the neighbourhood of $\bar{F}$ and $\bar{x} = 0$ since that was all that was needed for stability purposes and
for the purpose of deriving the saddle path. To allow for shifts in the $\dot{F} = 0$ locus

and the $\dot{e} = 0$ locus in (F, E) space we will need, first, to linearise E and w around $\bar{M}$ and $\bar{B}$ as well. Since M and B are exogenous variables under the control of the authorities, and to distinguish from changes in the endogenous E and F, we will use dM and dB to denote once-and-for-all discrete changes in these variables. Linearising E around $\bar{F}$, $\bar{x}$, $\bar{M}$ and $\bar{B}$, letting dM denote $M - \bar{M}$, dB denote $B - \bar{B}$ and solving for x allows us to rewrite (3.9) as follows:

$$x = \frac{(E - \bar{E}) - (\partial E/\partial F)(F - \bar{F}) - (\partial E/\partial M)(dM) - (\partial E/\partial B)(dB)}{\partial E/\partial x} \quad (3.9^*)$$

$$= \Phi_E(E - \bar{E}) + \Phi_F(F - \bar{F}) + \Phi_M(dM) + \Phi_B(dB)$$

where $\Phi_M \equiv - [(\partial E/\partial M)/(\partial E/\partial x)] < 0$, $\Phi_B \equiv -[(\partial E/\partial B)/(\partial E/\partial x)] \gtrless 0$.

Similarly, linearising w around $\bar{F}$, $\bar{x}$, $\bar{M}$ and $\bar{B}$ and using dM and dB to denote once-and-for-all discrete changes in M and B we will rewrite (3.7) as follows:

$$w = \bar{w} + (\partial w/\partial F)(F - \bar{F}) + (\partial w/\partial x)x + (\partial w/\partial M)dM + (\partial w/\partial B)dB$$

where $\partial w/\partial M < 0, \partial w/\partial B > 0$. $\quad (3.7^*)$

The signs of $\partial w/\partial M$ and $\partial w/\partial B$ in (3.7*) require some explanation. As we have seen in Section 3.3 an (helicopter) increase in money serves to reduce the interest rate, given expectations. This suggests that, given expectations, the ratio F to w rises and, since F is predetermined, real wealth must fall to accommodate the shift in portfolios. As we have also seen in Section 3.3, an (helicopter) increase in domestic bonds serves to increase the interest rate, given expectations. This suggests that, given expectations, the ratio of F to w falls and, since F is predetermined, real wealth must rise to accommodate the shift in portfolios. Taking account of (3.7*) we will rewrite (3.8) as follows:

$$\dot{F} = \Psi_F(F - \bar{F}) + \Psi_x(x) + \Psi_M(dM) + \Psi_B(dB);$$

$$\Psi_M \equiv (\partial S/\partial w)(\partial w/\partial M), \qquad \Psi_B \equiv (\partial S/\partial w)(\partial w/\partial B) \quad (3.8^*)$$

Finally, putting (3.8*) and (3.9*) in matrix form to rewrite (3.10b) we obtain:

$$\begin{bmatrix} \dot{F} \\ \dot{e} \end{bmatrix} = \begin{bmatrix} \Psi_F + \psi_x\Phi_F & \Psi_x\Phi_E \\ \Phi_F & \Phi_E \end{bmatrix} \begin{bmatrix} F - \bar{F} \\ E - \bar{E} \end{bmatrix}$$

$$+ \begin{bmatrix} (\Psi_M + \Psi_x\Phi_M)dM + (\Psi_B + \Psi_x\Phi_B)dB \\ (\Phi_M)dM \qquad + (\Phi_B)dB \end{bmatrix} \quad (3.10b^*)$$

which, upon substitutions, simplifies further to:

$$\begin{bmatrix} \dot{F} \\ \dot{e} \end{bmatrix} = \begin{bmatrix} \alpha_{11} & \alpha_{12} \\ \alpha_{21} & \alpha_{22} \end{bmatrix} \begin{bmatrix} F - \overline{F} \\ E - \overline{E} \end{bmatrix} + \begin{bmatrix} (\partial S/\partial w)(1/E)dM \ + \ (\partial S/\partial w)(1/E)dB \\ (\Phi_M)dM \hspace{2cm} + \ (\Phi_B)dB \end{bmatrix}$$

$$(3.11)$$

where $\alpha_{11} \equiv \partial S/\partial w$, $\alpha_{12} \equiv -(\partial S/\partial w)(M + B)(1/E^2)$, $\alpha_{21} \equiv \Phi_F$, $\alpha_{22} \equiv \Phi_E$.

Notice the rather interesting result in (3.11): *allowing for the effect of expectations on wealth, a unit increase in money and a unit increase in bonds have identical effects on wealth in the neighbourhood of the steady state; in both cases wealth rises by 1/E per unit increase in either of these assets.*

We are now in a position to conduct our analysis about responses of the exchange rate and the current account to $dB + dM = 0$, and to $dB + EdF = 0$.

Responses of the exchange rate and the current account to an unanticipated open-market purchase of domestic bonds for money

Our remarks at the end of the previous section indicate that the $\dot{F} = 0$ locus does not shift when money exchanges for domestic bonds; formally, $(\partial S/\partial w)(1/E)dM - (\partial S/\partial w)(1/E)dM = 0$. To ascertain the direction and the magnitude of the shift in the $\dot{e} = 0$ locus we have to evaluate $(\Phi_M - \Phi_B)dM = -[\partial E/\partial M - \partial E/\partial B](\partial E/\partial x)^{-1}$. Solving the short-run portfolio model for the response of the exchange rate to autonomous changes in M and in B we obtain the following results:

$$(\partial E/\partial M) = \frac{-[-(B/W)[\partial(FE/W)/\partial(r_b)^*] + (FE/W)[\partial(B/W)/\partial(r_b)^*]]}{F[[\partial(M/W)/\partial(r_b)^*](B/W) - [\partial(B/W)/\partial(r_b)^*](M/W)]} > 0$$

$$(3.12)$$

$$(\partial E/\partial B) = \frac{[-(M/W)[\partial(FE/W)/\partial(r_b)^*] + (FE/W)[\partial(M/W)/\partial(r_b)^*]]}{F[[\partial(M/W)/\partial(r_b)^*](B/W) - [\partial(B/W)/\partial(r_b)^*](M/W)]} \gtreqless 0$$

$$(3.13)$$

and, therefore,

$$(\partial E/\partial M) - (\partial E/\partial B) = \frac{\partial(FE/W)/\partial(r_b)^*}{F[[\partial(M/W)/\partial(r_b)^*](B/W) - [\partial(B/W)/\partial(r_b)^*](M/W)]} > 0$$

$$(3.14)$$

Thus $(\Phi_M - \Phi_B) dM < 0$. *At the initial steady state, an open market purchase of domestic bonds in exchange for money induces an expectation of an appreciating currency which requires a depreciation of the exhange rate to prevent the exchange rate from changing over time; in short the $\dot{e} = 0$ locus shifts up.* Across steady states the exchange rate depreciates and the stock of foreign bonds increases: since the propensity to save schedule remains unchanged real wealth remains unchanged across steady states and to accommodate the reduction in $(r_b)^*$, holdings of foreign assets must increase through the current account. To accommodate the increase in F at unchanged w the combined real holdings of money and domestic bonds must reduce and, given that $(M + B)$ remains constant throughout, E must rise. Notice that the impact depreciation of the exchange rate must exceed the depreciation across

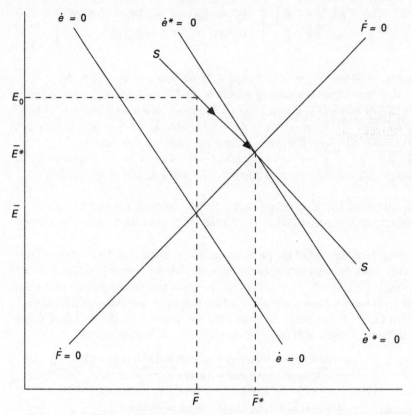

Figure 3.4 The current account and the exchange rate under rational expectations: responses to an unanticipated open-market purchase of domestic bonds for money

steady states since the stock of F in the short run is predetermined; in short, overshooting must occur. Figure 3.4 serves to illustrate adjustments to an open market increase of money in exchange for domestic bonds.

In Figure 3.4 the new steady state is defined by the intersection of the $\dot{e}^* = 0$ locus with the $\dot{F} = 0$ locus. Upon the announcement and the implementation of the open-market operations the exchange rate depreciates to E_0, overshooting its steady state by $E_0 - \bar{E}^*$; an incipient capital outflow induced by the reduction of the domestic interest rate depreciates the exchange rate to the point of generating an expectation of an appreciating exchange rate sufficient to induce agents to hold the existing stock of assets (after the operation) in their portfolios. The greater is the substitutability between bonds the smaller the risk premium required and the greater is the overshooting. At $(\bar{F}, E_0)$ wealth is below its steady state and agents run current account surpluses to acquire foreign assets.

Responses of the exchange rate and the current account to an
unanticipated, open-market purchase of domestic bonds for
foreign bonds

As we have seen, when we allow for the effect of expectations on real wealth, a
unit reduction in B reduces real wealth by $1/E$ units in the neighbourhood of the
steady state, whereas a unit increase in F increases real wealth by one unit in the
same neighbourhood. Hence, in order to maintain a balanced current account, a
unit decrease in B must be associated with $1/E$ units increase in F; at the initial
$\bar{E}$ the $\dot{F} = 0$ locus must shift to the right. Alternatively, at the initial $\bar{F}$ the $\dot{F} = 0$
locus must shift down; to maintain wealth constant at the initial $\bar{F}$ a unit reduc-
tion in B must be associated with $[E/(M + B)]$ units reduction in E after allowing
for the influence of expectations on real wealth.

To consider shifts in the $\dot{e} = 0$ locus we must distinguish between the case
where domestic and foreign bonds are 'relatively close substitutes' and the case
where they are not. In the former case, as we have already seen in Section 3.3, a
reduction in B will depreciate E, whereas in the latter case a reduction in B will
appreciate E. The intuitive reasoning for this is rather simple: loosely speaking,
in the case of 'close substitutes' a reduction in B resembles a reduction in F and,
therefore, the price of foreign exchange must rise to reflect the decreased supply.
The implications are the following. When foreign and domestic bonds are
relatively close substitutes a reduction in B will require the $\dot{e} = 0$ locus to shift to
the right; to prevent the exchange rate from changing over time at the initial $\bar{E}$,
F must increase to induce an appreciation sufficient to cancel the effects of the
depreciation associated with the reduction in B. When foreign and domestic
bonds are poor substitutes a reduction in B will require the $\dot{e} = 0$ to shift (down)
to the left to prevent the exchange rate from changing over time. Tedious
algebra confirms that when circumstances are such that the $\dot{e} = 0$ locus shifts
right the magnitude of this shift falls short of the magnitude of the shift in the
$\dot{F} = 0$ locus; at the initial $\bar{E}$, the increase in F required to prevent the exchange
rate from changing over time is not sufficient to maintain real wealth constant.
Similarly, when circumstances are such that the $\dot{e} = 0$ locus shifts down, the
magnitude of this shift falls short of the magnitude of the shift in the $\dot{F} = 0$
locus; at the initial $\bar{F}$, the appreciation required to prevent the exchange rate from
changing over time is not sufficient to maintain real wealth constant. In either
case, the stock of foreign assets increases across steady states and the exchange
rate appreciates across steady states. In either case the economy is running
current account deficits during the adjustment period; in either case part of the
initial increase in foreign assets through the open market is sold abroad through
the capital account. In the case where the two bonds are close substitutes, not
surprisingly, the appreciation across steady states is smaller and the cumulative
deficits are also smaller; when the two bonds are close substitutes agents have
less incentive to alter the yields of their asset holdings and the distribution of

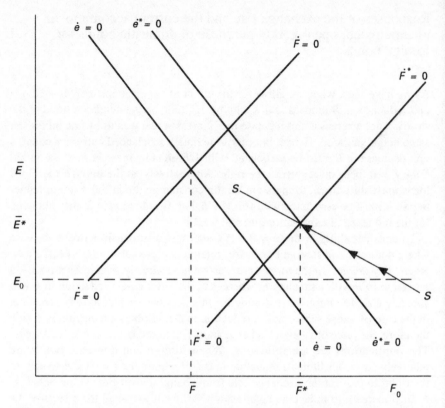

Figure 3.5a   Current account and exchange rate responses (under rational expectations) to an unanticipated open-market purchase of domestic bonds for foreign bonds: the 'close' substitutes case

these holdings immediately after an open-market exchange of one type of bond for the other. Figure 3.5a illustates adjustments when bonds are close substitutes, while Figure 3.5b illustrates adjustments when bonds are poor substitutes. In view of the explanations already provided there is very little comment attached to these figures.

In Figure 3.5a the initial steady state is defined by $(\bar{F}, \bar{E})$ at the intersection of the $\dot{e} = 0$ locus with the $\dot{F} = 0$ locus. Immediately after the open-market sale of foreign bonds the stock of these bonds increases to, say, F_0. Our detailed analysis in Section 3.3, together with our analysis above, explains why the initial position requires an appreciation of the exchange rate; in Figure 3.5a this initial position is defined by (F_0, E_0) on the saddle path SS. This initial appreciation raises initial wealth above its steady state and this explains the current account deficits that follow. Along the path of adjustment current account deficits serve to eliminate part of the increase in the stock of foreign bonds in portfolios and to moderate the initial appreciation; the new steady state is defined by $(\bar{F}^*, \bar{E}^*)$ at the intersection of the $\dot{e}^* = 0$ locus with the $\dot{F}^* = 0$ locus.

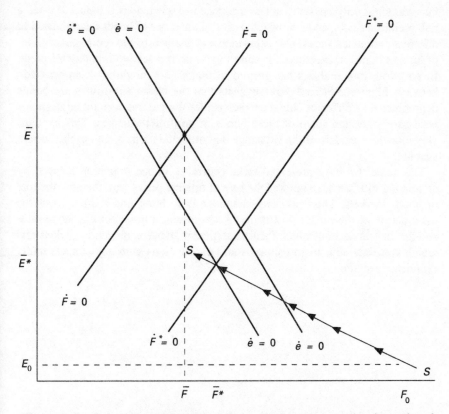

Figure 3.5b Current account and exchange rate responses (under rational expectations) to an unanticipated open-market purchase of domestic bonds for foreign bonds: the 'poor' substitutes case

In Figure 3.5b the initial steady state is defined in precisely the same way as in Figure 3.5a. Also the initial stock of foreign bonds outstanding after the open-market operations is precisely F_0, as before. However, when bonds are poor substitutes, a change in the share of these two bonds in portfolios would be expected to require a bigger adjustment in their relative price; in Figure 3.5b the exchange rate appreciates, on impact, to E_0. This relatively large appreciation explains why initial wealth rises by more in the case where the two bonds are poor substitutes and this accounts for the larger current account deficits that follow. Finally $(\bar{F}^*, \bar{E}^*)$ defines the new steady state.

3.7 Concluding remarks

As we have remarked repeatedly in this chapter, a feature which distinguishes portfolio balance models from monetary models is the fact that sterilised intervention is only possible (unless a change in expectations is induced) when a risk premium exists, and one which varies as the share of bonds denominated in different currencies varies. Our exposition and analysis of the open-market 'sale' of foreign bonds in exchange for domestic bonds has served to make this point. In addition, our analysis has served to make another point: a comparison between Figures 3.5a and 3.5b suggests that the closer substitutes are bonds denominated in different curencies the smaller the current account adjustments necessary when the share of these bonds in portfolios changes. This explains why monetary models of the exchange pay little attention, if any, to the current account.

The model we have presented lacks generality in one important respect: by embracing PPP we have ignored the role of relative prices and, thereby, the role of goods markets. This was done intentionally to bring into sharper focus the asset nature of the model. In Chapter 4 we present a model of exchange rates and the current account which focuses particular attention on goods markets and which contrasts adjustments under static expectations with adjustments under rational expectations.

Exchange Rates, Expectations and the Current Account

4.1 Introduction

In Chapter 1 we briefly looked into the relationship between the exchange rate and the current account required to maintain continuous balance in that account. This relationship is at the heart of exchange rate theories which build upon capital immobility since under capital immobility the role of the exchange rate is to preserve current account balance at all times. When capital is immobile internationally there is no asset role for the exchange rate to play; rather its role is to equate the (flow) demand for goods with the (flow) supply of goods and to balance absorption with income. The role of the exchange rate is to preserve flow equilibria. In Chapter 3 we looked, in some detail, into the relationship between the exchange rate and the current account in a world with perfect capital mobility, imperfect asset substitutability and continuous PPP. When capital is perfectly mobile internationally the exchange rate enters directly into the modelling of asset markets to equate the stock demand for assets denominated in different currencies with the stock supply of these assets and it continues with its role of bringing into equilibrium the flow demand for goods with the flow supply of goods. Given the existing supply of assets the role of the exchange rate is to preserve stock flow equilibria at any moment in time. However these momentary stock flow equilibria may not correspond with a balance between absorption and income and, as a result, current account imbalances may emerge. In a perfectly flexible exchange rate regime these current account imbalances mirror capital account imbalances. They reflect the disequilibrium dynamics of changes in the stock of net claims abroad designed to bring into balance the current stock of these claims with the steady-state demand for these claims. Thus, in a world of prefect capital mobility, the current account constitutes an important source of exchange rate dynamics. The other source of dynamics comes from the evolution of expectations about exchange rate changes.

However, when continuous PPP is the rule, as was the case with the analysis of Chapter 3, there is no way to examine adjustments to shocks that alter the distribution of a given absorption since the entire absorption is directed to a single commodity. An important feature of the present model is that it eschews PPP. Rather it distinguishes between a domestic and a foreign good whose relative price is endogenous, and it attempts to integrate portfolio balance with goods market equilibrium. Like Chapter 6, the present chapter develops a theory of the exchange rate which emphasises the dynamics of foreign asset accumulation and of exchange rate expectations. Unlike Chapter 6, however, the present chapter develops a model based on price flexibility and continuous full employment. The exchange rate may still overshoot its long-run equilibrium, not as a result of any price stickiness but rather as a result of the fact that foreign assets are short-run predetermined and, thus, evolve gradually over time in contrast to the forward-looking nature of the exchange rate.

The outline of this chapter is as follows. Section 4.2 describes the model which draws heavily on Dornbusch and Fischer (1980). The main difference in the structure of the present model from the structure of the Dornbusch-Fischer model is in the specification of asset demands. In the present model asset demands ignore transactions requirements. As a result, when expectations are static the short-run equilibrium nominal exchange rate is unaffected by shocks that influence the goods markets alone. However under rational expectations real shocks are transmitted instantly into the assets markets. Thus the by-product of our modelling of asset demands is to bring into sharper focus the role of expectations. Section 4.3 describes the characteristics of the short-run solution of the model under exogenous expectations. Section 4.4 examines the evolution of the economy under static expectations, whereas Section 4.5 examines the evolution of the economy under rational expectations and compares results with the previous section. To test for the robustness of the association between the exchange rate and the current account along the saddle path we assign a stronger role to expectations than do Dornbusch and Fischer. Section 4.6 concludes the chapter. To illustrate impact, dynamic and steady-state adjustments and compare adjustments under rational expectations with adjustments under static expectations we subject the model to the same two types of shock throughout our entire analysis; one type of shock involves an unanticipated open market purchase of foreign bonds, the other involves an unanticipated increase in the demand for the domestic good abroad.

4.2 A description of the model: setting the agenda

$$\lambda \equiv EP^*/P \tag{4.1}$$

$$w \equiv (H/P) + (\lambda \alpha /r^*) \tag{4.2}$$

$$r = r^* + x \tag{4.3}$$

$$(H/P) = k(r)w = k(r^* + x)w \qquad \partial k/\partial r < 0. \tag{4.4a}$$

$$(\lambda \alpha /r^*) = [1 - k(r)]w = [1 - k(r^* + x)]w \tag{4.4b}$$

$$\frac{(\lambda \alpha)/r^*}{H/P} = \frac{1 - k(r^* + x)}{k(r^* + x)} = \frac{(EP^*)\alpha}{r^* H} \tag{4.4c}$$

$$Y = A + T = A(w) + T(w,\lambda ;s) = D(w,\lambda ;s), \quad \partial A/\partial w > 0, \ \partial T/\partial w < 0, \ \partial T/\partial \lambda > 0$$
$$\partial T/\partial s > 0, \ \partial D/\partial w \equiv \partial A /\partial w + \partial T/\partial w > 0$$
$$\partial D/\partial \lambda \equiv \partial T/\partial \lambda, \partial D/\partial s \equiv \partial T/\partial s \tag{4.5}$$

$$S = S(w) \qquad \partial s/\partial w < 0, \tag{4.6}$$

$$(\lambda /r^*)(\dot\alpha) = S(w) \qquad \dot\alpha \equiv \partial \alpha /\partial t \tag{4.7}$$

Notation

λ = the real exchange rate.
E = the nominal exchange rate defined as the price of foreign currency in units of domestic currency.
P^* = the price of the foreign good in units of foreign currency.
P = the price of the domestic good in units of domestic currency.
w = the market value of wealth in units of the domestic good.
H = the stock of high-powered money in units of domestic currency.
α = the number of foreign bonds held domestically.
r^* = the nominal (and real) interest rate on foreign bonds.
x = the expected rate of depreciation of the nominal exchange rate.
r = the return on the foreign bond.
Y = the supply of the domestic good.
s = an index of tastes for the domestic good abroad.
S = private domestic saving in units of the domestic good.
A = absorption in units of the domestic good.
T = the trade balance in units of the domestic good.

Equation (4.1) identifies the real exchange rate with the price of the foreign good in units of the domestic good. A rise (fall) in λ corresponds to a depreciation (appreciation) of the real exchange rate or to an improvement (deterioration) in competitiveness. Equation (4.2) defines the wealth constraint of the domestic private sector. The menu of (net) assets for private residents to hold consists of high-powered money and of a foreign bond. By virtue of the assumption that the exchange rate floats freely and that government budgets always balance the stock of nominal high-powered money is taken to be fixed *over time*. Of course, barring the proverbial money rain through helicopter, *at a point in time* the stock of high-powered money can change but only through open-market operations. The number of foreign bonds held domestically is predetermined at any point in time by past saving or past open-market operations; over time α may increase (or decrease) through the accumulation of new saving (or dissaving). Each foreign bond entitles the holder to a unit of foreign output indefinitely. Thus the foreign bond is a real bond and it is also a perpetuity. Property income from abroad in real terms (that is, in units of domestic output) is equal to $\lambda\alpha$ and the capitalised value of this income given by $(\lambda\alpha/r^*)$ measures the market value of foreign bond holdings in real terms. Equation (4.3) states that the nominal return on the foreign bond r consists of the sum of the nominal interest rate on that bond r^* and of the expected rate of depreciation of the nominal exchange rate x which can measure the rate of expected capital gains on the foreign bond in nominal terms. By the small-country assumption we will take r^* to be exogenously given. On the assumption that high-powered money is non-interest bearing, r measures the opportunity cost of holding money. Equation (4.4a) models equilibrium in the market for (high-powered) money. For simplicity and to facilitate and illuminate exposition we model money demand to reflect portfolio considerations entirely. Ignoring transactions requirements in money demand does make some difference to some results but most of the key questions addressed in this chapter remain unaffected. We feel that the gain in clarity of exposition outweighs any loss in generality. According to (4.4a) the proportion of wealth held in money is a decreasing function of the opportunity cost of holding money. By virtue of the wealth constraint money market equilibrium is sufficient to ensure portfolio balance. Combining equations (4.2) and (4.4a) to eliminate real balances we obtain equation (4.4b) which expresses equilibrium in the bond market as well as overall portfolio balance. Equation (4.4c) yields an alternative formulation of portfolio balance designed to bring into sharp focus the view that the nominal exchange rate is first and foremost an asset price whose role is to balance the relative demand for assets with available relative supplies. In what follows it will prove convenient to work mainly with (4.4b) or (4.4c) to define portfolio balance. Equation (4.5) models equilibrium in the market for the domestic good. On the assumption that wages and prices adjust instantly to deliver full employment at all times the supply of the domestic good Y can be taken as exogenously given at its full employment level. For convenience and in the spirit of the absorption approach we model the demand for the domestic good as the sum of absorption and the trade balance. Wealth is taken to determine absorption and the real exchange rate is taken to determine the distribution of absorption between the domestic good and the foreign good. The real exchange rate (and the parameter s) also determines foreign demand for the domestic good. An increase in absorption generated by an increase in wealth is used partly to finance an increase in imports and partly to raise spending on the domestic good. A real exchange rate depreciation switches absorption from the foreign good to the domestic good and it also raises export demand. Hence a real exchange rate depreciation raises aggregate demand and it also improves the trade balance. Equation (4.6) models private saving along the lines of life-cycle principles and, thus, takes saving to be a decreasing function of wealth. Notice that our treatment of saving is consistent with our treatment of absorption; what motivates absorption and saving in this model is some measure of permanent income rather than current income. Since wealth can be viewed as a measure of the capitalised value of a permanent stream of income one can use wealth to capture the combined effects of permanent income and of the interest rate on absorption and on saving. On the assumption that no investment takes place and that government budgets always balance, realised private saving is identical with the realised surplus in the current account of the balance of payments, which is defined as the sum of the trade balance and of property income from abroad given by $T + \lambda\alpha$. *Thus when markets clear, using the definition of the current account surplus to evaluate $T + \lambda\alpha$ or evaluating $S(w)$ yields identical results.* The left-hand side of equation (4.7) measures the market value of net additions to foreign bond holdings through (net) purchases in the capital market which, in the absence of any domestic bonds, suffice to record the entire deficit in the capital account. By virtue of the fact that in a freely floating exchange rate regime the deficit in the capital account equals the surplus in the current account and in view of the role of saving in this model one can use the propensity to save schedule to model the capital account. There is another way of looking at equation (4.7); what it says is that the entire amount of saving is used to finance net acquisitions of claims on foreign resources. Whichever way we choose to look at it, equation (4.7) is a key dynamic relation which, together with the evolution of expectations, determines the path of the economy over time .

What is the association between the exchange rate and the current account along the adjustment path under static expectations? What difference does it make to this path if we assume rational expectations? In general, how can we derive the impact and the dynamic response of the exchange rate and the current account to an exogenous disturbance under static and under rational expectations? How can we determine the steady-state effects of a disturbance? The remainder of this chapter addresses these issues.

4.3 Short-run equilibrium responses under exogenous expectations

At any moment in time the number of foreign bonds held domestically is the result of past acquisitions or past open-market operations. Given this number and assuming for the moment expectations to be exogenous, equations (4.4b) and (4.5) can solve for the market value of wealth and for the real exchange rate which maintain equilibrium in the markets for assets and the domestic good. Using the equilibrium value of wealth in the propensity to save schedule, equation (4.6), we can determine the current account surplus and applying equation (4.7) we can trace the evolution of the number of foreign bonds over time which, given expectations, suffices to determine the path of the entire economy. As a by-product we can obtain the all-important association of the exchange rate and of the current account. When expectations are endogenous, specifically when they follow a rational expectations path, things are not as simple. For the moment we will focus on the simpler task of analysing the model under exogenous (in particular, static) expectations. To begin with we will analyse the characteristics of short-run equilibrium.

We will use Figure 4.1 to illustrate the determination of short-run equilibrium and the characteristics of short-run equilibrium responses to exogenous disturbances. The *GG* locus is intended to model equation (4.5). The combinations of wealth and of the real exchange rate along the *GG* locus are intended to depict equilibrium in the market for the domestic good given tastes abroad and given any other parameters that may affect this market and which are not explicitly modelled. Other things equal, an increase in wealth creates an excess demand for the domestic good, whereas an appreciation of the real exchange rate creates an excess supply. Hence to maintain equilibrium in the market for the domestic good an increase in w must be associated with a decrease in λ and this explains why the *GG* locus is downward-sloping. Now suppose that tastes for the domestic good abroad improve; that is, suppose that s increases. This development will create an excess demand for the domestic good and to restore equilibrium in the goods market the *GG* locus must shift down to the position occupied, say, by the *G*G** locus: at any initially given level of wealth the relative price of the domestic good must rise (λ must fall) sufficiently to eliminate the excess demand generated by the increase in export demand and to restore equilibrium at the fixed supply of output.

The *AA* locus is intended to model equation (4.4b). The combinations of wealth and of the real exchange rate along this locus can illustrate portfolio balance given expectations, given the number of foreign bonds held domestically at any particular time, given the foreign interest rate, and given any other factors that directly influence asset demands and which are not modelled explicitly. Other things equal, an increase in wealth raises the demand for bonds (and money) whereas a depreciation of the real exchange rate raises the market value of the existing number of bonds. Hence to maintain portfolio balance an increase in w must be associated with an increase in λ and this explains why the *AA* locus is upward-sloping. Now consider shifts in this locus. To start with, suppose that the monetary authorities conduct an open-market purchase of bonds in exchange for high-powered money. Portfolio balance considerations suggest that *at the initial level of wealth* and at the given return on bonds the reduction of bonds outstanding in private hands calls for a depreciation of the real exchange rate to restore the market value of bonds outstanding to its initial level: *at the initial level of wealth* the real exchange rate must depreciate in proportion to the number of bonds purchased by the authorities. In terms of Figure 4.1, the *AA* locus must shift up to the position

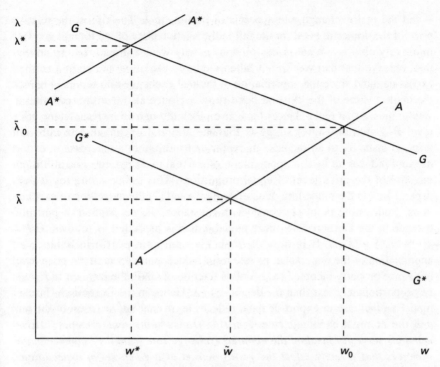

Figure 4.1   Short-run equilibrium in the markets for goods and assets

occupied, say, by the $A*A*$ locus. This time let us conduct a thought experiment in order to underline the role of expectations in the short run. Suppose that the economy is defined by the intersection of the AA locus with the GG locus when news arrives that leads agents to revise their expectations and to come to expect a higher rate of depreciation of the nominal exchange rate than the rate they expected at the intersection of these two loci. Such a development creates an excess demand for bonds at the initial equilibrium since it represents an increase in the return on bonds. To restore portfolio balance the AA locus must shift up: at the initial level of wealth the real exchange rate must depreciate to induce an increase in the market value of existing bonds and restore portfolio balance at the higher return on bonds relative to money. Without any loss in generality and for simplicity of exposition we may assume that the increase in the expected rate of depreciation of the nominal exchange rate causes the AA locus to shift to the position occupied by the $A*A*$ locus.

Let us now summarise the equilibrium responses in wealth and in the real exchange rate to the disturbances described above. Starting from a position of equilibrium defined, say, by the intersection of the AA locus with the GG locus, a shift in tastes abroad in favour of the domestic good places the economy immediately at the intersection of the AA locus with the $G*G*$ locus. Immediately after the disturbance the market value of wealth reduces from $\bar{w}_0$ to

$\tilde{w}$ and the real exchange rate appreciates from $\bar{\lambda}_0$ to $\tilde{\lambda}$. The rise in the relative price of the domestic good (or the fall in the relative price of the foreign good) is intuitively obvious. What is less obvious is why wealth should fall. To answer that, observe that had wealth not fallen the bond market would be in a state of excess demand since the appreciation of the real exchange rate serves to reduce the market value of the existing bond supply. Notice also that the reduction in wealth means that real balances have also fallen through an increase in the price level P. Equation (4.4c) suggests that the nominal exchange rate does not respond instantly to an increase in export demand; rather an increase in export demand induces an instant appreciation of the real exchange rate and an instant increase of the price level of equal proportions. This rather strong result does depend on: (1) the modelling of asset demands and (2) the modelling of expectations. Concerning point (1) consider, for instance, the description of portfolio balance in the Dornbusch-Fischer model which is modelled as follows: $H/P = k(r^* + x)(Y + \lambda\alpha.)$. It is now clear that to maintain portfolio balance an appreciation of the real exchange rate must induce an increase in the price level but, since property income, $\lambda\alpha$, is only a fraction of GNP, the increase in P must be proportionately less than the decrease in λ. Hence in the Dornbusch–Fischer model an increase in export demand induces an instant appreciation of the real *and* the nominal exchange rate. *Ignoring transactions requirements in asset demands serves to insulate the nominal exchange rate from the influence of parameters that directly affect the goods market at a given set of expectations.* Concerning point (2), and in anticipation of our discussion of the behaviour of the model under rational expectations, an increase in export demand will be shown to induce an expectation of an appreciation which, according to (4.4c), will require an instant appreciation of the nominal exchange rate. This result will serve to bring under sharper focus the role of expectations. To summarise: $\partial w/\partial s < 0$, $\partial\lambda/\partial s < 0$, $\partial(H/P)/\partial s < 0$, $\partial E/\partial s = 0$

Consider now the equilibrium responses to a reduction in the number of foreign bonds held domestically, α, through open-market operations. Starting from a position of equilibrium defined, say, by the intersection of the AA locus with the GG locus, the economy is placed immediately at the intersection of the A^*A^* locus with the GG locus. Wealth is reduced, immediately, from $\bar{w}_0$ to w^* and the real exchange rate depreciates immediately from $\bar{\lambda}_0$ to λ^*. To understand better the intuition behind this result notice, first, that by virtue of the fact that the foreign bond is a real perpetuity the real exchange rate can serve to measure the relative price of the perpetual stream of foreign output offered by the foreign bond. Hence a reduction in the supply of these bonds must raise their relative price; That is, it must depreciate the real exchange rate. *And although the depreciation of the real exchange rate serves to raise the real market value of the remainder of bonds it does not fully restore the real market value of bonds to its previous level*; had the real exchange rate depreciated proportionately to the reduction in the number of bonds to maintain the real market value of bonds and wealth unchanged, the goods market would be in a state of excess demand. Notice also that real balances must also reduce since wealth is reduced; in spite of the increase in nominal balances brought about by the open-market operations their equilibrium real value decreases owing to an increase in the price level which is proportionately more than the increase in H. Equation (4.4c) suggests that the nominal exchange rate must depreciate more than in proportion to the increase in money: (1) given the return on the bond relative to the return on money, relative demands remain unchanged and hence the relative supplies measured in the same unit must also remain unchanged; (2) to achieve this the nominal exchange rate must depreciate more than in proportion to the increase in money to make up for the reduced number of bonds and restore the market value of relative supplies. To summarise: $\partial w/\partial\alpha > 0$, $\partial\lambda/\partial\alpha < 0$, $-(\partial\lambda/\partial\alpha)(\alpha/\lambda) < 1$, $\partial(H/P)/\partial a > 0$, $\partial E/\partial\alpha < 0$. (NB $\partial E/\partial\alpha$ is intended to measure the response of E to a change in α, other things equal. Thus it is not intended to capture the total effect of open-market operations on E)

Consider finally the equilibrium response to an increase in the expected rate of depreciation of the nominal exchange rate. Starting from a position of equilibrium defined, say, by the intersection of the AA locus with the GG locus we may assume, without loss in generality, that the economy is placed immediately at the intersection of the A^*A^* locus with the GG locus. In view of the remarks we made above which explain why the real exchange rate can serve to measure the relative price of the income stream offered by the foreign bond, it is understandable why the real exchange rate depreciates: an increase in the return on these bonds induced by an increase in the expected rate of depreciation raises their demand and, hence, their price. Given this insight it is clear that wealth must reduce to preserve equilibrium in the goods market. As a result of the reduction in wealth and the increase in the opportunity cost of holding money, real balances must reduce by more than wealth does. Equation (4.4c) suggests that an increase in the expected rate of depreciation of the nominal exchange rate causes an instantaneous depreciation of the nominal exchange rate: an expectation of depreciation raises the demand for the foreign asset (bonds) relative to the domestic asset (money) and to restore equilibrium the nominal exchange rate depreciates to raise the market value of the foreign asset. In summary: $\partial w/\partial x < 0$, $\partial\lambda/\partial x > 0$, $\partial(H/P)/\partial x < 0$, $\partial E/\partial x > 0$.

Before we embark on further analysis we must pause to collect the results summarised above. Our analysis hitherto suggests that the reduced-form solutions of wealth, of the real and the nominal exchange rate, and of real balances that describe short-run equilibrium can be summarised as follows:

$$w = w(\alpha, x, s), \; \partial w/\partial\alpha > 0, \; \partial w/\partial x < 0, \; \partial w/\partial s < 0 \tag{4.8}$$

$$\lambda = \lambda(\alpha, x, s), \; \partial\lambda/\partial\alpha < 0, \; -(\partial\lambda/\partial\alpha)(\alpha/\lambda) < 1, \; \partial\lambda/\partial x > 0, \; \partial\lambda/\partial s < 0 \tag{4.9}$$

$$H/P \equiv h = h(\alpha, x, s), \; \partial h/\partial\alpha > 0, \; \partial h/\partial x < 0, \; \partial h/\partial s < 0 \tag{4.10}$$

$$E \equiv \lambda P/P^* \equiv (\lambda/h)(H/P^*) = E(\alpha, x, s, H/P^*), \; \partial E/\partial\alpha < 0, \; \partial E/\partial x > 0,$$
$$\partial E/\partial s = 0, \; \partial E/\partial(H/P^*) > 0 \tag{4.11}$$

4.4   Impact, dynamic and steady-state adjustments under static expectations

We are now able to illuminate the workings of the model and trace the path of the economy reflected in equations (4.4b) and (4.5)–(4.7) by the use of the diagrammatic apparatus developed in Figures (4.2)–(4.6). Figure 4.2, essentially, reproduces Figure 4.1; it is intended to show the simultaneous determination of the real exchange rate and the market value of wealth in the markets for assets and goods. Figure 4.4 is intended to illustrate the rate of saving consistent with market clearing; at any moment the real market value of wealth that is determined by the intersection of the appropriate *GG* locus with the appropriate *AA* locus in Figure 4.2 is projected onto Figure 4.4 to determine the appropriate rate of saving read from the propensity to save schedule defined by $S(w)$ in equation (4.6) and depicted by the *SS* locus. The vertical axis of Figure 4.5 is intended to measure the current account surplus $T + \lambda\alpha$ (capital account deficit) which, in this model, is identified with savings, and the horizontal axis measures the real exchange rate. So Figure 4.5 is intended to illustrate the association of the current account with the real exchange rate. With the aid of the 45° locus in Figure 4.3 we can project the market-clearing real exchange rate onto Figure 4.5. Similarly, with the aid of Figure 4.4 we can project the current account surplus (saving) consistent with market clearing onto Figure 4.5. Figure 4.6 is intended to depict the underlying reduced-form relationship between saving S, the number of bonds outstanding α and tastes s under static expectations; thus the vertical axis measures $S = \tilde{S}(\alpha, s)$, where $\tilde{S}(\ )$ defines this reduced-form relationship, and the horizontal axis measures α.

Suppose that we start from a position of steady-state equilibrium. In Figure 4.4 the intersection of the saving schedule *SS* with the wealth axis serves to define steady-state wealth at, say, $\bar{w}_0$; algebraically this is simply the solution obtained by setting $S(w) = 0$. Assuming that the index for tastes s takes the value, say, $s = \bar{s}_0$, and substituting $(\bar{w}_0, \bar{s}_0)$ into equation (4.5) we can solve for the real exchange rate consistent with steady-state equilibrium in the market for the domestic good. Letting this value of the real exchange rate be defined by, say, $\lambda = \bar{\lambda}_0$ we pass through point $(\bar{w}_0, \bar{\lambda}_0)$ in Figure 4.2, a *GG* locus intended to depict the combinations of the real exchange rate and wealth which serve to describe equilibrium in the market for the domestic good in the neighbourhood of the steady state defined by a given set of tastes. The portfolio balance locus consistent with steady-state equilibrium must also pass through point $(\bar{w}_0, \bar{\lambda}_0)$. Accordingly through point $(\bar{w}_0, \bar{\lambda}_0)$ in Figure 4.2 we pass an *AA* locus which is intended to depict the combinations of the real exchange rate and wealth which serve to describe equilibrium in the market for assets in the neighbourhood of the steady state defined by a given return. At the steady state expectations are realised regardless of how expectations are formed outside the steady state and, in the absence of steady-state inflation domestically or abroad, the expected rate of depreciation of the nominal exchange rate is zero. Substituting $x = 0$, $w = \bar{w}_0$ and $\lambda = \bar{\lambda}_0$ into equation (4.4b) serves to define the number of foreign bonds held

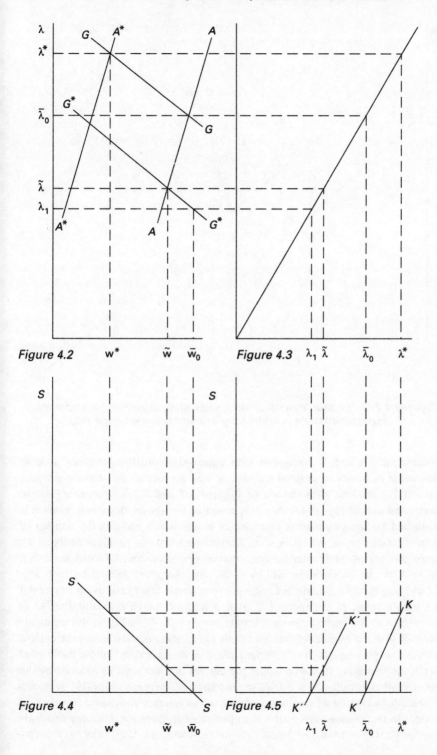

Figure 4.2

Figure 4.3

Figure 4.4

Figure 4.5

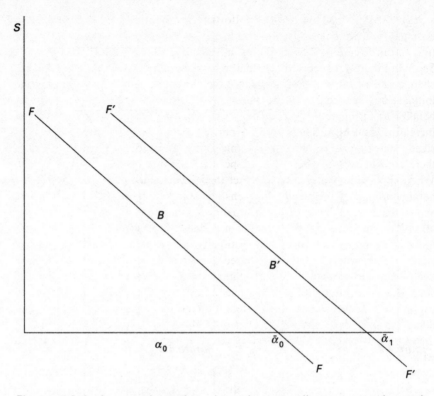

Figures 4.2–6   Impact, dynamic and steady-state adjustments under static expectations: the current accound and real exchange rate

domestically, which is consistent with steady-state portfolio balance. Letting this value of bonds be defined by, say, $\alpha = \bar{\alpha}_0$ we record $\bar{\alpha}_0$ on the horizontal axis of Figure 4.6. With the aid of Figures 4.2 and 4.3 we record $\bar{\lambda}_0$ on the horizontal axis of Figure 4.5. Now suppose that the above- described position is disturbed by an open-market purchase of bonds which reduces the number of bonds initially to α_0, where $\alpha_0 < \bar{\alpha}_0$. Borrowing from our previous analysis we know that immediately after the open-market operations the AA locus must shift up to A^*A^* to intersect the GG locus at, say, the point defined by (w^*, λ^*). Employing the SS schedule in Figure 4.4 to evaluate $S(w^*)$ and using Figure 4.3 we locate point K in Figure 4.5; at K a real exchange rate equal to λ^* is associated with a current account surplus equal to $S(w^*)$. In Figure 4.6 we locate point B; at B the number of foreign bonds outstanding equals α_0 and the current account surplus equals $S(w^*)$. What path does the economy follow thereafter? Well, the first thing to notice is that the current account surplus induced by the open-market purchase of bonds means that the private domestic sector is financing foreign bond purchases abroad in an attempt to rebuild its stock of bonds. In fact, immediately after the open-market operations, private residents are acquiring foreign bonds from abroad at the rate given by

$\dot{\alpha} = (r^*/\lambda^*)S(w^*)$. This has the following implications: in Figure 4.2 the economy is travelling down the GG locus from point (w^*, λ^*) towards point $(\bar{w}_0, \bar{\lambda}_0)$; in Figure 4.4 the economy is travelling down the SS locus towards $S(\bar{w}_0)$; in Figure 4.5 successively smaller surpluses are associated with a real exchange rate which is appreciating until the current account is in balance at the initial steady-state real exchange rate $\bar{\lambda}_0$; we illustrate this path with the locus labelled KK; In Figure 4.6 successively smaller surpluses are associated with an increasing number of bonds until the current account is in balance at the initial steady-state number $\bar{\alpha}_0$; we illustrate this path with the locus labelled FF. Hence there are forces in this model to propel the economy back to its steady state. When expectations are static the fact that $(\partial s/\partial w)(\partial w/\partial \alpha)$ is negative in the neighbourhood of the steady state ensures stability. In short the economy is shown to be stable. What permits us to draw all these loci as straight lines? After all is it not the case that the model is non-linear? The answer to this is that all these loci represent linear approximations in the neighbourhood of the steady state; all the partial derivatives required to construct each and every slope have been evaluated around the steady state. The reasoning behind this is that for small deviations around the steady state a linear approximation can adequately capture the model. Hence all the stability analysis conducted, and to be conducted, is an analysis applicable to local stability.

Let us now consider the impact, dynamic and steady-state effects associated with an autonomous increase in the demand for exports. Let us suppose, again, that the economy is at its initial steady state when the parameter s increases from, say, $s = \bar{s}_0$ to, say, $\bar{s}_1 > \bar{s}_0$. As a result the GG locus shifts to the position occupied by, say, the G^*G^* locus in Figure 4.2. In the same figure wealth is shown to reduce to $\tilde{w}$ and the real exchange rate to appreciate to $\tilde{\lambda}$. In Figure 4.4 saving is measured by $S(\tilde{w})$. In Figure 4.5 we record a surplus at the rate $S(\tilde{w})$ and, associated with it, a real exhange rate equal to $\tilde{\lambda}$; this is point K'. In Figure 4.6 we locate point B' at which a surplus of $S(\tilde{w})$ is associated with $\bar{\alpha}_0$. It is easy to show now that in Figure 4.2 adjustments follow along the G^*G^* locus until point $(\bar{w}_0, \bar{\lambda}_1)$ is reached and that in Figure 4.4 adjustments follow along the SS locus until $S(\bar{w}_0) = 0$ is reached. In Figure 4.5 adjustments follow along the $K'K'$ locus until a balanced current account is achieved at $\bar{\lambda}_1$. Finally in Figure 4.6 adjustments follow along the $F'F'$ locus until a current account balance is achieved at $\bar{\alpha}_1$. To summarise some key features: (1) at each and every real exchange rate the current account registers a higher surplus than before the increase in export demand and to bring the current account into balance the real exchange rate must appreciate across steady states; (2) also for each and every stock of foreign bonds held the current account registers a higher surplus and to bring this account into balance the number of bonds held across steady states must increase. Notice though that wealth is unchanged across steady states since the propensity to save schedule is not disturbed, which means that α must have increased proportionately to the fall in λ across steady states in order to preserve portfolio balance.

Since a very considerable interest is attached to the behaviour of the nominal exchange rate, how might one describe the joint path of the nominal exchange

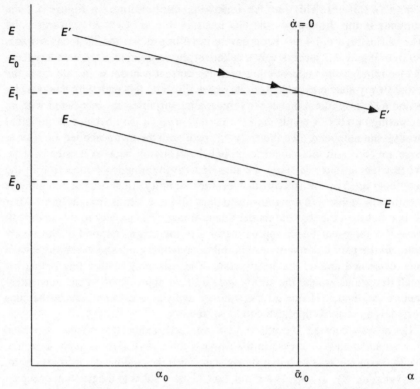

Figure 4.7a *The nominal exchange rate and the current account under static expectations: adjustments to an open-market operation*

rate and of foreign-issued claims held domestically? How might one illustrate impact, dynamic and steady-state adjustments in the nominal exchange rate when (1) the authorities conduct a once-and-for-all open-market purchase of foreign bonds and (2) foreign demand for the domestic good increases? To answer this we turn to equations (4.11) and (4.7). Armed with the reduced-form expressions for λ and for w, we will rewrite equation (4.7) to capture the path of foreign bonds consistent with market clearing. This rewritten equation will be numbered (4.7a). Thus the model to consider is given by:

$$\dot{\alpha} = [r*/\lambda(\alpha, x, s)]S[w(\alpha, x, s)] \tag{4.7a}$$

$$E = E(\alpha, x, s, H/P*) \tag{4.11}$$

(NB We leave s in $E(\ )$ although its contribution is zero.)

Setting $x = 0$ in (4.7a) we observe that $\dot{\alpha}$ depends only on α and s: *The current account is independent of the nominal exchange rate when expectations are static.* Rather it is the nominal exchange rate which is driven by the current account, as equation (4.11) suggests.

Figure 4.7a illustrates adjustments in the nominal exchange rate and the current account to an open-market purchase of bonds under static expectations. The vertical axis in Figure 4.7a measures the nominal exchange rate E, while the horizontal axis measures the number of foreign bonds held domestically, α. The *EE* locus graphs the association between E and α defined by equation (4.11) for given H/P^* and on the assumption that $x = 0$. At any moment in time, the economy is at some point on the *EE* locus: at any moment in time the nominal exchange rate takes the value consistent with market clearing at the predetermined α and the given H/P^*. Setting $\dot\alpha = 0$, $x = 0$ and, say, $s = \bar{s}_0$ in equation (4.7a) serves to define the steady-state number of bonds at, say, $\alpha = \bar\alpha_0$. At the thus determined $\bar\alpha_0$ we erect a vertical locus and label this the $\dot\alpha = 0$ locus. To the left of this locus the current account is in surplus, whereas to the right of this locus this account is in deficit: for any α less than (more than) $\bar\alpha_0$ wealth is below (above) its steady state and saving (dissaving) takes place. The initial steady-state nominal exchange rate is defined by the intersection of the *EE* locus with the $\dot\alpha = 0$ locus at $\bar{E}_0$. Consider now an open-market purchase of bonds that reduces the number of bonds outstanding to, say, α_0 initially. The increase in the stock of money coming from the open-market serves to induce an

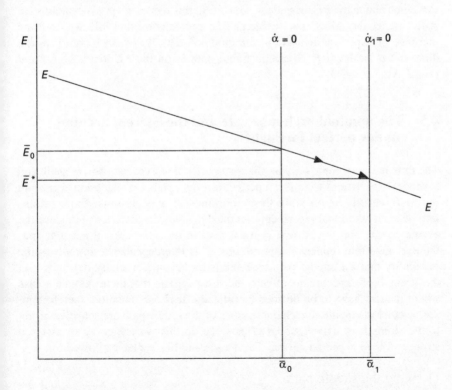

Figure 4.7b   The nominal exchange rate and the current account under static expectations: adjustments to an increase in export demand

upward shift in the *EE* locus to the position occupied by, say, the *E′E′* locus: at any level of α, E must depreciate in proportion to the rise in H to preserve portfolio balance. The initial market-clearing nominal exchange rate is defined by E_0, the point on the *E′E′* locus directly above α_0: immediately after the open-market purchase of bonds the exchange rate must depreciate sufficiently to accommodate portfolio balance at the reduced bond supply *and* the increased money supply. The path of the economy is along the *E′E′* locus from point (α_0, E_0) to $(\bar{\alpha}_0, \bar{E}_1)$. Along this path current account surpluses are associated with an appreciating nominal exchange rate: current account surpluses help to build the stock of bonds back to its initial steady state defined by the index of exogenous tastes and in the process the nominal exchange rate must be appreciating to accommodate portfolio balance at increasing stocks of foreign assets.

Consider now applying the diagrammatic apparatus developed in Figure 4.7a to an analysis of adjustments to an increase in export demand. Figure 4.7b reproduces the *EE* locus and the $\dot{\alpha} = 0$ locus and it adds an $\dot{\alpha}_1 = 0$ locus directly above $\bar{\alpha}_1$, where $\bar{\alpha}_1$ is the steady-state number of bonds found by setting $\dot{\alpha} = 0$, $x = 0$ and evaluating (4.7a) at $s = \bar{s}_1 > \bar{s}_0$. Starting from an initial steady state defined by the intersection of the *EE* locus with the $\dot{\alpha} = 0$ locus we have a shift in this locus to the position occupied by the $\dot{\alpha}_1 = 0$ locus. For the reasons explained above the *EE* locus does not shift in this model when expectations are static; rather the initial real exchange rate appreciation that follows from the increase in export demand is accommodated entirely by an increase in the domestic price level P. The adjustment path is on the *EE* locus from point $(\bar{\alpha}_0, \bar{E}_0)$ to $(\bar{\alpha}_1, \bar{E}^*)$.

4.5   The nominal exchange rate and the current account under perfect foresight

The time has now come to relax the assumption that expectations are static and to model expectations to follow a perfect foresight path. Our intention is to bring out as forcefully as possible the importance of expectations. Expectations introduce an additional ingredient into the dynamics. Expectations influence the exchange rate and the current account and, in turn, the current account and the exchange rate influence expectations. This interdependence introduces the possibility that the saddle path characteristics become crucially dependent on the strength of expectations effects and this suggests that there may be a case where matters have to be decided empirically. It is our intention, therefore, to see whether the qualitative characteristics of the saddle path are sensitive or not to the strength of expectational effects. To do this we are going to assign a stronger role to expectations than Dornbusch and Fischer have allowed for.

Deriving the saddle path

In what follows we will set the expected rate of depreciation equal to the actual rate to capture rational expectations in a non-stochastic framework. This requires setting $x = (\partial E/\partial t)/E = \partial(\log E)/\partial t$. To simplify notation we will define $e \equiv \log E$ and, therefore, we will set $x = \dot{e}$. To solve the model under perfect foresight let us first turn to equations (4.7a) and (4.11) and linearise these around the steady state, to obtain:

$$\dot{\alpha} = \Psi_\alpha (\alpha - \bar{\alpha}) + \Psi_x x \qquad \Psi_\alpha < 0, \quad \Psi_x > 0 \qquad (4.7a*)$$

$$E - \bar{E} = \Phi_\alpha (\alpha - \bar{\alpha}) + \Phi_x x \qquad \Phi_\alpha \equiv \partial E/\partial \alpha < 0, \quad \Phi_x \equiv \partial E/\partial x > 0 \qquad (4.11*)$$

A few comments about (4.7a*) and (4.11*) are in order. Firstly, the Ψs and the Φs are introduced to simplify the notation of the partial derivatives involved in obtaining the linear approximation. Secondly, the sign of the Ψs and Φs is self-explanatory in view of all our previous discussion and to avoid tedious repetition we do not attempt to provide yet again an additional explanation. Thirdly, the expressions $\bar{\alpha}$ and $\bar{E}$ *are* steady-state solutions predicated on particular values of the parameters entering these solutions so, for instance, $\bar{\alpha} = \bar{\alpha}\,(\bar{s})$, $\bar{E} = \bar{E}(\bar{H}, \bar{P}*, \bar{s})$. Setting $x = \dot{e}$ in (4.7a*) and (4.11*) and rewriting we obtain:

$$\begin{bmatrix} 1 & -\Psi_x \\ 0 & -\Phi_x \end{bmatrix} \begin{bmatrix} \dot{\alpha} \\ \dot{e} \end{bmatrix} = \begin{bmatrix} \Psi_\alpha & 0 \\ \Phi_\alpha & -1 \end{bmatrix} \begin{bmatrix} \alpha & -\bar{\alpha} \\ E & -\bar{E} \end{bmatrix} \qquad (4.12)$$

which yields, upon solution:

$$\dot{\alpha} = \tilde{\Psi}_\alpha (\alpha - \bar{\alpha}) + \tilde{\Psi}_e (E - \bar{E}) \qquad (4.12a)$$

$$\dot{e} = \tilde{\Phi}_\alpha (\alpha - \bar{\alpha}) + \tilde{\Phi}_e (E - \bar{E}) \qquad (4.12b)$$

Where $\tilde{\Psi}_\alpha \equiv [-\Phi_x \Psi_\alpha + \Psi_x \Phi_\alpha](-\Phi_x)^{-1} = \Psi_\alpha + \Psi_x \tilde{\Phi}_\alpha$? $\quad \tilde{\Psi}_e \equiv \Psi_x /\Phi_x > 0$,

$$\tilde{\Phi}_\alpha \equiv -\Phi_\alpha /\Phi_x > 0, \quad \tilde{\Phi}_e \equiv 1/\Phi_x > 0.$$

The sign of $\tilde{\Psi}_\alpha$ is ambiguous. On the one hand, a rise in α deteriorates the current account directly by Ψ_α; one may wish to label this the direct wealth effect on the current account. On the other hand, a rise in α induces an expectation of depreciation which reduces wealth and, thus, induces an improvement in the current account; one may wish to label this the expectations effect. The expectations effect on the current account due to a rise in α is captured by $\Psi_x\tilde{\Phi}_\alpha$. Dornbusch and Fischer have assumed that the sum of these two effects, measured by $\tilde{\Psi}_\alpha$, is negative. Had we followed their assumption we would have obtained, as they did, a saddle path along which surpluses are associated with an appreciating nominal exchange rate. Is their result robust within the confines of the present model? To answer this we have allowed for the possibility that expectations effects are strong enough to dominate the sign of $\tilde{\Psi}_\alpha$. Thus in what follows we are assuming $\tilde{\Psi}_\alpha > 0$. Armed with the expressions given by (4.12a) and (4.12b) we turn to Figure 4.8a to assist us in deriving the perfect foresight path.

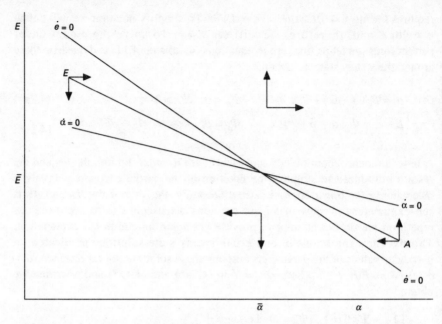

Figure 4.8a The nominal exchange rate and the current account under rational expectations: deriving the saddle path

In Figure 4.8a the $\dot{e} = 0$ locus gives the combinations of E and α which are required to prevent the nominal exchange rate from changing over time. To explain why this locus is downward-sloping we will argue as follows: (1) other things equal, an increase in α raises the market value of foreign assets at existing prices and to restore portfolio balance an expectation of a depreciating nominal exchange rate is required; (2) other things equal, an appreciation of the nominal exchange rate reduces the market value of the existing supplies of foreign assets and to restore portfolio balance an expectation of an appreciating nominal exchange rate is required; (3) hence a rise in α must be associated with a sufficient fall (appreciation) in E to prevent the nominal exchange rate either from appreciating or from depreciating over time. The $\dot{\alpha} = 0$ locus gives the combinations of E and α which are required to keep the current account in balance. Unlike Dornbusch and Fischer, who take the $\dot{\alpha} = 0$ locus to be positively-sloping we construct a negatively-sloping locus in Figure 4.8a. To explain this consider the following points. (1) Other things equal, an increase in α raises wealth and this reduces the rate of saving and causes the current account to deteriorate. At the same time, as we have seen above, a rise in α induces an expectation of a depreciating currency to preserve portfolio balance and this serves to reduce wealth and to improve the current account. *On the assumption that the expectations effects dominate, a rise in α will induce an improvement in the current account.* (2) Other things equal, an appreciation of the nominal exchange rate requires an expectation of an appreciating currency to restore portfolio balance and this serves to raise wealth and to deteriorate the current account. (3) Hence a rise in α must be associated with a sufficient fall (appreciation) in E to keep the current account in balance. This explains why the slope of the $\dot{\alpha} = 0$ locus is taken to be negative.

The slope of the $\dot{\alpha} = 0$ locus is given by $-\tilde{\Psi}_\alpha / \tilde{\Psi}_e$ which is negative by assumption and the slope of the $\dot{e} = 0$ locus is given by $-\tilde{\Phi}_\alpha / \tilde{\Phi}_e < 0$. Now it is simple to ascertain that $\tilde{\Phi}_\alpha / \tilde{\Phi}_e > \tilde{\Psi}_\alpha / \tilde{\Psi}_e$ and that, therefore, the $\dot{e} = 0$ locus is steeper than the $\dot{\alpha} = 0$ locus. To check this simply evaluate the determinant of the coefficient matrix formed by equations (4.12a) and (4.12b) to find that $\tilde{\Psi}_\alpha \tilde{\Phi}_e - \tilde{\Psi}_e \tilde{\Phi}_\alpha = \Psi_\alpha / \Phi_x < 0$. As it turn out, the fact that this determinant is negative ensures that this model must possess a unique saddle path. But more on this a little later. Consider now establishing the existence and uniqueness of a saddle path by the means of phase diagrams. At any point above (below) the $\dot{e} = 0$ locus the exchange rate is depreciating (appreciating) and, therefore, E is rising (falling). At any point above (below) the $\dot{\alpha} = 0$ locus expectations of a depreciating (appreciating) exchange rate improve (deteriorate) the current account and α is rising (falling). The arrows in Figure 4.8a point the direction the economy takes when it is off the steady state. It is now clear that the saddle path depicted by the EA locus is the unique stable path: *along the saddle path current account surpluses (deficits) are associated with an appreciating (depreciating) currency. It is easy to show that, had we assumed $\tilde{\Psi}_\alpha < 0$, we would also have obtained a downward-sloping saddle path, which points to the robustness of the characteristics of the saddle path in the context of this model.*

There is some more valuable information we can extract from Figure 4.8a. The $\dot{e} = 0$ locus turns out to have the exact same slope as the EE locus we have employed in Figures 4.7a and 4.7b to decribe the joint path of the nominal exchange rate and foreign assets under static expectations, since $-\tilde{\Phi}_\alpha / \tilde{\Phi}_e = \Phi_\alpha = \partial E / \partial \alpha$ This is no coincidence since both loci are derived by setting $x = 0$; of course the economics of these two loci is significantly different. The implication is that we can easily compare adjustments under static and rational expectations by comparing adjustments along the $\dot{e} = 0$ locus with adjustments along the saddle path. Notice that the saddle path is less steep than the $\dot{e} = 0$ locus. As a result, to the left (right) of the intersection of the EA locus with the $\dot{e} = 0$ locus the EA locus is below (above) the $\dot{e} = 0$ locus. The explanation is simple enough: under perfect foresight an expectation of an *appreciating (depreciating)* exchange rate induces an instant appreciation (depreciation) in the level of the exchange rate which is incorporated into the saddle path and which, obviously, cannot be incorporated into the static expectations path.

The nominal exchange rate and the current account under perfect foresight: adjustments across steady states.

We now examine adjustments of the nominal exchange rate and the current account under perfect foresight. To begin with we will focus attention on adjustments across steady states. The most illuminating way to deal with this is to rewrite the linearised expressions (4.7a*) and (4.11*) to allow for shifts at the initial steady state due to changes in the parameters or exogenous variables that define this initial steady state. If, for instance, $s = \bar{s}$ and $H = \bar{H}$ are the particular values that define the initial $\bar{\alpha}$ and $\bar{E}$, one may well ask how the $\dot{e} = 0$ locus and the $\dot{\alpha} = 0$ locus shift in response to a change in s or a change in H by $s - \bar{s}$ and $H - \bar{H}$, respectively. If we are able to establish, precisely, such shifts in the vertical and/or the horizontal direction then we are able to establish the steady-state effects of some disturbance qualitatively, at least, and perhaps quantitatively; recourse to algebra would be needed only to establish these effects quantitatively. Moreover, once the intersection of the new $\dot{e} = 0$ and $\dot{\alpha} = 0$ loci is located it is easy to draw a saddle path through this intersection to establish the path the economy traces following some shift. To incorporate the possibility of shifts due to changes in s and/or in H we write:

$$\dot{\alpha} = \Psi_\alpha(\alpha - \bar{\alpha}) + \Psi_x x + \Psi_s(s - \bar{s}), \qquad \Psi_s > 0 \qquad (4.7a^{**})$$

$$E - \bar{E} = \Phi_\alpha(\alpha - \bar{\alpha}) + \Phi_x x + \Phi_h(H - \bar{H}), \qquad \Phi_h > 0 \qquad (4.11^{**})$$

Other things equal, an incease in s by $s - \bar{s}$ improves the current account and generates purchases of α at the rate of, say, $\Psi_s(s - \bar{s})$ at the initial steady state. Other things equal, an increase in H by $H - \bar{H}$ increases E by, say, $\Phi_h(H - \bar{H})$ at the initial steady state. This is the interpretation of the terms we have added in (4.7a*) and (4.11*) to obtain (4.7a**) and (4.11**). Substituting out x by $\dot{e}$ and solving for $\dot{\alpha}$ and $\dot{e}$ we obtain:

$$\dot{\alpha} = \tilde{\Psi}_\alpha(\alpha - \bar{\alpha}) + \tilde{\Psi}_e(E - \bar{E}) + \tilde{\Psi}_h(H - \bar{H}) + \tilde{\Psi}_s(s - \bar{s}) \qquad (4.12a^*)$$

$$\dot{e} = \tilde{\Phi}_\alpha(\alpha - \bar{\alpha}) + \tilde{\Phi}_e(E - \bar{E}) + \tilde{\Phi}_h(H - \bar{H}) \qquad (4.12b^*)$$

Where $\tilde{\Psi}_h \equiv -(\Phi_h \Psi_x)/\Phi_x$, $\tilde{\Psi}_s \equiv \Psi_s$, $\tilde{\Phi}_h \equiv -\Phi_h/\Phi_x$.

A shift in the $\dot{\alpha} = 0$ locus vertically gives the magnitude and direction of the change in E required to restore current account balance following some exogenous disturbance. Similarly, a shift in the $\dot{e} = 0$ locus vertically gives the magnitude and direction of the change in E required to prevent the exchange rate from appreciating or depreciating over time following some exogenous disturbance.

Consider, first, the vertical shift in the $\dot{\alpha} = 0$ locus and the $\dot{e} = 0$ locus following an increase in H by $H - \bar{H}$. Setting $\dot{\alpha} = 0, \dot{e} = 0$ and $\alpha - \bar{\alpha} = 0$ (since we are evaluating *vertical* shifts) we find: (1) The vertical shift in the $\dot{e} = 0$ locus is $(-\tilde{\Phi}_h/\tilde{\Phi}_e)(H - \bar{H}) = \Phi_h(H - \bar{H})$; (2) the vertical shift in the $\dot{\alpha} = 0$ locus is $(-\tilde{\Psi}_h/\tilde{\Psi}_e)(H - \bar{H}) = \Phi_h(H - \bar{H})$. The shifts are identical, not surprisingly. In fact we can say something more: since we set $\dot{e} = 0$ to obtain these shifts, equations (4.4c) informs us that an increase in H, assuming $x = 0$, results in a nominal

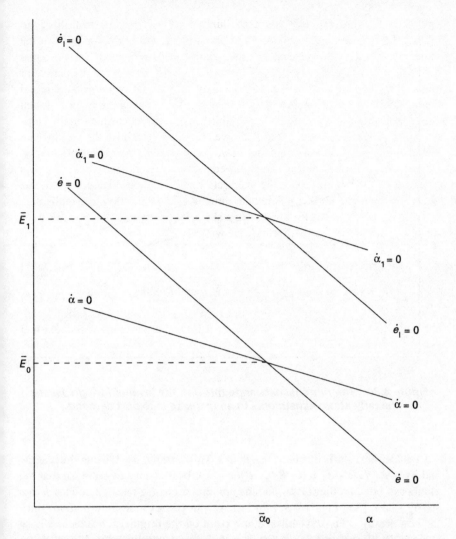

Figure 4.8b   *The nominal exchange rate and the level of foreign assets: steady-state adjustments to open-market operations*

exchange rate depreciation proportional to the increase in H at a given α . *An increase in the stock of money depreciates the nominal exchange rate proportionately across steady states and leaves the number of bonds unchanged across steady states.* Figure 4.8b illustrates adjustments across steady states associated with an increase in high-powered money. The $\dot{e}_1 = 0$ locus and the $\dot{\alpha}_1 = 0$ locus in this figure serve to locate the position of the $\dot{e} = 0$ locus and the $\dot{\alpha} = 0$ locus, respectively, *after* the shift induced by the increase in high-powered money. The old steady state is defined by ($\bar{\alpha}_0$, $\bar{E}_0$) whereas the new steady state is defined by ($\bar{\alpha}_0$, $\bar{E}_1$).

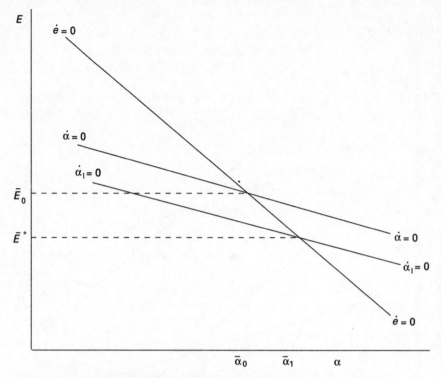

Figure 4.8c   The nominal exchange rate and the level of foreign assets: steady-state adjustments to an increase in export demand

Consider next shifts due to a change in s. This time the $\dot{\alpha} = 0$ locus shifts alone and by $(-\tilde{\Psi}_s / \tilde{\Psi}_e)(s - \bar{s}) = [(-\Psi_s \Phi_x)/\Psi_x](s - \bar{s}) < 0$. It is easy to establish that the number of bond holdings rises and the nominal exchange rate appreciates across steady states. (See Figure 4.8c). In fact we can extract more information: since the new steady state is established at a point on the original $\dot{e} = 0$ locus whose slope is $-\tilde{\Phi}_\alpha/\tilde{\Phi}_e = \Phi_\alpha$ it follows that $d\bar{E} = \Phi_\alpha d\bar{\alpha}$ across steady states. Moreover we have identified Φ_α with the slope of the EE locus encountered above and, given that neither the EE nor the $\dot{e} = 0$ locus shifts on account of the change in s, we can easily confirm that steady-state results are identical regardless of how expectations are formed. This should not surprise us, given that at the steady state $x = \dot{e} = 0$ regardless of how expectations are formed outside steady states. Figure 4.8c illustrates steady-state adjustments in foreign asset holdings and in the nominal exchange rate associated with an increase in export demand. The $\dot{\alpha}_1 = 0$ locus serves to illustrate the combinations of foreign asset holdings and the exchange rate that preserve current account balance *after* the shift in tastes. The old steady state is defined by $(\bar{\alpha}_0, \bar{E}_0)$ whereas the new steady state is defined by $(\bar{\alpha}_1, \bar{E}^*)$.

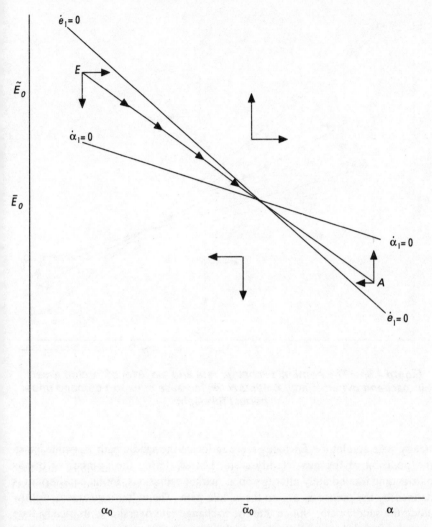

Figure 4.8d The nominal exchange rate and the level of foreign assets: impact and dynamic adjustments to open-market operations under perfect foresight

The nominal exchange rate and the current account under perfect foresight: impact and dynamic adjustments

Consider now employing Figure 4.8d for an analysis of impact and dynamic adjustments of the nominal exchange rate and the current account to an open-market purchase of bonds when expectations follow a perfect foresight path. Let the intersection of the $\dot{\alpha}_1 = 0$ locus with the $\dot{e}_1 = 0$ locus serve to locate the new

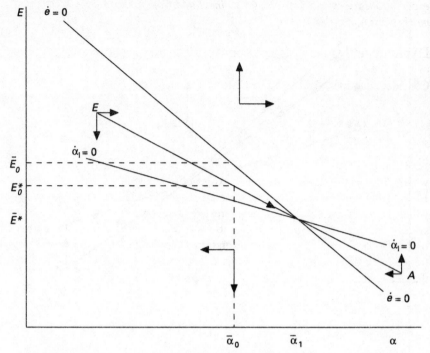

Figure 4.8e   The nominal exchange rate and the level of foreign assets: impact and dynamic adjustments to an increase in export demand under perfect foresight

steady state and let the *EA* locus serve to locate the saddle path associated with the position of the new steady state. Let α_0 define the number of bonds outstanding immediately after the open-market operations. Initial equilibrium is defined by the point $(\alpha_0, \tilde{E}_0)$ on the saddle path. Thereafter adjustments follow along the saddle path. Notice that the exchange rate overshoots its steady state initially; initial depreciation exceeds the amount of depreciation across steady states and this calls for an appreciating exchange rate along the saddle path. Notice also that along the saddle path the level of the exchange rate is below the level it would have been under static expectations.

In Figure 4.8e we illustrate impact and dynamic adjustments to an unanticipated increase in export demand when expectations are rational and compare these with adjustments under static expectations. In this figure the intersection of the $\dot{\alpha}_1 = 0$ with the $\dot{e} = 0$ locus serves to define the new steady state at $(\bar{\alpha}_1, \bar{E}^*)$; the old steady state is defined by $(\bar{\alpha}_0, \bar{E}_0)$. Initial equilibrium is defined by point $(\bar{\alpha}_0, E_0^*)$ on the saddle path *EA*. Thereafter adjustments follow along the saddle path until $(\bar{\alpha}_1, \bar{E}^*)$ is reached. The crucial thing to note is that the nominal exchange rate appreciates instantly in response to the increase in export demand since $E_0^* < \bar{E}_0$. This contrasts with our earlier analysis of the same thought experiment conducted under static expectations. *Under rational* *expectations assets markets cannot be insulated from disturbances in the goods markets even in the short run.*

Dynamic and steady-state responses derived algebraically

Consider equations (4.12a*) and (4.12b*) in matrix form:

$$\begin{bmatrix} \dot{\alpha} \\ \dot{e} \end{bmatrix} = \begin{bmatrix} \tilde{\Psi}_\alpha & \tilde{\Psi}_e \\ \tilde{\Phi}_\alpha & \tilde{\Phi}_e \end{bmatrix} \begin{bmatrix} \alpha - \bar{\alpha} \\ e - \bar{e} \end{bmatrix} + \begin{bmatrix} \tilde{\Psi}_h & \tilde{\Psi}_s \\ \tilde{\Phi}_h & 0 \end{bmatrix} \begin{bmatrix} dH \\ ds \end{bmatrix}$$

(4.13)

where $dH \equiv H - \bar{H}$ serves to define an exogenous change in high-powered money H, and where $ds \equiv s - \bar{s}$ serves to define an exogenous change in the parameter s which measures tastes. If we are interested in solving for adjustments across steady states we simply have to set $\dot{\alpha} = \dot{e} = 0$ and solve for $\alpha - \bar{\alpha}$ and for $e - \bar{e}$ as functions of dH and ds. To avoid confusion let this solution for $\alpha - \bar{\alpha}$ be denoted by $d\bar{\alpha}$ and let this solution for $e - \bar{e}$ be denoted by $d\bar{e}$. Then the steady-state response of α and of e to changes in H and/or s is given by:

$$\begin{bmatrix} d\bar{\alpha} \\ d\bar{e} \end{bmatrix} = - \begin{bmatrix} \tilde{\Psi}_\alpha & \tilde{\Psi}_e \\ \tilde{\Phi}_\alpha & \tilde{\Phi}_e \end{bmatrix}^{-1} \begin{bmatrix} \tilde{\Psi}_h & \tilde{\Psi}_s \\ \tilde{\Phi}_h & 0 \end{bmatrix} \begin{bmatrix} dH \\ ds \end{bmatrix}$$

(4.14)

If, on the other hand, we are interested in solving for the time path of α and e then we have to follow a number of steps. Firstly, we must solve for the unique stable root that drives the system. As explained in the Appendix, the existence of a unique and stable saddle path is predicated on the existence of a number of stable roots equal to the number of short-run predetermined state variables. In the context of the present model, α is the only short-run predetermined variable, whereas e is a forward-looking variable. Thus we require the existence of a single stable root. As we have also explained in the Appendix, the roots that drive the system are simply the solutions to the characteristic equation formed by the coefficient matrix of the state variables α and e. And since the determinant of this matrix is equal to the product of these roots, the sign of this determinant will help to indicate the existence or otherwise of a unique saddle path. In the present model we have been able to verify that the sign of this determinant is negative and hence the system possesses one unstable and one stable root, a condition which satisfies the existence and uniqueness of a saddle path. Secondly, observe that along the saddle path $\dot{\alpha} = \rho(\alpha - \bar{\alpha})$ and $\dot{e} = \rho(e - \bar{e})$ where ρ denotes the stable root. Thirdly, there remains to locate the initial position of the forward-looking variable, given that the initial position of the predetermined variable is defined by the initial steady state. Notice that locating the initial condition for the forward-looking variable(s) is equivalent to solving for the saddle path. The most illuminating way to solve for the saddle path in the present context is to arrive at a formula that makes it easy to compare the slope of the saddle path with the slope of the path under static expectations. To this effect we will set $dH = ds = 0$ in (4.13) and combine the second equation in (4.13) with the condition that $\dot{e} = \rho(e - \bar{e})$ to arrive at:

$$(e - \bar{e}) = (\alpha - \bar{\alpha}) \, \tilde{\Phi}_\alpha \, (\rho - \tilde{\Phi}_e)^{-1} = (\alpha - \bar{\alpha}) \, \Phi_\alpha \, (1 - \rho\Phi_x)^{-1} \tag{4.15}$$

Since the slope of the path under static expectations is equal to Φ_α and since $-\rho\Phi_x > 0$ we can verify our earlier finding that the saddle path is less steep.

4.6   Concluding remarks

In Chapter 3 we developed a model of the current account under PPP. That model was shown to possess a unique stable path along which an appreciating (depreciating) exchange rate was shown to be associated with current account surpluses (deficits). This association, which some authors prefer to call 'conventional', has survived in the present model which distinguishes between a domestic and a foreign good, and it has also proved to be robust under both static and rational expectations. However such an association may not survive in more complicated dynamic structures, such as the structure discussed in Chapter 6, for instance. A richer dynamic structure would incorporate investment in physical capital and would allow claims on domestically located physical capital to be traded internationally. This subject will be dealt with in chapter 7.

The present chapter has served to underline the integrating role of rational expectations. Under rational expectations, shocks that impinge upon one market have their influence felt, instantly, upon all other markets. As we have shown, this is not generally true under static expectations.

The reader will have noticed that the present model retains features to be found in monetary models and features to be found in portfolio balance models. This was done intentionally to draw attention to the often neglected fact that the current account, together with the evolution of rational expectations, is an important source of dynamics for *all* types of models of the exchange rate under capital mobility. We could, for instance, have augmented our menu of assets to allow for the presence of a non-tradeable domestic bond B and we could have taken this bond to be a perfect substitute for the foreign bond α so that $[B + EP^*(\alpha)]$ would constitute a single bond with a single return equal to $r \equiv r^* + x$. This specification, which would conform precisely with specifications to be found in monetary models of the exchange rate, would have yielded very similar results to those obtained by the model adopted in the present chapter.

CHAPTER 5

The Cost of Disinflation in a Floating Exchange Rate Regime

5.1 Introduction

It is widely accepted that sticky prices can allow monetary policy to have a systematic effect on output and can explain persistent departures of output from its natural level, rational expectations notwithstanding. This position applies with equal force to open economies with flexible exchange rates, perfectly mobile capital internationally and forward-looking agents. The experience with floating exchange rates has dashed any early hopes that monetary policy, freed from the objective of pegging the exchange rate, can be used effectively for internal stabilisation purposes. Dornbusch (1976) and more recently Buiter and Miller (1981), (1982), (1983) have explained the stylised facts of sharp and persistent departures of competitiveness from fundamentals and the associated sharp and persistent departures of output from 'natural' levels. For instance, a policy of reducing the level of money supply or its trend rate of growth applied to an economy where expectations are rational, exchange rates are perfectly flexible, assets are perfectly mobile internationally and substitutable and prices are sticky is shown to be associated with a sharp and persistent loss in competitiveness. In turn, and to the extent that output is demand-determined, the sharp and persistent loss in competitiveness is shown to be associated with and is thought to contribute to a sharp loss in output which persists as long as competitiveness deviates from fundamentals. Although such deviations in output are seen to be transitory there is little comfort from this when the cumulative loss in output is substantial. The next section of this chapter focuses on the basic Buiter–Miller model which addresses the issue of the cost of disinflation in a floating exchange rate regime.

Hitherto relatively little attention has been focused on the internal stabilisation properties of non-sterilised foreign exchange intervention. Accordingly, Section 5.3 aims to show that monetary rules of non-sterilised intervention when widely known by forward-looking agents can become a powerful means of reducing the cumulative loss in output associated with disinflation, sticky prices notwithstanding. The speed of adjusting the money supply to offset transitory departures of the real exchange rate from fundamentals is crucial to the degree of output stability. Of course, the saying that there is no such thing as a free lunch applies here as well since the cost of minimising output loss through non-sterilised intervention is a higher inflation rate along the adjustment path. However it is still desirable to know what is the precise trade-off between output and inflation outside steady states.

5.2 The basic Buiter–Miller model

The most appropriate vehicle for the discussion of the cost of a disinflationary policy in a floating exchange rate regime is the Buiter–Miller model which builds upon a version of the Dornbusch model. The Buiter–Miller model belongs to the class of monetary models of the exchange rate which allow for a core or trend rate in monetary growth, for price stickiness and, therefore, the possibility of deviations in output from natural rates and the possibility of permanent departures from PPP. The simplest 'basic' version of the Buiter-Miller model is presented immediately below.

$$y = -\gamma(r - Dp) + \delta(e + p^* - p) \qquad \gamma > 0, \ \delta > 0 \qquad (5.1)$$

$$m - p = ky - \lambda r \qquad k > 0, \ \lambda > 0 \qquad (5.2)$$

$$r = r^* + De \qquad (5.3)$$

$$Dp = D\bar{p} + \psi(y - \bar{y}) \qquad \psi > 0 \qquad (5.4)$$

$$D\bar{p} = D\bar{e} = D\bar{m} = Dm = \mu \qquad (5.5)$$

Notation

y = the logarithm of the volume of the domestic product.

$\bar{y}$ = the 'natural' level of y, assumed exogenous.

m = the logarithm of the nominal stock of domestic money taken as exogenous.

p = the logarithm of the price of the domestic product.

$\bar{p}$ = the long-run equilibrium path of p.

p^* = the logarithm of the price of the foreign product.

e = the logarithm of the price of foreign currency in units of domestic currency.

$\bar{e}$ = the long-run equilibrium path of e.

r = the domestic nominal interest rate.

r^* = the foreign nominal and real interest rate.

D = the differential operator so that, for example, $Dp = dp/dt$.

Equation (5.1) is a version of an open-economy *IS* relation. Output, which is demand-determined, is taken to be a decreasing function of the real interest rate $(r - Dp)$ and an increasing function of the relative price of the foreign good $(e + p^* - p)$. Notice how perfect foresight, which is the special case of rational expectations that assumes away random shocks, is being utilised to equate the expected rate of inflation with the actual rate Dp. Equation (5.2) is a standard textbook version of an *LM* relation. Equation (5.3) expresses an uncovered interest parity condition together with the assumption that expectations about the rate of depreciation of the nominal exchange rate follow a perfect foresight path. To put it differently, when the domestic and the foreign bond differ only in the currency in which they are denominated their expected returns must be equalised if both types of bonds are to be held in portfolios of risk-neutral investors. Equation (5.4) is a version of a Phillips curve-type relation reflecting the slow adjustment of the price level towards equilibrium. According to (5.4) the rate of inflation consists of the sum of an equilibrium or trend component $D\bar{p}$ and a disequilibrium component captured by $\psi(y - \bar{y})$. Thus the excess of the current rate of inflation over its trend rate is taken to be proportional to the excess of the current level of production over the 'natural' level. Equation (5.5) states that the trend rate of inflation and the trend rate of depreciation are equal to the rate of monetary growth which is set to some constant μ.

To facilitate exposition it will prove convenient to define liquidity, competitiveness and the real interest rate as follows: $m - p \equiv \ell$ (liquidity), $e + p^* - p \equiv c$ (competitiveness), $r - Dp \equiv i$ (the real interest rate). Note that with p^* taken to be constant one can chose units so that $p^* = 0$ and so that $c = e - p$. With these definitions in mind we will rewrite the entire model as follows:

$$y \quad = -\gamma i + \delta c \tag{5.1'}$$

$$\ell \quad = ky - \lambda(i + Dp) = ky - \lambda(i + Dp + Dm - Dm) = ky - \lambda i + \lambda D\ell - \lambda\mu \tag{5.2'}$$

$$i \quad = r^* + De - Dp = r^* + Dc \tag{5.3'}$$

$$Dm - Dp \equiv D\ell = Dm - \mu - \psi(y - \bar{y}) = -\psi(y - \bar{y}) \tag{5.4'}$$

We can further reduce the size of the model by substituting out the expression for $D\ell$ given by equation (5.4') into equation (5.2') to obtain:

$$\ell = (k - \lambda\psi)y - \lambda i - \lambda\mu + \lambda\psi\bar{y} \tag{5.2*}$$

Thus the model to consider consists of equations (5.1'), (5.2*) and (5.3'). Equation (5.1') requires no particular explanation; it is simply the open-economy *IS* relation encountered before. Equation (5.2*) expresses money market equilibrium adjusted for inflation; we will refer to this relation as the '*LM* adjusted for inflation'. Accordingly $(\partial i/\partial y)_{LM} = [(k - \lambda\psi)/\lambda]$ gives the slope of the *LM* curve adjusted for inflation in (i, y) space. Notice, next, that $(\partial i/\partial y)_{IS} = (-1/\gamma)$ gives the slope of the *IS* curve in the same space. Thus, whereas the *IS* is always downward-sloping in (i, y) space the slope of the *LM* can be positive or negative depending on whether $(k - \lambda\psi)$ is positive or negative, that is, depending on whether the total effect of an increase in output on money demand, *given the real interest rate*, is positive or negative. Notice that this total effect consists of the direct 'transactions effect' k plus the indirect 'inflation effect' $- \lambda\psi$. To explain this so-called 'inflation effect' notice that at a given real interest rate a unit rise in output will raise inflation and the nominal interest rate by ψ units, as the Phillips curve suggests, and this will reduce money demand by $\lambda\psi$ units in absolute terms. The stability analysis to be conducted shortly will suggest that when the *LM* is downward-sloping its slope must be less steep than the slope of the *IS*; that is, it will be shown that $(\lambda\psi - k) < (\lambda/\gamma)$ is sufficient for the model to exhibit saddle path stability. This condition is intuitively appealing since it suggests that an increase in aggregate demand, given competitiveness, raises output. In what follows we will assume stability. Equation (5.3′) is a version of the uncovered interest parity condition cast in terms of real interest rate differentials; to preserve the uncovered interest parity condition an excess (shortfall) of the domestic real interest rate over the foreign real interest rate must be matched with an expectation of a depreciating (appreciating) real exchange rate. Since the foreign interest rate is taken to be constant, variations in the domestic real interest rate suffice to induce variations in the rate of depreciation or appreciation of the real exchange rate. Figure 5.1 can help to illustrate adjustments to a previously unanticipated reduction in the core rate of monetary growth on the assumption that $(\lambda\psi - k) < (\lambda/\gamma)$.

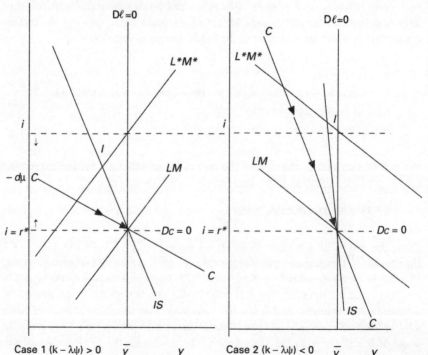

Figure 5.1   IS–LM adjustments in (i, y) space: the stable cases considered

   To start with let us assume that the economy is initially at the steady state defined by $i = r*$ and $y = \bar{y}$. We have constructed a $Dc = 0$ locus to indicate that only along this locus is the real exchange rate constant over time; above the $Dc = 0$ locus $i > r*$ and c is rising (depreciating) whereas below this locus $i < r*$ and c is falling (appreciating). We have also constructed a $D\ell = 0$ locus located vertically above steady-state output $\bar{y}$ to indicate that only along this locus are real balances constant over time; to the left of this locus inflation falls below the core rate of monetary growth μ and real balances are rising, whereas to the right of this locus inflation exceeds μ and real balances are falling. Cases 1 and 2 depict the two possible stable cases; in either case a shift in the *IS* to the right (not shown above), given competitiveness, will raise output. Consider now a reduction in the core rate of monetary growth μ. In both cases the *LM* must shift up by $-d\mu$ to, say, $L*M*$, to reflect the increase in the demand for money induced by the reduction in the opportunity cost of holding money associated with the policy of disinflation. Given competitiveness the intersection of the *IS* with the $L*M*$ at, say, point *I* would seem to determine the initial point. *However point I cannot serve as the initial point; if it did we would have ended up with an improvement in competitiveness across steady states which clearly is not the case since this model is 'superneutral' (to inflation) across steady states.* Competitiveness must deteriorate initially so the *IS* must shift to the left initially (not shown above). Loci like the *CC* loci can serve to describe the saddle path in each of the two cases depicted and the intersection of a *CC* locus with the $L*M*$ locus can serve to locate the initial point. To recap: initially competitiveness deteriorates, the real interest rate rises and output falls. Along the adjustment paths *CC* the real interest rate is falling, competitiveness is improving (since $Dc > 0$ along these paths), real balances are building up (since to the left of $\bar{y}$ inflation falls short of the core rate and $D\ell > 0$) and output is rising.

The conditions for stability and the steady-state characteristics of disinflation: a more formal analysis

Returning to equations (5.1′)–(5.4′) and substituting out i and y the dynamics of the model can be conveniently expressed in matrix form as follows:

$$\begin{bmatrix} D\ell \\ Dc \end{bmatrix} = \begin{bmatrix} \dfrac{-\psi\gamma}{\Delta} & \dfrac{-\psi\delta\lambda}{\Delta} \\ \dfrac{-1}{\Delta} & \dfrac{\delta(k-\lambda\psi)}{\Delta} \end{bmatrix} \begin{bmatrix} \ell \\ c \end{bmatrix}$$
$$+ \begin{bmatrix} \dfrac{\psi(k\gamma+\lambda)}{\Delta} & 0 & \dfrac{-\psi\gamma\lambda}{\Delta} \\ \dfrac{\psi\gamma}{\Delta} & -1 & \dfrac{-\lambda}{\Delta} \end{bmatrix} \begin{bmatrix} \bar{y} \\ r* \\ \mu \end{bmatrix}$$

$$(5.6)$$

where $\Delta = \gamma(k - \lambda\psi) + \lambda$. With liquidity taken as predetermined and competitiveness forward-looking there exists a unique saddle path converging to the long-run equilibrium provided there is one stable and one unstable characteristic root. Formally the necessary and sufficient condition for equilibrium to be a saddle point is that the determinant of the coefficient matrix associated with the state variables is negative. Accordingly it is required that $-\delta\psi/\Delta < 0$ or that $\Delta > 0$. As we have seen immediately above, the assumption that Δ is positive corresponds to the appealing assumption that an autonomous increase (decrease) in aggregate demand will increase (decrease) output, given competitiveness.

Assuming that the conditions for the existence of a unique saddle path converging towards equilibrium are satisfied, let us briefly look into the characteristics of the steady-state. In this respect it will be instructive to rewrite equation (5.6) as follows:

$$\begin{bmatrix} D\ell \\ Dc \end{bmatrix} = A \begin{bmatrix} \ell \\ c \end{bmatrix} + B \begin{bmatrix} \bar{y} \\ r* \\ \mu \end{bmatrix}$$

(5.6′)

In the above A is a 2×2 matrix whereas B is a 2×3 matrix whose coefficients are given in (5.6) above. Setting $D\ell = Dc = 0$ in (5.6′) and solving for the steady-state values of liquidity and of competitiveness $(\bar{\ell}, \bar{c})$, one obtains:

$$[\bar{\ell} \quad \bar{c}]' = - (A^{-1})(B)[\bar{y} \quad r* \quad \mu]', \text{ or}$$

(5.7)

$$\begin{bmatrix} \bar{\ell} \\ \bar{c} \end{bmatrix} = \begin{bmatrix} k & -\lambda & -\lambda \\ \dfrac{1}{\delta} & \dfrac{\gamma}{\delta} & 0 \end{bmatrix} \begin{bmatrix} \bar{y} \\ r* \\ \mu \end{bmatrix}$$

(5.7')

Notice first that variations in the rate of monetary growth are 'superneutral' in this model; that is, a change in the steady-state rate of inflation has no effect on the steady-state level of competitiveness. However a reduction in the rate of monetary growth raises steady-state liquidity; this is because a reduction in inflation reduces the opportunity cost of holding money and thereby raises its demand. Accordingly along the path of adjustment following a deceleration in the rate of monetary growth prices are rising at a lower rate than money grows to allow real balances to build to their higher level. In particular $d\bar{\ell} = -\lambda d\mu$.

Constructing the phase diagram and locating the saddle path

Equations (5.6′) and (5.7) suggest that we can rewrite the dynamics as follows:

$$\begin{bmatrix} D\ell \\ Dc \end{bmatrix} = \begin{bmatrix} \alpha_{11} & \alpha_{12} \\ \alpha_{21} & \alpha_{22} \end{bmatrix} \begin{bmatrix} \ell & \bar{\ell} \\ c & \bar{c} \end{bmatrix}$$

(5.6*)

where $\alpha_{11} = (-\psi\gamma/\Delta)<0$, $\alpha_{12} = (-\psi\delta\lambda/\Delta)<0$, $\alpha_{21} = (-1/\Delta)<0$, $\alpha_{22} = [\delta(k - \lambda\psi)/\Delta)] \gtrless 0$.

We are now in a position to explain the signs of the above coefficients. Let us begin our analysis from a position of steady state. To this effect notice the following. First, a rise (fall) in liquidity is associated with a negative (positive) rate of growth of real balances given competitiveness ($\alpha_{11} < 0$). This is because a rise (fall) in liquidity, that is, a shift of the *LM* adjusted for inflation downwards (upwards), will raise (reduce) output which in turn will raise (reduce) inflation above (below) the rate of nominal money growth, causing a negative (positive) growth rate in real balances. Second, an improvement (deterioration) in competitiveness is associated with a negative (positive) rate of growth of real balances given liquidity ($\alpha_{12} < 0$). This is because an improvement (deterioration) in competitiveness, that is, a shift of the *IS* to the right (left), will raise (reduce) output which in turn will raise (reduce) inflation above (below) the rate of nominal money growth, resulting in a negative (positive) growth rate in real balances. Accordingly to prevent real balances from changing over time a rise (fall) in liquidity must be associated with a deterioration (improvement) in competitiveness; the $D\ell = 0$ locus must be negatively sloping. Third, a rise (fall) in liquidity is associated with an appreciating (depreciating) real exchange rate ($\alpha_{21} < 0$). This is because a rise (fall) in liquidity, other things equal, will reduce (raise) the domestic real interest below (above) the foreign interest rate and to preserve equality of expected returns agents must be expecting real capital gains (capital losses) on their holdings of interest-bearing assets denominated in domestic currency. Finally an improvement (deterioration) in competitiveness may be associated with either an appreciating or a depreciating real exchange rate ($\alpha_{22} \lesseqgtr 0$). Specifically, when the *LM* adjusted for inflation is upward- (downward-) sloping in (i, y) space a rise in competitiveness will raise (reduce) the domestic real interest rate above (below) the foreign interest rate and this will require an expectation of a depreciating (appreciating) real exchange rate to preserve the uncovered interest parity condition. Thus the $Dc = 0$ locus may slope up or down. However saddle path stability requires that the $Dc = 0$ locus is steeper than the $D\ell = 0$ locus. Figure 5.2 reflects the two cases mentioned.

Having ascertained the characteristics of the saddle path with the aid of phase diagrams we will now attempt to do so in a slightly more formal way that introduces the stable root that drives the economy along the saddle path. This will prove useful when we come to discuss the path of prices and of output associated with disinflation. To this effect consider first that the path of liquidity and of competitiveness along the unique saddle path can be represented in the following way:

$$\ell - \bar{\ell} = (\ell_0 - \bar{\ell})e^{\rho t}, \quad c - \bar{c} = (c_0 - \bar{c})e^{\rho t} \tag{5.8}$$

where ℓ_0 and c_0 are the initial values of liquidity and competitiveness and where ρ is the stable root that drives the economy along the saddle path. Applying the operator D on the expressions given by (5.8) we obtain:

$$D\ell = \rho(\ell - \bar{\ell}), \quad Dc = \rho(c - \bar{c}) \tag{5.8'}$$

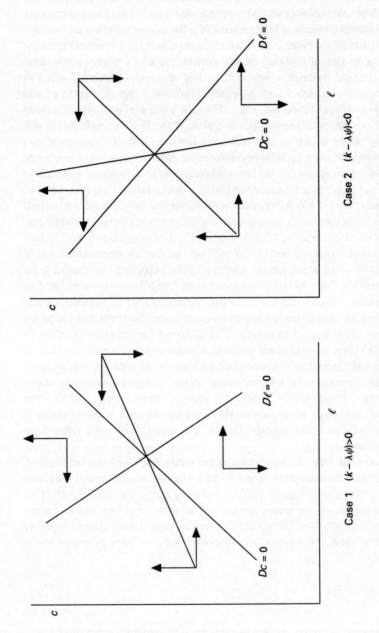

Figure 5.2 Phase diagrams in (c, ℓ) space

Case 1 $(k - \lambda \psi) > 0$

Case 2 $(k - \lambda \psi) < 0$

Using (5.6*) we have:

$$\rho(\ell-\bar{\ell})=\alpha_{11}(\ell-\bar{\ell})+\alpha_{12}(c-\bar{c}), \quad \rho(c-\bar{c})=\alpha_{21}(\ell-\bar{\ell})+\alpha_{22}(c-\bar{c}) \tag{5.9}$$

which upon substitution yields the slope of the saddle path as follows:

$$\frac{c-\bar{c}}{\ell-\bar{\ell}}=\frac{\rho-\alpha_{11}}{\alpha_{12}}=\frac{\alpha_{21}}{\rho-\alpha_{22}}>0$$

Consider now, with the aid of Figure 5.3, the adjustment of liquidity and of competitiveness to a previously unanticipated policy of disinflation which is announced at $t = 0$ and is implemented upon announcement.

In Figure 5.3, ℓ_0 stands for the initial steady-state liquidity whereas $\bar{\ell}$ stands for the new steady-state liquidity, so that $\bar{\ell} - \ell_0 = -\lambda d\mu$. Since this policy is shown to be 'superneutral' in this model! $\bar{c}$ can serve to indicate both the old and the new steady-state level of competitiveness. Let S_0S_0 stand for the initial saddle path. Our *IS–LM* diagrams in (i,y) space suggest that immediately upon the announcement and implementation of the policy of disinflation the *LM* curve must shift up by $-d\mu$ to reflect the rise in the demand for real balances associated with a policy designed to reduce the opportunity cost of holding such balances. Given competitiveness, the domestic real interest rate will rise above the

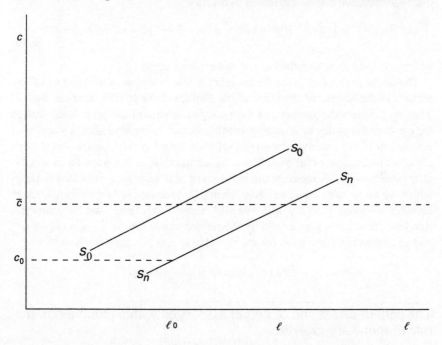

Figure 5.3 Adjustments in competitiveness and liquidity to an unanticipated reduction in μ

foreign interest rate. This, in turn, will bring about an incipient shift in the composition of portfolios from foreign currency-denominated assets into assets denominated in domestic currency until the rise in the price of domestic currency (the fall in e) is sufficient to bring the bond markets back into equilibrium and re-establish the uncovered interest parity condition; given p, the fall in e means a real exchange rate appreciation sufficient to bring about an expectation of a depreciating real exchange rate that will re-establish the uncovered interest parity condition. In terms of Figure 5.3, c must fall to, say, c_0 so that the locus of points connecting (c_0, ℓ_0) with $(\bar{c}, \bar{\ell})$ must have the same slope as the $S_0 S_0$ locus. The path labelled $S_n S_n$ is the new saddle path locus. Accordingly immediately upon the announcement and the implementation of the policy of disinflation there is a real exchange rate appreciation followed by a depreciating real exchange rate; in short the real exchange rate overshoots its equilibrium value. Along the adjustment path real balances are building up as the rate of inflation is below the rate of nomimal money growth. It is the build-up of real balances over time that allows for a reduction in the price of these balances in terms of foreign currency-denominated real balances.

Computing the cumulative loss in output

Since $D(p - \bar{p}) = \psi (y - \bar{y})$ by the Phillips curve, the cumulative loss in output due to disinflation can be expressed as follows:

$$\int_0^\infty (y - \bar{y}) dt = 1/\psi \int_0^\infty D(p - \bar{p}) dt = 1/\psi \int_0^\infty \rho (p_0 - \bar{p})(e^{\rho t}) dt = -(1/\psi)(p_0 - \bar{p}) \tag{5.10}$$

where e is used to denote the base of natural logarithms.

The above expression gives the cumulative loss in output as the product of two terms: (1) the inverse of the slope of the Phillips curve in (Dp, y) space and (2) The gap between the current and the steady-state path of the price level created the moment the policy of unanticipated disinflation is implemented. To obtain an estimate of (5.10) based on parameter values we need to compute $(p_0 - \bar{p})$. To this effect we will argue as follows. Since, by assumption, m is always on its steady-state path $(p_0 - \bar{p})$ can measure the build-up of real balances across steady states which we know to be equal to $-\lambda d\mu$. Hence the cumulative loss in output due to disinflation is equal to $(\lambda/\psi) d\mu$. We will return to this result and its interpretation later. Since y is also driven by the unique stable root ρ, $y - \bar{y} = (y_0 - \bar{y})e^{\rho t}$ and an alternative expression for the cumulative loss in output is given by

$$\int_0^\infty (y - \bar{y}) dt = (y_0 - \bar{y})(-1/\rho) = (\rho/\psi)(p_0 - \bar{p})(-1/\rho)$$

The path of prices and of output associated with a reduction in the rate of monetary growth

Figures 5.4a and 5.4b illustrate the paths of money, prices and of output following a previously unanticipated reduction in μ. In Figure 5.4a and for

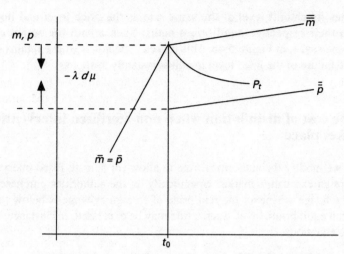

Figure 5.4a   The paths of money and prices

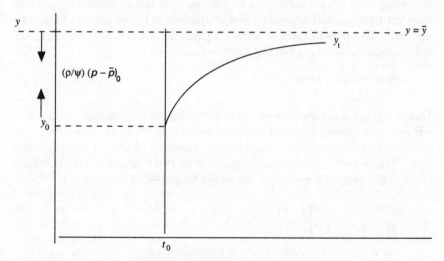

Figure 5.4b   The path of output

illustration purposes we are using two bars over a variable to depict its new steady-state path and a single bar to depict its old steady–state path. Like Buiter and Miller we are assuming, for simplicity, that for $t < t_0, \bar{m}(t) = \bar{p}(t)$. At t_0 the authorities announce and implement a previously unanticipated reduction in μ. Accordingly steady-state real balances must rise by $-\lambda d\mu$ and this measures the vertical gap between $\bar{m}(t)$ and $\bar{p}(t)$ for $t \geq t_0$. The actual path of prices is depicted by p_t. Consider now the evolution of output. Since $D(p - \bar{p}) = \psi(y - \bar{y}) = \rho(p - \bar{p})$, $y - \bar{y} = (\rho/\psi)(p - \bar{p})$; in particular, $y_0 - \bar{y} = (\rho/\psi)(p - \bar{p})_0 = -(\rho/\psi)\lambda d\mu$ measures the initial loss in output. Along the path of adjustment output approaches its natural level at the same rate as the price level and liquidity approach their respective equilibrium paths. Such a path for output can be depicted by, say, y_t in Figure 5.4b. This makes it clear that what explains output loss is the failure of the price level to adjust instantly to shocks.

5.3   The cost of disinflation when non-sterilised intervention takes place

Suppose we modify the authorities' rule to allow for non-sterilised intervention in the foreign exschange market. Specifically let the authorities purchase (sell) foreign exchange whenever the real price of foreign exhange is below (above) its long-run equilibrium level. Such a rule may be expressed, for instance, by the following equation:

$$Dm = D\overline{m} + \theta[(\overline{e} - \overline{p})] - (e - p)] = \mu + \theta(\overline{c} - c), \quad \theta > 0 \tag{5.5*}$$

According to (5.5*) the authorities let the rate of monetary growth exceed (fall short of) its target rate whenever competitiveness is below (above) its steady-state path. This may describe a 'leaning against the wind' type of non-sterilised intervention. Combining (5.4) and (5.5*) we write:

$$D\ell = -\psi(y - \overline{y}) - \theta(c - \overline{c}) \tag{5.4*}$$

That is, deviations of the growth rate of real balances from its zero trend reflect not only deviations of inflation from trend (the Phillips curve) but also deviations of competitiveness from trend. Equation (5.4*) replaces equation (5.4'). Taking in the modifications suggested by (5.4*) and (5.5*) the dynamics of this non-sterilised intervention model can be described as follows:

$$\begin{bmatrix} D\ell \\ Dc \end{bmatrix} = \begin{bmatrix} \tilde{\alpha}_{11} & \tilde{\alpha}_{12} \\ \tilde{\alpha}_{21} & \tilde{\alpha}_{22} \end{bmatrix} \begin{bmatrix} \ell & \overline{\ell} \\ c & \overline{c} \end{bmatrix}$$

where $\tilde{\alpha}_{11} = (-\psi\gamma/\Delta) < 0, \tilde{\alpha}_{12} = -\theta - (\psi\delta\lambda/\Delta) < 0, \tilde{\alpha}_{21} = (-1/\Delta) < 0,$

$\tilde{\alpha}_{22} = [\delta(k - \lambda\psi)/\Delta] \gtrless 0$ and $\tilde{\alpha}_{11}\tilde{\alpha}_{22} - \tilde{\alpha}_{12}\tilde{\alpha}_{21} = -(\psi\delta + \theta)/\Delta.$ (5.11)

Thus the assumption that Δ is positive turns out, again, to be necessary and sufficient to guarantee a unique and stable saddle path. Obviously the numerical value of the stable root will be different from ρ; in fact it will be larger than ρ in absolute value, suggesting, not surprisingly, a faster adjustment. To distinguish this root from ρ we will call it $\tilde{\rho}$. The paths of prices, money and output (and obviously the exchange rate) will be affected by non-sterilised intervention. We will examine the characteristics of these paths shortly. However it is still the case that the saddle path is upward-sloping; that is, it is still the case that

$$\frac{c-\bar{c}}{\ell-\bar{\ell}} = \frac{\tilde{\rho}-\tilde{\alpha}_{11}}{\tilde{\alpha}_{12}} = \frac{\tilde{\alpha}_{21}}{\tilde{\rho}-\tilde{\alpha}_{22}} = \frac{\alpha_{21}}{\tilde{\rho}-\alpha_{22}} > 0$$

In fact the saddle path in the non-sterilised model will be less steep: with an absolute value for $\tilde{\rho}$ larger than the absolute value of ρ, the absolute value of $\tilde{\rho} - \alpha_{22}$ will be larger than the absolute value of $\rho - \alpha_{22}$, suggesting a less steep saddle path. But this is what we would have expected: when the authorities intervene with a view to minimising fluctuations in the real exchange rate, a given size of disinflation (inflation) will be associated with a smaller initial appreciation (depreciation).

Let us now turn our attention to the cumulative loss in output in this model with a view to showing and explaining why this will be less than $(\lambda/\psi)d\mu$. To compute this cumulative loss in output consider, first, that (5.4*) suggests that

$$\begin{aligned} D\ell &= -\psi(y-\bar{y}) - \theta[(c-\bar{c})(\ell-\bar{\ell})^{-1}](\ell-\bar{\ell}) = -\psi(y-\bar{y}) - \theta[(\tilde{\alpha}_{21})(\tilde{\rho}-\tilde{\alpha}_{22})^{-1}](\ell-\bar{\ell}) \\ &= -\psi(y-\bar{y}) - \theta[(\tilde{\rho}-\tilde{\alpha}_{11})(\tilde{\alpha}_{12})^{-1}](\ell-\bar{\ell}) = \tilde{\rho}(\ell-\bar{\ell}) \end{aligned}$$

$$(5.4**)$$

Accordingly

$$\begin{aligned} (y-\bar{y}) &= -(\tilde{\rho}/\psi)[1+(\theta/\tilde{\rho})(\tilde{\alpha}_{21})(\tilde{\rho}-\tilde{\alpha}_{22})^{-1}](\ell-\bar{\ell}) \\ &= -(\tilde{\rho}/\psi)[1+(\theta/\tilde{\rho})(\tilde{\rho}-\tilde{\alpha}_{11})(\tilde{\alpha}_{12})^{-1}](\ell-\bar{\ell}) \end{aligned}$$

$$(5.12)$$

Since along the saddle path output and real balances are moving in the same direction the expression enclosed by both sets of square brackets in (5.12) is positive but, necessarily, less than one since it is the sum of one plus a negative number. Thus we can write,

$$(y-\bar{y}) = -(\tilde{\rho}/\psi)\pi(\ell-\bar{\ell}), \quad 1 > \pi > 0$$

$$(5.12*)$$

Hence

$$\int_0^\infty (y-\bar{y})dt = -(\tilde{\rho}/\psi)\pi \int_0^\infty (\ell-\bar{\ell})dt = -(\tilde{\rho}/\psi)\pi \int_0^\infty (\ell_0-\bar{\ell})e^{\rho'}dt = \pi(\lambda/\psi)d\mu$$

$$(5.13)$$

When the authorities intervene and do not sterilise they can reduce the cumulative loss in output associated with disinflation to a fraction of what this loss would otherwise be.

To get a better understanding of what is involved behind this result consider, again, equation (5.10) which suggests that the cumulative loss in output can also be expressed by $-(p_0-\bar{p})(1/\psi) = -[(p-\bar{p})_0](1/\psi)$. Thus it must be the case that a policy of disinflation that is accompanied by a policy of non-sterilised intervention, such as that described by (5.5*), must be associated with a smaller initial gap between the current and the steady-state path of prices. To explain this consider that

$$(p - \bar{p})_0 \equiv -(\ell - \bar{\ell})_0 + (m - \bar{m})_0 = -\lambda d\mu + (m - \bar{m})_0 \tag{5.14}$$

Since, in this model, the initial appreciation associated with the policy of disinflation will induce the authorities, who follow the rule suggested by (5.5*), to raise the rate of monetary growth above its trend rate $(m - \bar{m})_0$ will be negative. Specifically, using (5.5*) and taking account of (5.12) and (5.12*),

$$(m - \bar{m})_0 = -(\theta / \tilde{\rho})(c - \bar{c})_0 = -(\theta / \tilde{\rho})[(c - \bar{c})_0 / (\ell - \bar{\ell})_0](\ell - \bar{\ell})_0 = (1 - \pi)\lambda d\mu \tag{5.15}$$

Combining (5.14) and (5.15) we arrive, again, at the result given by (5.13); that is, $-(1/\psi)(p - \bar{p})_0 = \pi(\lambda/\psi)d\mu$ can measure the cumulative loss in output. To recap: (1) although steady-state ℓ is independent of intervention the steady-state paths of m and p are not; (2) with non-sterilised intervention both m and p follow higher steady-state paths; (3) as a result the gap between the current and the steady-state value of p is initially smaller in the intervention model. *Other things equal, the smaller the gap between the initial price level and its equilibrium path the smaller the cumulative change in output following some disturbance. In the extreme case of perfect price flexibility the price level jumps onto its equilibrium path instantly following a disturbance and, hence, the gap is zero. Barring discrete jumps in the price level the gap can only be narrowed by devising policies which bring the equilibrium path closer to the initial price level. This is precisely what happens in the model with non-sterilised intervention.*

Figures 5.5a and 5.5b illustrate adjustments under non-sterilised intervention. Again, and for the purposes of illustration, in Figure 5.5a we are using two bars over a variable to depict its new steady state and one bar to depict its old steady state. The comparison with Figures 5.4a and 5.4b brings into sharper focus the contrast between the two models. Notice how non-sterilised intervention reduces the gap between the current path of prices and the steady-state path and how, as a result, the cumulative loss in output is reduced. The reader should be warned, however, that a reduction in the cumulative loss in output is achieved at a cost: along the path of adjustment the rate of inflation is higher in the intervention model.

5.4 Conclusion

We all know that the long-run Phillips curve is vertical. This finding, however, should not obscure the fact that short-run trade-offs have cumulative effects and that the cumulative loss in output associated with disinflation policies can be substantial. Clearly there is a need to know the precise terms and costs of achieving a possible reduction in the cumulative loss of output across steady states. This chapter addresses that need. Clearly it is for the public at large to

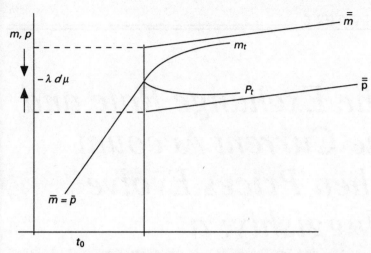

Figure 5.5a   The paths of money and prices in a model of non-sterilised intervention

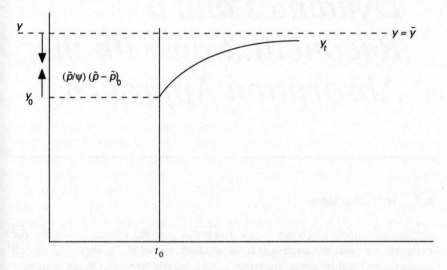

Figure 5.5b   The path of output in a model of non-sterilised intervention

decide which precise trade-off minimises aggregative welfare loss. A more complete analysis would incorporate stochastic shocks. But this subject is partly addressed in Chapter 8.

CHAPTER 6

The Exchange Rate and the Current Account when Prices Evolve Sluggishly: a Simplification of the Dynamics and a Reconciliation with the Absorption Approach

6.1 Introduction

On the occasions when we focused attention on the relation between the exchange rate and the current account we took output to be always at its full employment level by assuming prices to be perfectly flexible. On the occasions when prices were taken to be sticky in the short run and attention was focused on the relation between output and the exchange rate the current account was neglected completely. The time has come to enrich our analysis by looking into the relation between the current account, the exchange rate and other variables within a model where prices are sticky in the short run and expectations are rational. One of our main motives in this chapter is to develop a rather comprehensive and not too complicated framework of dynamic analysis that allows us to extract further results without much sacrifice in intuition or analytic tractability.

Models of the exchange rate and the current account under rational expectations, or perfect foresight, and sluggishly adjusting prices typically involve a relationship between at least three state variables. A minimum menu of the state variables involved includes two predetermined variables, namely the price of the domestic good and the stock of residents' holdings of net claims abroad, and one forward-looking variable, the exchange rate. Equilibrium in such models is typically a saddle point and the path that describes adjustments in the state variables and in the endogenous variables to disturbances which were previously unanticipated is a unique and stable saddle path. A formal derivation of such a saddle path requires the solution of a system of three difference or differential equations and model builders often resort to simulation exercises for a description of adjustments along such a path. However simulation exercises are not a very convenient tool of analysis, nor are they very helpful in gaining an intuitive understanding of the characteristics of the saddle path. Fortunately, as we will show, when the object of analysis is a description of the qualitative characteristics of the saddle path and when the model concerned does not involve more than two predetermined state variables, simulation exercises are not necessary. The qualitative characteristics of the saddle path can be derived from phase diagrams drawn in a two-dimensional space defined by the two predetermined variables. Such phase diagrams are relatively easy to draw and the information they provide enhances intuition. One objective of this chapter is to give a brief exposition of this technique and illustrate some of its advantages.

More often than not open-economy models are cast in linear or, more frequently, in log-linear semi-reduced form at the outset. Imposing linearity at the outset rather than performing the linearisation of an otherwise non-linear structural model can easily introduce pitfalls into the analysis with potentially serious consequences. Consider, for instance, the relationship between the current account and the goods market. When the market for goods clears the current account surplus (deficit) equals the excess (shortfall) of income over absorption. In turn, this income–absorption relationship with the current account imposes certain restrictions on the relationship between the structural parameters of the IS equation and the structural parameters of the current account equation. Failure to observe these restrictions may lead to serious errors and the possibility of committing such errors is always present when the *IS* equation is cast, at the outset, in a linear semi-reduced form, as is the common practice. Accordingly another objective of this chapter is to identify some of these restrictions and highlight the importance of observing them.

The structure of this chapter is as follows. In Section 6.2 we first present a log-linear model of the exchange rate and the current account which introduces three important dynamic extensions to the basic Mundell–Fleming model. These extensions involve the evolution, over time, of the price level, of the exchange rate and of the stock of residents' holdings of net claims abroad. The evolution of the price level reflects the gap of current output from its natural level along the lines of an augmented Phillips curve. The exchange rate is assumed to evolve along a perfect foresight path. Finally, residents' holdings of net claims abroad accumulate (decumulate) with a current account surplus (deficit). The model presented is 'superneutral'. We next explain why superneutrality runs contrary to the principles of monetary economics and go on to allow for the possibility of a non-neutral inflation at the steady state by introducing real balances into aggregate demand via the government budget constraint. The government budget constraint dispenses with 'helicopter' money, allows for a richer menu of fiscal policies and highlights the fiscal implications of varying the rate of monetary growth. We then examine the stability conditions of the model and end the section by looking into the characteristics of the steady state in some detail. In Section 6.3 we attempt a reconciliation of the Mundell–Fleming model with the absorption approach to the current account to highlight the restrictions on the parameters of the model that such a reconciliation requires and to show that the answer to certain questions crucially hinges on observing these restrictions. In Section 6.4 we illustrate the steps required for the construction of phase diagrams in a two-dimensional space for an analysis of short-run and dynamic adjustment of the three state variables and of the endogenous variables along the stable saddle path. To illuminate the advantages of phase diagrams over simulation exercises we use these diagrams to illustrate an analysis of adjustments to a previously unanticipated pure fiscal expansion. Section 6.5 concludes the chapter.

6.2 An extended version of a Mundell–Fleming model and the current account

The structure of the model

$$y = -\gamma(r - Dp) + \delta(e + p^* - p) + \epsilon_1 g + \epsilon_2 F + \nu y^*, \quad \gamma > 0,\ \delta > 0,\ \epsilon_1 > 0,\ \epsilon_2 > 0,\ \nu > 0 \quad (6.1)$$

$$m - p = ky - \lambda r, \quad\quad\quad\quad\quad\quad\quad\quad\quad\quad\quad\quad k > 0,\ \lambda > 0 \quad\quad\quad\quad\quad\quad\quad (6.2)$$

$$r = r^* + De \quad\quad\quad\quad\quad\quad\quad\quad\quad\quad\quad\quad\quad\quad\quad\quad\quad\quad\quad\quad\quad\quad\quad\quad (6.3)$$

$$Dp = \psi(y - \bar{y}) + \mu, \quad\quad\quad\quad\quad\quad\quad\quad\quad\quad\quad \psi > 0 \quad\quad\quad\quad\quad\quad\quad\quad\quad (6.4)$$

$$\mu = D^+ m, \quad\quad\quad\quad\quad\quad\quad\quad\quad\quad\quad\quad\quad\quad\quad\quad\quad\quad\quad\quad\quad\quad\quad (6.5)$$

$$DF = -\theta y + f(e + p^* - p) + \sigma y^* + \epsilon_3 F, \quad\quad \theta > 0,\ f > 0,\ \epsilon_3 < r^*,\ \sigma > 0 \quad (6.6)$$

Notation

y = the logarithm of domestic production.

$\bar{y}$ = the logarithm of the natural level of domestic production.

m = the logarithm of the nominal stock of domestic money.

p = the logarithm of the price of the domestic product.

e = the logarithm of the price of foreign currency in units of domestic currency.

p^* = the logarithm of the price of the foreign product in foreign currency.

r = the domestic norminal interest rate.
r^* = the foreign nominal and real interest rate.
y^* = the logarithm of foreign production.
g = the logarithm of government expenditure on the domestic product.
μ = the core or trend rate of inflation.
F = the number of (net) foreign bonds held by residents, each of which
      represents a claim on one unit of foreign product.
D = the differential operator, so that, for example, $Dp = \partial p/\partial t$.
D^+ = the right-hand side of the differential operator, so that, for example,
      $D^+m(t) = \text{Lim} \, [\, [(m(T) - m(t)]/(T - t)]$ as $T \rightarrow t, T > t$.

Equation (6.1) is a version of an open-economy *IS* relation. Output, which is demand-determined, is taken to be a decreasing function of the real interest rate but an increasing function of the relative price of the foreign good, of the level of foreign production, of government spending on the domestic good and of residents' holdings of net claims on the foreign product. The influence of F on aggregate demand is taken to reflect the effect of net property income from abroad as well as a direct wealth effect. In what follows we will take p^* to be fixed and by an appropriate choice of units we will set it equal to zero. Equation (6.2) describes a textbook-type *LM* relation. Before turning to (6.3) it is worthwhile noting that the foreign bond is, by assumption, a real bond whose real rate of return measured in units of the domestic good is $r^* + De - Dp$. On the assumption that the domestic bond is a perfect substitute for the foreign bond its real rate of return must also be equal to $r^* + De - Dp$ and, hence, the domestic nominal interest rate, denoted by r, must be equal to $r^* + De$. Equation (6.3) reflects the combined assumptions of perfect capital mobility, perfect substitutability between the domestic and the foreign bond and perfect foresight about the expected rate of depreciation of the exchange rate. Under these conditions risk-neutral speculators equate the uncovered interest differential in favour of the domestic bond with the rate of depreciation of the domestic currency. Equation (6.4) is a version of a Phillips curve. The excess of the current rate of inflation above the core rate is taken to rise proportionately with the excess of the current level of production above the natural level. Equation (6.5) identifies the core rate of inflation with the right-hand side time derivative of the money supply. This is one way of imposing short-run stickiness in the price level. Thus, even if the money supply were allowed to make discrete jumps, the price level (though not its rate of change) would not. On the assumption that domestic bonds are not traded internationally, the current account surplus measured in units of the domestic product is defined by τDF where $\tau = \exp(e - p)$. Equation (6.6), which models a reduced-form expression for this account in which the explicit role of τ is suppressed, takes the surplus in this account to be a decreasing function of domestic production but an increasing function of the relative price of the foreign product and of the level of foreign production. The influence of residents' net claims abroad on this account is captured by ϵ_3 which would be identified with the foreign interest rate only if there were no wealth and/or income effects on import demand working their influence through F. The restrictions imposed on ϵ_3 allow for the influence of these effects on the current account.

Why inflation superneutrality does not generally hold

The reader familiar with the influential writings of Buiter and Miller, especially their 1981, 1982 and 1983 papers, can easily verify that the model we have presented above shares one common characteristic with their 'basic' model and that is 'superneutrality': variations in the core rate of inflation that stem from variations in the rate of monetary growth are shown to be neutral in their long-run effects except for their effect on real balances. As we will argue immediately below, superneutrality runs contrary to a long-established body of monetary theory. It can also be particularly misleading in dealing with the macroeconomics of the open economy.

One tradition in monetary theory treats real balances like a consumers' durable good which yields a flow of services in the form of leisure or convenience. In this tradition it seems natural to include real balances in the utility function. Another tradition treats real balances like a producers' durable good which allows for a more efficient utilisation of labour in the production of goods and services by reducing the labour requirement necessary to effect transactions. In this case it is natural to include real balances in the production function. In either case variations in real balances have 'real' effects since they influence aggregate demand or aggregate supply and in either case superneutrality cannot hold, in general. However both of these approaches have attracted criticism and it is for this reason that we find it more attractive to introduce real balances in aggregate demand via the government budget constraint, a practice frequently used in the literature on money and growth. After all one cannot ignore the fact that inflation imposes a tax on real balances. In the case where the entire money stock is of the 'outside' variety the entire yield of the inflationary tax is appropriated by the government. However there is a maximum to the amount of resources a government can extract through inflationary taxes, this maximum occurring at the point where the long-run elasticity of money demand with respect to inflation is equal to one. Unless this elasticity is constant and happens to be equal to one, a change in the trend rate of inflation will induce a redistribution of resources between the public sector and the private sector at the steady state. To accommodate this redistribution of resources one or more determinants of private aggregate demand must adjust. In general, inflation cannot be superneutral.

Introducing the government budget constraint

To keep the analysis as simple as possible we will be assuming that budget deficits are fully monetised and we will write

$$G = T + (\partial M/\partial t)/P = T + (D^+ m)(M/P) = T + \mu(M/P) \tag{6.7}$$

where G is the flow of government spending on the domestic good, T is the flow of tax revenue net of transfers and M/P is the stock of real balances. For simplicity we are assuming that there are no government expenditures on the foreign good. Since μ is effectively under the control of the monetary authorities and M/P is predetermined in the short run the government can choose to control either G or T but not both. In what follows we are assuming, for convenience, that the authorities choose to control the fraction of G to be financed by taxation. Denoting this fraction h, we write:

$$T = hG, \qquad 0 < h < 1 \tag{6.8}$$

and therefore

$$G(1 - h) = \mu(M/P) \tag{6.9}$$

Taking logarithms to rewrite (6.9) we get:

$$g = \hat{\mu} + m - p + \varphi \tag{6.10}$$

where $\hat{\mu}$ is the logarithms of μ and φ is minus the logarithms of $1 - h$. An attractive feature of the budget constraint described by (6.10) is that it allows for an analysis of 'pure' fiscal policy, a policy in which expenditures and net taxes are varied so as to achieve a 'marginally balanced budget'. A pure fiscal expansion, for instance, is captured by a rise in φ. In this model a change in the rate of monetary growth has important fiscal implications. Without helicopter money a reduction in the rate of monetary growth, say, is identified with a reduction in the rate at which the monetary authorities extend interest-free credit (per unit of outstanding M) to the treasury to finance public spending. If the treasury were to adhere to a constant φ public spending would have to be reduced in the short run. In the long-run, however, real balances would rise and if, say, the long-run elasticity of money demand with respect to inflation (measured by $\lambda\mu$) were to exceed unity inflationary taxes would expand, permitting increased public spending across steady states. At any rate the treasury can always choose to insulate public spending from monetary policy by varying φ to achieve a target of public spending.

An analysis of the stability of equilibrium

In what follows it will prove convenient and illuminating to work entirely in terms of the real interest rate, the real exchange rate or competitiveness, and liquidity (real balances). To this effect we will define, $i \equiv r - Dp$, $c \equiv e - p$, $\ell \equiv m - p$, and we will take (6.10) into account to rewrite the model as follows:

$$y = -\gamma i + \delta c + \epsilon_1(\hat{\mu} + \ell + \varphi) + \epsilon_2 F + \nu y^* \qquad (IS) \qquad (6.11)$$

$$\ell = ky - \lambda(i + Dp) = ky - \lambda i - \lambda\mu - \lambda\psi(y - \bar{y}) \qquad (LM \text{ adjusted for inflation}) \quad (6.12)$$

$$i = r^* + Dc \qquad \text{(uncovered interest parity)} \quad (6.13)$$

$$D\ell = -\psi(y - \bar{y}) \qquad \text{(Phillips curve)} \qquad (6.14)$$

$$DF = -\theta y + fc + \sigma y^* + \epsilon_3 F \qquad \text{(current account)} \qquad (6.15)$$

Letting a bar (–) over a variable denote the steady-state value of that variable, we will rewrite (6.11)–(6.15) as follows:

$$\bar{y} = -\gamma\bar{i} + \delta\bar{c} + \epsilon_1(\hat{\mu} + \bar{\ell} + \varphi) + \epsilon_2\bar{F} + \nu y^* \qquad (6.16)$$

$$\bar{\ell} = k\bar{y} - \lambda\bar{i} - \lambda\mu \qquad (6.17)$$

$$\bar{i} = r^* + D\bar{c} = r^* \qquad (6.18)$$

$$D\bar{\ell} = 0 \qquad (6.19)$$

$$D\bar{F} = -\theta\bar{y} + f\bar{c} + \sigma y^* + \epsilon_3\bar{F} = 0 \qquad (6.20)$$

Taking deviations from the steady state we write:

$$y - \bar{y} = -\gamma(i - \bar{i}) + \delta(c - \bar{c}) + \epsilon_1(\ell - \bar{\ell}) + \epsilon_2(F - \bar{F}) \qquad (6.21)$$

$$\ell - \bar{\ell} = (k - \lambda\psi)(y - \bar{y}) - \lambda(i - \bar{i}) \qquad (6.22)$$

$$i - \bar{i} = Dc \qquad (6.23)$$

$$D\ell = -\psi(y - \bar{y}) \qquad (6.24)$$

$$DF = -\theta(y - \bar{y}) + f(c - \bar{c}) + \epsilon_3(F - \bar{F}) \qquad (6.25)$$

Solving out $y - \bar{y}$ and $i - \bar{i}$ from (6.21)–(6.25) the dynamics are as follows:

$$\begin{bmatrix} D\ell \\ DF \\ Dc \end{bmatrix} = \begin{bmatrix} \dfrac{\psi(\gamma + \lambda\epsilon_1)}{B} & \dfrac{\psi\lambda\epsilon_2}{B} & \dfrac{\psi\lambda\delta}{B} \\[2ex] \dfrac{\theta(\gamma + \lambda\epsilon_1)}{B} & \dfrac{\epsilon_3 B + \theta\lambda\epsilon_2}{B} & \dfrac{fB + \theta\lambda\delta}{B} \\[2ex] \dfrac{1 + \epsilon_1(\psi\lambda - k)}{B} & \dfrac{\epsilon_2(\psi\lambda - k)}{B} & \dfrac{\delta(\psi\lambda - k)}{B} \end{bmatrix} \begin{bmatrix} \ell - \bar{\ell} \\ F - \bar{F} \\ c - \bar{c} \end{bmatrix}$$

$$(6.26)$$

The determinant of (6.26) is given by $[\psi(\delta\epsilon_3 - f\epsilon_2)/B]$ with B equal to $\gamma(\lambda\psi - k) - \lambda$. Like Buiter and Miller we will be assuming that $B < 0$. This corresponds to the intuitively appealing assumption that an autonomous increase (reduction) in aggregate demand raises (reduces) output, given competitiveness. Having assumed that $B < 0$ we will also need to assume that $(\delta\epsilon_3 - f\epsilon_2) < 0$ if the model is to possess a stable saddle path. This proves an attractive assumption to make because, as we will show in some detail shortly, it corresponds to the requirement that the total effect of an increase (decrease) in F, given y, is to deteriorate (improve) the current account around the steady state. Accordingly we will be assuming that $(\delta\epsilon_3 - f\epsilon_2) < 0$. Having ruled out the existence of three stable roots there remains to rule out that all three roots are positive. To do so it will be sufficient to claim that the trace of the coefficient matrix is negative, which we shall do on empirical grounds. To summarise, we are assuming that the determinant of the coefficient matrix in (6.26) is positive and that the trace of this matrix is negative on empirical grounds. These combined assumptions are sufficient to ensure that a model which possesses two variables predetermined in the short run, such as F and ℓ, and one forward-looking variable, such as c, has a unique and stable saddle path.

The characteristics of the steady state

The model expressed by equations 6.16–6.20 can be written out more compactly to yield the following steady-state solution:

$$
\begin{bmatrix} \bar{\ell} \\ \bar{F} \\ \bar{c} \end{bmatrix} = \begin{bmatrix} -\lambda & 0 & 0 & 0 & k & -\lambda \\ \dfrac{-\lambda f\epsilon_1}{\Delta} & \dfrac{f\epsilon_1}{\Delta} & \dfrac{f\epsilon_1}{\Delta} & \dfrac{f\nu - \delta\sigma}{\Delta} & \dfrac{f(k\epsilon_1-1)+\delta\theta}{\Delta} & \dfrac{-f(\gamma+\lambda\epsilon_1)}{\Delta} \\ \dfrac{\lambda\epsilon_1\epsilon_3}{\Delta} & \dfrac{-\epsilon_1\epsilon_3}{\Delta} & \dfrac{-\epsilon_1\epsilon_3}{\Delta} & \dfrac{-\nu\epsilon_3+\sigma\epsilon_2}{\Delta} & \dfrac{\epsilon_3(1-k\epsilon_1)-\theta\epsilon_2}{\Delta} & \dfrac{\epsilon_3(\gamma+\lambda\epsilon_1)}{\Delta} \end{bmatrix} \begin{bmatrix} \mu \\ \hat{\mu} \\ \varphi \\ y^* \\ \bar{y} \\ r^* \end{bmatrix}
$$

(6.27)

In (6.27) $\Delta = \delta\epsilon_3 - f\epsilon_2$ which is negative by the stability assumption. Since the solution for steady-state liquidity is straightforward, we will focus attention on the joint determination of $\bar{F}$ and $\bar{c}$. To this effect, and to bring out more clearly the forces that determine the relation between F and c across steady state, we make use of Figure 6.1.

In this figure the *GM* locus, which is derived from equations (6.16)–(6.18), depicts the combinations of competitiveness and of net claims abroad required to clear the market for the domestic good and the money market at the steady state. The position of this locus depends on the exogenously determined $\bar{y}$, y^* and r^* and on the policy instruments φ and μ (and $\hat{\mu}$).Other things equal, a unit rise in F raises aggregate demand above its natural level by ϵ_2 units and to restore aggregate demand to its natural level competitiveness must deteriorate by ϵ_2/δ units. This explains why this locus is downward-sloping and why the slope of this locus is equal to $-\epsilon_2/\delta$. In the same figure the $\dot{F} = 0$ locus, which can be derived from equation (6.20), depicts the combinations of competitiveness and of net claims abroad required to keep the current account in balance. Other things equal, a unit rise in F improves the current account by ϵ_3 units and to restore equilibrium in this account competitiveness must deteriorate by ϵ_3/f units. This explains why this locus is downward-sloping and why the slope of

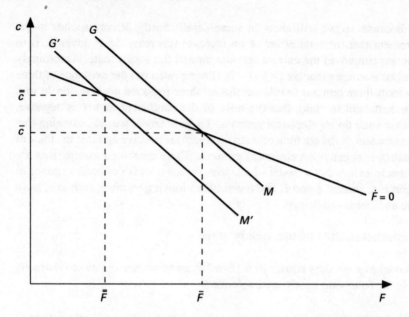

Figure 6.1   The joint determination of F and c across steady states: adjustments to a reduction in μ when λμ > 1, and to an increase in φ

this locus is equal to $-\epsilon_3/f$. By the stability condition the *GM* locus must be steeper than the $\dot{F} = 0$ locus. Notice here that the position of the $\dot{F} = 0$ locus depends on the exogenously determined $\bar{y}$ and y^*. In what follows we will consider four types of shocks and their effects on competitiveness and on residents' net claims abroad across steady states. These experiments will help illustrate that the relationship between competitiveness, the trade balance and the cumulative balance in the current account across steady states depends on the type of shock and, in some cases, on whether inflation is superneutral or not.

Consider, first, the adjustments across steady states that are induced by a reduction in the rate of monetary growth on the assumption that the long-run elasticity of money demand with respect to inflation $\lambda\mu$ exceeds one. In such a situation the proportion by which liquidity rises at the steady state exceeds the proportion by which the rate of monetary growth reduces. As a result inflationary taxes increase across steady states and this enables public spending to expand. At the initial equilibrium level of F competitiveness must deteriorate to release enough resources from private use to public use to allow this redistribution of demand to take place and preserve aggregate demand at the natural level of output. In Figure 6.1, above, the *GM* locus must shift down to the position occupied by, say, the *G'M'* locus. To compute the magnitude of, say, the vertical shift we must take into account that $d\hat{\mu} = d\mu/\mu$. This results in a vertical shift equal to $(\epsilon_1/\delta)\,(d\mu/\mu)\,(1 - \lambda\mu)$, in absolute terms. Notice, first, that F is reduced across steady states and, therefore, property income from abroad is also reduced, allowing the trade balance to improve; second, that the improvement in the trade balance across steady states is associated with an improvement in competitiveness, as one would expect; and third, that *on average* the economy must be running deficits in its current account along the adjustment path and, *on average*, the real exchange rate must be depreciating along this path. The reader can readily verify that, had we assumed that $\lambda\mu$ is less than one, the *GM* locus would have had to shift upwards and we would have obtained the exact opposite results. Only in the special case where $\lambda\mu$ is equal to one does neither the *GM* locus nor the $\dot{F} = 0$ locus shift and superneutrality hold.

Next consider long-run adjustments to a pure fiscal expansion using the same figure to illustrate results. In this model such a policy is captured by an increase in the instrument φ. At a given equilibrium level of competitiveness this policy results in an excess demand. To restore aggregate demand to its natural level competitiveness must deteriorate sufficiently to reduce private demand by an amount just enough to offset the increase in public demand. Again the *GM* locus must shift down and the vertical distance by which this locus shifts amounts to $(\epsilon_1/\delta)d\varphi$. Except for liquidity, which remains unchanged across steady states, in all other respects the long-run effects of such a policy duplicate, qualitatively, the effects of the previous policy. What the two policies examined have in common is an increase in public sector absorption at the given long-run equilibrium level of competitiveness.

Now consider the effects of an increase in income abroad, y^*. Figure 6.2 illustrates the case where the loss in competitiveness required to balance the current account is equal to the loss in competitiveness required to restore aggregate demand to its natural level. Formally the *GM* locus shifts down by a vertical distance equal to $v/\delta \; dy^*$ and the $\dot{F} = 0$ locus shifts down by a vertical distance equal to $\sigma/f \; dy^*$ and $\sigma/f = v/\delta$ by assumption. As a result competitiveness deteriorates by $\sigma/f \; dy^* = v/\delta \; dy^*$ while residents' net claims abroad remain unchanged. Moreover the balance on net property income from abroad and the balance of trade remain at whatever level each of these balances attained at the previous steady state. Hence each component of the current account remains unchanged notwithstanding a deterioration in competitiveness. We will shortly demonstrate that $\sigma/f = v/\delta$ is an assumption which can be validated by the restrictions imposed on the parameters of a structural model that observes the income-absorption relationship with the current account.

6.3 A reconciliation with the absorption approach

Buiter (1987) asks whether an improvement in the current account or the trade balance at full employment requires a depreciation of the real exchange rate. The short answer he gives, and to which this model subscribes, is no. Let us invert this question and ask whether a depreciation (appreciation) of the real

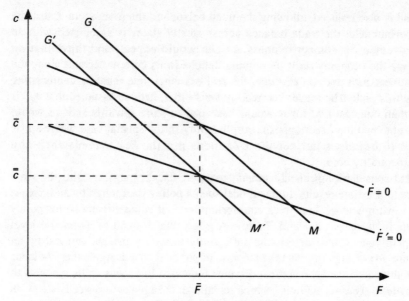

Figure 6.2   The joint determination of F and c across steady states adjustments to an increase in foreign income when $\sigma_{\!/\!f} = \nu/\delta$

exchange rate at full employment brings about an improvement (deterioration) in the current account or the trade balance. Figure 6.2 illustrates a case where the answer is no. To demonstrate that this result is not artificially contrived and to bring further insight into the forces that determine the relation between the current account, the trade balance and the real exchange rate at the steady state, and the restrictions that some of the model parameters must observe, consider a streamlined version of a structural model of the current account of the balance of payments. To illustrate, consider rewriting equations (6.1) and (6.6) in the following way:

$$Y = A + T = A(Y,i,F) + T(Y,F,\tau,Y^*) \tag{6.28}$$

where
$\partial A/\partial Y > 0,\ \partial A/\partial \tau < 0,\ \partial A/\partial F > 0,\ \partial T/\partial Y < 0,\ \partial T/\partial F < 0,\ \partial T/\partial \tau > 0,\ \partial T/\partial Y^* > 0$
and

$$DF = 1/\tau[T(Y,F,\tau,Y^*) + r^*\tau F] \tag{6.29}$$

where
$Y\ = \exp(y),$
$Y^* = \exp(y^*),$
$\tau\ = \exp(e - p) = \exp(c),$
$A\ = \text{private absorption and}$
$T\ = \text{the trade balance.}$

Equation (6.28) is a version of the *IS* relation. In an *ex ante* sense, equilibrium in the market for the domestic product requires that absorption plus the trade balance is equal to the domestic product. The influence of F in absorption and in the trade balance is designed to capture the influence of a wealth effect and of net property income from abroad. The influence of valuation changes on spending is ignored. Equation (6.29) models the current account surplus in the neigbourhood of the steady state. Differentiating (6.28) and (6.29) and applying whatever log-linearisations are required to cast these equations in the form of (6.1) and (6.6) one obtains, among other results:

(a) $\delta\epsilon_3 - f\epsilon_2 < 0$ if $r^* \tau < \partial A / \partial F$.

(b) $\epsilon_3 = 1/\tau \, [\partial T / \partial F + r^* \tau] \lessgtr 0$.

(c) $\sigma / f = v / \delta = (\partial T / \partial Y^*) / (\partial T / \partial \tau)(Y^* / \tau)$.

The first result makes it clear that stability (of the saddle path) hinges upon the assumption that a unit increase (decrease) in F raises (reduces) absorption by more than it raises (reduces) interest income from abroad and, thus, GNP. The second result states that the direct effect of a unit increase in F on the current account is the sum of the improvement of net property income from abroad and the marginal propensity to import associated with such a unit increase in F. Finally the third result imposes a restriction on the relative magnitude of the coefficients σ, f, v and δ. Thus the assumption we made about the relative magnitude of these coefficients to illustrate the workings of Figure 6.2 turns out to be validated. Let us dwell a little longer on this third result to stress the

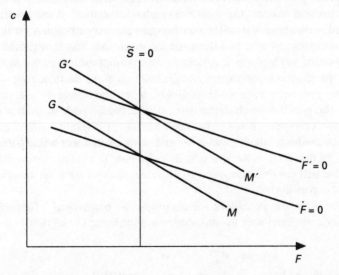

Figure 6.3 Adjustments across steady states to a shift in preferences towards the foreign good at the expense of the domestic good

importance of observing the restrictions imposed by the absorption approach to the analysis of the current account. To this effect consider Figure 6.3. Here the $\tilde{S} = 0$ locus describes the combinations of competitiveness and of residents' holdings of net claims abroad required to maintain aggregate saving and aggregate investment equal to zero at the steady state. The locus is vertical because revaluation effects arising from variations in competitiveness are ignored. It shifts only if there is a shift in the propensity to save or to invest by the private or the public sector. Now consider a shift in residents' preferences towards the foreign good and at the expense of the domestic good. Such a shock cannot disturb the $\tilde{S} = 0$ locus. From a position of initial steady state described by the intersection of the *GM* locus with the $\dot{F} = 0$ locus the economy is placed, instantaneously, at the new steady state described by the intersection of the *G'M'* locus with the $\dot{F}' = 0$ locus. Again this is an instance where a depreciation of the real exchange at full employment has failed to improve (or deteriorate) the current account or the trade surplus. This is because the shock that brought about this depreciation has not disturbed any of the propensities to save or to invest and because revaluation effects from changes in competitiveness are ignored.

6.4 A phase diagram analysis of the saddle path: an illustration

How to construct such phase diagrams

Perhaps it has not been widely appreciated that, when a model possesses one forward-looking and two short-run predetermined state variables, as is the case with the present model, the qualitative characteristics of the saddle path associated with these variables can be conveniently obtained from phase diagrams constructed in a two-dimensional space. All that is required for the construction of such phase diagrams is an assumption about the numerical values of the structural parameters and the solution of the unstable root obtained from these parameter values. Accordingly, when the object of analysis is to ascertain the qualitative characteristics of the saddle path in such a model, simulation exercises are not necessary. Moreover phase diagrams enhance intuition, something which cannot be said with equal force about simulation exercises. In this section we will first describe how to construct such diagrams and then we will use these diagrams to illustrate adjustments to an unanticipated pure fiscal expansion.

Consider, first, the procedure for obtaining the normalised left-hand (row) eigenvector associated with the unstable root. Following Dixit (1980) we write:

$$(M_{31} \quad M_{32} \quad -1)\begin{bmatrix} a_{11}-\rho u & a_{21} & a_{13} \\ a_{21} & a_{22}-\rho u & a_{23} \\ a_{31} & a_{32} & a_{33}-\rho u \end{bmatrix} = (0\,0\,0)$$

$$(6.30)$$

where ρ_u is the unstable root, a_{ij} ($i = 1, 2, 3, j = 1, 2, 3$) is the ijth element of the coefficient matrix in the system of equations described in (6.26) and M_{31}, M_{32} and -1 are the elements of the normalised left-hand (row) eigenvector associated with ρ_u.

Notice, next, that the stable path of the forward-looking variable can be uniquely determined by:

$$c - \bar{c} = M_{31}(\ell - \bar{\ell}) + M_{32}(F - \bar{F})$$ (6.31)

Substituting (6.31) back into the system of equations described by (6.26) we can write:

$$D\ell = (a_{11} + a_{13}M_{31})(\ell - \bar{\ell}) + (a_{12} + a_{13}M_{32})(F - \bar{F})$$ (6.32a)

$$DF = (a_{21} + a_{23}M_{31})(\ell - \bar{\ell}) + (a_{22} + a_{23}M_{32})(F - \bar{F})$$ (6.32b)

$$Dc = (a_{31} + a_{33}M_{31})(\ell - \bar{\ell}) + (a_{32} + a_{33}M_{32})(F - \bar{F})$$ (6.32c)

Let us rewrite (6.32a) and (6.32b), for convenience, as follows:

$$\begin{bmatrix} D\ell \\ DF \end{bmatrix} = \begin{bmatrix} \beta_{11} & \beta_{12} \\ \beta_{21} & \beta_{22} \end{bmatrix} \begin{bmatrix} \ell - \bar{\ell} \\ F - \bar{F} \end{bmatrix}$$

where

$$\beta_{11} = a_{11} + a_{13}M_{31}, \qquad \beta_{12} = a_{12} + a_{13}M_{32}$$
$$\beta_{21} = a_{21} + a_{23}M_{31}, \qquad \beta_{22} = a_{22} + a_{23}M_{32}$$ (6.33)

The intuitively obvious and yet remarkable fact about (6.33) is that the solution of the characteristic equation formed by the coefficient matrix in (6.33) yields the two stable roots. Accordingly one can construct a $D\ell = 0$ locus and a $DF = 0$ locus in the (ℓ, F) space and use these loci to derive the characteristics of the paths of liquidity and of residents' holdings of net claims abroad along the stable path. Turning to equation (6.31) and setting $t = 0$ one can solve for the initial and discrete jump in competitiveness that is required to place the system onto the stable path. Finally, turning to equation (6.32c) and setting $Dc = 0$, one derives a locus of combinations of ℓ and F along which competitiveness is constant. Accordingly this locus can serve to derive the motion of competitiveness along the stable path after the initial and discrete jump in this variable.

Adjustments following an unanticipated pure fiscal expansion: an illustration

To illustrate adjustments to this type of disturbance consider, first, the following parameter values:

Assumed parameter values

$$\psi = 0.5, \quad \delta = 0.5, \quad \gamma = 0.5, \quad k = 1, \quad \lambda = 6$$
$$\epsilon_1 = 0.04, \quad \epsilon_2 = 0.3, \quad \epsilon_3 = 0.05, \quad \nu = 0.3$$
$$\theta = 0.2, \quad f = 0.3, \quad \sigma = 0.18$$

The value of the unstable root associated with the above parameter values

$$\rho_u = 0.154693$$

The elements of the normalised eigenvector associated with the unstable root

$$M_{31} = 0.9867 \quad M_{32} = -0.3260 \quad M_{33} = -1$$

The slopes of the $D\ell = 0$, $DF = 0$ and $Dc = 0$ loci

$$\left. \frac{d\ell}{dF} \right|_{D\ell = 0} = -\frac{(\beta_{12})}{(\beta_{11})} = -\frac{(-0.0822)}{(-0.3700)} = -0.2222$$

$$\left. \frac{d\ell}{dF} \right|_{DF = 0} = -\frac{(\beta_{22})}{(\beta_{21})} = -\frac{(-0.0807)}{(-0.1480)} = 0.5453$$

$$\left. \frac{d\ell}{dF} \right|_{Dc = 0} = -\frac{(a_{32} + a_{33}M_{32})}{(a_{31} + a_{33}M_{31})} = -\frac{(-0.0548)}{(-0.4133)} = -0.1326$$

Let us now turn to Figure 6.4 to describe the characteristics of the adjustment path associated with an unanticipated pure fiscal expansion.

Here we are depicting a $DF = 0$ locus, a $Dc = 0$ locus and a $D\ell = 0$ locus going through point T which we take to describe the new steady state. Notice that the relative slopes of these loci reflect the assumed numerical values of the parameters. The analysis of the steady state presented above has revealed that a pure fiscal expansion reduces residents' holdings of net claims abroad while it leaves real balances unchanged. Thus a point such as 0 can serve to describe the initial steady state. Since below (above) the $DF = 0$ locus $DF < 0$ (> 0) and since above (below) the $D\ell = 0$ locus $D\ell < 0$ (> 0), the path of liquidity and of residents' claims abroad can be described by the path marked by arrows which originates at 0 and terminates at T. Notice that along the entire path the current account is in deficit. Liquidity reduces over time until point B and then rises steadily to its original level. This path of liquidity implies that until point B inflation exceeds its trend rate and output exceeds its natural level. At point B output equals its natural level and inflation equals its trend rate. After point B output falls below its natural level to reach gradually some minimum level and then climb back gradually to its natural level. Similarly after point B inflation falls below its trend rate to reach gradually some minimum level and then climb back gradually to its trend rate. Figures 6.5a and 6.5b illustrate these paths.

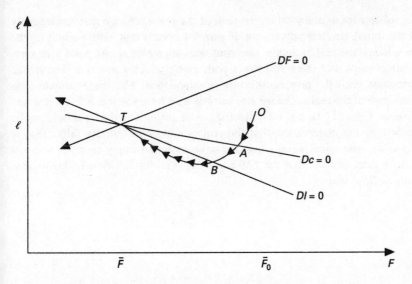

Figure 6.4   The characteristics of the stable path of ℓ, F and c associated with an unanticipated pure fiscal expansion

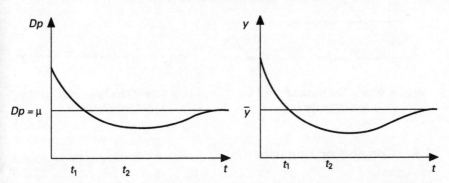

Figure 6.5a   The path of inflation   Figure 6.5b   The path of output

Finally consider the path of the real exchange rate, focusing first on the initial, discrete adjustment. Upon the announcement and the simultaneous implementation of the pure fiscal expansion the real exchange rate jumps below its new steady state since, by equation (6.31),

$$c_0 - \bar{c} = M_{32}(F_0 - \bar{F}) = -0.326(F_0 - \bar{F}) < 0 \tag{6.34}$$

Moreover this initial adjustment places the real exchange rate below its old steady state as well, since

$$
\begin{aligned}
c_0 - \bar{c}_0 &= -0.326(F_0 - \bar{F}) + \bar{c} - \bar{c}_0 \\
&= [-0.326(-f\epsilon_1\,d\varphi) + (-\epsilon_1\,\epsilon_3 d\varphi)]/\Delta = d\varphi(-0.029)
\end{aligned}
\tag{6.35}
$$

where $\bar{c}_0$ denotes the old steady-state real exchange rate.

Let us now focus attention on the path of the real exchange rate immediately after the initial, discrete adjustment. Figure 6.4 reveals that, until point A on the $Dc = 0$ locus, the real exchange rate continues appreciating. At point A this appreciation stops and there follows a path along which there is a continuous depreciation until the new equilibrium is established. The reader should note that the path of the real exchange rate implies a path for the real interest rate and vice versa. Figures 6.6a and 6.6b illustrate these paths. The reader should not be disturbed by the observation that the real interest rate initially falls. This is because the numerical values that we have assumed imply that $\lambda\psi - k > 0$ which, in turn, implies that the LM curve adjusted for inflation is downward-sloping in (i, y) space.

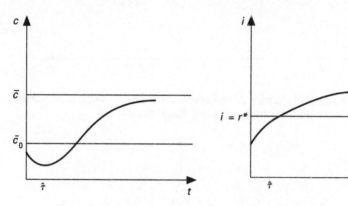

Figure 6.6a   The time path of the real exchange rate

Figure 6.6b   The time path of the real interest rate

6.5   Concluding remarks

It is interesting to note that the above exercise has captured rather well some of the recent behaviour of the American economy. The fiscal expansion in the United States in the earlier part of the 1980s, albeit not of the pure type, induced a sharp appreciation of the dollar which continued appreciating for a while longer before it began to depreciate. Meanwhile the US current account was registering persistent deficits. This should serve to warn us that the association between the exchange rate and the current account derived in Chapters 3 and 4 may not survive richer dynamic structures. And although it is comforting to know that the model can capture some of the observed features in actual economies, the more general message that seems to emerge from our analysis is that, apart from the assumed Phillips-type relation that links output to inflation, there is no simple and unique association that connects pairs of variables along the adjustment path. A lot depends on the type of shock and the numerical value of the structural parameters. Take, for instance, the association between output, the real exchange rate and the stock of net claims abroad following a change in tastes between the domestic and the foreign good or following a change in foreign income. For these types of shocks, and provided that the propensity to save and to invest remains unchanged and revaluation effects can be assumed away, the model seems to suggest that flexibility in the real exchange rate plays a stabilising rather than a destabilising role since in these circumstances the real exchange rate alone adjusts to absorb the shock, leaving no further adjustments to be borne by other variables. This serves to highlight the special role assigned to revaluation effects in the literature (see Chapter 4). If these effects were to prove empirically insignificant in affecting spending then the present analysis would become all the more relevant.

CHAPTER 7

Growth and the Balance of Payments under Alternative Exchange Rate Regimes: the Case of a Small Economy

1.1 Introduction

When secular growth and secular inflation are absent the current account and the capital account in the balance of payments each register a zero balance at the steady state. In such models, responses to any disturbance trace a sequence of stock flow equilibria along which agents are adjusting their stock of assets at the rate necessary to bring the current level of these assets to the level where any further accumulation or decumulation ceases. Viewed from a long-run perspective, imbalances in the current and the capital account of the balance of payments are a disequilibrium phenomenon since they cease to exist in the long run. In models where secular growth is present in the form of, say, population growth, secular imbalances in the balance of payments are the rule. For instance, unless all sectors other than the monetary authorities register a net indebtedness position of zero, secular imbalances in the capital account will prevail. Furthermore, unless the economy's target level of wealth coincides with its target level of capital, secular imbalances in its current account will prevail. Finally a small and growing economy that pursues a fixed exchange rate policy which makes it necessary for it to hold foreign reserves will experience secular surpluses in its overall balance of payments. Only in this way can such an economy acquire the money balances necessary to equip every member of its growing population with the level of money balances desired and preserve the desired ratio of foreign reserves to money. Viewed from a long-run perspective, secular flows in the balance of payments are an equilibrium phenomenon.

From a more general perspective, one could view each account in the balance of payments as the sum of a cyclical plus a secular component. For an economy without secular inflation or growth the secular component in the current account and the capital account of its balance of payments is zero. For a growing economy the secular component reveals the underlying forces of tastes and productivity that shape portfolio balance, saving and investment in the long run.

In a growing economy under flexible exchange rates the domestic government can determine the rate of monetary growth and thereby determine the secular growth rate of the price of the domestic product and of the price of foreign exchange. Revenues from money creation can accrue to the domestic government alone which can use them to boost consumption. In a growing economy under fixed exchange rates at least part of the revenue from money creation accrues to the foreign government. When foreign reserves are not interest-bearing the rest of the world enjoys a welfare gain unless, of course, there are arrangements to rebate its seigniorage.

The objective of this chapter is to study the characteristics and the determinants of the secular components in the balance of payments of a small and growing economy, first, under a regime of fixed exchange rates and, second, under a regime of perfectly flexible exchange rates. In our analysis we particularly focus attention on the effects of a change in the natural rate of growth on the composition of the balance of payments at the steady state. In each case examined we ascertain, first, that local stability can be assured under the restrictions imposed.

The structure of this chapter is as follows. After presentation of the notation used throughout this chapter, Section 7.2 explores the secular components of the balance of payments of a small and growing economy whose exchange rate is fixed and whose capital is immobile internationally. Section 7.3 extends the model of the previous section to the case where capital is perfectly mobile internationally. Section 7.4 explores the secular components of the balance of payments of a small and growing economy under flexible exchange rates and compares results with the previous section. Section 7.5 contrasts, briefly, secular with cyclical movements in the balance of payments. Section 7.6 concludes the chapter by exploring, very briefly, the issue of seigniorage in the international economy.

Notation

Unless otherwise indicated, the stock and flow variables reported below are measured in units of the domestic product divided by the labour force.

y = domestic product.

L = the (inelastic) labour supply taken to be identical to the labour force and strictly proportional to population.

K = the stock of capital in existence.

k $\equiv K/L$, capital intensity.

$\bar{k}$ = the steady-state value of k.

n = the natural rate of growth of population and of the labour force.

$\dot{k} + nk$ ≡ $\dot{K}/L$, investment.

i_ω = warranted investment.

s_h = saving by households.

s_f = saving by firms.

s ≡ $s_h + s_f$, private saving.

M = the nominal stock of money in existence.

P = the price index of the domestic product.

m ≡ M/PL.

$\bar{m}$ = the steady-state value of m.

$(\dot{M}/PL)_h$ = the accumulation of money by households.

$(\dot{M}/PL)_f$ = The accumulation of money by firms.

$(\dot{M}/PL)$ ≡ $(\dot{M}/PL)_h + (\dot{M}/PL)_f$.

v = the market value of equity held by residents.

$q, \tilde{q}$ = the market price of capital and the shadow price of capital, respectively.

W = the stock of wealth in existence.

w = W/L.

$\tilde{w}$ = desired w.

r_e = the rate of return on equity.

r_f = The world rate of return on equity.

$\tilde{\theta}$ = unanticipated capital gains.

μ = the ratio of desired wealth to labour disposable income taken to be constant and greater than one.

σ = the propensity to dissave induced by a unit increase in wealth.

7.2 A growth model of an open economy with capital immobility and fixed exchange rates

Description of the model

The model consists of the following seven equations:

$$y = f(k), f'(k) > 0, f''(k) < 0, f'(k) \to 0 \text{ as } k \to \infty, f'(k) \to \infty \text{ as } k \to 0,$$
$$-f''(k)k \to 0 \text{ as } k \to \infty, -f''(k)k \to \infty \text{ as } k \to 0, -f'''(k)k - f''(k) < 0 \tag{7.1}$$

$$s = \sigma(\tilde{w} - w) + nw, \ 0 < \sigma < 1 \tag{7.2}$$

$$\tilde{w} = \mu[f(k) - f'(k)k] = \tilde{w}(k), \ \tilde{w}'(k) > 0, \ \tilde{w}''(k) < 0 \tag{7.3}$$

$$w \equiv v + m = qk + m \tag{7.4}$$

$$qk = \hat{v}(y, r_e)w, \ \partial\hat{v}/\partial y < 0, \ \partial\hat{v}/\partial r_e > 0 \tag{7.5}$$

$$r_e = [f'(k)k/qk] = f'(k)/q \tag{7.6}$$

$$\dot{K}/L \equiv \dot{k} + nk = i(q) + nk, \ i'(q) > 0, \ i(1) = 0 \tag{7.7}$$

Equation (7.1) models a well-behaved production function and, in addition, it imposes some restrictions on the first and second derivatives of the marginal product of labour. As we will show below, these restrictions help to ensure the existence, uniqueness and stability of steady-state equilibrium. The reader can readily verify that these restrictions are satisfied by a homogeneous-of-degree-one Cobb–Douglas production function and by a homogeneous-of-degree-one CES production function with an elasticity of substitution greater than one. Equation (7.2) models saving as the sum of a disequilibrium plus an equilibrium component: when desired wealth equals actual wealth, saving is just sufficient to maintain per capita wealth constant. In (7.3) we model desired wealth after Tobin and Buiter (1976) who observe that, 'On life cycle principles wealth is a multiple of labour disposable income.' In this model taxes or transfers of any kind are assumed away and labour markets are perfectly competitive. Therefore labour disposable income is equal to the marginal product of labour and, accordingly, desired wealth is taken to be equal to the marginal product of labour multiplied by the multiple μ. Equation (7.4) expresses the wealth constraint facing domestic agents; wealth can be held in the form of either equity or money. In this model capital is immobile internationally and the entire investment is financed by the issue of equity. Therefore the market value of equity held by residents, v, must coincide with the market value of capital, qk. As a result of the wealth constraint equilibrium in any one of the two asset markets suffices to ensure equilibrium in the remainder asset market; accordingly we need to model explicitly only one of these market equilibria. In (7.5) we model equilibrium in the market for equity. The proportion of wealth which residents wish to hold in the form of equity is taken to be an increasing function of the own return on equity and a decreasing function of domestic product (income). The assumption that desired equity holdings, as a proportion of wealth, reduce as income rises follows directly from the wealth constraint and the assumption that desired money holdings, as a proportion of wealth, increase with income. Equation (7.6) defines the market rate of return on equity. On the assumption that expectations about (real) capital gains on equity holdings are static and that capital does not depreciate, the rate of return on equity is simply the ratio of the marginal product of capital to the market price of capital. Taking the exchange rate to be fixed and to be expected to remain fixed and taking the world price of the domestic good to be exogenous (by the small-country assumption) and fixed (on the simplifying assumption of zero inflation abroad) P is effectively fixed. Hence r_e can also define the opportunity cost of holding money. Finally, in equation (7.7), we follow Tobin (1969) by specifying investment as an increasing function of the market price of capital. When the market price of capital equals the price of newly created investment goods (that is, when $q = 1$) the rate of investment is assumed to be just sufficient to maintain capital intensity constant. To put it differently, the higher the return on physical capital relative to the return on equity, the higher the profitability of converting domestic product into installed capital and the higher is the rate at which capital intensity expands. When these two returns are equalised firms no longer find it profitable to expand capital intensity.

Portfolio balance, the market price of capital and the short-run solution of the model

Observe now that at any moment in time $k \equiv K/L$ is (short-run) predetermined: at any moment in time K is given by past investment and L, by assumption, is identical to the predetermined labour force. At any moment in time real balances $m \equiv M/PL$ are also (short-run) predetermined in this model: at any moment in time M is given by the past monetisation of foreign and domestic assets and, as argued above, PL is effectively predetermined. As a result of the predetermined nature of k and m, once the solution for q is obtained the entire short-run solution will be shown to be easily obtainable, recursively. Consider, next, obtaining the solution for q. Using (7.1) and (7.6) to substitute out y and r_e from $\hat{v}(\ )$ and making use of (7.4) to replace wealth with the sum of its constituent components, we can rewrite portfolio balance as follows:

$$qk = \hat{v}\,[f(k), f'(k)/q](m + qk) = \varphi(k,q)(m + qk), \quad \varphi_k < 0, \quad \varphi_q < 0, \quad \text{or} \quad (7.5')$$

$$qk/m = (\varphi(\ )/[1 - \varphi(\ )]) \tag{7.5*}$$

As equation (7.5′) or (7.5*) makes clear, the price of capital in the short run is determined by portfolio balance considerations alone. These equations can give rise to a reduced-form expression in q with the following properties:

$$q = q(m,k), \quad \partial q/\partial m > 0, \quad \partial q/\partial k < 0 \tag{7.5**}$$

Although the precise expressions for the partial derivatives in (7.5**) are cumbersome, the explanation as to why q falls with k but rises with m is rather straightforward: a rise in k creates an excess supply in the equity market; it raises qk/m and reduces $\varphi(\ )/[1 - \varphi(\ )]$. On the other hand, a fall in q creates an excess demand in the market for equity; it reduces qk/m and raises $\varphi(\ )/[1 - \varphi(\ )]$. Hence, to maintain portfolio balance a rise in k must be associated with a fall in q. By a similar argument, a rise in m creates an excess demand for equity whereas a rise in q creates an excess supply; hence, to maintain portfolio balance, a rise in m must be associated with a rise in q.

By several substitutions the short-run solution of the model can now read as follows:

$$y = f(k)$$
$$q = q(m, k)$$
$$w = qk + m$$
$$s = \sigma\tilde{w}(k) + (n - \sigma)w$$
$$\dot{k} = i[q(m, k)]$$

Before turning our attention to the dynamics of the model it will prove convenient, for the purpose of future reference, to define an iso-q locus and look into its properties. An iso-q locus shall be defined as the locus of combinations of m and k required to maintain portfolio balance at a constant q. It is quite clear that iso-q loci in (k, m) space must be upward-sloping: to maintain portfolio balance at a given price of equity and a given set of tastes the increase in the supply of equity generated by an increase in k requires an increase in m sufficient to raise demand to the higher supply level. It is also quite clear that an x per cent increase (decrease) in k must be associated with a more than x per cent increase (decrease) in m along an iso-q locus. This is because an equiproportionate increase (decrease) in k and m generates an excess supply (excess demand) at the initial q and this can only restore portfolio balance at a lower (higher) q; hence m must increase (decrease) proportionately more than k if portfolio balance is to be restored at the initial q. Among the family of iso-q loci particular interest is attached to the member obtained by linearising around $q = 1$, since this is the requirement for maintaining capital intensity constant. As it turns out, the slope of an iso-q locus evaluated around $q = 1$ is measured by

$$\partial m / \partial k \big|_{q=1} = [-(m\varphi_k)(1 - \varphi(k,1))^{-2} + 1](m/k) > (m/k)$$

Dynamics of the model

It should be clear by now that, if we are able to trace the paths of k and m, we should be able to trace the path of all the endogenous variables. As we already know, equations (7.7) and (7.5**) give rise to a reduced-form equation that defines the path of k as follows:

$$\dot{k} = i(q(k,m)) = \pi(k,m), \quad \pi_k < 0, \quad \pi_m > 0 \tag{7.7*}$$

By construction, the expressions that define π_k and π_m are obtained by evaluating $\partial \dot{k}/\partial k$ and $\partial \dot{k}/\partial m$ around the steady state; that is around $q = 1$. To obtain the path of m in a manner that is intuitively appealing we will first have to define saving by households, S_h, and saving by firms, S_f, which are given below:

$$S_h \equiv q(\dot{K}/L) + (\dot{M}/PL)_h \tag{7.8}$$

$$S_f + q(\dot{K}/L) \equiv \dot{K}/L + (\dot{M}/PL)_f \tag{7.9}$$

According to (7.8) households use their saving to acquire money balances and newly issued equity. According to (7.9) firms use their saving and the revenue from the sale of newly issued equity to increase their capital stock and to acquire money balances. Combining (7.8) and (7.9) we can then write the flow budget constraint facing the private sector as follows:

$$s \equiv \dot{K}/L + \dot{M}/PL \tag{7.10}$$

Since $\dot{M}/PL \equiv \dot{m} + nm$ and $\dot{K}/L \equiv \dot{k} + nk$, it follows (using (7.10)) that $\dot{m}$ can be derived from

$$\dot{m} = s - \dot{k} - n(k+m) = \sigma\tilde{w}(k) + (n-\sigma)[m+q(k,m)k] - \pi(k,m) - n(k+m)$$

$$= \psi(k,m), \ \psi_k \gtrless 0, \ \psi_m \gtrless 0 \tag{7.11}$$

Again the expessions that define ψ_k and ψ_m are obtained by evaluating $\partial\dot{m}/\partial k$ and $\partial\dot{m}/\partial m$ around the steady state. Linearising around the steady state we can express (7.7*) and (7.11) as follows:

$$\begin{bmatrix} \dot{m} \\ \dot{k} \end{bmatrix} = \begin{bmatrix} \psi_m & \psi_k \\ \pi_m & \pi_k \end{bmatrix} \begin{bmatrix} m-\bar{m} \\ k-\bar{k} \end{bmatrix} \tag{7.12}$$

Since both m and k are predetermined, local stability can only be assured if both of the two roots that drive the system are stable and this, in turn, requires the coefficient matrix in (7.12) to have a trace which is negative and a determinant which is positive. Technically the requirements for local stability are:

$$\psi_m + \pi_k < 0 \quad \text{and} \tag{7.13}$$

$$\pi_k\psi_m - \pi_m\psi_k > 0 \tag{7.14}$$

If, for instance, we are assuming that $n - \sigma < 0$ the condition given by (7.13) is unambiguously satisfied. The assumption that $n - \sigma < 0$ is simply the assumption that the marginal propensity to save out of wealth (in the context of growth with no expected capital gains) is negative. This assumption, which is sufficient but by no means necessary to satisfy (7.13), would seem to be supported by empirical evidence. After algebraic manipulations the expression given by (7.14) reduces to

$$-\pi_k/\pi_m > \tilde{w}'(\bar{k}) - 1 \tag{7.14*}$$

The left-hand side in (7.14*) records the increase in m *necessary* to maintain $\dot{k} = 0$ following an increase in k by one unit above its steady-state value. In other words,

$$-\pi_k/\pi_m = \partial m/\partial k \big|_{\dot{k}} = 0 = \partial m/\partial k \big|_{q=1} > m/k \tag{7.15}$$

The right-hand side in (7.14*) records the increase in m *available* after allowing for wealth to adjust to its new steady state following such a unit increase in k. The stability requirement states that in the neighbourhood of the steady state an increase in k by one unit must be associated with an increase in m which is insufficient to support this increase in k. Only then will forces be generated to drive the system back to the equilibrium from which it was displaced. There is an alternative way to read (7.14*): in the neighbourhood of the steady state, an increase in k by one unit requires wealth to increase by $-\pi_k/\pi_m + 1$ units in order to sustain this increase in k. However, if the actual increase in wealth generated by such a unit increase in k, measured by $\tilde{w}'(\bar{k})$, falls short of the required increase forces will be generated to drive the system back to the equilibrium from which it was displaced. To evaluate the right-hand side of (7.14*) it will prove convenient, and also in accord with our earlier restrictions, to adopt a Cobb–Douglas production function. Letting α denote the share of profits in output in a Cobb–Douglas production function we can readily verify that

$$[\partial \tilde{w}(k)/\partial k][k/\tilde{w}(k)] = \alpha$$

Hence, around the steady state,

$$\tilde{w}'(\bar{k}) - 1 = \alpha(m + k)/k - 1 = (\alpha - 1) + \alpha(m/k) < m/k$$

Thus local stability can be assured under the restrictions of the model.

The steady-state growth path and the anatomy of the balance of payments along this path

The characteristics of the steady-state equilibrium, its determinants and the balance of payments defined by such an equilibrium can all be illustrated diagramatically. Before constructing the appropriate diagram it will prove convenient to define what we will call potential equilibria as follows: for any value of k there corresponds a potential equilibrium value for saving, investment, equity accumulation and the accumulation of real money balances that would obtain had (this) k been the equilibrium k. In this respect, $n\tilde{w} = n\tilde{w}(k)$ defines potential equilibrium saving and $\hat{v}$ $(f(k),\ f'(k))n\tilde{w} = \tilde{v}(k)n\tilde{w}(k),\ \tilde{v}'(k) < 0$, defines potential equilibrium accumulation of equities. That is what is known as the warranted rate of investment. Potential equilibrium investment is defined by $(\dot{K}/L) = nk$. Finally the potential equilibrium accumulation of real money balances is defined by $(1 - \tilde{v}(k))n\tilde{w}(k)$. Among all the potential equilibria there exists one which yields the steady-state solution. This is found by setting $nk = i_\omega = \tilde{v}(k)n\tilde{w}(k)$. Potential equilibria, the steady-state solution and the balance of payments are shown in Figure 7.1.

The drawing of the $n\tilde{w}(k)$ curve reflects the restrictions imposed on the production function according to which $\tilde{w}'(k) > 0,\ \tilde{w}'(k) < 0,\ \tilde{w}''(k) \to \infty$ as $k \to 0$ and $\tilde{w}'(k) \to 0$ as $k \to \infty$. The drawing of the $\tilde{v}(k)n\tilde{w}(k)$ curve reflects, in addition, the assumption that the proportion of wealth held in equities diminishes with k. Moreover as $k \to 0\ f'(k) \to \infty$ and all wealth is held in equity, whereas as $k \to \infty f'(k) \to 0$ and all wealth is held in money. These assumptions imply that the $\tilde{v}(k)n\tilde{w}(k)$ curve cuts the nk curve once and from above. Accordingly there is a unique steady state. By observation several inferences can be made about the behaviour of the steady-state solution. Firstly, the equilibrium k is independent of n. Secondly, a positive (negative) shift in $\tilde{v}(k)$ will lead to a rise (reduction) in steady-state k: a shift in tastes in favour of (against) equity will raise (reduce) the price required to hold existing capital in

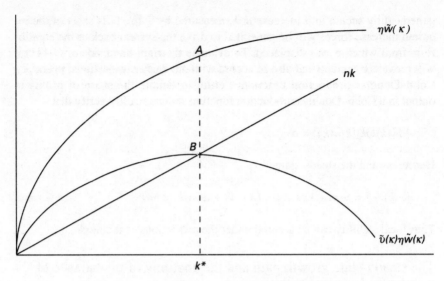

Figure 7.1   Growth, the balance of payments and capital immobility

portfolios and this will induce firms to expand (contract) capital intensity. Similarly a positive (negative) shift in $\tilde{w}(k)$ will raise (reduce) the demand price for equity and this will induce firms to expand (contract) capital intensity.

In a model where capital is immobile internationally and where net transfers to or from abroad are assumed away the trade balance coincides with the current account in the balance of payments and with the overall balance of payments. Assuming that the entire money supply is backed by international reserves the steady-state trade balance and the overall balance of payments are given by the distance AB which measures the steady-state accumulation of real money balances by residents: residents must be running balance of payments surpluses at the steady state since this is the only way that allows them to acquire the necessary money balances to keep real money balances per capita (and real international reserves per capita) constant. A rise in the growth rate n, for instance, will shift all three curves upwards, leaving the equilibrium k undisturbed. However, as a result of the rise in n, say by dn, the balance of payments surplus will rise by $dn[1 - \tilde{v}(k^*)]\tilde{w}(k^*)$. This confirms Mundell's findings.

7.3 A growth model of an open economy with perfect capital mobility and fixed exchange rates

Description of the model

Let us now abandon capital immobility and embrace, instead, perfect capital mobility and perfect substitutability between domestically issued and foreign-issued equity. In addition, the world product and the domestic product will also be assumed to be perfectly substitutable. Let the world return on equity be equal to r_f and the world real price of equity be equal to one. The domestic economy, being small, has no other option but to take as given the world return on equity and the world price of equity. However the rate of return on domestic physical capital can be allowed to deviate from r_f and, therefore, the 'shadow' price of capital, $\tilde{q}$, can be allowed to deviate from its market price whenever the economy is off its steady-state path. We may also note that, since titles to capital are priced at unity, the market value of such titles coincides with the number of such titles. Taking in these modifications our model now reads as follows:

$$y = f(k) \tag{7.16}$$

$$s = \sigma(\tilde{w} - w) + nw \tag{7.17}$$

$$\tilde{w} = \tilde{w}(k) \tag{7.18}$$

$$w = v + m \tag{7.19}$$

$$v = \tilde{v}(y, r_f)w \tag{7.20}$$

$$\tilde{q} = f'(k)/r_f \tag{7.21}$$

$$\dot{k} = i(\tilde{q}) \tag{7.22}$$

Since international trade in equities can take place at all times through the medium of foreign exchange and at a fixed price for foreign exchange and for equity, residents can change their wealth composition at any time without causing valuation changes in their wealth. This suggests that neither m nor v can be considered to be short-run predetermined; rather it is w and k which perform this role. Taking in these considerations and adding an equation to define the motion of w, we end up with the following model:

$$y = f(k)$$
$$s = \sigma(\tilde{w}(k) + (n - \sigma)w)$$
$$v = \hat{v}(f(k), r_f)w$$
$$\dot{k} = i(f'(k)/r_f)$$
$$\dot{w} = \dot{W}/L - nw \equiv s + \hat{\theta} - nw = \sigma[\tilde{w}(k) - w] + \hat{\theta}$$

Outside the steady state the paths of w and k, defined by $\dot{w}$ and $\dot{k}$, respectively, determine a sequence of short-run equilibria. To establish whether this sequence can lead the economy back to the steady-state path when this path is slightly disturbed we need to consider whether the conditions for local stability exist under reasonable restrictions. Linearising w and $\dot{k}$ in the neighbourhood of $k - \bar{k}$ and $w - \bar{w}$ and noting that $\hat{\theta} = 0$ in that neighbourhood we obtain:

$$\begin{bmatrix} \dot{w} \\ \dot{k} \end{bmatrix} = \begin{bmatrix} \alpha_{11} & \alpha_{12} \\ 0 & \alpha_{22} \end{bmatrix} \begin{bmatrix} w - \overline{w} \\ k - \overline{k} \end{bmatrix}$$

where $\alpha_{11} = -\sigma < 0, \alpha_{12} = \sigma\tilde{w}'(\overline{k}) > 0, \alpha_{22} = i'(1)[f''(\overline{k})/r_f] < 0.$

As is readily seen, in a model such as this with w and k both being short-run predetermined the conditions for local stability are easily satisfied.

The steady-state growth path and the anatomy of the balance of payments along this path

POTENTIAL STEADY-STATE EQUILIBRIA

Turning to potential steady states and the steady-state solution we can observe the following. For any k, $n\tilde{w}(k)$ defines potential equilibrium saving, $n\tilde{w}(k) \hat{v}(f(k), r_f) = n\tilde{w}(k)\tilde{v}(k)$, $\tilde{v}'(k) < 0$ defines potential equilibrium accumulation of equities, $\dot{K}/L = nk$ defines potential equilibrium investment and $(1 - \tilde{v}(k))n\tilde{w}(k)$ defines potential equilibrium accumulation of real money balances. The steady-state solution is obtained by setting $f'(k)$ equal to the given r_f. Notice, again, that the steady-state solution for k is independent of n. This

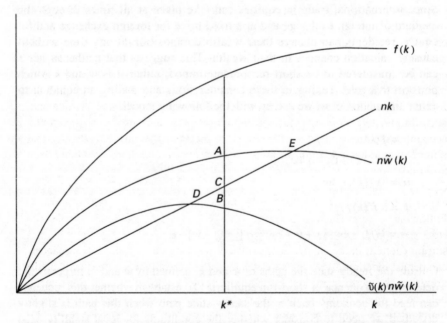

Figure 7.2 Growth, the balance of payments and capital mobility

solution depends on productivity and on the world return on equity. A positive shift in productivity or a reduction in the world return on equity, for instance, would serve to increase capital intensity at the steady state. Figure 7.2 illustrates potential equilibria, the steady-state solution and the anatomy of the balance of payments.

In the above figure we assume, for the sake of illustration, that the slope of the tangent to $f(k^*)$ equals r_f. In our example, equilibrium saving at the steady state is measured by Ak^*, which is divided into an equilibrium accumulation of equities measured by Bk^* and an equilibrium accumulation of real money balances measured by AB. Investment at the steady state and the issue of equity are measured by Ck^*. Thus, in our example, the economy is running a surplus in its current account which is measured by AC at the steady state and a surplus in its capital account which is measured by CB at the steady state. Consequently AB measures the surplus in the overall balance of payments at the steady state. Notice, again, that when money balances are fully backed by foreign reserves the surplus in the overall balance of payments is identified with and measured by the rate of accumulation of real money balances at the steady state.

THE NET FOREIGN INDEBTEDNESS POSITION, THE RELATION BETWEEN WEALTH AND CAPITAL INTENSITY AND THE BALANCE OF PAYMENTS

To the left of D the economy is a net creditor internationally since the number of claims on homogeneous capital held in the portfolios of residents, $\tilde{v}(k)\tilde{w}(k)$ exceeds the units of capital located domestically, k, while to the right of D the economy is a net debtor internationally since $\tilde{v}(k)\tilde{w}(k) < k$. If circumstances are such as to cause the steady-state solution to be located to the left (right) of D the economy must be running a persistent deficit (surplus) in its capital account to maintain its desired position. In our example residents desire to maintain a net foreign indebtedness position equal to $k^* - \tilde{v}(k^*)\tilde{w}(k^*)$ at the steady state and, accordingly, the economy must be running a persistent surplus in its capital account at the rate of $n[k^* - \tilde{v}(k^*)\tilde{w}(k^*)]$ to maintain this position. (Notice that point D would have determined the steady-state solution had the economy been a closed economy or had the economy not allowed for capital movements in equity). Coming to point E we note that to the left of E the value of wealth exceeds the value of capital, while to the right of E the opposite occurs. Following an argument similar to that employed above we can see why a steady-state solution that is located to the left (right) of E must be associated with a surplus (deficit) in the current account which, barring rather 'large' disturbances, can persist indefinitely. At the steady state, and in the absence of domestic credit creation, the economy must be running persistent surpluses in the overall balance of payments to accumulate real money balances at a rate sufficient to maintain its per capita real money balances constant at the desired level. We will conclude by observing that a rise in n causes surpluses in the balance of payments to improve and deficits to deteriorate.

7.4 A growth model of an open economy with perfect capital mobility and flexible exchange rates

Description of the model

We will continue to assume that the domestic economy is small, that domestically issued equity is perfectly substitutable for foreign-issued equity and that the domestic product is perfectly substitutable for the foreign product. For the world as a whole there are as many titles to capital as there are units of capital, each title trading at the real price of one and bearing a given real rate of return equal to r_f. Again we will allow the shadow price of domestic capital to deviate from unity whenever the domestic economy is off its steady-state path. With no loss in generality we will continue to assume that the price of commodities expressed in foreign currency is fixed at, say, P^* and that $P = EP^*$ where E is the price of foreign currency in units of domestic currency. In a model such as this, where the exchange rate is taken to be perfectly flexible at all times, there is no compelling reason for the authorities to hold any foreign reserves, particularly if foreign reserves are non-interest bearing, since there is no need for them to intervene in the foreign exchange market. Therefore, and for the sake of simplicity, we will be assuming that money balances are backed completely by domestic credit. Freed from any obligation to influence directly the price of foreign exchange the authorities are in complete command of monetary policy; they can set the rate of monetary growth to pursue their objectives. Let the authorities' objective be price stability which, as it turns out, guarantees the stability of the exchange rate as well. To accomplish this they must set the rate of monetary growth equal to n. To inject more realism into the model we will be assuming that the authorities' issue of money is used to finance lump sum transfers at the rate of g where $g = \dot{M}/PL = nm$. The complete model is now described by the following equations:

$$y = f(k) \tag{7.23}$$

$$s = \sigma(\tilde{w} - w) + nw \tag{7.24}$$

$$\tilde{w} = \tilde{w}(k) \tag{7.25}$$

$$w \equiv v + m \tag{7.26}$$

$$v = \hat{v}(y, r_f)w \tag{7.27}$$

$$\tilde{q} = f'(k)/r_f \tag{7.28}$$

$$\dot{k} = i(\tilde{q}) \tag{7.29}$$

$$\dot{M}/PL = g = nm \tag{7.30}$$

In models where the public sector neither saves nor dissaves, as was the case with the models we examined in Sections 7.2 and 7.3, there is no need to distinguish between national and private saving. Obviously this is no longer the case. Since the public sector is dissaving (at the rate $g = \dot{M}/PL = nm$) national saving is less than private saving by the amount of public sector dissaving and, other things equal, the surplus in the current account of the balance of payments is less (the deficit is more) by that same amount. In particular, national saving is measured by $s - \dot{M}/PL$ and the flow budget constraint facing the economy can be written as follows:

$$(s - \dot{M}/PL) - \dot{K}/L = (\dot{v} + nv) - \dot{K}/L \tag{7.31}$$

$$\sigma(\tilde{w} - w) = \dot{v} \tag{7.31*}$$

Equation (7.31) expresses the familiar national accounts identity: the excess of national saving over national investment measures the surplus in the current account of the balance of payments which, in turn, can record the rate at which residents are accumulating net claims on non-residents. Equation (7.31*), which follows directly from (7.24), (7.30) and (7.31), can be used to define the path of v. Notice that v is short-run predetermined in this model: since the authorities refuse to validate portfolio shifts through the foreign exchanges, any attempt by residents to exchange claims on capital for money can only result in altering the price level (identified with the exchange rate) and through the price level the level of real money balances and of wealth. In order to fully determine the path of v we must first replace w in (7.31*) by its short-run equilibrium value determined by (7.27). This yields

$$\dot{v} = \sigma[\tilde{w}(k) - v\hat{w}(f(k), r_f)] \tag{7.31**}$$

which together with

$$\dot{k} = i(\tilde{q}) = i(f'(k)/r_f) \tag{7.29*}$$

can adequately define the path of the entire economy near the steady state. Linearising (7.31**) and (7.29*) around the steady state we write:

$$\begin{bmatrix} \dot{v} \\ \dot{k} \end{bmatrix} = \begin{bmatrix} \beta_{11} & \beta_{12} \\ 0 & \beta_{22} \end{bmatrix} \begin{bmatrix} v - \bar{v} \\ k - \bar{k} \end{bmatrix}$$

where $\beta_{11} = -\sigma \hat{w} < 0$, $\beta_{12} = \sigma[\tilde{w}'(\bar{k}) + (v (\partial \hat{v} /\partial y)f'(\bar{k}))/\hat{w}(\ )^2)] \gtrless 0$, $\beta_{22} = i'(1)(f'(\bar{k}))/r_f < 0$ and where $\hat{v}(\ )$ is evaluated at the steady state. Again the conditions for local stability are satisfied, unambiguously.

Private saving, national saving and the balance of payments

In order to bring into sharper focus the features that distinguish a growing economy under floating exchange rates from a growing economy under fixed exchange rates we will continue to use Figure 7.2. In the present context it is easy to see that $n\widetilde{w}(k)$ can be identified with potential equilibria that measure private saving, that the vertical distance between $n\widetilde{w}(k)$ and $\widetilde{v}(k)n\widetilde{w}(k)$ can define potential equilibria that measure public sector dissaving and that, therefore, $\widetilde{v}(k)n\widetilde{w}(k)$ can define potential equilibria that measure national saving. In our example the economy is running a deficit in its current account which is fully financed by a surplus in its capital account, both accounts being measured by the distance CB. The crucial thing to note is that public sector dissaving crowds out fully potential surpluses in the current account. The net creditor–net debtor position at the steady state, which is determined by productivity and portfolio balance considerations, determines the characteristics of the balance of payments at the steady state. In our example the economy chooses to be a net debtor at the steady state and, in order to support the same level of (equilibrium) indebtedness for every individual among a population growing at the rate n, it is prepared to pay foreign lenders a perpetual flow of income streams that grows at the rate n. To put it differently, the rest of the world is prepared to maintain a net creditor position and increase the flow of lending to the domestic economy at the rate n to enable it to enjoy a perpetual flow of income streams that grow at the same rate n.

7.5   Secular and cyclical movement in the balance of payments

Suppose that circumstances are such that the economy chooses to maintain a net creditor position equal to $v - k$. This suggests that the economy is running a secular deficit in its capital account at the rate $nv - nk$. Let $\dot{\gamma}/L \equiv \dot{v} + nv$ and observe that $\dot{\gamma}/L - \dot{K}/L$ defines the observed deficit in the capital account. If we suppose that this deficit consists of a cyclical plus a secular component we can then measure the contribution of the cyclical component from $(\dot{\gamma}/L - \dot{K}/L) - n(v - k)$. In the absence of growth there is no secular component and observed measures of the balance of payments simply measure disturbances around a zero trend. In the presence of growth the cyclical and the secular components of the balance of payments may take opposite signs. For instance, a cyclical surplus in the capital account combined with a larger secular deficit in this account will register as a deficit in the capital account. This suggests that in the presence of secular growth it may become important to distinguish between secular and cyclical components in the balance of payments.

7.6   Seigniorage and the foreign exchange regime

It is customary to define seigniorage as the amount of revenue that a government can collect from the creation of money balances. It would be useful to distinguish, at the outset, between the revenue that a government can collect from the creation of money balances as a result of an inflation tax imposed on such balances and the revenue that a government can collect from a non-inflationary growth of money balances. In this chapter we have not considered inflationary finance because this would complicate the analysis and because there is not much to recommend this type of finance. Thus, in the models we have examined in this chapter, the maximum amount of seigniorage has amounted to nm.

When the economy pursues a fixed exchange rate policy it is reasonable to assume that there is a level of foreign reserves that the authorities and the public at large find it desirable to possess. The precise level of these reserves will, obviously, have to be determined endogenously, taking account of the costs and benefits associated with holding such reserves. When the economy pursues an exchange rate policy of perfectly flexible exchange rates it is not so obvious what level of reserves it is optimum to hold. In this chapter we have set aside these issues and have focused, instead, on two extreme positions: (1) money balances fully backed by foreign reserves when the exchange rate is fixed, and (2) money balances fully backed by domestic assets when the exchange rate is perfectly flexible. Accordingly the full amount of the seigniorage is collected by the foreign government under (1) above and by the domestic government under (2). Although this may not be entirely correct it would still be fair to say that a fixed exchange rate policy pursued by a growing economy allows some seigniorage to be collected by the rest of the world.

In general, if β is the proportion of money backed by foreign reserves in a small and growing economy that pursues a fixed exchange rate policy then βnm is the seigniorage collected from that economy by the rest of the world and $(1 - \beta)nm$ is the seigniorage collected by the domestic government. This suggests that, if the rest of the world were to rebate its seigniorage to the domestic economy and if this rebate were to be distributed to private agents as a lump sum transfer, then no welfare gain would be enjoyed by either of the two economies at the expense of the other, nor would the determinants of the net lender–borrower position be affected. One way to do this is to require the foreign government to pay interest on foreign reserves held domestically equal to its seigniorage and require the domestic government to rebate this interest to the private sector in a lump sum.

CHAPTER 8

Economic Stability under Fixed, Flexible and Managed Exchange Rates

8.1 Introduction

If a country wishes to attain greater economy stability, should it let its exchange rate float or would it be better off pegging its exchange rate? Is it the case that some type of managed floating can offer more advantages than either a flexible or a fixed exchange rate regime? These questions have received attention in the past and are receiving attention again because the experience with the recent floating regime has proved unsatisfactory. Unfortunately any attempt to resolve these issues is bound to stir controversy. Disagreements can arise about the objective function to be used to measure economic stability, the theoretical structure of the model to be used to compare regimes, the numerical values of the structural parameters to be used to obtain numerical solutions and the relative importance of the various shocks to which the economy under investigation is likely to be subjected. One way to begin to resolve these questions is to leave aside the issue of the precise form of the welfare function and simply state that agents value stability in output and in prices (both absolute and relative). One would then select some version of an open-economy *IS–LM* model with a wage–price adjustment equation and an interest parity condition attached to it, attempt to identify the channels via which random shocks transmit their influence on output and prices under alternative exchange rate regimes and attempt to give an estimate of the sensitivity of output and prices to the variance of these shocks.

The measure of economic stability offered by different exchange rate regimes is not independent of the size of an economy and an analysis based on a small-country model may produce results which do not apply to large or even medium-size economies. Moreover, if we are to be able to provide some measure of the relative influence of the different types of shocks which originate abroad, we need a systematic framework to handle such shocks and this is something which single-country models are not particularly good at. For these reasons our analysis in this chapter will be based on a two-country model.

Economies are subject to prolonged departures from their long-run equilibrium paths and this stylised fact ought to be captured in our modelling of exchange rate regimes, especially if it is found that some regimes produce more inertia in the wage–price process than other regimes do. The simplest way to capture this stylised fact is to postulate that wages and prices are partly backward looking and, as a result, previously unanticipated shocks that disturb the wage–price process can have prolonged effects even if these shocks are to last only for a single period. In the analysis which follows only unanticipated shocks that affect directly the supply side of the economy will give rise to persistence. For simplicity and analytic tractability all other types of shocks will have a purely transitory effect.

In general, no two economies share the same structure; nor would we expect policy makers to follow identical policies in any two countries. However if we are to be able to provide an analytically tractable solution to a two-country model which is stochastic and dynamic it is worth making the heroic and simplifying assumption that countries are symmetric so that private agents behave identically in the two economies and policy makers follow identical policies. One can then apply Aoki's method (1981) to solve the model.

The outline of this chapter is as follows. In Section 8.2 we present a stochastic and symmetric two-country model in which expectations are rational and supply shocks give rise to persistent deviations from steady states. We then proceed to obtain its solution. In Section 8.3 we focus, briefly, on the characteristics of the solution for the exchange rate when countries pursue a flexible exchange rate policy. In Section 8.4 we explain the modifications we need to impose on the structure of the model presented in order to solve the model under alternative exchange rate regimes. In Section 8.5 we report numerical solutions of the model when exchange rates are flexible, fixed and managed. Under managed floating we consider the Miller–Williamson proposal described in their (1988) paper and a proposal suggested by Pikoulakis (1992). In our report we provide measures of the sensitivity of output and of prices (absolute and relative) to the variance of each and every shock that can disturb the economy. We make no attempt to see how sensitive our results are to the numerical values we impose on the parameters. Section 8.6 concludes the chapter.

8.2 A symmetric two country model

Our analysis is based on a symmetric, two-country model in which each country specialises in the production of a single product and in the issue of two assets, bonds and money. Each country's product is taken to be an imperfect substitute for the other country's product. Similarly bonds denominated in one currency are taken to be imperfect substitutes for bonds denominated in the other currency and both types of bonds are taken to be traded internationally. The case of perfect substitutability in bonds can be regarded as the special case that arises when circumstances are such that no risk premium is required by agents. Each country's money is a non-interest bearing asset and monies are not traded internationally. The nominal wage rate in each country is modelled to adjust sluggishly towards equilibrium when the economy is subjected to supply shocks and this, in turn, imparts sluggishness in the process of price adjustment. As a result, the exchange rate and the output level in each country also adjust sluggishly in response to unanticipated supply shocks. Markets for goods, assets and labour are subjected to stochastic shocks and attention focuses, mainly, on the properties of the variances of output and of prices under alternative exchange rate regimes. One of the regimes examined takes the exchange rate to be perfectly flexible, while another regime examined takes the nominal exchange rate to be fixed and to be expected to remain fixed. Finally we consider two types of managed floating. One examines the case where monetary policy insulates aggregate demand from the real exchange rate without requiring the real exchange rate to be fixed, as was described by Pikoulakis in his 1992 paper. The other type of managed floating takes up the case of target zones with a fixed real exchange rate along the lines proposed by Williamson and Miller in their 1988 paper. The assumption of symmetry means that the two countries follow identical policies and that private sector behaviour is identical across countries. Without this strong assumption the solution of the model would not be analytically tractable.

The model below defines behaviour in the 'home' and in the 'foreign' country. The foreign country variables are marked with an asterisk.

The home country

$$y = -\gamma (r - EC_{+1} + EC) + \delta (e + p^* - p) + u \tag{8.1}$$

$$m = C + ky - \lambda r - v \tag{8.2}$$

$$w = w_{-1} + \pi (EC - C_{-1}) + \omega E(y - \bar{y}) + \epsilon, \quad 0 < \pi \leqslant 1 \tag{8.3}$$

$$p = w \tag{8.4}$$

$$m = \hat{m} - \theta_1 [(e + p^* - p) - (\bar{e} + \bar{p}^* - \bar{p})] + \theta_2 (C - \bar{C}) + \theta_3 (r - \bar{r}) + \theta_4 (y - \bar{y}) + \eta \tag{8.5}$$

$$C \equiv \varphi p + (1 - \varphi)(p^* + e) = p + (1 - \varphi)(p^* + e - p), \quad \frac{1}{2} < \varphi \leqslant 1 \tag{8.6}$$

The foreign country

$$y^* = -\gamma (r - EC^*_{+1} + EC^*) + \delta (e + p^* - p) + u^* \tag{8.1*}$$

$$m^* = C^* + ky^* - \lambda r^* - v^* \tag{8.2*}$$

$$w^* = w^*_{-1} + \pi(EC^* - C^*_{-1}) + \omega E(y^* - \bar{y}^*) + \epsilon^*, \quad 0 < \pi \leq 1 \tag{8.3*}$$

$$p^* = w^* \tag{8.4*}$$

$$m^* = \hat{m} + \theta_1[(e + p^* - p) - (\bar{e} + \bar{p}^* - \bar{p})] + \theta_2(C^* - \bar{C}^*) + \theta_3(r^* - \bar{r}^*) + \theta_4(y^* - \bar{y}^*) + \eta^* \tag{8.5*}$$

$$C^* \equiv \varphi p^* + (1 - \varphi)(p - e) = p^* - (1 - \varphi)(p^* + e - p), \quad \frac{1}{2} < \varphi \leq 1 \tag{8.6*}$$

International bond markets: the risk premium equation

$$r = [r^* + Ee_{+1} - e] = \tilde{\beta}[b - (e + b^*)] \tag{8.7}$$

Notation

What follows is the notation for the home country model. As we mentioned above, foreign country variables are simply marked with an asterisk.

y	= the logarithm of output.
$\bar{y}$	= the steady-state value of y.
r	= the short-term nominal interest rate.
$\bar{r}$	= the steady-state value of r.
e	= the logarithm of the price of foreign currency in units of domestic currency.
$\bar{e}$	= the steady-state value of e.
p	= the logarithm of the price of output in units of domestic currency.
$\bar{p}$	= the steady-state value of p.
m	= the logarithm of the nominal stock of money.
$\hat{m}$	= the target value of m.
w	= the logarithm of the nominal wage rate.
C	= the logarithm of the consumer price index in units of domestic currency.
$\bar{C}$	= the steady-state value of C.
b	= the logarithm of the stock of bonds issued domestically and denominated in domestic currency.
E	= the operator on expectations conditional on an information set that is available to all private agents at time t.
u, v, ϵ, η	= white noise random variables.

Before proceeding with the description of the model we should make it absolutely clear that, by assumption, all private agents possess the same information set and this information set includes all the lagged values of the variables up to $t - 1$. To put it differently, none of the random disturbances occurring at time t is in the information set available to private agents at time t:

information is available with one period lag. However we do allow governments an informational advantage over private agents. Since the structure of the domestic economy is identical to the structure of the foreign economy it will suffice to explain behaviour in the domestic economy alone. Equation (8.1) is a version of an open-economy *IS* relation consisting of a systematic and a random component. The systematic component takes domestic output to be an increasing function of the relative price of the foreign good (the real exchange rate) and a decreasing function of the *ex ante* real interest rate. The consumer price index is taken, by assumption, to be the relevant index for computing expected inflation. Equation (8.2) is a standard-type *LM* relation to which a random shock in velocity is appended. Again the consumer price index is taken to be the relevant index for computing real balances. Equation (8.3) describes the wage-setting process and states that the nominal wage rate set at the start of the current period equals the nominal wage rate set at the start of the previous period plus adjustments. One of these adjustments reflects the expected price increase for the duration of this one-period contract and is captured by $\pi(EC - C_{-1})$. A second adjustment reflects the expected excess demand during the contract and is captured by $\omega E(y - \bar{y})$. Crucial to the wage dynamics is the assumption that π is less than one. When $\pi = 1$ the only stable solution is the full employment solution. This possibility is not explored in this chapter, primarily because it does not give rise to persistence. Finally a random shock is appended to the systematic components defining wage setting.

Admittedly it is rather difficult to motivate a value for π less than one in a single-period contract so it is worthwhile digressing for a moment to consider how an overlapping contract may deliver a π less than one. Suppose that half of the labour force negotiates at the beginning of the period for the entire period and that the other half of the labour force negotiates twice during the period: first, at the beginning of the period for the first half of the period and, again, at the middle of the period for the second half of the same period. Let $\hat{w}$ denote the wage rate set by the half of the labour force which negotiates once for the entire period and let w_b and w_m denote the wage rates set at the beggining and at the middle of the same period, respectively, by the other half of the labour force and assume the following very simple wage-setting structure:

$$(\hat{w})_t = w_{t-1} + EC_t - C_{t-1}$$
$$(w_b)_t = w_{t-1} + (1/2)(EC_t - C_{t-1}) \text{ and}$$
$$(w_m)_t = (w_b)_t + (1/2)(EC_t - C_{t-1})$$

The half of the labour force which negotiates once for the entire period asks for a wage rate $(\hat{w})_t$ which is designed to increase its nominal earnings, relative to w_{t-1} which is the average wage rate set at the last period, by an amount equal to the expected consumer price inflation for the period $EC_t - C_{t-1}$. The half of the labour force which negotiates at the beginning of the period for the first half of the period asks for a wage rate $(w_b)_t$ which is designed to increase its nominal earnings, relative to the average wage rate set at the last period, by an amount equal to the expected inflation multiplied by the fraction of the period the contract lasts. Finally, at the middle of the period, this same half of the labour force negotiates again for a wage rate $(w_m)_t$ which raises the wage rate it received at the beginning of the period by an amount equal to the expected inflation multiplied by the fraction of the period the contract lasts. The average wage rate for the period w_t is, accordingly, given by

$$w_t = (1/2)[\hat{w}_t + (1/2)[(\hat{w}_b)t + (w_m)_t]] = w_{t-1} + (7/8)(EC_t - C_{t-1})$$

where π is 7/8.

Equation (8.4) is a very simple mark-up of prices over labour costs. This equation reflects two simplifying assumptions: firstly, it reflects the assumption that the only costs in the production of output are wage costs and, secondly, it reflects the assumption that labour productivity is constant. Thus there is no loss in generality in setting the value of labour productivity at zero. Notice that the model implies a constant real wage rate. Equation (8.5) defines the money supply rule. According to this rule the monetary authorities have a target money supply $\hat{m}$ from which they can deviate, if they so wish, whenever output, the consumer price index, the interest rate and the real exchange rate deviate from their respective steady-state levels. The rule is sufficiently flexible to allow a wide range of options to the authorities. One option, for instance, is to set each and every θ equal to zero and thus adhere to a pure money target rule. By assumption the government has information on the current value of the variables. Nevertheless it can still make mistakes in monetary targeting and these mistakes are captured by η. Equation (8.6) defines the consumer price index as a weighted average of the prices of the two goods consumed by residents of each country. The restriction here is that the weight of the domestic good exceeds the weight of the foreign good. The description of the model ends with equation (8.7) which presents a hypothesis about the risk premium in favour of the domestic bond when bonds are short-term. This risk premium, defined by $r - [r^* + Ee_{t+1} - e]$, will only be zero if bonds denominated in different currencies are considered to be perfect substitutes. This special case of perfect substitutability, which is identified with uncovered interest rate parity, can be obtained by setting $\tilde{\beta} = 0$. To put it differently, when bonds denominated in different currencies are considered to be perfect substitutes no risk premium is required and variations in their relative quantities does not affect the spot exchange rate unless, of course, these variations were to induce a change in expectations. In general, however, we would expect $\tilde{\beta} > 0$ and, thus, a rise in the quantity of domestic bonds relative to foreign bonds will require either an increase in the risk premium in favour of the domestic bond or a depreciation of the exchange rate.

Each of the random variables considered is taken to be serially uncorrelated and independent of the other random variables so that $E(u) = E(v) = E(\epsilon) = E(\eta) = E(uv) = E(u\epsilon) = E(u\eta) = E(v\eta) = E(v\epsilon) = E(\eta\epsilon) = 0$. These same properties are assumed to apply to random shocks in the foreign country as well. In addition we are assuming that each and every shock in the domestic economy is independent of each and every shock in the foreign economy.

Substituting out equations (8.4)–(8.6) in the home economy and (8.4*)–(8.6*) in the foreign economy, using a tilde over a variable to denote the deviation of this variable from its steady state, letting $c \equiv \tilde{e} - (\tilde{w} - \tilde{w}^*)$ define the deviation of the real exchange rate from its steady state measured in wage units and letting $\tilde{\theta}_2 \equiv \theta_2 - 1, \tilde{\theta}_3 \equiv \theta_3 + \lambda, \tilde{\theta}_4 \equiv k - \theta_4$ we write:

The home economy

$$\tilde{y} = -\gamma \tilde{r} + \gamma E(\tilde{w}_{+1} - \tilde{w}) + \gamma (1 - \varphi)E(c_{+1} - c) + \delta c + u \qquad \text{GOODS} \qquad (8.1a)$$

$$\tilde{w} = \tilde{w}_{-1} + \pi (E\tilde{w} - \tilde{w}_{-1}) + \pi (1 - \varphi)(Ec - c_{-1}) + \omega E\tilde{y} + \epsilon \qquad \text{WAGES} \qquad (8.2a)$$

$$\tilde{r} = (\tilde{\theta}_3)^{-1}[-\tilde{\theta}_2 \tilde{w} + \tilde{\theta}_4 \tilde{y} + [\theta_1 - (1 - \varphi)\tilde{\theta}_2]c - v - \eta] \qquad \text{MONEY} \qquad (8.3a)$$

The foreign economy

$$\tilde{y}^* = -\gamma \tilde{r}^* + \gamma E(\tilde{w}^*_{+1} - \tilde{w}^*) - \gamma (1 - \varphi)E(c_{+1} - c) + \delta c + u^* \qquad \text{GOODS} \qquad (8.1a^*)$$

$$\tilde{w}^* = \tilde{w}^*_{-1} + \pi (E\tilde{w}^* - \tilde{w}^*_{-1}) - \pi (1 - \varphi)(Ec - c_{-1}) + \omega E\tilde{y}^* + \epsilon^* \qquad \text{WAGES} \qquad (8.2a^*)$$

$$\tilde{r}^* = (\tilde{\theta}_3)^{-1}[-\tilde{\theta}_2 \tilde{w}^* + \tilde{\theta}_4 \tilde{y}^* - [\theta_1 - (1 - \varphi)\tilde{\theta}_2]c - v^* - \eta^*] \qquad \text{MONEY} \qquad (8.3a^*)$$

Since the structural parameters are identical in each country, by assumption, the dynamic analysis can conveniently be conducted at two separate stages, as Aoki (1981) has shown. One stage involves aggregation whereas the other involves taking differences. For instance, if we can derive the behaviour of, say, $r + r^*$ and of $r - r^*$ we can then derive the behaviour of r from $r = (1/2)[(r + r^*) + (r - r^*)]$.

The global economy

Using (8.1a)–(8.3a) and (8.1a*)–(8.3a*) to aggregate the levels of output, of wages, and of interest rates in the two economies we obtain:

$$\tilde{y}_\alpha = -\gamma \tilde{r}_\alpha + \gamma E(\tilde{w}_{\alpha+1} - \tilde{w}_\alpha) + u_\alpha \qquad \text{GOODS} \qquad (8.8)$$

$$\tilde{w}_\alpha = \tilde{w}_{\alpha-1} + \pi(E\tilde{w}_\alpha - \tilde{w}_{\alpha-1}) + \omega E\tilde{y}_\alpha + \epsilon_\alpha \qquad \text{WAGES} \qquad (8.9)$$

$$\tilde{r}_\alpha = (\tilde{\theta}_3)^{-1}[-\tilde{\theta}_2 \tilde{w}_\alpha + \tilde{\theta}_4 \tilde{y}_\alpha - v_\alpha - \eta_\alpha] \qquad \text{MONEY} \qquad (8.10)$$

where $\tilde{y}_\alpha = \tilde{y} + \tilde{y}^*, \tilde{w}_\alpha = w + \tilde{w}^*, \tilde{r}_\alpha = r + \tilde{r}^*,$

$u_\alpha = u + u^*, v_\alpha = v + v^*, \epsilon_\alpha = \epsilon + \epsilon^*, \eta_\alpha = \eta + \eta^*.$

Solving for the reduced form wage equation we obtain:

$$\tilde{w}_\alpha = \tilde{w}_{\alpha-1} - \pi\tilde{w}_{\alpha-1} + (\gamma\tilde{\theta}_4 + \tilde{\theta}_3)^{-1}[[\pi(\tilde{\theta}_3 + \tilde{\theta}_4) + \omega\gamma(\tilde{\theta}_2 - \tilde{\theta}_3)](E\tilde{w}_a)$$
$$+ \omega\gamma\tilde{\theta}_3 E\tilde{w}_{\alpha+1}] + \epsilon_\alpha$$

(8.11)

Applying the operator E on (8.11) we arrive at a second-order difference equation in $E\tilde{w}_\alpha$. Since the model contains only one initial condition, namely $\tilde{w}_{\alpha-1}$, there will exist a unique stable path provided that there exists a single stable root. Letting ρ denote the stable root of this difference equation and observing that $E\tilde{w}_{\alpha-1} = \tilde{w}_{\alpha-1}$ we can arrive at a solution for $\tilde{w}_\alpha$ which is given by:

$$\tilde{w}_\alpha = E\tilde{w}_\alpha + \epsilon_\alpha = \rho\tilde{w}_{\alpha-1} + \epsilon_\alpha$$

(8.12)

If we wished we could use the solution in (8.12) to obtain the paths of $\tilde{y}_\alpha$ and of $\tilde{r}_\alpha$. Next we focus attention on international differences.

International differences

To express the difference in the levels of output, of wages and of rates of interest in the two economies as deviations from their respective steady-state levels we will use, again, (8.1a)–(8.3a) and (8.1a*)–(8.3a*) to obtain:

$$\tilde{y}_d = -\gamma\tilde{r}_d + \gamma E(\tilde{w}_{d+1} - \tilde{w}_d) + 2\gamma(1-\varphi)E(c_{+1} - c) + 2\delta c + u_d \qquad \text{GOODS} \quad (8.13)$$

$$\tilde{w}_d = \tilde{w}_{d-1} + \pi(E\tilde{w}_d - \tilde{w}_{d-1}) + 2\pi(1-\varphi)(Ec - c_{-1}) + \omega E\tilde{y}_d + \epsilon_d \qquad \text{WAGES} \quad (8.14)$$

$$\tilde{r}_d = (\tilde{\theta}_3)^{-1}[-\tilde{\theta}_2\tilde{w}_d + \tilde{\theta}_4\tilde{y}_d + 2[\theta_1 - \tilde{\theta}_2(1-\varphi)]c - v_d - \eta_d] \qquad \text{MONEY} \quad (8.15)$$

where $\tilde{y}_d = \tilde{y} - \tilde{y}^*, \tilde{w}_d = \tilde{w} - \tilde{w}^*, c = \tilde{e} + \tilde{w}_d, \tilde{r}_d = \tilde{r} - \tilde{r}^*,$
$u_d = u - u^*, \eta_d = \eta - \eta^*, v_d = v - v^*, \epsilon_d = \epsilon - \epsilon^*.$

Next let us focus on equation (8.7) which determines the risk premium in favour of the domestic bond. Taking deviations from steady-state levels and assuming that the bond supplies b and b^* are constant, one obtains:

$$\tilde{r}_d = E\tilde{e}_{+1} - \tilde{e} - \tilde{\beta}\tilde{e} = E\tilde{e}_{t+1} - (1+\tilde{\beta})\tilde{e} \qquad \text{RISK PREMIUM} \quad (8.7a)$$

Adding and subtracting $E\tilde{w}_{d+1}$ and $(1+\tilde{\beta})\tilde{w}_d$ we can write:

$$\tilde{r}_d = Ec_{+1} + E\tilde{w}_{d+1} - (1+\tilde{\beta})c - (1+\tilde{\beta})\tilde{w}_d$$

(8.7b)

Armed with the above information, and for the sake of brevity, we will merely indicate the steps involved in obtaining the solution to international differences. In this respect firstly, use equation (8.15) to substitute out $\tilde{r}_d$ from the qoods market and apply the operator E to the resulting expression in $\tilde{y}_d$; secondly, substitute out the resulting expression in $E\tilde{y}_d$ from the wage equation and apply the operator E to the resulting expression in $\tilde{w}_d$. This will yield a second-order difference equation in $E\tilde{w}_d$ and Ec. To obtain the other second-order difference equation the following steps are needed: firstly, use (8.13) to substitute out $\tilde{y}_d$ from the interest rate differential determined by the money markets; secondly, equate the resulting expression in $\tilde{r}_d$ with the $\tilde{r}_d$ determined by the risk premium equation (8.7b) and apply the operator E. The above steps give the following matrix expression:

$$A\begin{bmatrix} E\tilde{w}_{d+1} \\ Ec_{+1} \end{bmatrix} = B\begin{bmatrix} E\tilde{w}_d \\ Ec \end{bmatrix} + \Gamma \begin{bmatrix} E\tilde{w}_{d-1} \\ Ec_{-1} \end{bmatrix}$$

(8.16)

where $a_{11} = \gamma\tilde{\theta}_3$, $a_{12} = 2\gamma(1-\varphi)\tilde{\theta}_3$, $a_{21} = \tilde{\theta}_3(\tilde{\theta}_3 + \gamma\tilde{\theta}_4)^{-1}$

$a_{22} = 1 - 2\gamma(1-\varphi)\tilde{\theta}_4(\tilde{\theta}_3 + \gamma\tilde{\theta}_4)^{-1}$, $b_{11} = [(1-\pi)/\omega](\tilde{\theta}_3 + \gamma\tilde{\theta}_4) + \gamma(\tilde{\theta}_3 - \tilde{\theta}_2)$

$b_{12} = 2[[-\pi(1-\varphi)/\omega](\tilde{\theta}_3 + \gamma\tilde{\theta}_4) + \gamma[(1-\varphi)(\tilde{\theta}_3 - \tilde{\theta}_2) + \theta_1] - \delta\tilde{\theta}_3]$

$b_{21} = (1+\tilde{\beta}) - (\tilde{\theta}_2 + \gamma\tilde{\theta}_4)(\tilde{\theta}_3 + \gamma\tilde{\theta}_4)^{-1}$

$b_{22} = (1+\tilde{\beta}) + 2(\tilde{\theta}_3 + \gamma\tilde{\theta}_4)^{-1}[\theta_1 + \delta\tilde{\theta}_4 - (1-\varphi)(\tilde{\theta}_2 + \gamma\tilde{\theta}_4)]$

$\gamma_{11} = -[(1-\pi)/\varphi(\tilde{\theta}_3 + \gamma\tilde{\theta}_4)^{-1}]$, $\gamma_{12} = [2\pi(1-\varphi)/\omega](\tilde{\theta}_3 + \gamma\tilde{\theta}_4)$, $\gamma_{21} = 0$, $\gamma_{22} = 0$.

The solution to (8.16) follows Chow (1975): letting $\tilde{A} = A^{-1}B$, and $\tilde{B} = A^{-1}\Gamma$, provided that A^{-1} exists, we can rewrite (8.16) as follows:

$$Z' = \tilde{C}Z'_{-1}$$

where $Z = E[\tilde{w}_{d+1}\, c_{+1}\, \tilde{w}_d\, c]$, $\quad Z_{-1} = E[\tilde{w}_d\, c\, \tilde{w}_{d-1}\, c_{-1}]$

$$\tilde{C} = \begin{bmatrix} \tilde{A} & \tilde{B} \\ I & 0 \end{bmatrix}$$
and where I is a 2×2 identity matrix, and 0 is also 2×2.

As it turns out, one root of the characteristic equation formed by $\tilde{C}$ is by construction equal to zero and for a considerable range of plausible parameter values $\tilde{C}$ yields real valued eigenvalues of which only one is within the unit circle and this turns out to be positive. Denoting this eigenvalue by $\tilde{\lambda}$, imposing stability and ignoring the possibility of oscillations, the stable solution to (8.16) is of the form:

$$E\tilde{w}_{d+i} = (\tilde{\lambda}^i)E\tilde{w}_d = (\tilde{\lambda}^i)(\tilde{\lambda}E\tilde{w}_{d-1}) = (\tilde{\lambda}^i)(\tilde{\lambda}\tilde{w}_{d-1})$$

(8.17a)

$$Ec_{+i} = (\tilde{\lambda}^i)Ec = (\tilde{\lambda}^i)(\tilde{\lambda}Ec_{-1}) = (\tilde{\lambda}^i)(\tilde{\lambda}c_{-1})$$

(8.17b)

$$Ec = \tilde{s}E\tilde{w}_d$$

(8.17c)

Since $\tilde{w}_d = E\tilde{w}_d + \epsilon_d$ according to rational expectations, and since $E\tilde{w}_d = \tilde{\lambda}\tilde{w}_{d-1}$ according to the solution of the model, it must be the case that

$$\tilde{w}_d = \tilde{\lambda}\tilde{w}_{d-1} + \epsilon_d \tag{8.18}$$

Let us now return to (8.17c) to draw attention to the fact that $1 + \tilde{s}$ can be identified with the slope of the saddle path in perfect foresight models drawn in (e, w_d) space or in $(e, p - p^*)$ space. Armed with information provided by (8.17a)–(8.17c) and by (8.18) we can use, say, (8.7b) and (8.15) to solve for $\tilde{s}$ and for the real exchange rate. The solution for $\tilde{s}$ turns out as follows:

$$\tilde{s} = -[[z + \tilde{\theta}_3(1 - \tilde{\lambda})]/[\xi + (1 - \tilde{\lambda})\tau^{-1}]]$$

$$\text{where } \tau = [\gamma\tilde{\theta}_4(1 - 2(1 - \varphi)) + \tilde{\theta}_3]^{-1}$$

$$z = \tilde{\beta}(\gamma\tilde{\theta}_4 + \tilde{\theta}_3) - \tilde{\theta}_2$$

$$\xi = 2[\theta_1 - \tilde{\theta}_2(1 - \varphi)] + \tilde{\beta}(\gamma\tilde{\theta}_4 + \tilde{\theta}_3) + 2\delta\tilde{\theta}_4.$$

And, finally, the solution for the real exchange rate is given by:

$$c = \tilde{s}E\tilde{w}_d + (1/\zeta_0)[\zeta_1(v_d + \eta_d) + \zeta_2 u_d + \zeta_3\epsilon_d] \tag{8.19}$$

$$\text{where}$$

$$\zeta_0 = -[(1 + \tilde{\beta})(\tilde{\theta}_3 + \gamma\tilde{\theta}_4) + 2[\theta_1 - (1 - \varphi)\tilde{\theta}_2 + \delta\tilde{\theta}_4]]$$

$$\zeta_1 = -1$$

$$\zeta_2 = \tilde{\theta}_4$$

$$\zeta_3 = (1 + \tilde{\beta})(\tilde{\theta}_3 + \gamma\tilde{\theta}_4) - \tilde{\theta}_2.$$

We will postpone any discussion on the solution for the real exchange rate until the next section.

The asymptotic variance of output, of prices and of the real exchange rate

Since the two economies are symmetric we can focus attention on only one economy, say the domestic economy. Letting $\tilde{E}$ denote the unconditional expectations operator appropriate for computing asymptotic variances and observing that the deviation of the domestic wage rate from its long-run mean $\tilde{w}$ can be computed from $\tilde{w} = (1/2)(\tilde{w}_a + \tilde{w}_d)$, the asymptotic variance of the wage rate, or of the GDP deflator, in the domestic economy is computed from the expression:

$$\tilde{E}(\tilde{w})^2 = \tilde{E}[(1/2)(\tilde{w}_\alpha + \tilde{w}_d)]^2 \tag{8.20}$$

Since $\tilde{w}_\alpha$ and $\tilde{w}_d$ follow an AR(1) process, their variances and their covariance are as follows:

$$\tilde{E}(\tilde{w}_d)^2 \quad = [\tilde{E}(\epsilon_d)^2][1-\tilde{\lambda}^2]^{-1} = [\tilde{E}(\epsilon^2 + \epsilon^{*2})][1-\tilde{\lambda}^2]^{-1} \qquad (8.20a)$$

$$\tilde{E}(\tilde{w}_\alpha)^2 \quad = [\tilde{E}(\epsilon_\alpha)^2][1-\rho^2]^{-1} = [\tilde{E}(\epsilon^2 + \epsilon^{*2})][1-\rho^2]^{-1} \qquad (8.20b)$$

$$\tilde{E}(\tilde{w}_\alpha \tilde{w}_d) = [\tilde{E}(\epsilon_\alpha \epsilon_d)][1-\rho\tilde{\lambda}]^{-1} = [\tilde{E}(\epsilon^2 - \epsilon^{*2})][1-\rho\tilde{\lambda}]^{-1} \qquad (8.20c)$$

From (8.19), (8.18) and (8.20a), the expression for the asymptotic variance of the real exchange rate is given by:

$$\tilde{E}c^2 = [(\tilde{s}\tilde{\lambda})^2(1-\tilde{\lambda}^2) + (\zeta_3/\zeta_0)^2][\tilde{E}(\epsilon)^2 + \tilde{E}(\epsilon^*)^2] + (\zeta_1/\zeta_0)^2[\tilde{E}(v)^2 + \tilde{E}(v^*)^2]$$
$$+ (\zeta_1/\zeta_0)^2[\tilde{E}(\eta)^2 + \tilde{E}(\eta^*)^2] + (\zeta_2/\zeta_0)^2[\tilde{E}(u)^2 + \tilde{E}(u^*)^2]$$
$$(8.21)$$

Since we know how to compute $\tilde{E}(\tilde{w}_\alpha)^2$, $\tilde{E}(\tilde{w}_d)^2$, and $\tilde{E}c^2$ and since $\tilde{y}$ can be computed from $\tilde{y} = (1/2)(\tilde{y}_\alpha + \tilde{y}_d)$, the asymptotic variance of output can be derived from

$$\tilde{E}(\tilde{y})^2 = \tilde{E}[(1/2)(\tilde{y}_\alpha + y_d)]^2$$
$$(8.22)$$

Finally, if we so wished, we could calculate the asymptotic variance of the other variables from the information provided above.

8.3   The solution of the exchange rate under pure floating

The exchange rate theories developed in previous chapters were drawn from non-stochastic models cast in continuous time and, until now, our analyses have focused on adjustments to disturbances which were permanent and expectations evolved along a perfect foresight path. In the present model time flows discretely and the economy is subjected to shocks which are serially uncorrelated and independently distributed random variables with zero mean and constant variance. When time runs discretely the rational expectations solution crucially depends on the assumption one makes about the information set available to agents and therefore our results do depend on this assumption. The reduced-form solution for the real exchange rate in this model is given by equation (8.19) and our main objective in this section will be to explain the behaviour captured by this solution for the case where the exchange rate is perfectly flexible. This particular case is obtained by setting $\theta_1 = \theta_2 = \theta_3 = \theta_4 = 0$.

As will be recalled the solution given by (8.19) is based on the assumption that all private agents share the same information set which, at time t, includes all the variables realised up to period $t - 1$ and that the information set of the two governments at time t includes all the variables realised at t as well as their lagged values. Any mistakes of the governments are captured by the error term in monetary targeting. However, since we are focusing only on the flexible exchange rate case, the information set of governments is irrelevant since each government follows a given fixed target for its money supply. To simplify matters we will restrict our attention to the case where assets are perfect substitutes and where agents use the GDP deflator, rather than the consumer price index, to compute their real balances and to forecast inflation. Thus we restrict attention to the case where $\tilde{\beta} = 0$ and $\varphi = 1$. For convenience we will reproduce the solution for the real exchange rate modified to reflect the case where the exchange rate is perfectly flexible and $\tilde{\beta} = 0$ and $\varphi = 1$. This is expressed by

$$c = \tilde{s}E\tilde{w}_d + (1/\tilde{\zeta}_0)[\tilde{\zeta}_1(v_d + \eta_d) + \tilde{\zeta}_2 u_d + \tilde{\zeta}_3 \epsilon_d] =$$
$$(\tilde{s}\tilde{\lambda})\tilde{w}_{d-1} + (1/\tilde{\zeta}_0)[\tilde{\zeta}_1(v_d + \eta_d) + \tilde{\zeta}_2 u_d + \tilde{\zeta}_3 \epsilon_d]$$

where

$$\tilde{\zeta}_0 = -[(\lambda + \gamma k + 2\delta k], \tilde{\zeta}_1 = -1, \tilde{\zeta}_2 = k, \tilde{\zeta}_3 = (\lambda + \gamma k + 1).$$

(8.19*)

To fix ideas consider first the response of c to an unanticipated increase in the domestic money supply equal to $\Delta \eta$. To simplify matters we will assume that the economy was in equilibrium before this disturbance. Keeping the exchange rate constant but allowing for all other adjustments to take place in response to the increase in η, we can solve for the reduction in the interest rate differential required to clear goods and money markets at unchanged c: from equations (8.13) and (8.15) we arrive at $(\lambda + \gamma k)\Delta(\tilde{r}_d) = -\Delta \eta$. Turning attention to the bond markets we require an expectation of an appreciating real exchange rate to clear this market. By the assumption that the economy was in equilibrium prior to this disturbance and barring any other disturbances $\tilde{w}_d = \tilde{w}_{d-1} = Ec_{+1} = E\tilde{w}_{d+1} = 0$ and the real exchange rate must depreciate by the full amount of the reduction in the interest rate differential so that $\Delta c = -\Delta(\tilde{r}_d)$ is the response required in the bond market to clear this market. Allowing for the effects of this depreciation on output and, through output, on the interest rate differential (see (8.13) and (8.15)) we finally arrive at $\Delta c = -\Delta(\tilde{r}_d) = (\Delta \eta)[\lambda + \gamma k + 2\delta k]^{-1}$ which measures the impact depreciation of the real exchange rate associated with an unanticipated increase in the domestic money supply after allowing all endogenous variables to adjust to this disturbance. Barring any supply disturbances the economy will be in equilibrium at $t + 1$.

Consider next the response of c to an unanticipated increase in domestic demand. From (8.13) and (8.15) we find that the increase in the interest rate differential required to clear the goods and money markets at unchanged c is given by $(\lambda + \gamma k)\Delta(\tilde{r}_d) = k\Delta(u)$. Turning attention to the bond market we require an expectation of a depreciating exchange rate to clear this market. By the assumption that the economy was in equilibrium prior to this disturbance and barring any other disturbances $\tilde{w}_d = \tilde{w}_{d-1} = Ec_{+1} = E\tilde{w}_{d+1} = 0$ and the real exchange rate must appreciate by the full amount of the increase in the interest rate differential so that $\Delta c = -\Delta(\tilde{r}_d)$ is the response required in the bond market to clear this market. Allowing for the effects of this appreciation on output and, through output, on the interest rate differential (see (8.13) and (8.15)) we finally arrive at $\Delta c = = -\Delta(\tilde{r}_d) = -k\Delta(u)[\lambda + \gamma k + 2\delta k]^{-1}$ which measures the appreciation of the real exchange rate associated with an unanticipated increase in domestic demand after allowing all endogenous variables to adjust to this disturbance. Barring any supply disturbances the economy will be in equilibrium at $t + 1$.

Consider, finally, the response of the real exchange rate to an unanticipated disturbance which raises domestic wages and prices by $\Delta\tilde{w}_d = \Delta\epsilon$. As before, we are assuming that prior to this disturbance the economy was in equilibrium. From (8.13) and (8.15) we learn that the relationship between $\Delta(\tilde{r}_d)$, Δc and $\Delta\epsilon$ associated with equilibrium in the markets for goods and money is given by $(\lambda + \gamma k)\Delta(\tilde{r}_d) = \Delta\epsilon + (2\delta k)\Delta c$. In the bond markets the relationship between $\Delta(\tilde{r}_d)$, Δc and $\Delta\epsilon$ that is required to preserve equilibrium, given that $\tilde{w}_{d-1} = 0$, is given by $\Delta(\tilde{r}_d) = -\Delta c - \Delta\epsilon$. Substituting out $\Delta(\tilde{r}_d)$ we find that $\Delta c = -(\Delta\epsilon)(1 + \lambda + \gamma k)(\lambda + \gamma k + 2\delta k)^{-1}$ measures the appreciation in the real exchange rate associated with an unanticipated increase in domestic prices when short-run equilibrium is restored. However this is not the end of the adjustment; $\tilde{w}_{d+1}$ is positive but falling and from $t + 1$ onwards the economy is on its saddle path. Along this path domestic prices and wages, relative to foreign prices and wages, are falling, real money balances are rising and the real exchange rate is depreciating towards its initial equilibrium level. This is precisely what we should expect to find if we were to subject the Buiter–Miller model to an unanticipated price increase.

The behaviour of the nominal exchange rate is defined by $\tilde{e} \equiv \tilde{w}_d + c$, where c is described by (8.19). As we remarked earlier, the slope of the saddle path drawn in $(\tilde{e}, \tilde{w}_d)$ space or in $(\tilde{e}, \tilde{p}_d)$ space equals $(1 + \tilde{s})$ which turns out to be positive for the parameter values we have used to solve the model. That is, for the parameter values we have used to solve the model the nominal exchange rate exhibits undershooting. This means that falling prices are associated with an appreciating nominal exchange rate but a depreciating real exchange rate.

8.4 Solving the model under alternative exchange rate regimes

Solving the model when exchange rates are perfectly flexible

This solution is simply accomplished by setting $\theta_1 = \theta_2 = \theta_3 = \theta_4 = 0$. No other adjustments are necessary. Under this regime each country's monetary authority adheres to a money target rule.

Solving the model when the nominal exchange rate is fixed

Suppose that both countries agree to set e equal to some given $\bar{e}$ at all times and they have the means to do so. Under these circumstances equations (8.5) and (8.5*) are inappropriate and, hence, they must be eliminated; to support this exchange rate regime each country must let its money supply be demand-determined. At the global economy level no qualitative adjustments to the model presented are necessary since, as before, the non-stochastic part of the global money supply is fixed. When it comes to international differences, though, one must set $\tilde{r}_d = 0$; interest rate differentials must be constant when relative bond supplies are taken to be constant and when the exchange rate is fixed and is expected to remain fixed. One implication of this is that r can be computed from $= (1/2)\tilde{r}_\alpha$. Moreover, since one country's money supply can expand at the expense of the other country's money supply, equation (8.15) cannot describe the difference between money market equilibria at home and abroad. This equation must now be replaced by $m - m^* = C - C^* + k(y - y^*) + (\eta - \eta^*) - (v - v^*)$ from which one could solve for the difference in money supplies. Notice that $c \equiv \tilde{e} - \tilde{w}_d$ can no longer define competitiveness since, by assumption, $\tilde{e} = 0$. It is wage differentials that now play the role of competitiveness. Needless to say, one must set $\theta_1 = \theta_2 = \theta_3 = \theta_4 = 0$.

Managed floating designed to insulate aggregate demand from the real exchange rate

If the authorities are concerned that real exchange rate variability causes 'excessive' variability in output, one way for them to manage the exchange rate would be to design policies that insulate aggregate demand from the real exchange rate without requiring the real exchange rate to be fixed. To see how this might be accomplished in some detail it would be useful to distinguish between the case where $\varphi = 1$ and the more general case where $1/2 < \varphi < 1$.

INSULATING AGGREGATE DEMAND FROM THE REAL EXCHANGE RATE WHEN $\varphi = 1$.

Under a very strict interpretation, when $\varphi = 1$ residents of each country comsume only the domestic good. However this is a rather silly interpretation. A more useful interpretation is to say that , when a country's imports are a 'small' fraction of the comsumption basket, residents find it more convenient to use the GDP deflator for the purpose of measuring their real balances, for setting their wage claims and for calculating their expectations of inflation. This special case deserves attention because of its simplicity and because economists have been using it more often than not. When $\varphi = 1$ the main role of the exchange rate is to determine the relative price of goods. To appreciate the workings of the policy to be examined, and for the sake of future reference, it would be useful to focus

$$\tilde{y}_\alpha = (\tilde{\theta}_3 + \gamma\tilde{\theta}_4)^{-1}[\gamma\tilde{\theta}_2\tilde{w}_\alpha + \gamma\tilde{\theta}_3(E\tilde{w}_{\alpha+1} - E\tilde{w}_\alpha) + \tilde{\theta}_3 u_\alpha + (\gamma v_\alpha + \gamma\eta_\alpha)] \tag{8.23}$$

and

$$\tilde{y}_d = (\tilde{\theta}_3 + \gamma\tilde{\theta}_4)^{-1}[\gamma\tilde{\theta}_2\tilde{w}_d - 2\gamma\,[\theta_1 - (1-\varphi)\tilde{\theta}_2 - \tilde{\theta}_3(\delta/\gamma)]c +$$
$$2\gamma(1-\varphi)\tilde{\theta}_3(Ec_{+1} - Ec) + \gamma\tilde{\theta}_3(E\tilde{w}_{d+1} - E\tilde{w}_d) + \tilde{\theta}_3 u_d + (\gamma\eta_d + \gamma v_d)] \tag{8.24}$$

Insulating output from the variability of the real exchange rate without requiring the real exchange rate to be fixed can be accomplished by devising policies that make $\tilde{y}_d$ independent of c or Ec. As equation (8.24) makes clear, when $\varphi = 1$ this is simply accomplished by setting $\theta_1 = \tilde{\theta}_3(\delta/\gamma)$. To appreciate the workings of this policy consider, first, the goods market and observe that, other things equal, a unit increase (decrease) in the real exchange rate must be associated with δ/γ units increase (decrease) in the nominal interest rate to maintain this market in equilibrium and leave aggregate demand unchanged. That is, $\Delta\tilde{r} = (\delta/\gamma)\Delta c$ measures the vertical shift in the *IS* locus required to preserve goods market equilibrium at the initial level of aggregate demand whenever the real exchange rate changes by Δc. Consider, next, the money market and observe that, other things equal, the relationship between changes in the nominal interest rate, the real exchange rate and output that maintains this market in equilibrium is given by:

$$-\tilde{\theta}_3\Delta\tilde{r} + \tilde{\theta}_4\Delta\tilde{y} = -\theta_1\Delta c$$

Accordingly, by setting $\theta_1 = \tilde{\theta}_3(\delta/\gamma)$, the monetary authorities succeed in producing the change in the money supply required to cause the *LM* locus to shift and intersect the *IS* locus at the initial equilibrium level of output whenever this equilibrium is disturbed by changes in the real exchange rate. The reader is asked to observe that in this special case the root that governs the global economy, ρ, is equal to the root that governs international differences, $\tilde{\lambda}$. All feedbacks between the two economies are broken.

INSULATING AGGREGATE DEMAND FROM THE REAL EXCHANGE RATE WHEN $1/2 < \varphi < 1$

Under this more general case, the insulation of aggregate demand from the real exchange rate can be accomplished by setting $\theta_1 = (1 - \varphi)\tilde{\theta}_2$ and $\tilde{\theta}_3 = 0$ as equation (8.24) suggests. By setting $\theta_1 = (1 - \varphi)\tilde{\theta}_2$ the monetary authorities prevent the *LM* locus from shifting whenever the real exchange rate changes. Furthermore, by setting $\tilde{\theta}_3 = 0$, they cause the money market equilibrium condition to be independent of the interest rate so that the *LM* locus becomes vertical and, in effect, it determines the level of output independently of the real exchange rate. As the reader can readily confirm, under this type of policy output is simply determined by

$$y = (\tilde{\theta}_4)^{-1}[\tilde{\theta}_2 w + v + \eta]$$

and, therefore,

$$\tilde{E}(\tilde{y})^2 = (\tilde{\theta}_4)^{-2}[(\tilde{\theta}_2)^2 \tilde{E}(\tilde{w})^2 + \tilde{E}(v)^2 + \tilde{E}(\eta)^2] \qquad (8.25)$$

As (8.25) makes abundantly clear, different values for $\tilde{\theta}_2$ and $\tilde{\theta}_4$ change the price–output trade-off along familiar lines: greater output stability can be achieved at the expense of price stability and vice versa!. Notice also that, as $\tilde{\theta}_4$ becomes larger and larger, the influence of errors in monetary targeting and of velocity shocks on the variance of output becomes smaller and smaller.

The Miller–Williamson model

To model the Miller–Williamson proposals two fundamental changes in the structure of the model presented in Section 8.2 are required. Firstly, fixing the real exchange rate would deprive the economy of a nominal anchor rendering the price level indeterminate and to prevent this we must modify equations (8.1) and (8.1*) to include an index of fiscal stance s or $s*$, designed to reduce the deviation of nominal GDP in each country from a constant target, ζ or $\zeta *$, such that:

$$s = -\sigma(p + y - \zeta) \qquad (8.26)$$
$$s* = -\sigma(p* + y* - \zeta*) \qquad (8.27)$$

Secondly, equations (8.5) and (8.5*) must be replaced by alternative monetary rules designed to achieve a constant, *ex ante*, real interest rate in each country. As it turns out, these rules are sufficient to 'produce' a constant real exchange rate, not only in an *ex ante* sense, but also *ex post*. To see this assume that each country pursues the following interest rate rules:

$$r = E_0(p_{+1} - p) - (1/2)\tilde{\beta}[b - (e + b*)] + \eta \qquad (8.28)$$
$$r* = E_0(p*_{+1} - Ep*) + (1/2)\tilde{\beta}[b - (e + b*)] + \eta * \qquad (8.29)$$

Consistency with the assumption made previously that a government's information set includes current values requires that expectations formed by the government are dated accordingly; hence the operator E_0 denotes expectations formed on the basis of information that includes current values. Equations (8.28) and (8.29) imply that the interest differential set by the authorities expressed in deviation form is given by:

$$r_d = E_0(\tilde{w}_{d+1} - \tilde{w}_d) - \tilde{\beta}\tilde{e} + \eta_d \qquad (8.30)$$

where p has been substituted out by w. Let us turn now to equation (8.7a) which expresses the interest rate differential that would equilibrate the bond markets and observe that the private agents' best guess is that the interest rate differential consistent with the objectives of the two governments must coincide, in an *ex ante* sense, with the interest rate differential that equilibrates the bond markets. Specifically, applying the private agents' expectations operator E on the expressions given by (8.7a) and (8.30) yields $Ec_{+1} = Ec$. Substituting this result into the goods and labour markets further suggests that $Ec_{+1} = Ec = c_{-1} = 0$. *Thus the monetary authorities' rules summarised by (8.28) and (8.29) succeed in producing a constant real exchange rate not only in an ex ante but also in an ex post sense.* For the sake of brevity we will only report the solution of this model which the reader can readily verify. Thus

$$\tilde{w}_\alpha = \mu \tilde{w}_{\alpha-1} + \epsilon_\alpha, \qquad \mu = (1+\sigma)(1-\pi)[(1-\pi)(1+\sigma)+\varphi\sigma]^{-1} \qquad (8.31)$$

$$\tilde{w}_d = \nu \tilde{w}_{d-1} + \epsilon_d \qquad \nu = (1+\sigma)(1-\pi)[(1-\pi)(1+\sigma)+\omega(\sigma-\gamma\tilde{\beta}]^{-1} \qquad (8.32)$$

$$\tilde{y}_\alpha = (1+\sigma)^{-1}[\gamma(1-\mu)\epsilon_\alpha - \sigma\tilde{w}_\alpha + (u_\alpha - \gamma\eta_\alpha)] \qquad (8.33)$$

$$\tilde{y}_d = (1+\sigma)^{-1}[\gamma(1-\nu)\epsilon_d + (\gamma\tilde{\beta}-\sigma)\tilde{w}_d + (u_d - \gamma\eta_d)] \qquad (8.34)$$

It is worth noting that the first term inside the brackets in (8.33) and (8.34) is wholly attributable to the governments' superior information. As it turns out this informational advantage produces smaller output variances. Finally observe that behaviour in this model is independent of the parameter φ.

8.5   Reporting and commenting on results

To compare the relative efficiency of alternative exchange rate regimes we need to know the following pieces of information: (1) the precise form of the welfare function that agents attempt to maximise; (2) how sensitive is each of the determinants of this welfare function to the variance of each and every random disturbance; and (3) the magnitude of the variance of one random disturbance relative to the magnitude of the variance of each and every other random disturbance. In addition we need to be certain that our ranking of efficiency is not sensitive to the precise values we assign to the structural parameters. This is rather an impossible task. What is possible is to say that agents value stability in output and in prices (both absolute and relative prices) and proceed to measure how sensitive is the variance of ouput and of prices to the variance of each and every random shock under alternative exchange rate regimes and under specific parameter values. We could, of course, experiment with different sets of structural parameters but for the sake of brevity and simplicity we will not do so. We will also attempt to identify the channels via which shocks transmit their influence on output and prices under alternative regimes. Throughout the remainder of this chapter, and for the purpose of simplicity and brevity, we restrict attention to the case where $\varphi = 1$ and $\tilde{\beta} = 0$.

Table 8.1 Asymptotic variances under fixed exchange rates

Assumed parameter values: $\gamma = \delta = 0.5$, $\lambda = 2$, $\pi = 0.6$, $\omega = 0.4$, $k = 1$,

$$\varphi = 1, \tilde{\beta} = 0, \theta_1 = \theta_2 = \theta_3 = \theta_4 = 0.$$

Other parameters: $\rho = 0.775$, $\tilde{\lambda} = 0.438$.

THE SENSITIVITY OF THE VARIANCE OF OUTPUT TO THE VARIANCES OF THE RANDOM SHOCKS

$\tilde{E}(\epsilon)^2$	$\tilde{E}(\epsilon*)^2$	$\tilde{E}(u)^2$	$\tilde{E}(u*)^2$	$\tilde{E}(v)^2$	$\tilde{E}(v*)^2$	$\tilde{E}(\eta)^2$	$\tilde{E}(\eta*)^2$
0.584	0.193	0.810	0.010	0.010	0.010	0.010	0.010

THE SENSITIVITY OF THE VARIANCE OF THE GDP DEFLATOR TO THE VARIANCES OF THE RANDOM SHOCKS

$\tilde{E}(\epsilon)^2$	$\tilde{E}(\epsilon*)^2$	$\tilde{E}(u)^2$	$\tilde{E}(u*)^2$	$\tilde{E}(v)^2$	$\tilde{E}(v*)^2$	$\tilde{E}(\eta)^2$	$\tilde{E}(\eta*)^2$
1.692	0.177	zero	zero	zero	zero	zero	zero

THE SENSITIVITY OF THE VARIANCE OF GDP DIFFERENTIALS TO THE VARIANCES OF THE RANDOM SHOCKS

$\tilde{E}(\epsilon)^2$	$\tilde{E}(\epsilon*)^2$	$\tilde{E}(u)^2$	$\tilde{E}(u*)^2$	$\tilde{E}(v)^2$	$\tilde{E}(v*)^2$	$\tilde{E}(\eta)^2$	$\tilde{E}(\eta*)^2$
1.238	1.238	zero	zero	zero	zero	zero	zero

Table 8.2 Asymptotic variances under pure float

Assumed parameter values: $\gamma = \delta = 0.5$, $\lambda = 2$, $\pi = 0.6$, $\omega = 0.4$, $k = 1$,

$$\varphi = 1, \tilde{\beta} = 0, \theta_1 = \theta_2 = \theta_3 = \theta_4 = 0.$$

Other parameters: $\rho = 0.775$, $\tilde{\lambda} = 0.472$, $\tilde{s} = -0.886$.

THE SENSITIVITY OF THE VARIANCE OF OUTPUT TO THE VARIANCES OF THE RANDOM SHOCKS

$\tilde{E}(\epsilon)^2$	$\tilde{E}(\epsilon*)^2$	$\tilde{E}(u)^2$	$\tilde{E}(u*)^2$	$\tilde{E}(v)^2$	$\tilde{E}(v*)^2$	$\tilde{E}(\eta)^2$	$\tilde{E}(\eta*)^2$
0.575	0.188	0.470	0.013	0.099	0.013	0.099	0.013

THE SENSITIVITY OF THE VARIANCE OF THE GDP DEFLATOR TO THE VARIANCES OF THE RANDOM SHOCKS

$\tilde{E}(\epsilon)^2$	$\tilde{E}(\epsilon^*)^2$	$\tilde{E}(u)^2$	$\tilde{E}(u^*)^2$	$\tilde{E}(v)^2$	$\tilde{E}(v^*)^2$	$\tilde{E}(\eta)^2$	$\tilde{E}(\eta^*)^2$
1.736	0.159	zero	zero	zero	zero	zero	zero

THE SENSITIVITY OF THE VARIANCE OF THE REAL EXCHANGE RATE TO THE VARIANCES OF THE RANDOM SHOCKS

$\tilde{E}(\epsilon)^2$	$\tilde{E}(\epsilon^*)^2$	$\tilde{E}(u)^2$	$\tilde{E}(u^*)^2$	$\tilde{E}(v)^2$	$\tilde{E}(v^*)^2$	$\tilde{E}(\eta)^2$	$\tilde{E}(\eta^*)^2$
1.225	1.225	0.082	0.082	0.082	0.082	0.082	0.082

COMMENTING ON THE ABOVE RESULTS

Our comments below draw heavily upon our analysis in Section 8.3.

1. A regime of fixed nominal exchange rates performs better than a regime of flexible exchange rates at insulating output from random shocks in domestic velocity v and in domestic money supply η. One of the main reasons for this has to do with the fact that in a flexible exchange rate regime a random shock in domestic velocity or in domestic money supply requires a change in the exchange rate to restore equilibrium which, in turn, reinforces the effect of the initial shock on output.

2. A regime of floating exchange rates performs better than a regime of fixed nominal exchange rates at insulating output from random shocks in domestic demand u. One of the main reasons for this has to do with the fact that in a flexible exchange rate regime a random shock in domestic demand has a direct as well as an indirect effect. The indirect effect works through the real exchange rate and is stabilising since a positive (negative) disturbance in u, say, causes an appreciation (depreciation) which works towards offsetting the direct effect.

3. When the exchange rate is fixed random shocks in domestic or foreign velocity and in domestic or foreign money supply change global output in the first instance and this change, in turn, is distributed symmetrically between the two economies.

4. When the nominal exchange rate is fixed variations in competitiveness are captured by variations in the GDP deflator or in wage differentials, whereas when the exchange rate is floating variations in competitiveness are captured by variations in the real exchange rate. Thus competitiveness in this model is

subject only to supply shocks when the nominal exchange rate is fixed but is subject to all the types of shocks when the exchange rate is floating. Obviously domestic and foreign supply shocks affect price–wage differentials symmetrically.

5. The coefficient that measures the sensitivity of the asymptotic variance of c to the variance of v, v^*, η, η^* is $(\zeta_1/\zeta_0)^2$. The coefficient that measures the sensitivity of the asymptotic variance of c to u or u^* is $(\zeta_2/\zeta_0)^2$. Notice that ζ_1/ζ_0 gives the change in c required to equilibrate goods, money and bond markets following a unit shock in v, v^*, η or η^*, whereas (ζ_2/ζ_0) gives the change in c required to equilibrate goods, money and bond markets following a unit shock in u or u^*.

6. Whether or not output is more sensitive to supply shocks in a fixed exchange rate regime compared to a flexible exchange rate regime is an empirical matter.

7. The larger are the measures of persistence ρ and $\tilde{\lambda}$ the larger the sensitivity of the asymptotic variance of the GDP deflator to domestic supply shocks.

Table 8.3 Asymptotic variances under managed floating: insulating aggregate demand from the real exchange rate without requiring a fixed real exchange rate

Assumed parameter values: $\gamma = \delta = 0.5$, $\lambda = 2$, $\pi = 0.6$, $\omega = 0.4$, $k = 1$,

$$\varphi = 1, \bar{\beta} = 0, \theta_2 = \theta_3 = \theta_4 = 0, \theta_1 = \lambda = 2.$$

Other parameters: $\rho = 0.775$, $\tilde{\lambda} = 0.775$, $\tilde{s} = -0.261$.

THE SENSITIVITY OF THE VARIANCE OF OUTPUT TO THE VARIANCES OF THE RANDOM SHOCKS

$\tilde{E}(\epsilon)^2$	$\tilde{E}(\epsilon^*)^2$	$\tilde{E}(u)^2$	$\tilde{E}(u^*)^2$	$\tilde{E}(v)^2$	$\tilde{E}(v^*)^2$	$\tilde{E}(\eta)^2$	$\tilde{E}(\eta^*)^2$
0.166	zero	0.640	zero	0.040	zero	0.040	zero

THE SENSITIVITY OF THE VARIANCE OF THE GDP DEFLATOR TO THE VARIANCES OF THE RANDOM SHOCKS

$\tilde{E}(\epsilon)^2$	$\tilde{E}(\epsilon^*)^2$	$\tilde{E}(u)^2$	$\tilde{E}(u^*)^2$	$\tilde{E}(v)^2$	$\tilde{E}(v^*)^2$	$\tilde{E}(\eta)^2$	$\tilde{E}(\eta^*)^2$
2.504	zero	zero	zero	zero	zero	zero	zero

THE SENSITIVITY OF THE VARIANCE OF THE REAL EXCHANGE RATE TO THE VARIANCES OF THE RANDOM SHOCKS

$\tilde{E}(\epsilon)^2$	$\tilde{E}(\epsilon^*)^2$	$\tilde{E}(u)^2$	$\tilde{E}(u^*)^2$	$\tilde{E}(v)^2$	$\tilde{E}(v^*)^2$	$\tilde{E}(\eta)^2$	$\tilde{E}(\eta^*)^2$
0.142	0.142	0.040	0.040	0.040	0.040	0.040	0.040

COMMENTING ON THE ABOVE RESULTS

1. When the monetary authorities manage the money supply with a view to insulating aggregate demand from the influence of the real exchange they, in effect, insulate aggregate demand from shocks originating abroad since these shocks would normally transmit their effects through the real exchange rate.

2. In this regime of managed floating, disturbances in ϵ, v and η produce a smaller variability in output than they do in a regime of perfectly flexible exchange rates. To better appreciate the reasons for this consider, for instance, a positive disturbance in velocity v. Other things equal, this would raise output through a reduction in money demand and through a real exchange rate depreciation (see the specification of c given by (8.19)). However to insulate aggregate demand from the real exchange rate the monetary authorities would have to reduce the money supply to prevent this depreciation from happening and this would act to reduce the impact of the positive disturbance in velocity on output.

3. A regime of purely floating exchange rates seems to outperform this regime of managed floating at insulating output from shocks in domestic demand u. As we remarked above, this is because the real exchange rate has a stabilising influence when shocks in domestic demand u are concerned, and this stabilising influence is removed under the type of managed floating considered here.

4. Greater stability of output to domestic supply disturbances ϵ can be associated with greater instability of the GDP deflator to these disturbances: the more insensitive is output to domestic supply shocks the more persistence there is, and the more persistence there is the higher the sensitivity of the GDP deflator to these supply shocks. However, when $\varphi = 1$, wage setting is independent of foreign supply shocks ϵ^* and since monetary policy can insulate demand from foreign shocks it follows that managed floating can insulate the GDP deflator from disturbances in ϵ^*.

5. Notice, finally, how managed floating can offer more stability to the real exchange rate than pure floating can: technically, this is achieved through a positive value of θ_1 causing ξ to take a larger value. To put it differently, the authorities manage the exchange rate by following a 'leaning against the wind' policy.

Table 8.4   Asymptotic variances under managed floating: the Miller–Williamson proposals of fixing the real exchange rate

Assumed parameter values: $\gamma = \delta = 0.5$, $\lambda = 2$, $\pi = 0.6$, $\omega = 0.4$, $k = 1$,

$$\sigma = 0.408.$$

Other parameters: $\mu = \nu = 0.775$.

THE SENSITIVITY OF THE VARIANCE OF OUTPUT TO THE VARIANCES OF THE RANDOM SHOCKS

$\tilde{E}(\epsilon)^2$	$\tilde{E}(\epsilon\,*)^2$	$\tilde{E}(u)^2$	$\tilde{E}(u*)^2$	$\tilde{E}(v)^2$	$\tilde{E}(v\,*)^2$	$\tilde{E}(\eta)^2$	$\tilde{E}(\eta\,*)^2$
0.171	zero	0.504	zero	zero	zero	0.126	zero

THE SENSITIVITY OF THE VARIANCE OF THE GDP DEFLATOR TO THE VARIANCES OF THE RANDOM SHOCKS

$\tilde{E}(\epsilon)^2$	$\tilde{E}(\epsilon\,*)^2$	$\tilde{E}(u)^2$	$\tilde{E}(u*)^2$	$\tilde{E}(v)^2$	$\tilde{E}(v\,*)^2$	$\tilde{E}(\eta)^2$	$\tilde{E}(\eta\,*)^2$
2.504	zero	zero	zero	zero	zero	zero	zero

A BRIEF COMMENT

To facilitate comparison between the Pikoulakis proposal and the Miller–Williamson proposal we have chosen the value of σ to produce the same value for the stable root under both of these proposals. Thus $\rho = \tilde{\lambda} = \mu = \nu = 0.775$ and the two proposals produce identical results with repect to the stability of the GDP deflator. With respect to output stability there is hardly a difference significant enough to comment upon. The main drawback with the Pikoulakis proposal, apart from the fact that it does not remove the variability in the real exchange rate entirely, is that it makes monetary policy rather more difficult to implement and the main drawback with the Miller–Williamson proposal is that it requires fiscal policy to target nominal GDP which makes this policy rather unattractive and, therefore, less likely to be accepted politically. It would seem that both proposals can compete favourably with the two other regimes explored.

8.6 Concluding remarks

Our choice of parameter values has been particularly favourable to the flexible exchange rate regime because these parameter values imply exchange rate undershooting in this model. Taking this observation into account, one could say that a fixed exchange rate regime can provide more stability than a floating exchange rate regime except, of course, against shocks in domestic demand. To put it more generally, the more important are foreign originating shocks and the less important are shocks in domestic demand the less attractive are flexible exchange rates as far as output stability is concerned. Given that there seems to be a trade-off between price and output stability when the economy is subjected to domestic supply shocks there is no obvious way to compare the price-stabilising properties of exchange rate regimes independently of their output-stabilising properties. For instance, we could have obtained a greater price stability than we did under managed floating if we were prepared to sacrifice some output stability against supply shocks. At this abstract level one should guard against any more generalisations. Besides there are several questions unanswered. Here are a few: what difference would it have made to the stability of output, of prices and of competitiveness had bonds been taken to be less than perfect substitutes, that is, had $\tilde{\beta}$ taken a positive value? Had we allowed agents to use the consumer price index rather than the GDP deflator to guide their bahaviour, that is, had we allowed φ to take a value of less than one (but more than half), would our results be substantially different?. In particular, which regime would provide better insulation from import penetration? Unfortunately these questions were left unexplored but, it is hoped, the interested reader should be able to pursue them.

However the most important issue that needs addressing is an empirical one. We need, at least, to obtain estimates of the variance of the random errors in *LM*, in *IS* and in wage setting to be able to attempt some ranking of regimes.

CHAPTER 9

International Interdependence and Macroeconomic Policy Coordination

Frederick van der Ploeg

9.1 Introduction

The global economy is more and more integrated. Not only are countries interconnected by trade in goods and service, but also by trade in financial assets. Many restrictions on international capital flows have been eliminated, so that the world is more and more characterised by one global capital market. The capital markets of many individual countries have thus become integrated in one global market. This means that interest rates through the world move up and down together. Within this setting of international capital movements, we investigate what the appropriate nominal exchange rate regime is. Chapter 8 argued that the answer to this question depends crucially on where the shocks hitting the economy originate from. For example, if most shocks derive from changes in money demand, a regime of fixed nominal exchange rates is most desirable. However, if most of the shocks occur in goods demand, a regime based on a target for nominal national income is desirable, although this poses severe data problems in view of the lags in collecting national income data. In this chapter we are concerned with a related question: what is the scope for international coordination of macroeconomic policies *given* that a particular exchange rate regime is in force?

Some ardent believers and advocates of the market mechanism argue that such questions are to a large extent irrelevant. If all market clear instantaneously, that is, there are no nominal price or wage rigidities, and all nominal assets are indexed, only relative prices matter in general equilibrium and any form of nominal exchange rate regime is irrelevant. For example, if there is a country-specific adverse shock to the aggregate demand for goods, unemployment occurs abroad and inflationary pressure occurs. According to the market view, this situation clearly resolves itself as wages and prices fall at home and rise abroad. In short, if the market mechanism works, there is no role for government intervention and thus no role for exchange rate policy. According to many classical economists, the particular type of exchange rate regime is irrelevant from the point of view of macroeconomic stabilisation irrespective of whether unilateral or multilateral policy actions are concerned. If one really believed this, one might as well argue that one should move ahead with one currency for the global economy in order to save on transactions costs, hedging costs, information costs, and so on.

However, even under a Panglossian view of the global economy, there may be a role for international coordination of monetary policies under fixed nominal exchange rates. Indeed, the classic and pioneering work on the game-theoretic approach to international policy coordination, Hamada (1985), uses the monetary approach to the balance of payments (see Chapter 3) and the classical assumptions of full employment and PPP to discuss how different central banks who are concerned about their balance of payments and inflation rate should coordinate their monetary policies under pegged exchange rates. The crucial externality in such a multi-country world is that under fixed exchange rates there is a common global inflation rate, which rises if any one of the countries boosts domestic credit. Hence, an expansion of domestic credit in one country directly hurts the inflation target of other countries. Such a policy also leads to a deficit on the balance of payments at home and surpluses abroad. Clearly, even under fixed nominal exchange rates, there are substantial international spill-over effects. The setting of monetary policies is a highly interdependent affair and can be modelled as a game between the various central banks. Indeed, if there is an excessive (too low) expansion of world reserves, international policy coordi- nation requires central banks to reduce (boost) their rates of domestic credit expansion below (above) the rates that would be prevail in a non-cooperative outcome. Intuitively, domestic credit expansion is, as far as inflation is concerned, an international public bad (good) so that under international policy cooperation countries defend themselves against excessive (deficient) reserve accumulation by depressing (raising) domestic credit expansion and exporting (importing) inflation. If a regime of floating exchange rates is in force, the domestic economy is insulated from changes in domestic credit expansion abroad. Hence, as long as all labour and goods markets clear instantaneously and all contracts are indexed, there is no need to coordinate monetary policies under flexible exchange rates.

The classic work of Hamada (1974 and 1985) is particularly relevant for the very long run which is not plagued by involuntary unemployment. In this chapter we are, however, concerned with economies in which markets, and the labour market in particular, do not clear immediately. The appropriate framework for the short-run analysis of economies with involuntary unemployment is the familiar work-horse of international macroeconomics, the two-country extension of the Mundell–Fleming model. We thus investigate economies in which wages and prices are rigid in the short run in order to analyse policies that can deal with Keynesian unemployment. We also consider stagflation caused by adverse supply shocks. In such situations macroeconomic stabilisation is called for and, given the interdependencies in the global economies, international coordination of budgetary and/or monetary policies may be required.

In a world of floating exchange rates, we show that monetary expansion is a *beggar-thy-neighbour* policy. In other words, a monetary expansion destroys jobs abroad. The reasoning is as follows. Monetary expansion induces a downward pressure on the domestic interest rate, thereby inducing incipient capital outflows. Consequently, the exchange rate depreciates, making home goods more competitive than foreign goods. This is why a monetary expansion under floating exchange rates has a strong beneficial effect on home employment, but adversely affects net exports and employment in foreign countries. Unilateral monetary expansion leads to a depreciation of the currency, thereby boosting the consumer price index at home and reducing it abroad.

What do such interdependencies in monetary policies imply for international policy coordination? If there is widespread Keynesian unemployment, monetary policies are likely to be too expansionary relative to the cooperative outcome. Intuitively, each country attempts to export unemployment by depreciating its currency. Of course, if all countries do this together such attempts are futile and the world eventually ends up with too much inflation. However, if the global economy is plagued by inflation (for example, caused by shocks in oil prices), each country will attempt to export inflation by appreciating its currency. If all countries do this together, such disinflationary policies do not work. In other words, absence of international policy coordination leads to too contractionary monetary policies relative to the cooperative outcome.

Fiscal policies also have strong international spill-over effects. In particular, a unilateral fiscal expansion (achieved by cutting taxes or boosting public spending) is a *locomotive* policy in the sense that employment rises abroad as well as at home. Intuitively, a fiscal expansion has a tendency to push domestic interest rates above foreign interest rates and thus to attract foreign capital flows. This induces an appreciation of the domestic currency, so that part of the fiscal stimulus is crowded out by a reduction in net exports of the home country. Conversely, net exports of the foreign country increase and thus employment abroad rises. This is why many commentators argue for a coordinated fiscal policy expansion in times of globally demand-induced recessions. Indeed, the outcome under international policy cooperation has looser budgetary policies than under the non-cooperative outcomes as countries internalise the beneficial employment effects for other countries.

This chapter discusses such international policy games under a variety of nominal exchange rate regimes. In particular, detailed attention is paid to managed exchange rate regimes. A good example is the European Monetary System. Although this system was meant to be symmetric, in practice it has worked for many years as an asymmetric system in which the German Bundesbank sets monetary policy for Europe and the other members of the European Monetary System follow by dedicating their monetary policy to fixing the value of their currency in terms of the Deutschmark (or DM: see, for example, Giavazzi and Giovannini, 1989a). Similarly, the Gold Standard was characterised by UK hegemony and Bretton Woods by US hegemony. It is therefore of interest to study the needs and nature of international monetary policy coordination under such asymmetric systems of managed exchange rates. In addition, it is of some interest to investigate the effects of more symmetric systems of fixed exchange rates. An example of this ought to be the future European Monetary Union.

This chapter therefore examines the effectiveness and need for international coordination of monetary policies, in the face of unemployment and inflation caused by demand and/or supply shocks, under three alternative nominal exchange rate regimes: (1) floating exchange rates; (2) managed exchange rates and hegemony of a centre country; and (3) irrevocably fixed exchange rates and a common centralised monetary policy. The framework of analysis assumes perfect capital mobility. Given that the European Community has decided that from 1 July 1990 onwards most member countries should fully liberalise their cross-country capital movements, this does not seem too unrealistic for Europe. To keep matters tractable, attention is restricted to monetary policy while fiscal policies are assumed to be passive in the exercises discussed in this chapter. Of course, as one moves to relatively fixed exchange rates, there may be a greater need to rely on fiscal policies to stabilise the economy. We discuss the international aspects of fiscal policy, but only discuss analytical results for the optimal setting of monetary policies.[1]

The outline of the chapter is as follows. Section 9.2 sets up a two-country Mundell–Fleming model and uses both a graphical and an algebraic approach to investigate the international spill-over effects of budgetary and monetary policies under floating exchange rates and perfect international capital mobility. Section 9.3 uses this two-country framework to discuss the nature of international policy coordination under floating exchange rates. Section 9.4 does the same for an asymmetric regime of managed exchange rates, such as the Gold Standard, Bretton Woods or the European Monetary System. Section 9.5 interprets and compares the results of sections 9.3 and 9.4 and compares them with the outcome under monetary union. Section 9.6 demonstrates that international policy coordination may be counterproductive, because international cooperation effectively destroys part of the credibility of central banks. To demonstrate this formally, a two-country model with pre-negotiated nominal wage contracts and rational expectations in labour and foreign exchange markets is formulated. This specification allows a comparison of situations in which the government can commit and in which they cannot commit. Section 9.7 investigates the robustness of the results by allowing for rational expectations and wage–price dynamics (compare the Buiter–Miller model discussed in Chapter 5). Differential game theory and numerical simulation are used to extend the analysis of Sections 9.2–9.4. Sections 9.2–9.7 focus on the examination of the relative merits of floating, managed and fixed exchange rate regimes if all economies are hit by common adverse supply shocks which cause stagflation in all countries. Floating exchange rates turned out to be not very desirable. However, if shocks are country-specific rather than global, it is easier to make a case for floating exchange rates. Hence, Section 9.8 studies to what extent idosyncratic shocks harm the case for a monetary union or fixed exchange rates. Section 9.9 concludes the chapter with a summary of results, and also offers a more general assessment of the case for a monetary union.

9.2   Monetary interdependence under floating exchange rates

A short-run Keynesian two-country model with nominal wage rigidity, international immobility of labour, imperfect substitution between home and foreign goods, perfect capital mobility and, for the time being, static expectations can be written as follows (compare Chapter 8):

$$y \quad = -\bar{\sigma} r + \bar{\delta}(p^* + e - p) + \bar{f} + \gamma y^*, \quad 0 \le \gamma < 1 \tag{9.1}$$

$$y^* \quad = -\bar{\sigma} r^* - \bar{\delta}(p^* + e - p) + \bar{f}^* + \gamma y, \quad \bar{\sigma} > 0, \bar{\delta} > 0 \tag{9.2}$$

$$m - p_c = y_c - \lambda r, \quad y_c \equiv y + p - p_c, \lambda > 0 \tag{9.3}$$

$$m^* - p^* = y^* - \lambda r^* \tag{9.4}$$

$$p_c \quad = (1 - \alpha)p + \alpha(p^* + e), \quad 0 < \alpha < 1 \tag{9.5}$$

$$p_c^* = (1 - \alpha)p^* + \alpha(p - e) \tag{9.6}$$

where y, y_c and $\bar{f}$ stand for real output, real national income (deflated by the cost-of-living index) and a fiscal shock, respectively; r, e and m represent the interest rate, the nominal exchange rate (price of foreign exchange in terms of domestic currency) and the nominal money supply, respectively; and p and p_c denote the producer price level and consumer price level, respectively. Variables are expressed as percentage deviations from their initial steady-state values, except the rate of interest, r, which is expressed as an arithmetic deviation from its initial steady-state value. Foreign variables are indicated with an asterisk. The real exchange rate (relative price of foreign goods in terms of home goods) will be denoted by $c \equiv p^* + e - p$.

Equations (9.1) and (9.2) are the familiar *IS*-curves, which show that aggregate demand in each country depends on the interest rate, the real exchange rate, fiscal policy and income abroad. We assume that the Marshall–Lerner condition holds (that is, the sum of the price elasticities for exports and imports exceeds unity), so that an appreciation of the real exchange rate (lower c) lowers net exports and thus reduces the demand for domestic goods ($\bar{\delta} > 0$). Equations (9.3) and (9.4) are the *LM*-curves, which show that the real supply of money must equal real money demand, and furthermore that the latter depends positively on income and negatively on the interest rate. We assume a unit income elasticity of money demand and the semi-elasticity of money demand with respect to the interest rate is denoted by λ. We assume that changes in the nominal money supply are due to open market operations. For example, a monetary expansion is achieved through a government purchase of bonds on the open market. We also assume that additional government spending and tax cuts (that is, a higher value of $\bar{f}$) are financed by issuing government bonds. Equations (9.5) and (9.6) define the cost-of-living (or consumer price) indices as weighted averages of domestic and foreign prices (converted into home currency). The parameter α stands for the value share of imports in final expenditures.

To keep the analysis tractable, we initially abstract from wage–price dynamics. To capture the Keynesian flavour of the analysis, we assume that nominal wages in both countries are rigid in the short run. Since firms set prices as a mark-up on unit labour costs and we assume that labour productivity is exogenous, prices (p and p^*) are exogenous in the analysis as well. Adverse supply shocks – such as a higher wage level, an adverse shock of labour productivity or a rise in the employers' labour tax rate – cause firms to set higher prices. Hence, an increase in the price level may be interpreted as an adverse supply shock.

Under floating exchange rates both money supplies are exogenous policy instruments, since the nominal exchange rate adjusts to keep the balance of payments in equilibrium. International capital mobility implies that the returns on home and foreign bonds are equalised, that is, $r = r^*$. Effectively, speculators ensure that there are no unexploited arbitrage opportunities.[2] Upon substitution of the condition for perfect capital mobility ($r = r^*$) into the IS-curves (9.1) and (9.2) and the LM-curve (9.3), the condition for equilbrium in the home goods market can be written as:

$$m - p + \lambda r = -\sigma r + \delta(p^* + e - p) + f + \gamma f^* \qquad (GME)$$

where $\sigma \equiv \bar{\sigma}/(1 - \gamma)$, $\delta \equiv \bar{\delta}/(1 + \gamma)$ and $f \equiv \bar{f}/(1 - \gamma^2)$. The goods market equilibrium locus is plotted in Figure 9.1 as the GME-locus with the interest rate on the vertical axis and the real exchange rate, or competitiveness ($c \equiv p^* + e - p$), on the horizontal axis.

The left hand side of (GME) corresponds to the aggregate 'supply' (AS) schedule. For a given price level, the AS-schedule slopes upwards (see Figure 9.1). the reasoning is as follows. A higher interest rate depresses money demand and thus allows a higher level of national income in order to restore equilibrium in the money market. Alternatively, a higher interest rate chokes off the demand for money which puts upwards pressure on the price level. This erodes the real value of the wage, thereby boosting the aggregate supply of goods. This chain of reasoning explains why the left hand side of (GME) – that is, the supply of goods (y) – is a positive function of the interest rate and the nominal money

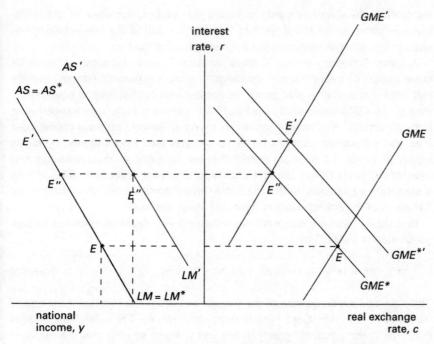

Figure 9.1   The two-country Mundell–Fleming model

Key: A home budgetary expansion shifts the equilibrium from *E* to *E"* thereby
       inducing an appreciation of the real exchange rate (lower *c*), a rise in the
       interest rate and a boost to both home and foreign economic activity. Fiscal
       expansion is thus a locomotive policy. A home monetary contraction shifts the
       equilibrium from E to E", thereby leading to an appreciation of the real
       exchange rate, a rise in the interest rate, a fall in home output and a rise in
       foreign output. Conversely, a monetary expansion is a beggar-thy-neighbour
       policy.

supply and a negative function of the price level. Hence, a monetary expansion
or a beneficial supply shock shifts the AS-schedule outwards.

The right hand side of (*GME*) amounts to the aggregate demand (AD)
schedule. The AD-schedule shows that aggregate demand for domestic goods
(y) is a negative function of the global interest rate (r) and a positive function of
competitiveness (c) and the fiscal stances at home (f) and abroad ($f*$). Since the
demand for home goods depends on foreign income, there is a positive effect of
the foreign fiscal stance on the demand for domestic goods.

Intersection of the AD- and AS-schedules yields the *GME*-locus. On the one
hand, a higher interest rate boosts the supply of goods. On the other hand, a
higher interest rate boosts private saving and depresses private consumption and
thus reduces the aggregate demand for domestic goods. To choke off the excess
supply for goods, the real exchange rate must depreciate (c rises) in order to
stimulate net exports and the aggregate demand for domestic goods. This is why

the *GME*-locus slopes upwards in Figure 9.1. In fact, the slope of the *GME*-locus is given by $\partial r/\partial c = \delta/(\sigma + \lambda) > 0$ and is small if the semi-elasticity of money demand with respect to the interest rate (λ) is large.

A looser budgetary policy at home or abroad boosts aggregate demand for home goods, so either the real exchange rate must appreciate (lower c) or the real interest rate must rise to return the home goods market back to equilibrium. Hence, the *GME*-locus shifts backwards if there is a budgetary expansion at home or abroad. A monetary expansion exerts an upward pressure on the price level and a downward pressure on the real wage, thereby boosting the aggregate supply of goods. To maintain equilibrium on the goods market, either the real interest rate must fall or the real exchange rate must depreciate. This is why a monetary expansion shifts the *GME*-locus downwards. In addition, the *LM*-curve or the AS-schedule in figure 9.1 shifts outwards.

In a similar way we can write the condition for equilibrium on the foreign goods market (*GME**) as:

$$m^* - p^* + \lambda r = -\sigma r - \delta(p^* + e - p) + f^* + \gamma f \qquad (GME^*)$$

Since the real exchange rate of the foreign country is the inverse of the one of the home country, the *GME**-locus slopes downwards. The *GME**-locus shifts outwards if there is a budgetary expansion at home or abroad and inwards if there is a monetary expansion.

For changes in home policy, the shifts in the *GME*-locus are less than in the *GME**-locus. This depends on the spill-over paramer (γ) being less than unity. In that case, a looser budgetary policy at home (higher f) shifts the *GME*-locus more backwards than it shifts the *GME**-locus outwards. The equilibrium in Figure 9.1 shifts from E to E'. The expansion of the demand for home produced goods raises the relative price of home goods; that is, the real exchange rate appreciates (c falls). Since the budget deficit is bond financed, the home interest rate and thus the foreign interest rate rises. The contraction in money demand puts upward pressure on prices and thus downward pressure on real wages. Consequently, world economic activity expands. Home employment and output expand, but are crowded out somewhat by the falls in private investment and net exports. Foreign employment and output expand, because the rise in net exports outweighs the fall in investment. In other words, a budgetary expansion is a *locomotive* policy. In the new equilibrium the home country shows a deficit on the current account and thus a surplus on the capital account of the balance of payments. Also, the appreciation of the real exchange rate associated with the home budgetary expansion reduces the consumer price index (CPI) at home, while it increases the foreign CPI (p_c^*). Hence, a fiscal expansion at home boosts both employment and consumer price inflation abroad.

A tighter monetary policy at home shifts both the *GME*-locus and the *LM*-curve back, thereby shifting the equilibrium in Figure 9.1 from E to E''. The upward pressure on world interest rates depresses world economic activity. However, the incipient capital inflows induce an appreciation of the real exchange rate. This reduces net exports of the home country. Together with the rise in the interest rate, this gives a severe blow to the aggregate demand for home goods and to home employment. However, foreign economic activity benefits from the boost to the foreign country's net exports. This effect dominates the adverse effect on investment of the higher rate of interest. Hence, a monetary contraction at home boosts economic activity abroad. The CPI at home falls while it rises abroad. Conversely, a domestic expansion of monetary policy is a *beggar-thy-neighbour policy* in the sense that the accompanying depreciation of the home currency yields a big boost to domestic output but a fall to foreign employment and output. Naturally, the home CPI increases while the foreign CPI falls.

This graphical and intuitive discussion of the international spill-over effects of budgetary and monetary policy relied on the intersection of the *GME*- and *GME**-loci. The results are confirmed by the analytical solution of equations (9.1) – (9.6):

$$r = \frac{1}{2}[(1+\gamma)(f+f^*)-(m-p)-(m^*-p^*)]/(\sigma+\lambda) \tag{9.7}$$

$$c = p^*+e-p = \frac{1}{2}[(m-p)-(m^*-p^*)+(1-\gamma)(f^*-f)]/\delta \tag{9.8}$$

$$y = \frac{1}{2}[(2\sigma+\lambda)(m-p)-\lambda(m^*-p^*)+(1+\gamma)\lambda(f+f^*)]/(\sigma+\lambda) \tag{9.9}$$

These results build on the pioneering analysis of Mundell (1968).

9.3 International policy coordination under floating exchange rates

In this section we use the results of Section 9.2 to analyse the potential benefits of international coordination of monetary policies. We assume that fiscal policies are exogenous and consider the consequences of two different types of preferences for the government.

Towards full employment and monetary stability

We first assume that each central bank is concerned about achieving, on the one hand, full employment and, on the other hand, ensuring a stable money supply. Hence, the problem for the home central bank is to set its monetary policy (m) in such a way as to minimise its welfare loss (W):

$$\text{Min} W \equiv (y-y^d)^2 + \theta m^2 \tag{9.10}$$

where y^d denotes the full-employment value of output and θ stands for the weight attached to the price target. The foreign country has a similar welfare loss criterion. We assume that, initially, there is too much unemployment $(y^d = y^{d*} > 0)$ caused by a global adverse demand shock. From the solution for national income (9.9) and the first-order condition $\partial W/\partial m = 0$, we obtain the following reaction function for the home central bank:

$$m = \hat{\sigma}(\hat{\sigma}^2 + \theta)^{-1}(y^d + \hat{\sigma}\hat{\lambda}m^*)$$

(9.11)

where $\frac{1}{2} < \hat{\sigma} \equiv (\sigma + \frac{1}{2}\lambda)/(\sigma + \lambda) < 1$ and $0 < \hat{\lambda} \equiv \lambda/(2\sigma + \lambda) < 1$. If the economies are far removed from full employment (that is y^d large and positive), the central banks loosen their monetary policies. If the foreign central bank implements a monetary expansion, this induces (in the absence of domestic policy intervention) unemployment at home. This is why the home central bank reacts by loosening its monetary policy as well. In other words, the reaction function (9.11) slopes upwards.

Intersection of (9.11) with the corresponding foreign reaction function yields the non-cooperative (or Nash–Cournot) outcome, say $m = m_F$. The cooperative outcome under floating exchange rates, say m_U, follows from choosing domestic and foreign monetary policies, m and $m*$, to minimise the global welfare loss, $W + W*$, so that the relevant first-order conditions for the central banks are $\partial(W + W*)/\partial m = \partial(W + W*)/\partial m* = 0$. With some elementary algebra, it can be shown that as $\hat{\sigma}(1-\hat{\lambda}) = \sigma/(\sigma+\lambda)$:

$$m_F = \hat{\sigma}[\hat{\sigma}^2(1 - \hat{\lambda}) + \theta]^{-1}y^d > m_U = \hat{\sigma}[\hat{\sigma}^2(1 - \hat{\lambda}) + \theta(1 - \hat{\lambda})^{-1}]^{-1}y^d > 0$$

(9.12)

This analytical result leads to the following propositions for an international system with flexible exchange rates, perfect capital mobility, Keynesian unemployment and governments that are concerned with full employment and monetary stability:

(a) the non-cooperative policy outcome induces too expansionary monetary policies and thus too low interest rates and too high levels of employment and output, because each central bank ignores the advers effects on foreign unemployment;

(b) international policy coordination would encourage countries to pay more attention to their objective of monetary stability and thus induce countries to reduce their money supplies.

Although international policy cooperation yields a superior outcome (that is, $W_U < W_F$), individual countries have an incentive to deviate from the co-operative outcome. If other countries adhere to tight monetary policies, individual countries have an incentive to cheat and loosen their monetary policies.

Canzoneri and Gray (1985) use a similar welfare loss function and also find that non-cooperative monetary policies are too expansionary.

Towards consumer price stability

In the 1970s inflation was an important policy issue in the Western world and, not surprisingly, many central banks engaged in monetary disinflation (witness, for example, the Medium Term Financial Strategy adopted in the UK economy under Mrs Thatcher). Many studies have been inspired to analyse the potential for international coordination of disinflation programmes (see Oudiz and Sachs, 1984, Canzoneri and Henderson, 1991, and Oudiz and Sachs, Miller and Salmon and others in Buiter and Marston, 1985). These studies have, typically, applied differential or difference game theory to multiple-country versions of Dornbusch's (1976) famous real exchange rate overshooting model (see also Section 9.7). In such models a cut in home monetary growth induces on impact an appreciation of the home real exchange rate, a fall in home employment and an increase in foreign employment (compare Section 9.2). Each central bank starts off with full employment, but inherits inflation from the past. Disinflation, however, leads to transient job losses. The literature cited above finds that an absence of international policy cooperation leads to excessively fast disinflation in all countries. Such a finding may seem counterintuitive at first sight, because one could think that excessive disinflation is a public good as far as employment is concerned and thus one would expect that non-cooperation would yield an undersupply of that public good. However, this argument ignores the fact that a cut in monetary growth induces a higher foreign consumer price level. Hence, from this point of view, monetary disinflation is a public bad as it amounts to exporting consumer price inflation. If these external effects are not internalised, it is no surprise that absence of international policy cooperation leads to excessive disinflation.

To understand this insight within the context of our two-country model, we need to modify the objective function by including a concern for consumer price (or exchange rate) stability. Hence, consider the alternative (and, perhaps, more realistic) welfare loss criterion for the home central bank:

$$W \equiv (y - y^d)^2 + \bar{\theta}(p_c + \bar{\omega})^2 \tag{9.10'}$$

where $\bar{\omega} > 0$ stands for the desired reduction in the consumer price index and $\bar{\theta} > 0$ now represents the relative aversion to consumer price inflation. A global recession caused by a fall in world trade (say, $\epsilon > 0$) may be modelled by a negative shock to the demand for goods in each countries (that is, $f = f^* = -\epsilon < 0$). Such a global demand shock induces world-wide unemployment, but leaves the cost-of-living indices unaffected. Hence, the relevant targets for the goverments after such a shock are $y^d = (1 + \gamma)\lambda(\sigma + \lambda)^{-1}\epsilon$ and $\bar{\omega} = 0$. However, a global adverse supply shock ($p = p^* = \epsilon > 0$) causes unemployment and inflation (stagflation). Hence, the relevant output and price reduction targets for the government are $y^d = \sigma(\sigma + \lambda)^{-1}\epsilon < \epsilon$ and $\bar{\omega} = \epsilon > 0$, respectively.

Upon substitution of the solutions for national income (9.9) and the CPI (9.5) (using the expression for the real exchange rate (9.8)), we obtain the reduced-form expression for the welfare loss:

$$W \equiv [\hat{\sigma}(m - \hat{\lambda}m^*) - y^d]^2 + \theta(m^* - m - + \omega)^2$$
(9.10'')

where $\theta \equiv \frac{1}{4}\bar{\theta}\alpha^2/\delta^2 > 0$ and $\omega \equiv 2\delta\,\bar{\omega}/\alpha$.

In the non-cooperative (or Nash–Cournot) outcome the home central bank unilaterally sets its money supply on the assumption that the other country does not adjust its money supply. The first-order condition $\partial W/\partial m = 0$ yields the following reaction function for the home central bank:

$$m \equiv (\hat{\sigma}^2 + \theta)^{-1}[(\hat{\sigma}y^d + (\hat{\sigma}^2\lambda + \theta)m^*) - \theta\,\omega]$$
(9.11')

A wish to boost employment and a bigger foreign money supply still induces a looser monetary policy. In fact, the reaction coefficient is larger than in (9.11). Intuitively, a foreign monetary expansion induces an appreciation of the home currency and thus a lower home cost-of-living index so that the home central bank can permit a looser monetary stance. The main difference with (9.11) is, however, the term $-\theta\omega$. This captures that a central bank that wishes to disinflate ($\omega > 0$) pursues a more stringent monetary policy.

The non-cooperative outcome follows from the intersection of the home reaction function (9.11') and the corresponding foreign reaction function. The cooperative outcome follows from simultaneously choosing m and m^* to minimise the global welfare loss ($W + W^*$). It is straightforward to establish the following result for the case of $\omega > 0$:

$$m_F = (\sigma + \lambda)\sigma^{-1}[y^d - (\theta/\hat{\sigma})\omega] < m_U = (\sigma + \lambda)\sigma^{-1}y^d$$
(9.12')

One interesting point emerges straight away. A global demand shock does not affect inflation (so $\omega = 0$) and thus creates no need for short-run international coordination of monetary policies. Indeed, non-cooperative decision making already achieves full employment (that is, $m_F = m_U = (1 + \gamma)\lambda\sigma^{-1}\epsilon$ and $y_F = y_U = y_d$). Since the price level is not affected by an adverse global demand shock, there is one policy instrument to attain one target and international policy coordination is unnecessary. World interest rates fall ($r_F = r_U = -(1 + \gamma)\sigma^{-1}\epsilon < 0$, both because of the fall in the demand for goods caused by the global adverse demand shock and by the induced monetary expansions.

If goverments are concerned with monetary disinflation and care about avoiding unemployment and consumer price stability (that is $y^d = 0$ and $\omega > 0$) and face a world with floating exchange rates and international capital mobility, we have the following propositions:

(a) the non-cooperative outcome leads to a too tight monetary stance and thus to too much unemployment (that is, $y_F = y^d - (\theta/\hat{\sigma})\omega < y_U = y^d$), because each central bank attempts to export inflation by appreciating its exchange rate, (of course, in equilibrium such beggar-thy-neighbour attempts are futile);

(b) the outcome under international policy coordination realises that such competitive appreciations of the currency are futile and therefore brings about a looser monetary policy which achieves full employment.

These propositions are in striking contrast with those obtained when the central banks care about money supply stability rather than cost-of-living stability. The lesson is that the nature of the bias in non-cooperative decision making and the gains from international policy coordination depend crucially on the nature of the preferences of the various governments and on the source of the shocks that hit the global economy.

9.4 Managed exchange rates

Sections 9.2 and 9.3 investigated the international coordination of monetary policies under a regime of floating exchange rates. This section analyses an asymmetric regime of managed exchange rates (in contrast to the clean float considered so far), which is also known as a reserve currency system. Such a regime of managed exchange rates may be quite realistic, because since 1980 more than 140 countries seem to be classified by the International Monetary Fund as pegging their currencies in some way or another. Perhaps this is not so surprising in view of the '$N-1$ problem' which says that not all of the N countries can independently control their nominal exchange rate as only $N-1$ of them are independent bilateral exchange rates: see Mundell (1968). However, managing or pegging the exchange rate *vis-à-vis* a centre currency may be problematic under unrestricted international capital flows in view of the vulnerability to speculative attacks on the currency and balance-of-payments crises. We abstract from such problems in this chapter. The foreign central bank is assumed to be in full control of its money supply whilst the home central bank manages its exchange rate and thereby gives up an independent monetary policy. This is in accordance with the view that the European Monetary System operates as a greater DM zone (Giavazzi and Giovannini, 1989a); the Bundesbank determines the monetary policy for the whole of Europe whilst the other central banks of Europe peg and periodically realign their currencies *vis-à-vis* the DM. Similarly, it can be argued that the Gold Standard was characterised by UK hegemony and Bretton Woods by US hegemony. If there is pressure on the home currency to devalue ($e\uparrow$), the home central bank sells foreign currency in exchange for home currency in order to meet the deficit on the balance of payments and thereby defends its exchange rate. There is a corresponding fall in the home money supply, so that the home central bank cannot have an independent monetary policy. When e and m^*, rather than m and m^*, are exogenous policy instruments, (GME) and (GME^*) can be solved as:

$$r = [-\delta e - m^* + \gamma f + f^* + \delta p + (1-\delta)p^*]/(\sigma + \lambda) \tag{9.13}$$

$$m = 2\delta e + m^* + (1-\gamma)(f - f^*) + (1-2\delta)(p - p^*) \tag{9.14}$$

$$y = [\sigma m^* + ((1-\gamma)\sigma + \lambda)f - ((1-\gamma)\sigma - \gamma\lambda)f^*) + (2\sigma + \lambda)\delta(e - p)$$
$$-((1-2\delta)\sigma - \delta\lambda)p^*]/(\sigma + \lambda) \tag{9.15}$$

$$y^* = [\sigma m^* + \lambda(\gamma f + f^*) - \lambda\delta(e - p) - (\sigma + \lambda\delta)p^*]/(\sigma + \lambda) \tag{9.15'}$$

For the sake of concreteness, we will cast our discussion in terms of the European Monetary System. The foreign country will be called Germany while the home country will be called France. A contraction in the German money supply $(m^* \downarrow)$ leads to an equal fall in, say, the French money supply, because the French are defending themselves against a depreciating currency by buying up francs. Hence, the increase in European interest rates and the associated crowding out of private consumption and investment throughout Europe is twice as large as under a clean float. With a fixed exchange rate, there is no adverse effect on German net exports and employment arising from an appreciation of the DM and therefore monetary contraction in Germany increases unemployment throughout Europe by the same amount. Conversely, a German monetary expansion is now a locomotive (rather than) a beggar-thy-neighbour policy.

A devaluation of the currencies of the rest of Europe *vis-à-vis* the DM $(e \uparrow)$ improves net exports to Germany and thus boosts non-German employment and output and increases unemployment in Germany. To choke off the resulting excess supply of German money, European interest rates fall and as a consequence non-German money demand increases in line with non-German money supplies. Since the European money supplies increase and European interest rates fall, the increase in the non-German levels of production and employment exceed the fall in German output and employment. Clearly, from such a point of view, a devaluation *vis-à-vis* the DM is a beggar-thy-neighbour policy. However, it increases the cost of living at home and decreases the cost of living in Germany.

We assume that each central bank is concerned about unemployment and the cost of living in its own country, so that the welfare loss function is given by (9.10'). We consider the situation where the central banks of Europe other than the Bundesbank periodically realign and adjust their exchange rate *vis-à-vis* the DM (e) to minimise their welfare loss function (W). Similarly, the Bundesbank sets its monetary policy (m^*) to minimise its welfare loss function (W^*). Any complications arising from speculative attacks, such as agents selling off liras for DMs if a devaluation of the lira is anticipated, are ignored, even though the recent abolishing of most capital controls in Europe raises the likelihood of such attacks. In such a regime of managed exchange rates, the reduced-form welfare loss functions can, with the aid of (9.15) and (9.15'), be expressed as:

$$W = [2\hat{\sigma}\delta e + \sigma(\sigma + \lambda)^{-1}m^* - y^d]^2 + \bar{\theta}\alpha^2[e + (\bar{\omega}/\alpha)]^2 \tag{9.10'''}$$

$$W^* = [-2\hat{\sigma}\lambda\delta e + \sigma(\sigma + \lambda)^{-1}m^* - y^d]^2 + \bar{\theta}\alpha^2[e - (\bar{\omega}/\alpha)]^2 \tag{9.10''''}$$

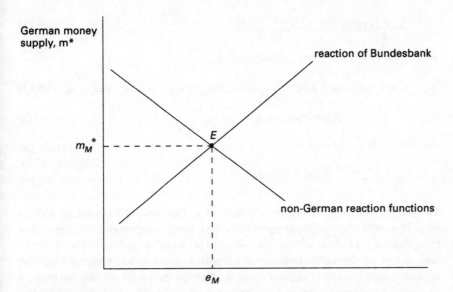

Figure 9.2   Reaction functions under managed exchange rates

The Bundesbank has given up manipulating the nominal exchange rate, so cannot influence the German cost of living in the short run. The reaction function for the Bundesbank follows from setting $\partial W^*/\partial m^* = 0$. This yields:

$$m^* = (\sigma + \lambda)\sigma^{-1}y^d + (\lambda\delta / \sigma)e \tag{9.11''}$$

The reaction function of the Bundesbank slopes upwards (see Figure 9.2). Intuitively, a devaluation of the other currencies causes German unemployment and a fall in the German cost of living. Hence, the Bundesbank responds by loosening its monetary policy. The reaction functions of the non-German central banks follow from setting $\partial W/\partial e = 0$:

$$e = [4\hat{\sigma}\delta^2 + \bar{\theta}\alpha^2]^{-1}\{2\hat{\sigma}\delta[y^d - \sigma(\sigma + \lambda)^{-1}m^*] - \bar{\theta}\alpha\,\bar{\omega}\} \tag{9.11'''}$$

The non-German reaction functions slope downwards (see Figure 9.2). The reason is that a German monetary expansion boosts employment elsewhere in Europe and therefore the non-German central banks can afford to pay more attention to their cost-of-living targets. Hence, they appreciate their currencies *vis-à-vis* the DM. Furthermore, a wish to disinflate ($\bar{\omega} > 0$) induces non-German central banks to appreciate their currencies and to export inflation to Germany.

Intersection of the reaction functions (9.11'') and (9.11''') yields the outcome for a non-cooperative managed exchange-rate regime, which we denote by the subscript *M*. The resulting solution is given by:

$$e_M = -\frac{1}{2}(\theta/\delta)(\theta+\hat{\sigma})^{-1}\omega \le e_F = e_U = 0 \qquad (9.16)$$

$$m_M^* = (\sigma+\lambda)\sigma^{-1}y^d - \frac{1}{2}\lambda\theta\sigma^{-1}(\theta+\hat{\sigma})^{-1}\omega \le m_U^* \qquad (9.17)$$

$$m_F = m_F^* \le m_M = (\sigma+\lambda)\sigma^{-1}y^d - \frac{1}{2}(2\sigma+\lambda)\theta\sigma^{-1}(\theta+\hat{\sigma})^{-1}\omega \le m_M^* \le m_U = m_U^* \qquad (9.18)$$

$$r_U \le r_M = -[y^d - \frac{1}{2}\theta(\hat{\sigma}+\theta)^{-1}\omega]/\sigma \le r_F \qquad (9.19)$$

$$y_M = y^d - \theta(\hat{\sigma}+\theta)^{-1}\omega \le y_U = y^d \qquad (9.20)$$

$$y_M^* = y_U^* = y^d \ge y_M \ge y_F = y_F^* \qquad (9.21)$$

The cooperative outcome chooses e and m^* to minimise the European welfare loss $(W + W^*)$ and yields the same full-employment outcomes as a cooperative clean float: $e_U = 0$, $y_U = y_U^* = y^d$, $m_U = m_U^* = (\sigma+\lambda)y^d/\sigma$ and $ru = r_U^* = -y^d/\sigma$. In fact, it can be shown that international policy coordination under a managed exchange-rate system or under a clean float yields the same outcome as under a European Monetary Union and are therefore all denoted by the subscript U. The associated welfare losses are:

$$0 \le W_M = \theta\omega^2[(\theta+\hat{\sigma}^2)/(\theta+\hat{\sigma})^2] \le W_U = W_U^* = \theta\omega^2 \le \frac{1}{2}(W_M + W_M^*) \le$$

$$W_M^* = \theta\omega^2[(2\theta+\hat{\sigma})/(\theta+\hat{\sigma})]^2 \qquad (9.22)$$

In addition, it can be shown that[3]

$$\frac{1}{2}(W_M + W_M^*) \le W_F = W_F^*$$

One cannot say whether $W_F = W_F^*$ is less or greater than W_M^*. However, one can show that $W_F = W_F^*$ is less (greater) than or equal to W_M^*, whenever θ is small (large).[4]

9.5   Interpretation of results and comparison with monetary union

The interpretation of the above results is as follows. First, coordination of monetary policies in the face of a common adverse demand or supply shock leads to full employment throughout Europe, irrespective of whether intra-European exchange rates float, are managed or are irrevocably fixed. This is achieved with an equal increase in all European money supplies and a fall in European interest rates, whilst intra-European exchange rates are unaffected. Hence, international coordination of monetary policies within Europe may facilitate the move towards a European Monetary Union.

Second, in the face of a global adverse demand shock ($y^d > 0$, $\omega = \bar{\omega} = 0$), there is no need for international policy coordination as it does not create international conflict over the cost of living. This result holds for a clean float, the European Monetary System and a European Monetary Union.

Third, a global adverse supply shock leads under a non-cooperative European managed exchange-rate system to an appreciation of the lira, franc and guilder *vis-à-vis* the DM even though the European economies are assumed to have symmetric structures and are hit by identical shocks. Hence, the non-German economies use an appreciation of the real exchange rate to disinflate away the consequences of an adverse supply shock. This occurs because the Bundesbank expands its money supply by more than the other European central banks. Germany achieves full employment but does not score on its cost-of-living target, whilst the rest of Europe scores less well on the unemployment target, but scores somewhat on its cost-of-living target. The rest of Europe achieves a smaller welfare loss than Germany, so that the exchange-rate realignment allows the rest of Europe to reduce the damage to its welfare at the expense of Germany.

Fourth, comparison of a non-cooperative managed exchange-rate system or a European Monetary Union with a non-cooperative float shows that the latter leads to lower money stocks, higher interest rates and more unemployment because the latter leads to futile attempts to engage in competitive appreciations of the exchange rate and export inflation abroad.

Fifth, comparison of a non-cooperative managed exchange-rate system with a European Monetary Union shows that the latter leads to higher money supplies and lower interest rates and thus to full employment in both Germany and the rest of Europe. A managed exchange-rate system is worse for Germany (despite the fact that there is full employment in Germany) and better for the rest of Europe than a monetary union, and for Europe as a whole it is worse than a monetary union. This is a reason why Germany may be keen on the recommendations for a more symmetric European System of Central Banks, as proposed by the Delors Committee (1989), and why the rest of Europe may be less keen.

Sixth, a European Monetary Union yields exactly the same outcome as a cooperative float or a cooperative European Monetary System and yields the smallest welfare loss. A non-cooperative float yields the highest welfare loss, which is due to each central bank engaging in competitive, futile attempts to appreciate the currency and export inflation. Under the European Monetary System France and Italy are better off than under monetary union whilst Germany is worse off, but on average Europe is better off with the European Monetary System than with a non-cooperative float and worse off with the European Monetary System than with a monetary union.

Finally, when countries are very conservative, (that is, they care relatively much more about the cost of living than unemployment), Germany prefers the European Monetary System to a non-cooperative float, or else Germany prefers a floating exchange-rate regime. The reason is, of course, that the European Monetary System avoids to a certain extent competitive, futile attempts to appreciate the currency and thus leads to looser monetary policies and less unemployment.

Giavazzi and Giovannini (1989b) also show that the non-German economies in a European managed exchange-rate system use an appreciation of the real exchange rate to disinflate a common adverse supply shock. However, their model does not have the real exchange rate affecting the cost of living but affecting aggregate supply through the usage of imported raw materials, and their analysis does not fully compare welfare of the countries concerned for the alternative exchange-rate regimes. They also argue that with a country-specific demand shock, Germany can be better rather than worse off than the rest of Europe under a managed exchange-rate system. This result arises from the negative spill-over effects which in part relieve Germany from the bias in non-cooperative decision making. Basevi and Giavazzi (1987) perform a number of numerical exercises when the European economies are not symmetric – that is, do not have identical structures – and then, even under a monetary union, intra-European exchange rates need not remain fixed. This suggests that the completion of a common European market is a prerequisite for full monetary union within Europe. Kenen (1987) uses a two-country portfolio balance model (PBM) to analyse the question which nominal exchange rate regime allows individual governments to achieve their national objectives without international policy coordination, and finds that the answer depends both on the nature and the origin of the shock (cf. Section 9.7).

9.6   Can international policy coordination be counter-productive?

Here the analysis conducted in Sections 9.2–9.4 is extended in two directions within a simple two-period framework along the lines of Barro and Gordon (1983) and Rogoff (1985). This specification introduces pre-negotiated nominal wage contracts and allows for rational expectations in labour and foreign exchange markets. By modifying the model in this way, it is possible to distinguish situations in which the government can commit to announced monetary policies and situations in which the government cannot commit. This permits an analysis of how the credibility of government policy affects macroeconomic outcomes and the need for international policy coordination.

Aggregate demand revisited

First, risk-neutral arbitrage between home and foreign government bonds leads to the condition of uncovered interest parity (UIP):

$$r = r^* + E(e_{+1}) - e \tag{9.23}$$

where $E(.)$ denotes the expectations operator. Hence, the return on home bonds (that is, the home interest rate, r) equals the expected return on foreign bonds (that is the foreign interest rate plus the expected future rate of depreciation of the nominal exchange rate). Period two is the steady state, so that in period two there are no shocks and all markets clear and thus $E(e_{+1}) = 0$. Solution of the *IS-LM* block (9.1)–(9.4), together with the parity UIP condition (9.23), yields expressions for the interest rate, competitiveness and national income:

$$r = r^* - e = \frac{1}{2}[(1+\gamma)(f+f^*) - (m-p) - (m^*-p^*)](\sigma+\lambda)^{-1} - \frac{1}{2}e \qquad (9.5')$$

$$c \equiv p^* + e - p = [(m-p) - (m^*-p^*) + (1-\gamma)(f^*-f) - \lambda(p-p^*)](2\delta+\lambda)^{-1} \qquad (9.6')$$

$$y = \hat{\sigma}(m-p) - (1-\hat{\sigma})(m^*-p^*) + (1+\gamma)(1-\hat{\sigma})(f+f^*) - \frac{1}{2}\lambda e \qquad (9.7')$$

Upon substitution of (9.6′) into (9.7′), we obtain the following expression for the aggregate demand for domestic goods:

$$y = (\hat{\sigma}-\lambda)(m-p) - (1-\hat{\sigma}-\lambda)(m^*-p^*) + (1+\gamma)(1-\hat{\sigma})(f+f^*) - (1-\gamma)\hat{\lambda}(f^*-f)$$
$$+2\delta\hat{\lambda}(p-p^*) \qquad (9.7'')$$

where $0 < \hat{\lambda} \equiv \frac{1}{2}\lambda(\lambda + 2\delta)^{-1} < \frac{1}{2}$. The main difference with the analysis of Sections 9.2–9.5 is that an appreciation of the nominal exchange rate implies an expected depreciation of the exchange rate and thus raises the home interest rate. As long as money demand is sensitive to changes in the interest rate (that is λ strictly positive), this raises money demand so that aggregate demand and national income must rise to restore equilibrium in the money market. It follows that a rise in the home prices relative to foreign prices increases aggregate demand (see equation (9.7″)).

Aggregate supply

The second direction in which the analysis of Section 9.2–9.5 is extended is to allow for a more detailed explanation of aggregate supply rather than to simply assume exogenous wages and prices. Assume a Cobb–Douglas production function (in percentage deviations):

$$y = (1-\beta)n + \epsilon, \qquad E(\epsilon) = 0 \qquad (9.24)$$

where n represents employment, $1-\beta$ stands for the share of labour in value added, and ϵ denotes a general productivity shock. The profit-maximising demand for the labour then follows from setting the marginal productivity of labour equal to the real producer wage, so that

$$-\beta n + \epsilon = w - p \qquad (9.25)$$

where w denotes the nominal wage rate. Hence, labour demand is a negative function of the real producer wage $(w-p)$ and a positive function of productivity. Notional labour supply, say n^s, is exogenous. Workers agree *ex post* to supply whatever labour is demanded by firms, provided firms pay workers the *ex ante* negotiated wage. The wage contract may contain a partial indexation clause, so that the actual wage contract can be written as follows:

$$w = w' + \zeta(p_c - w'), \quad 0 \le \zeta < 1 \tag{9.26}$$

where w' denotes the (negotiated) base wage rate and ζ stands for the indexation coefficient. No indexation corresponds to $\zeta = 0$ and full indexation corresponds to $\zeta = 1$. Upon substitution of equations (9.8) and (9.26) into (9.25), we obtain the following expression for (equilibrium) employment:

$$n = \beta^{-1}\epsilon - \zeta\alpha\beta^{-1}c + (1 - \zeta)\beta^{-1}(p - w') \tag{9.27}$$

Hence, equilibrium employment falls if there is an adverse productivity shock (lower ϵ) or a rise in the *ex ante* negotiated producer wage $(w' - p)$. A depreciation of the real exchange rate (higher c) also lowers equilibrium employment as long as wages are not full indexed to the cost of living $(\zeta < 1)$, because then the relative price of imports rises, the real comsumer wage falls and thus workers negotiate a higher wage. Effectively, a depreciation of the real exchange rate raises the wedge between producer and consumer wages and thus lowers employment.

Workers set the base wage so as to minimise the expected deviation of actual employment from the notional supply of labour: that is, they choose w' to minimise $E[(n - n^s)^2]$ subject to the expression for equilibrium employment (9.27). The first-order optimality condition yields the following negotiated base wage rate:

$$w' = E[p - \alpha\zeta(1 - \zeta)^{-1}c] - \beta(1 - \zeta)^{-1}n^s \tag{9.28}$$

because *ex ante* workers do not know the realisation of the productivity shock. Workers thus set their base wage in anticipation of what they expect prices to be. Also, if workers expect a real depreciation of the currency and higher prices, they negotiate a higher base wage as well. A high notional supply of labour pushes down the negotiated wage. Upon substitution of (9.28) into (9.27) and then into (9.24), we obtain an expression for the aggregate supply of goods:

$$y = \beta^{-1}\{\epsilon + (1 - \beta)((1 - \zeta)[p - E(p)] - \zeta\alpha[c - E(c)])\} + (1 - \beta)n^s \tag{9.29}$$

Hence, an unanticipated increase in prices or, alternatively, an unanticipated appreciation of the real exchange rate boosts employment and output. Adverse productivity shocks and falls in notional labour supply also reduce employment and output. Equation (9.29) may be interpreted as an open economy version of a New Classical aggregate supply schedule.

Market equilibrium

To keep matters simple, assume that there is no automatic indexation of wages to the cost-of-living index $(\zeta = 0)$ and that the velocity of circulation is constant

($\lambda = 0$, so that $\hat{\lambda} = 0$ and $\hat{\sigma} = 1$). The latter assumption implies the quantity theory of money, so that both the demand and supply sides of our two-country model are thoroughly classical. Equating aggregate demand (9.7″), that is $y = m - p$, to aggregate supply (9.29) then yields the price level which clears the goods market:

$$p = (1-\beta)E(p) - \epsilon - \beta(1-\beta)n^s + \beta m \qquad (9.30)$$

Taking expectations and solving for the expected price level, $E(p)$, yields:

$$E(p) = -\beta^{-1}\epsilon - (1-\beta)n^s + E(m) \qquad (9.31)$$

Substitution of (9.31) into (9.30) and subsequently into (9.29) gives the following expressions for the equilibrium price and output levels:

$$p = (1-\beta)E(m) + \beta m - \beta^{-1}\epsilon - (1-\beta)n^s$$
$$y = \beta^{-1}\epsilon + (1-\beta)n^s + (1-\beta)[m - E(m)] \qquad (9.32)$$

Clearly, unanticipated increases in the nominal money supply boost output and employment. Anticipated increases in the nominal money supply leave output unaffected and give rise to a one-for-one increase in the price level. An adverse productivity shock (lower ϵ) causes stagflation: that is, the price level rises and output falls.

Real wage income falls if there is an unanticipated increase in the home relative to the foreign nominal money supply or if there is an increase in the nominal supply of labour:

$$w - p_c = w - p - \alpha c = E(p) - p - \beta n^s - \frac{1}{2}\alpha\delta^{-1}(y - y^*)$$
$$= \beta[E(m) - m] - \beta n^s \frac{1}{2}\alpha\delta^{-1}[(m - m^*) - E(m - m^*)] \qquad (9.33)$$

Each government minimises a welfare loss function of the form (9.10′), which attempts to stabilise both output and the cost-of-living index.

Rules versus discretion

Following Barro and Gordon (1983), two outcomes are distinguished: *rules* (indicated by the superscript R) and *discretion* (indicated by the superscript D). The rules outcome supposes that each government can credibly commit itself to a pre-announced monetary policy, so that $E(m) = m$. This means that there can be no price (or exchange exchange) rate surprises, hence output in each country is given by its 'natural' level (that is, $y^R = \beta^{-1}\epsilon + (1-\beta)n^s$ from equation (9.32)). Clearly, the central bank of each country then has no incentive to try to boost output through an expansionary monetary policy. It thus contracts the money supply in the presence of adverse (stagflationary) supply shocks in order to ensure that the cost-of-living index is not affected (that is, $m^R = m^{*R} = \beta^{-1}\epsilon +$

$(1 - \beta)n^s$ so that $p_c^R = p_c^{*R} = 0$, which is the case for a clean float as well as for a monetary union). The welfare loss under rules is thus given by the unavoidable loss, that is, $W^R = [\beta^{-1}\epsilon + (1 - \beta)n^s]^2$.

However, in practice not all central banks have built up a reputation for stringent monetary discipline. Such central banks are vulnerable to renege and cheat on their announced policies. The central banks, then, cannot manipulate the expectations of private agents. This proposition can be demonstrated by comparing the optimal discretionary monetary policy under competitive decision making with that under international policy cooperation. Under competitive decision making each central bank takes the policy of the other central bank as given. This yields for the symmetric non-cooperative Nash equilibrium:

$$m^{DN} = m^{*DN} = \left(\frac{\bar{\theta}\left[\dfrac{1-\beta}{2\delta}+\beta\right]-(1-\beta)}{\bar{\theta}\left[\dfrac{1-\beta}{2\delta}+\beta\right]} \right)\left[\frac{1}{\beta}\epsilon + (1-\beta)n^s\right]$$

(9.34)

$$p_c^{DN} = p_c^{*DN} = -\left(\frac{1-\beta}{\bar{\theta}\left[\dfrac{1-\beta}{2\delta}+\beta\right]} \right)\left[\frac{1}{\beta}\epsilon + (1-\beta)n^s\right]$$

(9.35)

while the output levels are the same as under rules. Clearly, the absence of credibility means that the central banks are open to the invitation of raising the money supply in an unanticipated fashion in order to boost employment and output. Of course, any such attempts are in equilibrium futile and only lead to higher prices. This is why under discretion the money supply is contracted less than under rules in the face of adverse, staflationary supply shocks. The CPI and the welfare loss for each country are therefore higher under discretion than under rules.

Under international policy coordination the central banks minimise the global welfare loss. This leads to the following optimal outcomes:

$$m^{DC} = m^{*DC} = \left(\frac{\bar{\theta}\beta - (1-\beta)}{\bar{\theta}\beta} \right)\left[\frac{1}{\beta}\epsilon + (1-\beta)n^s\right]$$

(9.34′)

$$p_c^{DC} = p_c^{*DC} = -\left(\frac{1-\beta}{\bar{\theta}\beta} \right)\left[\frac{1}{\beta}\epsilon + (1-\beta)n^s\right]$$

(9.35′)

and the output levels are again the same as under rules. Again, the absence of credibility induces central banks to pursue laxer monetary policies than under rules. As a result the cost-of-living indices and welfare losses are higher than under rules.

The most surprising feature is, however, that comparison of (9.34)–(9.35) and (9.34′)–(9.35′) reveals that international policy coordination is counterproductive if central banks cannot pre-commit themselves. Under policy coordination monetary policies are less contractionary than under competitive decision making, so that prices and welfare losses are higher. For adverse, stagflationary supply shocks this may be summarised as follows:

$$p_c^{DC} > p_c^{DN} > p_c^R = 0, \quad W^{DC} > W^{DN} > W^R \tag{9.36}$$

The main lesson of this analysis is that international coordination of monetary policies may be counterproductive because it worsens the credibility and destroys the discipline of central banks (see Rogoff, 1985; van der Ploeg, 1988). The reason is that, when a central bank reneges and implements a surprise increase in the nominal money supply, this induces a depreciation of the currency and thus a higher cost-of-living index. This disincentive to renege does not exist if there is international policy coordination, because then the exchange rate is unaffected. Since the cost of reneging are thus less under international policy coordination than under competition, monetary policies are looser and prices are higher in equilibrium. As a result, it does not pay to coordinate policies at summit meetings of government cannot commit to their announced policies.

9.7   Rational expectations and wage–price dynamics

The analysis conducted in Sections 9.2–9.5 of this survey is relevant for the understanding of non-cooperative stabilisation policies under alternative exchange-rate regimes and finds that a European Monetary Union is the most desirable regime, but is of limited interest as the analysis did not consider wage–price and/or exchange-rate dynamics. The studies in Buiter and Marston (1985) report numerical policy coordination exercises that allow for rational expectations and wage–price dynamics, but are unfortunately restricted to regimes of floating exchange rates. This section therefore uses numerical methods to examine the robustness of our analytical results with respect to rational expectations and wage–price dynamics. The extended model[5] is given by: (9.1), (9.5), (9.6),

$$m - p = y - \lambda r, \lambda > 0 \tag{9.37}$$
$$r \equiv i + E\dot{p}_c = r^* + E\dot{e} \tag{9.38}$$
$$\dot{w} = \varphi(y - \bar{y}), \bar{y} \equiv \bar{n} - s, \varphi > 0 \tag{9.39}$$
$$p = w + s \tag{9.40}$$

and the foreign equivalents of equations (9.1), (9.37), (9.39) and (9.40), where r, i, w, s, $\bar{y}$ and $\bar{n}$ denote the real interest rate, the nominal interest rate, the nominal wage, a deterioration in labour productivity (an adverse supply shock), full-employment output and the labour force, respectively. Equation (9.38) captures UIP ensured by risk-neutral arbitrageurs in foreign-exchange markets, whilst equation (9.39) captures sluggish wage–price dynamics. Wages and prices in each country are predetermined and historically given. Under a clean float each central bank can control its money supply and the exchange rate is non-predetermined and jumps in response to 'news' about future events. Under a managed float Germany has full control of its money supply, m^*, and the rest of Europe pegs their currencies to the DM. Under monetary union the European Central Bank sets the European money supply, $m_E \equiv \frac{1}{2}(m + m^*)$, and sets the intra-European exchange rate once and for all. Under the latter two regimes the private sector does not expect adjustments in the exchange rate.

The short-run effects of supply shocks and monetary policy under the three regimes are, apart from initial jumps in the exchange rate and inflation, as before. In the long run output is at its full-employment level, $y(\infty) = \bar{n} - s$, inflation is zero, interest rates are given by

$$r(\infty) = r^*(\infty) = \frac{1}{2\bar{\sigma}}[\bar{f} + \bar{f}^* + (1-\gamma)(s + s^* - \bar{n} - \bar{n}^*)]$$

(9.41)

the real exchange rate is given by

$$c(\infty) = \frac{1}{2\bar{\delta}}[(1+\gamma)(s^* - s + \bar{n} - \bar{n}^*) - \bar{f} + \bar{f}^*]$$

(9.42)

and real wage income, $w - pc$, is given by

$$w(\infty) - p_c(\infty) = -s + \left[\frac{\alpha}{2\bar{\delta}}\right][(1+\gamma)(s - s^* - \bar{n} + \bar{n}^*) + \bar{f} - \bar{f}^*]$$

(9.43)

Table 9.1 illustrates the effects of a common adverse supply shock ($s = s^* > 0$). Initially output falls, but by less than the fall in full-employment output. Hence, subsequently wages and real interest rates rise so that output falls until the lower equilibrium value has been reached. Real income falls immediately by the full extent of the adverse supply shock. Policy follows from minimising the intertemporal welfare loss function:

$$w = \int_0^\infty \exp(-\rho t)[y^2 + \theta_1(w - p_c)^2 + \theta_2 m^2]dt$$

(9.44)

where ρ denotes the rate of discount. The loss function captures the usual targets of achieving full employment and maintaining real wage income (or CPI stability). The money supply target is included to avoid excessive instrument instability in a dynamic game; this does not affect a qualitative comparison with the results obtained for the games considered in Sections 9.2–9.6. The various outcomes are calculated as the outcome of a differential game (van der Ploeg and Markink, 1991) and are reported in Table 9.1.[6]

Most of the recent literature on international coordination of macroeconomic policies has focused on the coordination of monetary policies in a regime of

Table 9.1 Policy responses to a common adverse supply shock (s = s = 1)
under alternative exchange-rate regimes*

Variable	No policy	FLOAT: no pre-commitment	FLOAT: pre-commitment	EMS in Germany	EMS in rest of Europe	EMU
Output						
time 0	−0.500	−0.501	−0.557	−0.636	−0.719	−0.636
time 5	−0.857	−0.726	−0.846	−0.774	−0.829	−0.774
time ∞	−1.0	−1.0	−1.0	−1.0	−1.0	−1.0
loss	36.840	34.041	35.972	34.565	35.824	34.565
Real wage income						
time 0	−1.0	−1.0	−1.0	−1.045	−0.955	−1.0
time 5	−1.0	−1.0	−1.0	−1.029	−0.971	−1.0
time ∞	−1.0	−1.0	−1.0	−1.0	−1.0	−1.0
loss	40.0	40.0	40.0	40.833	39.188	40.0
Nominal wage rate						
time 0	0.0	0.0	0.0	0.0	0.0	0.0
time 5	0.357	0.470	0.329	0.362	0.277	0.362
time ∞	0.5	1.043	0.682	0.955	0.708	0.955
Nominal exchange rate						
time 0	0.0	0.0	0.0	0.180	−0.180	0.0
time 5	0.0	0.0	0.0	0.203	−0.203	0.0
time ∞	0.0	0.0	0.0	0.246	−0.246	0.0
Nominal money supply						
time 0	0.0	−0.001	−0.057	−0.136	−0.219	−0.136
time 5	0.0	0.244	−0.017	0.088	−0.052	0.088
time ∞	0.0	0.543	0.182	0.455	0.208	0.455
loss	0.0	8.832	0.771	5.418	1.126	5.418
Real interest rate						
time 0	0.125	0.125	0.139	0.164	0.175	0.159
time 5	0.214	0.181	0.211	0.197	0.204	0.194
time ∞	0.25	0.25	0.25	0.25	0.25	0.25
Welfare loss	76.840	75.807	76.216	76.482	75.237	75.649

Parameters: $\bar{\sigma} = 1.0$; $\bar{\delta} = 0.375$; $\gamma = 0.75$; $\lambda = 2.0$; $\varphi = 0.25$; $\alpha = 0.25$; $\theta_1 = 1.0$; $\theta_2 = 0.2$; $\rho = 0.025$

Notes: 1. International policy coordination under a FLOAT (with or without credibility) and under the EMS (European Monetary System) yield the same outcomes as under EMU (European Monetary Union); the table presents the non–cooperative (Nash–Cournot) outcomes under FLOAT and EMS.
   2. The losses for output, real income and the money supply refer to the discounted squared deviations from desired values.

floating exchange rates and has used two-country real-exchange-rate overshooting models as a framework of analysis (for example, Miller and Salmon, 1985;
Oudiz and Sachs, 1985). One of the lessons is that international coordination of
monetary policies can be counterproductive, because it worsens the credibility
and destroys the discipline of central banks (Rogoff, 1985; van der Ploeg, 1988;

see Section 9.6). If a central bank reneges unilaterally, this leads to a depreciation of the currency and thus to inflation. This is a disincentive to renege, which
does not exist when there is international policy coordination. Hence, with international policy cooperation one obtains looser monetary policies and higher
prices in equilibrium. Effectively, international coordination of monetary policies destroys a discipline device of central banks. The results presented in Table
9.1 for a regime of floating exchange rates show, however, that coordination in
the absence of credibility need not always be counterproductive. One does have,
in the absence of pre-commitment, higher money supplies and thus higher
prices, but this also leads to less output losses and thus to smaller welfare losses
than when central banks can pre-commit themselves to their announced
monetary policies.

When one compares a non-cooperative float without commitment with the
EMU or alternatively a cooperative float (with or without commitment), one
notes higher money supplies and thus higher wages and prices, and in the short
run lower real interest rates and smaller output losses. It is clear that, as monetary policies are not looser, cooperation does pay in the example of Table 9.1.

Table 9.1 suggests that the main result of Section 9.5 is robust as regards extending the model by allowing for wage–price and exchange-rate dynamics: a
non-cooperative float yields the highest welfare loss and European Monetary
Union corresponds to a cooperative float or a cooperative European Monetary
System and yields the lowest welfare loss. The reason is again that under a
regime of floating exchange rates each central bank tries to export inflation by
engaging in competitive, futile attempts to appreciate the currency, whilst a
regime of irrevocably fixed exchange rates avoids such beggar-thy-neighbour
inefficiencies. Table 9.1 confirms the result that on average Europe is better off
with monetary union and worse off with a regime of floating exchange rates
than with a regime of managed exchange rates. Furthermore, under the
European Monetary System central banks other than the Bundesbank implement
a tighter monetary stance and cause higher interest rates than in Germany and
thus manage to appreciate their currencies *vis-à-vis* the DM and export inflation.
In fact, Table 9.1 also confirms the result that Germany is worse off under the
European Monetary System than under monetary union, whilst the rest of
Europe is better off. Table 9.1 shows that Germany obtains the same amount of
unemployment under managed exchange rates as under monetary union – that is,
less than the rest of Europe – but nevertheless the deterioration of real wage
income (more than the initial impact of the shock) ensures that Germany suffers
a greater welfare loss than the rest of Europe.

9.8   Idiosyncratic supply shocks and the case for monetary union

So far, the non-cooperative responses of monetary policies to a common adverse
supply shock under three alternative exchange-rate regimes for Europe have

been considered. The main finding has been that for such a shock a monetary union is the preferred arrangement for exchange rates. A second-best exchange regime may be the European Monetary System, because then the futile, non-cooperative attempts to appreciate the currency and export inflation by tightening monetary policy that occur under a regime of floating exchange rates are also avoided. However, if there is an asymmetric shock, say a shift in preferences away from the goods of country 1 towards the goods of country 2, matters are not so simple. The initial effects of this shock are unemployment and a trade deficit for country 1 and overemployment and a trade surplus for country 2. If labour markets function properly, then wages in country 1 fall immediately and wages in country 2 increase to ensure full employment. In that case, one should proceed to monetary union and reap all the benefits of a greater common currency area (lower transaction costs, lower information costs, no exchange-rate risk, saving on exchange reserves, and so on). However, nominal wage rigidities may prevent labour markets from adjusting immediately to full employment. This is why the Delors Committee resorts to the theory of optimum currency areas (Mundell, 1961) and emphasises the role of international labour mobility. In effect, workers may migrate from country 1 to country 2 and restore balance in this way. Unfortunately, Europe is neither characterised by a smooth functioning of its labour markets nor by high degrees of labour mobility (due to differences in language and culture),and therefore some form of policy adjustment is required. The most obvious policy adjustment, in the absence of wage flexibility and labour mobility, is a loosening of monetary policy in country 1, tightening of monetary policy in country 2 and a depreciation of the exchange rate of country 1, for this boosts net exports of country 1 and restores equilibrium. Of course, this is not possible under a monetary union with irrevocably fixed exchange rates and is only possible to a limited extent under the European Monetary System. This is the main reason why in the presence of asymmetric real shocks and nominal wage rigidities a regime of floating exchange rates is to be preferred to a monetary union or, to a lesser extent, to a regime of managed exchange rates.

The case for floating exchange rates is convincing if the shock consists of a shift in preferences away from goods of country 1 towards goods of country 2, but if nevertheless the traditional advantages of a greater common currency area are large enough to warrant the move towards monetary union then another form of policy adjustment must be used. One possibility is that the establishment of a European Monetary Union must go hand in hand with the establishment of a European Federal Transfer Scheme, whose task it is to transfer income from country 2 to country 1 when there are such shifts in preferences. Such a scheme must be budget-neutral on a European level. Initial evidence suggests that one-third of stage-specific shocks in the USA are cushioned by the federal tax system (Sachs and Sala-i-Martin, 1989). Problems of moral hazard and adverse selection suggest that such schemes carry the danger of incentives to free ride on European funds and rewards for government failure. Most of these problems can, however, be avoided by making transfers contingent on the local govern-

Table 9.2   *Effects of an idiosyncratic adverse supply shock under alternative exchange-rate regimes*

Variable			FLOAT (s=1)	EMS (s=1)	EMS (s*=1)	EMU (s=1)
y:	time	0	−0.75	−0.135	−0.365	−0.442
	time	5	−0.928	−0.583	−0.274	−0.756
	time	∞	−1.0	−1.0	0.0	−1.0
y^*:	time	0	0.25	0.25	−0.75	−0.058
	time	5	0.072	0.072	−0.928	−0.101
	time	∞	0.0	0.0	−1.0	0.0
$w - P_c$:	time	0	−0.417	−0.75	−0.25	−0.75
	time	5	−0.417	−0.604	−0.396	−0.604
	time	∞	−0.417	−0.417	−0.583	−0.417
$w^* - P_c^*$:	time	0	−0.583	−0.25	−0.75	−0.25
	time	5	−0.583	−0.396	−0.604	−0.396
	time	∞	−0.583	−0.583	−0.417	−0.583
w:	time	0	0.0	0.0	0.0	0.0
	time	5	0.178	0.763	−0.406	0.471
	time	∞	0.25	1.583	−1.083	0.917
w^*:	time	0	0.0	0.0	0.0	0.0
	time	5	0.178	0.178	0.178	−0.114
	time	∞	0.25	0.25	0.25	−0.417
e:	time	0	−1.333	0.0	0.0	0.0
	time	5	−1.333	0.0	0.0	0.0
	time	∞	−1.333	0.0	0.0	0.0
m:	time	0	0.0	0.615	−0.615	0.308
	time	5	0.0	0.930	−0.930	0.465
	time	∞	0.0	1.333	−1.333	0.667
m^*:	time	0	0.0	0.0	0.0	−0.308
	time	5	0.0	0.0	0.0	−0.465
	time	∞	0.0	0.0	0.0	−0.667

Parameters: $\bar{\sigma} = 1.0$; $\bar{\delta} = 0.375$; $\gamma = 0.75$; $\lambda = 2.0$; $\varphi = 0.25$; $\alpha = 0.25$
Note: Abroad corresponds to Germany and home to the rest of Europe.

ment having to invest in training and work-experience programmes for the (long-term) unemployed (van der Ploeg, 1991a, 1991b). It is therefore a pity that the Delors Report does not contain any recommendations for the establishment of a European Federal Transfer Scheme, for without this regional imbalances induced by shifts in preferences may persist.

However, when asymmetric shocks correspond to adverse supply shocks to country 1, the case for a regime of floating exchange rates is a bit more subtle.

The reason is that such a shock leads both to unemployment and to higher prices and a lower real wage income in country 1, so that on the one hand a depreci ation of the currency is required as this leads to more employment, but on the other hand an appreciation of the currency is required to depress prices and raise real wage income. It is therefore not clear a priori whether a depreciation or an appreciation of the currency is desirable from a welfare point of view. Table 9.2 shows the effects of an adverse supply shock in one of the two countries under the alternative exchange-rate regimes. The main point to note is that in a regime of floating exchange rates the excess demand for home goods induces an imme- diate appreciation of the exchange rate to its new long-run value,[7] so that the fall in real wage income is cushioned compared with the outcome under monetary union. The counterpart is that the other country suffers a greater increase in the cost of living and a fall in real wage income. Of course, the falls in employment and output are accelerated whilst the other country enjoys a temporary increase in employment and output as a result of the appreciation of the exchange rate. Hence, in the face of an adverse supply shock, a monetary union copes better with unemployment than with real wage income.[8] The reason is that a monetary union leads to an expansion of the money supply at home and a contraction abroad. As far as the European Monetary System is concerned. Table 9.2 shows that an adverse supply shock in Germany leads to a much sharper fall in German employment than the fall induced in, say, French employment by a French supply shock. In addition, a German supply deterioration leads to unemploy- ment in the rest of Europe, whilst an adverse supply shock in the rest of Europe leads to overemployment in Germany. The reason is that in the first case the central banks of the rest of Europe defend their currencies by buying them up and tightening their monetary policy, whilst in the latter case the central banks of the rest of Europe prevent their currencies from appreciating by buying DMs and loosening their monetary policy. The adverse effects on real incomes are symmetric because the greater increase in French wages arising from a French shock is exactly off-set by less of a fall (actually an increase) in German wages, so that the effect of a French supply shock on the real exchange rate is exactly the opposite of the effect of a German supply shock.[9]

Table 9.3 presents the non-cooperative and cooperative policy responses to an idiosyncratic supply deterioration under the alternative exchange-rate regimes.[10] As far as average welfare is concerned, the welfare ranking in decreasing order of magnitude is a cooperative float, a cooperative monetary union or a coopera- tive European Monetary System, a non-cooperative European Monetary System, a non-cooperative float and a European Monetary Union. European Monetary Union performs so badly because appreciation of the exchange rate can no longer be used as an instrument to remove the excess demand for home goods. As a result the greater expansion of the home money supply leads to a larger in- crease in prices, a larger fall in (and overshooting of) real wage income and less unemployment than in the regimes where the exchange rate is allowed to appre- ciate. Hence, the occurrence of idiosyncratic shocks make monetary union an undesirable regime. This can, of course, be attenuated if the exchange rate is

Table 9.3   Policy responses to an idiosyncratic adverse supply shock under alternative exchange-rate regimes

Variable			FLOAT Nash (s=1)	FLOAT Pareto (s=1)	EMS Nash (s=1)	EMS Nash (s*=1)	EMU fixed e (s=1)	Symmetric EMS managed e (s=1)
y:	time	0	−0.705	−0.765	−0.786	0.067	−0.510	−0.749
	time	5	−0.873	−0.838	−0.863	0.034	−0.714	−0.837
	time	∞	−1.0	−1.0	−1.0	0.0	−1.0	−1.0
	loss		36.505	35.704	36.470	0.015	33.591	35.749
y^*:	time	0	0.148	0.129	0.095	−0.732	−0.126	0.113
	time	5	0.027	0.064	0.059	−0.833	−0.060	0.063
	time	∞	0.0	0.0	0.0	−1.0	0.0	0.0
	loss		0.031	0.053	0.042	35.870	0.049	0.048
$w - P_c$:	time	o	−0.498	−0.408	−0.481	−0.474	−0.75	−0.492
	time	5	−0.472	−0.472	−0.459	−0.512	−0.604	−0.471
	time	∞	−0.417	−0.417	−0.417	−0.582	−0.417	−0.419
	loss		7.685	7.729	7.456	12.507	9.358	7.680
$w^* - P_c^*$:	time	0	−0.502	−0.502	−0.519	−0.526	−0.25	−0.508
	time	5	−0.528	−0.528	−0.541	−0.488	−0.396	−0.529
	time	∞	−0.583	−0.583	−0.583	−0.418	−0.583	−0.582
	loss		12.667	12.603	12.946	7.839	11.275	12.670
w:	time	0	0.0	0.0	0.0	0.0	0.0	0.0
	time	5	0.240	0.248	0.216	0.061	0.473	0.255
	time	∞	0.599	0.766	0.602	0.106	1.144	0.746
w^*:	time	0	0.0	0.0	0.0	0.0	0.0	0.0
	time	5	0.089	0.114	0.095	0.267	−0.111	0.107
	time	∞	0.083	0.189	0.25	0.705	−0.189	0.207
e:	time	0	−1.009	−1.078	−1.076	0.897	0.0	−1.033
	time	5	−0.959	−0.978	−1.044	0.841	0.0	−0.968
	time	∞	−0.818	−0.757	−0.981	0.735	0.0	−0.797
m:	time	0	0.035	−0.053	−0.036	−0.183	0.240	0.001
	time	5	0.108	0.147	0.103	−0.154	0.509	0.168
	time	∞	0.349	0.516	0.352	−0.144	0.894	0.496
	loss		3.109	6.649	3.292	0.828	24.811	6.487
m^*:	time	0	−0.093	−0.084	−0.155	0.019	−0.376	−0.138
	time	5	−0.127	−0.059	−0.096	0.184	−0.421	−0.081
	time	∞	−0.167	−0.061	0.0	0.455	−0.439	−0.041
	loss		0.882	0.096	0.111	5.851	7.643	0.113
Welfare loss			44.811	44.763	44.584	12.687	47.910	44.726
Welfare loss*			12.874	12.676	13.011	44.879	12.853	12.740
Average welfare loss			57.685	57.439	57.595	57.566	60.763	57.466

Parameters: $\bar{\sigma} = 1.0; \bar{\delta} = 0.375; \gamma = 0.75; \lambda = 2.0; \varphi = 0.25; \alpha = 0.25; \theta_1 = 1.0; \theta_2 = 0.2; \rho = 0.025$

Notes: 1. The EMS outcomes under international policy coordination correspond to the EMU outcomes under international policy coordination and under floating exchange rates. The FLOAT outcomes assume that central banks can pre-commit to their announced monetary policies.

2. The losses for output, real income and the money supply refer to the discounted squared deviations from desired values.

allowed to appreciate in the face of the adverse supply shock in the home country (see the column headed 'Symmetric EMS' in Table 9.3). There is not much difference between a cooperative and a non-cooperative float. In the former case the home money supply expands somewhat more, which leads to somewhat smaller output losses and higher losses in real income. As far as the European Monetary System is concerned, when Germany is hit by a supply shock, it expands its money supply by more than when the rest of Europe is hit by a supply shock, so that this leads to smaller output losses and larger losses in real income for Germany.

9.9   Concluding remarks

Both a standard two-country Mundell–Fleming model and a similar model extended to allow for wage–price and exchange-rate dynamics have been used to compare the responses of monetary policy and the effects on welfare under a regime of floating exchange rate, an asymmetric regime of managed exchange rates (such as the European Monetary System) and a symmetric regime of irrevocably fixed exchange rates (such as European Monetary Union). It has been assumed that capital markets are fully liberalised and that there is no labour mobility. In the face of a common adverse demand shock monetary policy expands to ensure full employment. There is no conflict over the cost of living, so that there is no need for international policy coordination under any of the three exchange-rate regimes. In the face of a change in preferences away from the goods of country 1 towards the goods of country 2, monetary union performs very badly compared with the other two regimes because the exchange rate is not able to depreciate. This is the main reason why, when there are rigidities in labour markets, one might advocate the establishment of a contingent and budget-neutral Federal Transfer Scheme in conjunction with the establishment of a Federal Monetary Authority. Its task should, in the presence of such a shock, be to transfer income from country 2 to country 1. It is a pity that the Delors Report did not advocate the establishment of such a Federal Transfer Scheme.

In the face of a common adverse supply shock, however, a monetary union performs much better than a regime of floating exchange rates. The reason is that the competitive, futile attempts to appreciate the currency and export inflation are avoided. A non-cooperative float then leads to too tight monetary stances, too high interest rates and too much unemployment. Under the European Monetary System, the central banks of Europe other than the Bundesbank manage to appreciate their currencies *vis-à-vis* the DM and thus disinflate away some of the adverse consequences of a common supply shock. Because Germany suffers a large loss in real wage income, it experiences a greater welfare loss than the rest of Europe. In addition, Germany is worse off under the European Monetary System than under monetary union, whilst the rest of Europe is better off. This may be one of the few reasons why Germany may be keen to join a more symmetric European System of Central Banks. The rest of Europe is better off than with a non-cooperative float, but Germany is only better off when countries care relatively more about the cost of living than unemployment. In the face of an idiosyncratic supply shock, a monetary union performs, in terms of the average welfare loss, much worse than either a cooperative or a non-cooperative regime of floating or managed exchange rates. The reason is, of course, that the currency cannot appreciate in response to the excess demand for goods.

The move towards monetary union in Europe is thus much more justified in the presence of common shocks than in the presence of idiosyncratic shocks. This means that the establishment of a Federal Transfer Scheme may be essential in order to off-set idiosyncratic shocks. As long as such a scheme is budget-neutral on a European level and contingent on the government concerned taking action to improve the productivity and work-experience of its unemployed, there should not be too many political problems with such a scheme.

However, a preferable solution is to make sure that labour markets clear immediately through structural labour market policies, or to make sure that factor (in particular labour) mobility is very high throughout Europe.[11] Unfortunately, labour markets do not function properly and cultural and language barriers prevent a high degree of labour mobility,[12] so that the move towards monetary union must be accompanied by the appropriate design of a fiscal institution at a European level in order to compensate for giving up monetary and exchange-rate policy as an independent instrument of economic policy. The other advantages of moving towards full monetary union in Europe can then be obtained as well: reduction in exchange-rate risk and the associated costs of hedging; fewer speculative capital flows and no more speculative attacks, thus facilitating the liberalisation of capital markets throughout Europe; saving on foreign-exchange reserves; a greater weight in negotiations about the global management of exchange rates with Japan and the USA; the efficiency of a single currency as a unit of account, medium of exchange and store of value; weakening of the German hegemony in monetary policy may mean that Germany is more likely to have a looser fiscal stance, carry its full burden of fighting unemployment in Europe and be 'a locomotive engine of growth'; lower transaction and information costs; better monetary discipline and lower inflation rates (for example, van der Ploeg, 1991b).

Three problems then remain. The first problem is that the presence of a large black economy in southern Europe justifies a higher optimal inflation tax for southern Europe than for northern Europe and thus justifies a crawling peg between southern and northern Europe (for example, Dornbusch, 1988; Canzoneri and Rogers, 1990). However, it can be argued that countries with a large public nominal debt, such as Italy, have a big temptation to use surprise inflation to erode the real value of debt which, as the private sector anticipates this, leads to higher inflation rates in equilibrium (Gros, 1988). A clear commitment to peg the exchange rate to a low-inflation common currency area eliminates this inefficiency and may thus be optimal, despite a reduction in seigniorage revenues. In a monetary union arguments of this type provide a justification for an independent and autonomous common central bank, along the lines advocated by the Delors Committee (1989). The second problem is that under monetary union there also is a need to coordinate monetary policies from a public finance point of view, because without it excessive inflation occurs throughout the region. The reason is that each country ignores the adverse effects of higher inflation on the other members of the common currency area and thus grabs too much seigniorage from the common central bank (van der Ploeg, 1991a). The third problem is that, even when the countries of a monetary union are hit by a common adverse supply shock, there may be potential advantages associated with international coordination of fiscal policies so that appropriate supranational institutions must be founded in order to ensure that this happens (Cohen and Wyplosz, 1989; van der Ploeg, 1991a, 1991b). This need arises *either* when a European System of Central Banks is independent and is not willing to use the European money supply for stabilisation purposes and thus fiscal policy must be called upon, *or* when the countries forming a European Monetary Union strategically interact with the USA. The latter situation arises because Europe's trade balance determines its real exchange rate *vis-à-vis* the USA and thus effectively is a public good; its povision may in the absence of international coordination of fiscal policies be inefficient.[13]

Notes

1. For a more formal analysis of international coordination of fiscal policies, see van der Ploeg (1992) and Jensen (1991).
2. Strictly speaking, risk-neutral arbitrage yields the condition of uncovered interest parity (UIP). This condition says that the home interest rate (r) should equal the foreign interest rate (r^*) plus the expected rate of depreciation of the home currency. Hence, a country which currently has a higher interest rate than abroad thus faces the risk of a depreciating currency in the future. We postpone a treatment of expectations in currency markets to Sections 9.6 and 9.7. A short cut to rational expectations would be to consider temporary shocks (occurring only in 'period 1') and assume that in the future ('period 2') all markets clear. In that case, the exchange rate returns to its equilibrium value (that is zero) in the future and the UIP condition reads $r = r^* - e$ instead of $r = r^*$. Hence, the current exchange rate is overvalued $(e < 0)$ if the home interest rate is higher than the foreign interest rate. In Section 9.2–9.5 we assume static expectations in foreign markets $(r = r^*)$, but in Section 9.6 we assume rational expectations $(r = r^* - e)$.
3. The proof is that this inequality requires for $\omega > 0$ that $g(\theta) \equiv \theta^2 + \hat{\sigma}(2 - \hat{\sigma}) \theta + \frac{1}{2} \hat{\sigma}^2 > 0$, which is the case as $g(0) = \frac{1}{2} \hat{\sigma}^2 > 0$ and $g'(0) = 2\theta + \hat{\sigma}(2 - \hat{\sigma}) > 0$.
4. $W_F = W_F^* < W_M^*$ requires that $f(\theta) \equiv \theta^2 + (2\hat{\sigma} - 3\hat{\sigma}^2)\theta + \hat{\sigma}^2 - 2\hat{\sigma}^3 < 0$, so that $f(0) = \hat{\sigma}^2(1 - 2\hat{\sigma}) < 0$ and $f''(0) = 2$. Hence, this inequality holds for small θ and is violated for large θ.
5. An extended model with micro foundations and overlapping generations may be found in van der Ploeg (1993).
6. These differential games are under floating exchange rates characterised by two predetermined, backward-looking state variables, namely $m - p$ and $m^* - p^*$ and one non-predetermined, forward-looking state variable, namely c. Time inconsistency problems arise because c responds to credible announcements about future policy changes. Under managed and fixed exchange rates, the exchange rate is either a policy instrument or fixed, and the game is thus characterised by two backward-looking state variables only and no time inconsistency problems arise.

7. This is a general result, which arises because $\Delta w(\infty) = \Delta w^*(\infty) = \lambda \Delta i(\infty)$ implies that e must jump immediately to its new steady state.

8. This is exactly the opposite of what happens under a shift of preferences from home to foreign goods, because then the depreciation of the currency that occurs under a float softens the adverse effects on unemployment but leads to a further fall in real income.

9. This is a general result, which arises because it is easy to show that the effects of $s-s^*$ on $w - w^*$, c, $m - m^*$ and $y - y^*$ are the same under monetary union as under the European Monetary System.

10. Similar exercises have recently been performed by McKibbin (1988) McKibbin and Sachs (1988), John Taylor (1988) and Frenkel, Goldstein and Masson (1989).

11. It also helps to make the move towards monetary union a success when countries have a high proportion of traded goods in domestic output, a high degree of product diversification, a high degree of financial integration, similar optimal inflation rates, and a high degree of policy and political integration (Ishiyama, 1975).

12. Workers, when they make migration decisions, consider both variable costs (missing friends, and so on) and fixed costs (removal costs, and so on). When the wage differential exceeds full costs, workers migrate. When the wage differential becomes smaller, they stay abroad as long as they can cover variable costs as fixed costs are then sunk. The presence of fixed costs thus leads to a zone of inaction. This zone expands when there is a lot of exchange-rate uncertainty, because then there is option value attached to staying where you are (Bertola, 1989). The move towards a regime of irrevocably fixed exchange rates reduced hysteresis phenomena of this sort and should thus enhance international labour mobility.

13. For example, in the face of a common adverse supply shock, each country attempts to get the other country to accept more of an increase in unemployment in order to achieve the appreciation of the European currency that is desirable for both countries. It follows that in a non-cooperative outcome not enough action is taken relative to the cooperative outcome.

CHAPTER 10

Monetary and Portfolio Balance Models: Which does the Empirical Evidence Support?

Ronald MacDonald

10.1 Introduction

In this chapter we seek to survey the empirical evidence on the two main classes of exchange rate models considered in previous chapters, namely the monetary (in both its flexible and sticky price versions) and the portfolio balance models. As has been demonstrated in previous chapters, the key distinguishing feature of these two classes of model concerns whether non-money assets (in particular government bonds) are perfect substitutes, and this may be summarised again with reference to equations (10.1) and (10.2),

$$r_t = r_t^* + \Delta e_{t+k}^\epsilon + \lambda_t \tag{10.1}$$

$$\lambda_t = \vartheta \, [b_t - (e_t + b_t^*)] \quad \vartheta > 0 \tag{10.2}$$

where (10.1) is a representation of risk adjusted UIP, and λ denotes the risk premium which is determined in (10.2) by relative bond supplies (in this chapter all variables, apart from interest rates, are defined in natural logarithms). In the monetary class of models the bonds entering (10.2) are presumed perfect substitutes (that is, $\vartheta \to 0$) and therefore for this class of models $\lambda_t = 0$ and (10.1) reduces to simple UIP:

$$r_t = r_t^* + \Delta e_{t+k}^\epsilon \tag{10.1'}$$

The whole motivation of the portfolio class of models is that bonds are, in fact, imperfect substitutes and therefore the appropriate way to define the relationship between domestic and foreign interest rates is given by (10.1). The issue of which of the two models is the most valid may therefore be seen to boil down to the issue of the existence of the risk premium, λ_t. In this chapter we categorise the empirical exchange rate literature which has a bearing on this issue in the following way.

First, there is a (relatively small) literature which seeks to test (10.1) and (10.2) directly. Thus, a number of researchers have tested UIP, and its risk adjusted version, for a variety of key currencies. This literature is surveyed in the next section. A related literature to that on UIP is concerned with testing whether the forward exchange rate premium contains information about the expected change in the exchange rate. This literature relates to (10.1) in the following way. Consider again the condition of covered interest rate parity (CIP):

$$f_t - e_t = r_t - r_t^*$$
(10.3)

where $f_t - e_t$ may be thought of as the (logarithmic) forward premium. If this condition holds then we may substitute for the interest differential in (10.1) to obtain an alternative definiton of the risk premium as the difference between the forward premium and the expected exchange rate change:

$$(f_t - e_t) - \Delta e_{t+k}^\epsilon = \lambda_t$$
(10.4)

Thus UIP is only equivalent to CIP in circumstances where individuals are risk-neutral, or there is an absence of the risk premium, λ_t. The evidence that this relationship has to shed on the existence of a risk premium is considered in Section 10.3. The remainder of the evidence which we consider in this chapter concerns the reduced form work on the monetary and portfolio models. Rather than testing for the existence of a risk premium, this body of work seeks to discriminate between the monetary and portfolio classes of model by testing the reduced form representation of the relevant model. In particular, the idea is to test whether a reduced form version of, say, the flexible-price model performs better than a reduced form version of the Portfolio Balance Model (PBM). The criteria used to assess the relative merits of the different classes of models is how well they fit, or explain, the data on an in-sample basis and, second, how they perform in an out-of-sample forecasting context. As we have indicated, the focus of this chapter is an attempt at reviewing elements of the exchange rate literature which have a direct bearing on which class of asset market model of the exchange rate is the most relevant. This inevitably means we are not providing a comprehensive survey of the exchange rate literature;[1] such comprehensive surveys are to be found in MacDonald (1988, 1990b) and MacDonald and Taylor (1992).

10.2 Uncovered and risk-adjusted uncovered interest rate parity

As we noted in the introduction to this chapter one way of thinking about the difference between the monetary and portfolio classes of exchange rate model concerns whether UIP holds exactly or whether it has to be modified to incorporate a risk premium (the so-called risk-adjusted UIP). In this section we consider a number of different tests of UIP.

In testing the UIP condition a researcher is immediately confronted with how to model the expected change in the exchange rate. A common practice in this regard is to assume that expectations are formed rationally and therefore (10.5) holds

$$\Delta e_{t+k}^{\epsilon} = \Delta e_{t+k}^{\epsilon} + \varphi_{t+k} \tag{10.5}$$

where φ_{t+k} is the rational expectations forecast error. On substituting (10.5) in (10.1') and rearranging we may obtain

$$\Delta e_{t+k} = (r - r^*)_t - \varphi_{t+k} \tag{10.6}$$

or, as a regression equation,

$$\Delta e_{t+k} = \alpha + \beta(r - r^*)_t + u_{t+k} \tag{10.6'}$$

Thus under rational expectations and risk neutrality, (10.6') suggests that the interest differential should be an optimal predictor of the rate of exchange rate depreciation. In equation (10.6') a test of this hypothesis would amount to testing whether $\alpha = 0$, $\beta = 1$ and the residuals were orthogonal to publicly available information (dated t or earlier). Note the jointness of the test under consideration here. Thus a finding that β deviates substantially from unity in an estimated version of (10.6') may indicate some expectational failure (be it a 'peso' problem[2] or simple irrationality) rather than a failure of the UIP itself (that is, rather than a time-varying risk premium being the explanation).

Hacche and Townend (1983) test equation (10.6) for sterling's effective exchange rate over the period July 1972–Febuary 1980, and find that the a priori constraints on α and β are supported by the data. The error orthogonality property was not, however, supported lagged values of domestic credit expansion and the change in the exchange rate proved to be statistically significant (similar results for the sterling dollar rate, February 1973–December 1980, are reported in Davidson, 1985). Similarly, Loopesko (1984), in testing the error orthogonality property, found that it did not hold for the majority of currencies studied. Taylor (1987) tests UIP for a selection of six bilateral exchange rates, using the bivariate vector autoregression (BVAR) framework, and reports that UIP is easily rejected for all exchange rates, with the exception of dollar–DM.

Cumby and Obstfeld (1981) estimate whether the error term u_{t+k} in equation (10.6') is in fact white noise when $k = 1$ by using Box-Pierce and likelihood ratio tests on $[e_t - e_{t-1} - (r - r^*)_{t-1}]$ for six bilateral dollar exchange rates (weekly data for the period 5 July 1974 to 27 June 1980). For only one exchange market, the UK pound–US dollar, is it demonstrated that the residuals are white (a further rejection of UIP is given in Cumby and Obstfeld, 1984). Cumby and Obstfeld rationalise these deviations from UIP by suggesting the existence of a variable risk premium.

However, as we have indicated, the interpretation that Cumby and Obstfeld place on their findings is, because of the joint nature of the hypothesis under consideration, just that: an interpretation. MacDonald and Torrance (1988b) have argued that one potential way around the jointness of the hypothesis tested in the above-noted trials would be to use an independent measure of expectations. In fact, MacDonald and Torrance utilise survey data gathered by Money Market Services (MMS), UK, to test (10.1') directly (using an analogous regression equation to (10.5') in which the expected exchange rate change features as the dependent variable). In particular, they decompose β into a component due to risk aversion and that due to expectational failures. MacDonald and Torrance (1988b) utilise this decomposition and find, using four bilateral dollar currencies (the British pound, the German DM, the Swiss franc and the Japanese yen) that deviations of β from unity for the early 1980s are explained in terms of both risk and expectational failures. They suggest that the latter could arise either from a peso effect or simple irrationality.

In an attempt to extract the risk premium from the serially correlated errors reported by Cumby and Obstfeld a number of researchers have conducted their UIP tests by estimating versions of equation (10.2). Hence if assets are imperfect substitutes the portfolio balance approach to modelling the exchange rate suggests that if, say, the supply of home country assets increases (the b term in equation 10.2), then either the domestic rate of interest will have to rise or the currency must be expected to appreciate for the asset to be willingly held. Thus, if assets are imperfect substitutes, relative asset stocks should be systematically related to expected returns. If, however, assets are perfect substitutes then there should be no systematic relationship: we are back in a world in which UIP holds continuously. In order to test the substitutability of home and foreign assets a number of researchers have estimated a simple regression equation of the following form:

$$(r_t - r_t^* - \Delta e_{t+k}) = \alpha + \beta[b - (e + b^*)]_t + \varphi_{t+k}$$

(10.7)

where deviations from UIP define the risk premium and rational expectations have been assumed. Thus, if the portfolio balance story is correct, it is expected that the estimated value of the β coefficient should differ significantly from zero. However, a further assumption needs to be invoked before (10.7) can be empirically implemented: namely, the identity of the investors whose portfolios are examined. Frankel (1983) lists three possible assumptions concerning portfolio preferences. First, if residents of each country in the world have the same portfolio preferences, and if the market under consideration is the whole world, then b and b^* are simply net domestic government indebtedness and net foreign government indebtedness, respectively. Such a view of portfolio choice, classified in the literature as uniform preference, implies that the changes in the indebtedness of residents of one country to residents of another has no effect on the risk premium. A second assumption concerning preferences, used in the studies by Branson, Halttunen and Masson (1977), is that the domestic country is small and foreign residents do not hold domestic bonds, and thus the risk premium is determined only by home residents. Finally, it is presumably more realistic to allow residents in both countries to hold assets issued by both countries. Such models are usually classed as 'preferred habitat' models because domestic residents in each country are assumed to hold a greater proportion of their wealth in domestic assets.

Dooley and Isard (1982) test the uniform preference version of equation (10.7) for the German DM–US dollar over the period 1973–78 (quarterly data); they report insignificant coefficients and that only a small part of the discrepancy between $r - r^*$ and Δe can be explained by risk factors. Additionally, Dooley and Isard estimate (10.7) with the uniform preference assumption relaxed for the DM–dollar rate; however, the resulting estimates of the risk premium are still capable of explaining only a small part of observed changes in exchange rates. Frankel (1982) also estimates the uniform preference and preferred habitat versions of equation (10.7) for the DM–US dollar January 1974–October 1978 and reports that 'Many regressions were run ... [but] no coefficients appeared significantly different from zero.'

Frankel (1982b, 1983) develops equation (10.7) further by using an insight from finance theory: namely, that the parameters in asset demand functions such as (10.7) depend not only on the degree of risk-aversion but also on the conditional covariance matrix of returns. For example, in terms of equation (10.7), β should equal $\rho^*\Omega$ (see Frankel, 1985 for a derivation) where ρ is the Arrow-Pratt measure of relative risk aversion and Ω is the (conditional) covariance matrix of relative rates of return. Failure to account for this factor in estimates of (10.7) will give results which are biased against the PBM. But Frankel's incorporation of the variance term into an estimated version of equation (10.7) did not lead to a rejection of the null hypothesis of perfect substitutability. Rogoff (1984) replicates Frankel's study, using weekly data for the Canadian dollar–US dollar, but also reports a statistically insignificant relationship.

Although studies testing for the existence of a risk premium generally fail to reject the null hypothesis of perfect asset substitutability, it is important to note, following Frankel (1982a), the obvious point that failure to reject a hypothesis is not the same as acceptance. Indeed, tests of equation (10.7) are likely to have very low power to reject a false null hypothesis because of the variability of the error term, representing unexpected exchange rate changes or 'news'. News is an important feature of foreign exchange markets (and has indeed been an empirical regularity of the recent floating experience: see Mussa, 1979) and therefore perhaps the risk premium and news should be modelled jointly.

In addition to expectational errors, if there have been errors in the measurement of the right hand side variables, or if the asset demand equations have not been correctly specified, then the error term in equation (10.7) may also contain measurement or specification error. Further, the error term may be correlated with the right hand side variables if sumultaneity is an issue (if the asset equations have been correctly specified and expectations are rational then, even if the regressors are endogenous, they should be uncorrelated with the error term because they are known at the time expectations are formed). To the extent that there are simultaneity and errors-in-variables problems, least squares estimates of (10.7) are likely to be biased and inconsistent.

There are two main conclusions to be drawn from this section. First, direct tests of the UIP condition, conditional on rational expectations, suggest that this condition is very strongly violated for a broad range of currencies (over a number of time periods). Although most authors interpret this rejection as indicative of a time-varying risk premium, a study using survey data (which avoids the assumption of rationality) indicates that the explanation is due to both expectional errors (which may not, necessarily, imply irrationality) and time-varying risk premia. Second, researchers have been unable to find a statistically significant link between the excess of relative interest rates over the expected exchange rate change (the risk premium) and relative non-money asset stocks; there should be a link if the PBM is valid. At best, then, this evidence does not come down clearly in support of one particular class of model. We therefore turn to a related, but much more extensive, literature to ascertain if this can shed any further light on the topic.

10.3 Evidence for a risk premium from the literature on the optimality of the forward rate as a predictor of the future exchange rate

Evidence on the existence, or otherwise, of a foreign exchange risk premium may be gleaned from the vast literature on the efficiency of the forward exchange market. The pivotal relationship in this literature is equation (10.4). In evaluating the decomposition given by (10.4), a researcher is again (as in tests of UIP) faced with the unobservable nature of the expected change in the exchange rate and the thorny issue arises of making some assumption about the formation of expectations. A common practice is, as in the UIP literature, to assume that expectations are formulated rationally and therefore (10.5) holds. On using (10.5) in (10.4) we obtain

$$(f_t - e_t) = \Delta e_{t+k}^{\epsilon} + \lambda_t + \varphi_{t+k}$$

$$(10.8)$$

If agents are risk-neutral then an implication of (10.8) is that the forward premium should be an optimal predictor of the future exchange rate change. A popular way of testing this joint hypothesis of rational expectations and risk neutrality has involved estimating the following regression equation:

$$\Delta e^{\epsilon}_{t+k} = \alpha_0 + \beta_0 f p_t + u_{t+k} \tag{10.9}$$

Under the joint null hypothesis it is expected that $\alpha_0 = 0$, $\beta_0 = 1$ and, in the presence of non-overlapping data, the disturbance term should be a serially uncorrelated process, orthogonal to available information; if, however, agents are either risk-averse or 'irrational', or both, then such conditions will be violated.

A large number of researchers have implemented (10.9), using a variety of currencies and time periods, for the recent floating experience, and report results which are unfavourable to the unbiasedness hypothesis. For example, Bilson (1981), Longworth (1981), Fama (1984), Gregory and McCurdy (1984) and Taylor (1988a) all report a result which seems to suggest a resounding rejection of the unbiasedness hypothesis: namely, a significantly negative point estimate of β_0 (this result seems particularly robust given the variety of estimation techniques used by researchers and the mix of overlapping and non-overlapping data sets). A good example of the kind of result obtained by researchers is reported here as equation (10.10) (the result is from Fama, 1984), where standard errors are in parenthesis.

$$\Delta e_{t+k} = 0.81 - 1.15(f - e)_t$$
$$\phantom{\Delta e_{t+k} = }(0.42)\ (0.50) \tag{10.10}$$

Currency: Swiss franc–US dollar; Est. Tech.: ZSURE

A large amount of research effort has been expended in trying to rationalise this finding. Perhaps the most popular explanation lies in the existence of a non-zero time-varying risk premium which drives a wedge between the forward rate and future spot rate: that is, the assumption of risk neutrality, which underpins regression equation (10.9) is erroneous.

A useful starting point in any discussion of time-varying risk premia is Fama's novel way of analysing the degree of variability of the components of the forward premium. In addition to equation (10.9) Fama considers the 'companion' regression equation:

$$f_t - e_{t+k} = \alpha_1 + \beta_1(f_t - e_t) + \epsilon_{2,t+k} \tag{10.11}$$

Since the regressor in (10.9) and (10.11) is the same variable and the sum of the regressands equals the regressor, the equations are entirely complementary (that is, $\alpha_0 = -\alpha_1$ and $\beta_0 = 1 - \beta_1$). The usefulness in estimating both equations lies in their ability to interpret the data. By using the standard formula for β_0 and β_1, the definition of the risk premium given by (10.4) and the rationality equation (10.5), it is relatively easy to demonstrate that the probability limits of the βs may be written as (see Fama, 1984, and MacDonald and Taylor, 1989, for further details):

$$\beta_0 = \frac{\text{var}(e^{\epsilon}_{t+k} - e_t) + \text{cov}(\lambda_t, e^{\epsilon}_{t+k} - e_t)}{\text{var}(\lambda_t) + \text{var}(e^{\epsilon}_{t+k} - e_t) + 2\,\text{cov}(\lambda_t, e^{\epsilon}_{t+k} - e_t)} \tag{10.12}$$

$$\beta_1 = \frac{\text{var}(\lambda_t) + \text{cov}(\lambda_t, e^{\epsilon}_{t+k} - e_t)}{\text{var}(\lambda_t) + \text{var}(e^{\epsilon}_{t+k} - e_t) + 2\,\text{cov}(\lambda_t, e^{\epsilon}_{t+k} - e_t)} \tag{10.13}$$

In the rather extreme case where λ_t and $e^{\epsilon}_{t+k} - e_t$ are uncorrelated, β_1 would capture that component of the variance of the forward premium due to the variance of the risk premium, and β_0 would reflect that part of the variance of the premium due to variability of the expected change of the exchange rate. In practice the interpretation of the βs is unlikely to be so clear cut, since the covariance terms are unlikely to be zero. However, even in the presence of non-zero covariance terms, (10.12) and (10.13) offer a neat interpretation of the empirical finding of a negative β_1. Thus, since the denominator and the var term in the numerator of (10.12) must be positive, it follows that $\text{cov}(\lambda_t, e^{\epsilon}_{t+k} - e_t)$ must be negative and greater than $\text{var}(e^{\epsilon}_{t+k} - e_t)$ in absolute magnitude. This in turn implies that $\text{var}(\lambda_t)$ must be greater than $\text{var}(e^{\epsilon}_{t+k} - e_t)$. In order to get a feel for the magnitude of the difference we may subtract (10.12) from (10.13) to obtain:

$$\beta_1 - \beta_0 = \frac{\text{var}(\lambda_t) - \text{var}(e^{\epsilon}_{t+k} - e_t)}{\text{var}(f_t - e_t)} \tag{10.14}$$

Thus, the difference between the βs in (10.12) and (10.13) is determined by the relative variances of the risk premium and the expected rate of change of the exchange rate. Fama (1984) calculates this difference for nine major dollar rates and finds a range for (10.14) from 1.58 (Japanese yen) to 4.16 (Belgian franc). Moreover, in six out of nine cases the estimate of (10.14) is more than 2 standard errors away from zero, and in all cases it is more than 1½ estimated standard errors away from zero. Fama thus confidently concludes that the variance in the risk premium is reliably greater than the variance in the expected change in the exchange rate.

The negative covariation between the risk premium and the expected depreciation implied by most reported point estimates of β_0 proved puzzling to Fama (1984), who argued that 'A good story for negative covariation ... is difficult to tell.' Intuitively, a negative β_0 means that the greater the expected depreciation of the dollar, the greater the expected return that one should require for holding a dollar-denominated security (all exchange rates are defined as dollars per unit of currency). Hodrick and Srivastava (1986) provide a solution to this apparent paradox. They point out that the risk premium in this empirical work is the expected profit from an open forward *purchase* of dollars, and so this is in fact denominated in foreign currency (the maturing long dollar position is eventually sold in the spot market). The expected (dollar-denominated) profit from an open forward *sale* of dollars is $-\lambda_t$ and the widely reported negative estimate of β_0 suggest that this will be positively correlated with the expected rate of dollar depreciation.

Conditional on the assumption of rational expectations, a large number of researchers have sought to model the risk premium which seems to be suggested by the empirical evidence on (10.9). Some of these papers are based on a theoretical 'representative agent' model of the risk premium, whilst others are rather *ad hoc* implemenations; that is, the risk premium is assumed to be defined by (10.4) and the researcher uses some form of time series model in an attempt to capture it. Estimates of variants of the representative agent model have been conducted by, *inter alia*, Hansen and Hodrick (1983), Hodrick and Srivastava (1984), Campbell and Clarida (1987), Giovannini and Jorion (1987) and Mark (1985). Empirical models of the risk premium, not based on any theoretical underpinnings, are to be found in Domowitz and Hakkio (1985), Wolff (1987), Kaminsky and Peruga (1988), Nerlove *et al.* (1988), Taylor (1988a or b) and MacDonald and Taylor (1989); these *ad hoc* models of the risk premium use Kalman filter and GRACH modelling techniques. Although there is some slight support for the existence of time-varying risk premia (particularly in the papers by Kaminsky and Peruga and Nerlove *et al.*) the main conclusion to emerge from this literature is that if risk premia are important in foreign exchange markets other methods have to be used to capture them. One such method may lie in the use of survey-based data on foreign exchange expectations.

The problem with all of the above attempts at interpreting and modelling the risk premium is that they all rely on the assumption that foreign exchange market participants are endowed with rational expectations, and therefore the derived results could be simply reflecting some form of expectational failure, be it simple irrationality or some form of peso effect (we do not discuss the so-called expectational failures explanation for the failure of the joint null hypothesis in this paper; see the discussion in MacDonald, 1990a). It would therefore be advantageous in trying to define or model the risk premium if researchers had access to an independent measure of expectations. The existence of survey data on foreign exchange market participants' expectations would seem to offer researchers just such a measure and has, indeed, become a popular way of determining if the widely reported result for (10.9) is due to the existence of important time-varying risk premia (as purported by Fama, 1984) or some form of expectational failure.

One way of motivating survey-based tests of the bias in the forward premium is to consider again the coefficient β_0 in equation (10.9). By noting additionally that the actual exchange rate change may be defined by (10.5), this coefficient may be written as

$$\beta_0 = \frac{\text{Cov}[\varphi_{t+k}, (f-e)_t + \text{Cov}[\Delta e^{\varepsilon}_{t+k}, (f-e)_t]}{Var[(f-e)_t]}$$

(10.15)

On manipulating (10.15), β_0 may be written as equal to unity minus a term, β_0^{re}, arising from any failure of rational expectations minus a further term, β_0^{λ}, arising from the presence of a risk premium (see Frankel and Froot, 1989, for further details):

$$\beta_0 = 1 - \beta_0^{re} - \beta_0^{\lambda}$$

where

$$\beta_0^{re} = \frac{\text{Cov}[\varphi_{t+k}, (f-e)_t]}{\text{Var}[(f-e)_t]}$$

and

$$\beta_0^{\lambda} = \frac{\text{Var}[\lambda_t] + \text{Cov}(\Delta e_{t+k}^{\epsilon}, \lambda_t)}{\text{Var}[(f-e)_t]}$$

(10.16)

The availability of survey data means that both β_0^{re} and β_0^{λ} can be distinguished, and therefore, in principle, it should be possible to discern whether rejection of the null is due to risk or an expectational failure. Thus β_0^{re} may be estimated from a regression of the form

$$e_{t+k}^{\epsilon} - e_{t+k} = \alpha + \beta_0^{re}(f-e)_t + v_{t+k}$$

(10.17)

and β_0^{λ} may be estimated from a regression of the form

$$e_{t+k}^{\epsilon} - e_t = \gamma_0 + \gamma_1^{\lambda}(f-e)_t + u_{t+k}$$

(10.18)

as $1 - \gamma_1^{\lambda}$. Recently a number of researchers in the USA and UK have estimated (10.17) and (10.18) and obtained estimates of β_0^{re} and β_0^{λ}. Do their findings shed any light on the rejection of the joint null, noted earlier, and, in particular, the existence or otherwise of a risk premium? Frankel and Froot (1989) estimate (10.17) and (10.18) using a variety of survey data sets (AMEX, Economist and Money Market Services (MMS), US) for a period covering the early 1980s (the data sets are pooled across a number of currencies). The main conclusion to emerge from this work is that the unbiasedness proposition fails both because of deviations of β_0^{re} from unity and also because of the existence of a *constant* risk premium (that is, a significant estimate of γ_0 in (10.18); the hypothesis that γ_1^{λ} equals unity cannot be rejected (and therefore they conclude that the risk premium is not of the time-varying variety). In contrast to Frankel and Froot, MacDonald and Torrance (1988a, 1988b, 1990) find, using survey data generated by MMS (UK) Ltd, that the unbiasedness proposition fails both because of deviations of β_0^{re} from unity and also because of the existence of a time-varying risk premium (that is, estimates of γ_1^{λ} which differ significantly from unity). Indeed the estimates of the risk premium reported by MacDonald and Torrance are much larger than estimates obtained from standard mean-variance models (see, for example, Frankel, 1982b).

Taylor (1989) uses a survey data base, constructed by a firm of British management consultants, which consists of the expectations of over 50 London investment houses on the sterling effective exchange rate and the dollar – sterling rate, to test equations (10.19) (with the expected exchange rate substituted for the forward rate) and (10.18). It is demonstrated *inter alia* that rejection of the standard unbiasedness equation for the chosen currencies is due to the existence of a time-varying risk premium and not market 'irrationality'. Dominguez (1986) tests the efficiency of MMS (US) one-week, two-week, one-month, and three-month forecast data for the US dollar against the UK pound, the DM, the Swiss franc and the Japanese yen for the period 1983–5. Dominguez reports significant evidence of biasedness and violation of the error orthogonality condition. MacDonald (1990a) uses MMS (UK) survey data to estimate a number of error orthogonality conditions and finds that variables (particularly forward premia) in the period t information set remained unexploited.[3]

Canova and Ito (1988) use a weekly VAR model (sample period: 1979, week 1–1985, week 52) to generate a series for the expected Japanese yen–US dollar exchange rate. The main purpose is to use this series as an alternative independent means of generating the risk premium term. Of course, the procedure relies crucially on the variables entering the conditioning information set. Canova and Ito use Japanese and US stock prices and short-term interest rates and the yen–dollar spot rate in their VAR model.[4] Amongst their results, Canova and Ito show that their generated expectational series is much more accurate than the equivalent survey series described in Frankel and Froot (1989); they confirm the findings of Fama (1984) and Hodrick and Srivastava (1986) regarding the negative correlation between the risk premium and the expected appreciation of the yen;[5] and they also demonstrate that the time series of the risk premium exhibits time varying and non-stationary components. From the perspective of the survey data literature the import of the Canova and Ito study would seem to be that using simple mechanical forecasting formulae would have enabled speculators to improve their exchange rate forecasts.

One 'problem' with the above survey studies is that they all utilise median responses. This is fine if agents' forecasts are homogeneous, as they should be if the rational expectations model is correct; however, if forecasts are heterogeneous then concentration on the median may miss important insights into how agents process information. Ito (1988) uses a survey data base, collected by the Japanese centre for International Finance, which consists of the individual responses of a number of financial and non-financial institutions on their expectation of the yen–dollar exchange rate one, three, and six months ahead. Amongst Ito's results is the interesting finding that expectations appear to be highly heterogeneous: that is, exporters seem to have a significant depreciation bias whilst the insurance and banking sectors have a significant appreciation bias. Such heterogeneity can perhaps be interpreted as a rejection of the rational expectations hypothesis, or maintaining the rationality hypothesis it may reflect a slow learning process due to a strongly biased prior. MacDonald and Marsh (1993 and 1994) use a consensus survey data base, which is disaggregated both within and across countries, and they demonstrate that there is a substantial degree of heterogeneous behaviour amongst forecasters (some produce optimal forecasts, whilst others do not) and that combining such forecasts in a variety of 'optimal' ways does not produce consensus measures which are superior to such a measure based on the mean of the sample.

MacDonald and Taylor (1993a) exploit MMS (US) data to *model* the risk premium (as opposed to *testing* for its existence); this work may be seen as the counterpoint to the body of work which seeks to model the risk premium under the assumption of rational expectations. One of the striking findings of this paper is that, in contrast to much of the work noted earlier, there is considerable support for the existence of time-varying risk premia in two out of the three foreign exchange markets studied. Thus modelling the risk premium using survey data would seem to offer a useful avenue for future research.

In this section we have demonstrated that the forward exchange rate premium is not an optimal predictor of the future exchange rate. There are two inter-pretations that may be placed on this finding: either it is indicative of a time-varying risk premium or it is an expectational failure of some sort. This latter interpretation has become especially popular in the recent financial economics literature in which leading researchers have posited that non-rational agents have an important role to play in the determination of asset prices, such as the exchange rate (see, for example, De Long *et al.*, 1990). Indeed, models based on chartist techniques are becoming increasingly popular in the exchange rate liter-ature to explain exchange rate behaviour not apparently explicable by a standard menu of fundamentals (these fundamentals, and tests of fundamentals models, are considered in some detail in the next section). The other interpretation placed on the sub-optimal predictive properties of the forward rate is that it is due to the existence of important time-varying risk premia. Although tests, con-ditional on rational expectations, which seek to model such premia have not been particularly successful, more recent work which does not impose rationality has met with more success.

10.4   Reduced-form exchange rate modelling: some in-sample and out-of-sample evidence

As we noted in the introduction, a number of researchers have sought to test the relative merits of the monetary and portfolio class of models by testing their reduced form counterparts on an in- and out-of-sample context. Such tests may be motivated using a simple reduced form which may be derived from the stan-dard relationships underpinning asset market exchange rate models, introduced in earlier chapters. In particular,

$$\bar{m} - \bar{p} = \alpha_0 \bar{y} - \alpha_1 \bar{r} \tag{10.19}$$

$$\bar{m}^* - \bar{p}^* = \alpha_0 \bar{y}^* - \alpha_1 \bar{r}^* \tag{10.19'}$$

$$\bar{c} = \bar{s} - \bar{p} + \bar{p}^* \tag{10.20}$$

where (10.19) and (10.19′) denote, respectively, the home and foreign money demand functions, (10.20) defines the real exchange rate (assumed equal to zero in the monetary class of models, and therefore PPP is assumed to hold continuously) and a bar denotes an equilibrium value. In the empirical exchange rate literature, a common way of defining the expected exchange rate component of (10.1) is as (see Hooper and Morton, 1982, and Frankel, 1983)

$$\Delta e_{t+k}^{\epsilon} = \phi\,(\bar{e}_t - e_t) + \pi_t^{\epsilon} - \pi_t^{\epsilon*}, \quad 0 < \phi < 1 \tag{10.21}$$

where π_t^{ϵ} represents the current rate of expected long-run inflation. The first component on the right hand side of (10.21) represents regressive expectations: *ceterus paribus*, the exchange rate is expected to depreciate (appreciate) whenever the current spot rate is below (above) its steady state. The second component on the right hand side of (10.21) is the expected inflation differential and indicates that even when $e_t = \bar{e}_t$ the exchange rate will be expected to change if there is an expected inflation gap. In the Buiter–Miller (1981) model this second component reflects the core inflation differential. Assuming for the moment that UIP holds exactly, we may use (10.1) (with λ_t set to zero) to obtain

$$\bar{e}_t - e_t = \phi^{-1}[(r - \pi^{\epsilon})_t - (r* - \pi^{\epsilon*})_t] \tag{10.22}$$

Although π_t^{ϵ} and $\pi_t^{\epsilon*}$ refer to *long-run* inflationary expectations, (10.22) can be viewed as relating the exchange rate to real interest differentials. Given UIP and (long-run) PPP, the long-run interest differential must be equal to the long-run expected inflation differential.

$$(\bar{r}_t - \bar{r}_t^*) = (\pi_t^{\epsilon} - \pi_t^{\epsilon*}) \tag{10.23}$$

so that (10.21) can be alternatively expressed as

$$e_t = \bar{e} + \phi^{-1}[(\bar{r}_t - \bar{r}_t) - (\bar{r}_t^* - r_t^*)] \tag{10.24}$$

which demonstrates that the exchange rate will appreciate above its long-run level whenever the relative nominal interest differential is above its equilibrium value.

On using (10.19) and (10.19′) to solve for the home and foreign long-run price levels, substituting the resulting expressions into (10.20) (where it is assumed $c = 0$) and assuming that the long-run interest rates are equal to expected inflation rates we obtain an expression for the long-run exchange rate as:

$$\bar{e}_t = (\bar{m} - \bar{m}*)_t - \alpha_0(\bar{y} - \bar{y}*)_t + \alpha_1(\pi^{\epsilon} - \pi^{\epsilon*})_t \tag{10.25}$$

Substituting (10.25) into (10.24) and assuming, for simplicity, that the current equilibrium money supplies and income levels are given by their current actual levels (which amounts to assuming that they follow random walks), we obtain:

$$e_t = (m - m^*)_t - \alpha_0 (y - y^*)_t - \phi^{-1}(r - r^*)_t + (\phi^{-1} + \alpha_1)(\pi^\epsilon - \pi^{\epsilon^*})_t \qquad (10.26)$$

or, as a regression equation

$$e_t = \delta_1 (m - m^*)_t + \delta_2 (y - y^*)_t + \delta_3 (r - r^*)_t + \delta_4 (\pi^\epsilon - \pi^{\epsilon^*})_t + u_t \qquad (10.26')$$

Equation (10.26) has been labelled the real interest rate (RID) reduced form by Frankel (1979). Its advantage is that nested within it are the two versions of the monetary view of the exchange rate, namely the flexible and sticky price monetary models. Since both relative money supplies and income levels feature in both versions of the monetary model, their expected values will be the same in the flexible and sticky price versions (that is, δ_1 is expected to equal unity and δ_2 is expected to be around -0.8). The two models are, however, distinguished by the expected values of δ_3 and δ_4. Thus in the FLM interest rates always track expected inflation, and therefore the relative interest rate and relative expected inflation terms are synonymous. This is usually indicated by the hypothesis $\delta_3 = 0$ (see Frankel, 1979) although it would be more correct to hypothesise $\delta_3(r - r^*)_t = \delta_4(\pi^\epsilon - \pi^{\epsilon^*})_t$. In the sticky price monetary model δ_4 is expected to be zero. The RID formulation suggests that both the expected inflation and relative interest rate terms are relevant, and therefore $\delta_3 < 0$ and $\delta_4 > 0$.

Relationship (10.26) may be further generalised to incorporate portfolio balance effects by simply using (10.1), with no assumptions imposed on λ, instead of UIP to give

$$e_t = \delta_1 (m - m^*)_t + \delta_2 (y - y^*)_t + \delta_3 (r - r^*)_t + \delta_4 (\pi^\epsilon - \pi^{\epsilon^*})_t + \delta_5 \lambda_t + u_t \qquad (10.27)$$

Some of the empirical estimates of (10.26), and variants thereof, estimated using data for the period (approximately 1972–78), appeared to be relatively supportive of the monetary model in that estimated coefficients were correctly signed, close to their expected values and significant; the equations appeared to have good in-sample explanatory power as jduged by the adjusted coefficient of determination. For example, Bilson (1978a, 1978b), Hodrick (1978), Dornbusch (1979), Putnam and Woodbury (1979) and MacDonald (1983) all report reasonably successful estimates of the flexible price version of (10.26) (that is, an equation in which the last two terms of (10.26) become a composite term reflecting expected inflation); Driskell (1981) reports favourable estimates of the sticky price monetary reduced form[6] for the Swiss franc; Frankel (1979) reports results supportive of the more general RID model – equation (10.26 – for the DM–US dollar rate over the period July 1974 to February 1978. His estimated equation is:

$$e_t = 1.39 + 0.97(m - m^*)_t - 0.52(y - y^*)_t - 5.40(r - r^*)_t +$$
$$(0.12) \quad (0.21) \qquad\qquad (0.22) \qquad\qquad (2.04)$$
$$29.40(\pi^\epsilon - \pi^{\epsilon^*})_t \qquad R^2 = 0.91 \qquad \hat{\rho} = 0.46$$
$$(3.33)$$

$$(10.28)$$

where estimated standard errors are given in parenthesis and a long bond differential is used as an instrument for the expected inflation differential. One particularly noteworthy feature of (10.28) is that both interest rate differentials are significant. The fact that the short-term interest differential is significant is, Frankel argues, indicative that the flexible price monetary model is not a complete model of the exchange rate.

However, a less sanguine view of the monetary model emerges when a more complete up-to-date data set is employed. For example, Dornbusch (1980), Haynes and Stone (1981), Hacche and Townend (1981, 1983), MacDonald (1983), Backus (1984) and Frankel (1984) have tested (10.26), and variants thereof, beyond 1978 (or for currencies other than the DM–dollar rate, which tended to be the favoured rate for the pre-1978 period); very unsatisfactory results are obtained in that few coefficients are correctly signed, the equations have poor explanatory power, in terms of the coefficient of determination, and autocorrelation is a severe problem. One particularly disturbing feature of some of the estimates (particularly those for the DM–dollar) is that the sign of the coefficient on the relative money supply term is negative, suggesting that an increase in the home money supply results in an exchange rate *appreciation*. A representative result, due to Haynes and Stone (1981), is reported here as equation (10.29):

$$e_t = -4.08 - 0.57 \ (m - m^*)_t + 0.02 \ (y - y^*)_t + 0.22 \ (r - r^*)_t +$$
$$(23.40) \ (1.89) \qquad\quad (0.08) \qquad\qquad (0.13)$$
$$13.33(\pi^e - \pi^*)_t \qquad \bar{R}^2 = 0.38 \qquad \hat{\rho} = 0.77$$
$$(3.57) \tag{10.29}$$

which is for the DM–dollar rate and was estimated with a Cochrane Orcutt correction.

Estimates of variants of the PBM for the recent floating exchange rate appear to be little better than those based on the monetary model. For example, Isard (1980), Hooper and Morton (1982), Frankel (1983, 1984) and Hacche and Townend (1983) estimate versions of equation (10.27). Each of these researchers uses a different method of modelling the risk premium term. In Hooper and Morton's implementation of equation (10.28) the risk premium is assumed to be a function of the cumulated current account surplus net of the cumulation of foreign exchange market intervention. With this modification, the equation is estimated for the dollar effective rate 1973, second quarter, to 1978, fourth quarter, using an instrumental variables estimator, and is reported here as equation (10.30).

$$e_t = 4.55 + 0.77(m - m^*)_t - 1.84(y - y^*)_t - 0.15(r - r^*)_t +$$
$$(131.9) \ (2.56) \qquad\quad (2.72) \qquad\qquad (0.27)$$
$$2.41(\pi - \pi^*)_t - 1.69(ca - Eca)_t + 0.97\lambda_t, \quad \bar{R}^2 = 0.78 \quad DW = 1.87$$
$$(0.98) \qquad\qquad (3.90) \qquad (0.82) \tag{10.30}$$

where t-ratios are in parenthesis. Notice that all the monetary variables enter with the correct sign and two are statistically significant, but that of the portfolio balance variables only the current account news term is statistically significant (and correctly signed); the risk premium term is insignificant (and wrongly signed). Other similar estimated versions of (10.27) have been equally unsuccessful.[7]

10.5   The out-of-sample forecasting performance of asset approach reduced forms

So far we have considered only the in-sample performance of the various asset approach reduced forms. A much more stringent test of a model's validity is its ability to forecast better out-of-sample than, say, a simple time-series representation of the exchange rate, such as the random walk model, or the forward rate. Meese and Rogoff (1983) have conducted such a study for the dollar–pound, dollar–DM, dollar–yen and trade weighted dollar exchange rates using data running from March 1973 to June 1981. The reduced form asset equations tested by Meese and Rogoff are (10.26) (the RID model), the flexible price version of (10.26) and (10.27) (the hybrid equation). The out-of-sample performance of these equations is compared with the forecasting performance of the naive random walk model, the forward exchange rate, a univariate autoregression of the spot rate and a vector autoregression formed using lagged values of the explanatory variables of equation (10.26) plus cumulated home and foreign trade balances. The out-of-sample performance is gauged for three forecast periods (one, six and twelve months ahead) using three statistics: the mean error (ME); the mean absolute error (MAE); and the root mean square error (RMSE). The devastating conclusion to emerge from Meese and Rogoff's work is that *none* of the asset reduced forms considered outperform the simple random walk model. In a further paper, Meese and Rogoff (1984) consider possible explanations of why the reduced form models fail to beat the random walk model out of sample. In particular, Meese and Rogoff (1984) show – using the vector autoregressive methodology – that the instruments used in simultaneous estimates of asset reduced forms may not be truly exogenous and thus that the estimated parameters may be extremely imprecise. To overcome this problem Meese and Rogoff impose coefficient constraints, culled from the empirical literature on money demand equations, on asset reduced forms and re-estimate the RMSEs for the same period as Meese and Rogoff (1983). Interestingly, Meese and Rogoff find that although the coefficient constrained asset reduced forms still fail to outperform the random walk for most horizons up to a year, in forecasting beyond a year the asset reduced forms do outperform the random walk in terms of RMSE. As Salemi (1984) points out, this tends to suggest that the exchange rate acts like a pure asset price in the short term (that is, approximately a random walk) but that in the longer term its equilibrium is systematically related to other economic variables. One important point to bear in mind about Meese and

Rogoff's work is that their comparison of the random walk model with the structural models is a little unfair because the random walk predictions are one step ahead and therefore use information not available to the structural multi-step ahead forecasts.

10.6 Explanations for the poor performance of asset approach reduced forms

How may the poor performance of asset approach reduced forms be explained? Although a number of explanations have been proposed in the literature, we would argue that there are two key explanations. First, most of the reduced form estimates discussed above have been estimated with very limited data dynamics; indeed the majority have been estimated as static regressions. If these equations were being interpreted as long-run relationships then it may be permissible to study a static form (see our discussion of cointegration tests, below); however, it is clear that the above-noted researchers do not make a distinction between long- and short-run relationships, and indeed versions of the monetary model, such as the sticky price model, by definition, cannot represent a long-run relationship. As short-run relationships they are woefully inadequate because they ignore, for example, the often complex dynamics which are a feature of successfully estimated domestic asset market relationships (such as estimates of money demand functions) and the dynamics that will be introduced by a failure of parity conditions which underpin the asset market model, such as PPP and UIP (or risk-adjusted UIP), to hold continuously.

A second key explanation for the apparent failure of estimated asset reduced forms is that they are not true reduced forms and are, at best, quasi-reduced forms. In particular, there are at least two important simultaneous relationships in a reduced form like (10.26) which most researchers ignore in their estimation. The fact that the recent floating experience has been a dirty, or managed float, implies that money supplies will not be truly exogenous. Thus any non-sterilised intervention adopted by the authorities will impart a simultaneous relationship between the exchange rate and the home and foreign money supply. Similarly, it is widely accepted that central banks have manipulated interest rates to influence exchange rates, and this will impart a further simultaneity into an equation like (10.26). Such simultaneity issues are perhaps at their clearest for countries involved in the exchange rate mechanism of the European Monetary System, and the target zone literature (see Krugman, 1988; and Svensson, 1991) was spawned to explain the behaviour of exchange rates in a managed system with target bands (this literature is not surveyed in this chapter).

Recently researchers have begun to take account of the above critiques in their estimates of asset exchange rate equations. Recent developments in the time-series literature, and in particular the introduction of the concept of cointegration, have been helpful in this regard. The latter method allows a researcher to determine if a long-run static relationship does indeed exist for the kind of variables that enter an exchange rate equation and the information gleaned from the long-run relationship then allows a decision to be made on the appropriate short-run dynamic equation. Baillie and Selover (1987), Boothe and Glassman (1987a) , Meese (1987) and Kearney and MacDonald (1990) all use the Engle–Granger (1987) two-step cointegration procedure to test the monetary model and are unable to reject the null of no cointegration. These results would seem to suggest that the monetary model does not even have empirical support as a long-run relationship (to our knowledge no one has tested the PBM using the cointegration methodology). However, MacDonald and Taylor (1991b) have criticised the use of the two-step procedure to test the monetary model and have instead advocated the Johansen (1988) maximum likelihood procedure. Interestingly, in using this approach to test the monetary model for three currencies (dollar–DM, dollar–sterling and dollar–yen) MacDonald and Taylor (1991b) demonstrate that there is very strong support for the monetary model as a long-run relationship (indeed for the dollar–DM exchange rate they show that all of the restrictions implied by the monetary model are accepted by the data).

In a further paper, MacDonald and Taylor (1993b) use the evidence of significant long-run relationships for the monetary model to formulate an appropriate dynamic short-run model for the dollar–DM exchange rate, over the period January 1976 to December 1990. They demonstrate, *inter alia*, that their dynamic model (the model is a dynamic error correction model which uses the long-run information to define the error correction term) satisfies a battery of diagnostic tests, indicative of its sensible in-sample properties, and show that the random walk model is beaten in a Meese and Rogoff out-of-sample forecasting context. Both Wolff (1987) and Schinasi and Swamy (1987) capture the instabilities in the structural relationships underlying the monetary equation by using time-varying parameter techniques. Using such techniques, Wolff finds some limited improved forecasting performance, whilst Schinasi and Swamy show that the time-varying model produces consistently better forecasts than the random walk model; however, it is not clear if this latter finding is due to their use of the time-varying parameters technique or to the multi-step random walk forecast used instead of the one-step forecast as used by Meese and Rogoff.

A number of researchers have tried to improve on the reduced form empirical work by estimating both the monetary model and the PBM structurally. One of the first attempts at implementing the monetary model structurally was provided by Kearney and MacDonald (1986a, b) for the sterling–dollar rate and evidence from a simulation exercise suggested the estimated structure was supportive of the monetary model. Papell (1988) has estimated the Dornbusch sticky price model in a structural context with forward looking expectations for the effective exchange rates of Germany, Japan, the UK and the USA, and notes: 'The results of the estimation are moderately successful. Most of the structural coefficients have the expected sign, are of reasonable magnitude, and are significant ... Our results ... show that Dornbusch's model and its extensions provide a solid empirical, as well as theoretical, basis for understanding the functioning of the flexible exchange rate system.' As is evident, this conclusion is somewhat at variance with standard reduced form estimates. The Buiter–Miller (1981) version of the sticky price monetary model has been implemented structurally by Barr (1989) and Smith and Wickens (1988, 1990) for the sterling exchange rate and both sets of authors report favourable in-sample estimates of the model. The results reported in these papers are likely to be fairly robust since care has been taken in specifying the model dynamics. In simulating their model, Smith and Wickens find that the exchange rate overshoots its equilibrium level by 21 per cent in response to a 5 per cent change in the money supply. Some success has also been reported in structural estimates of the portfolio balance approach. For example, Kearney and MacDonald (1986a) estimate a structural portfolio model for the sterling–dollar rate and report simulation results which are supportive of the PBM. Obstfeld (1983) and Kearney and MacDonald (1986a) estimate a four-equation structural version of the PBM with forward looking expectations for, respectively, the dollar–DM and dollar–sterling exchange rates. The former author finds that in a simulation exercise sterilised intervention has an insignificant impact on the exchange rate (a finding which is not supportive of the portfolio class of models), whilst the latter authors find that such intervention does have a significant impact on the dollar–sterling rate. The structural evidence is therefore more supportive of the asset market approach than the reduced form evidence, although it is not particularly helpful in discriminating which version of the asset model is the more appropriate.

10.7   Tests of forward looking monetary and portfolio balance models

A number of researchers have advocated testing monetary and portfolio balance models using the forward looking restrictions that arise from the imposition of rational expectations. Such forward looking models may be illustrated with reference to the flexible price version of the monetary model:

$$e_t = (m - m^*)_t - \alpha_0 (y - y^*)_t + \alpha_1 (r - r^*)_t \tag{10.25a}$$

where no distinction is made between relative nominal interest rates and relative inflation (because the former are assumed always to reflect the latter) and actual values are always at their equilibrium levels. If we define x_t to equal the term $[(m - m^*)_t - \alpha_0 (y - y^*)_t]$ and assume that UIP holds (that is, equation (10.1') is assumed to hold continuously), we may rewrite (10.25a) as

$$e_t = x_t + \alpha_1 (e_{t+1}^\epsilon - e_t) \tag{10.25b}$$

$$e_t = z_t + \beta e_{t+1}^\epsilon \tag{10.25c}$$

where $z_t = 1. [1 + \alpha_1]^{-1}$ and $\beta = \alpha_1. [1 + \alpha_1]^{-1}$. Assuming expectations are formed rationally (that is, $e^\epsilon_{t+1} = E_t [e_{t+1}|I_t]$) then we may solve this expression recursively forward to obtain

$$e_t = \sum_{i=0}^{n} \beta^i E_t z_{t+i}$$

(10.31)

where the transversality condition – that $lim \ \beta^n e^\epsilon_{t+i+1} \to 0$ as $i \to \infty$ – has been imposed. Equation (10.31) simply states that the current spot rate is equal to the present discounted value of the expected future stream of fundamentals (discounted by β). Although (10.31) has been derived using the flexible price monetary model, it is, in fact, quite general and is equally valid for other classes of exchange rate models, such as the PBM (in this instance the z_t term would also include relative bond supplies). In implementing (10.31) empirically, the main task facing a researcher lies in the modelling of the expected fundamentals term and, in particular, obtaining a closed form solution.

For the monetary class of models (10.31) has been tested by Hoffman and Schlagenhauf (1983) using a time-series model for the stochastic evolution of the fundamentals contained in z_t; in particular, the money and income variables are assumed to be generated by ARIMA (1 1 0) processes. Using such ARIMA processes for the fundamental variables, it is straightforward to demonstrate that the closed form exchange rate equation is given by:

$$e = \gamma + (m - m^*)_t - \alpha_0(y - y^*)_t + \frac{\rho_m \alpha_1}{1 + \alpha_1 - \alpha_1 \rho_m} \Delta m_t -$$
$$\frac{\rho_m^* \alpha_1}{1 + \alpha_1 - \alpha_1 \rho_m} \Delta m_t^* - \frac{\alpha_0 \rho_y \alpha_1}{1 + \alpha_1 - \alpha_1 \rho_y} \Delta y_t + \frac{\alpha_0 \rho_y^* \alpha_1}{1 + \alpha_1 - \alpha_1 \rho_2^*} \Delta y_t^*$$

(10.32)

where the α terms have the same interpretation as in expression (10.25) and the ρ terms denote the parameters from the ARIMA process (that is ρ_m denotes the autoregressive parameter from the ARIMA process for the domestic money supply). Equation (10.32) is estimated jointly with the ARIMA process for each of the fundamental variables for France, Germany and the UK, and likelihood ratio tests are computed for the validity of the rational expectations hypothesis and the validity of this hypothesis *plus* the coefficient restrictions implied by the flexible price monetary model (such as the unitary coefficient on relative money supplies), and although the expectations restrictions are not rejected for any of the countries the flexible price restrictions are rejected for Germany, Kearney and MacDonald (1990) estimate (10.32) for the Australian dollar–US dollar and cannot reject the restrictions implied by the rational expectations appended FLM model. Woo (1985) and Finn (1986) test the out-of-sample forecasting performance of the forward looking flexible price monetary model, using similar criteria to Meese and Rogoff (1983). Finn reports that this model forecasts as well as the random walk model but fails to outperform the random walk, whilst Woo finds that his formulation outperforms the random walk model for one currency (the dollar–DM rate). The forward looking reduced form (10.31) using a set of portfolio balance fundamentals has been implemented and successful in-sample and out-of-sample properties have been reported. Hence the success of the forward looking asset approach reduced form would not seem to be model-specific but, rather, hinges crucially on the careful modelling of forward looking expectations.

The rational expectations solution to the FLM has spawned further empirical work which seeks to test for the presence of speculative bubbles. Thus, it is well known from the rational expectations literature that equation (10.31) is potentially one solution from an infinite sequence.[8] If we denote the exchange rate given in (10.31) as $\hat{e}_t$ then it is straightforward to demonstrate (see MacDonald and Taylor, 1989, for a fuller discussion) that equation (10.31) has multiple rational expectations solutions, each of which may be written in the form.

$$e_t = \hat{e}_t + b_t \tag{10.33}$$

where b_t is the bubble term which will be important if agents believe it to be so. Such a rational bubble may arise where the market exchange rates have been bid away from the fundamental solution.[9] Many view the dramatic appreciation of the US dollar in the early 1980s as due, at least in part, to a speculative bubble.[10]

Meese (1986) attempts to test for bubbles by applying a version of the Hausman (1978) specification test originally suggested by West (1986) for present value models. The test involves estimating a version of (10.25c)[11] which produces consistent estimates of β in the presence or absence of bubbles, and a closed form version of (10.31) which produces a consistent estimate of β only in the absence of a bubble. Hausman's specification test is used to determine if the two estimates of β are significantly different. If they are, then this is suggestive of the existence of a speculative bubble. For the dollar–yen, dollar–DM and dollar–sterling exchange rates Meese in fact finds that the two estimates of β are significantly different and therefore rejects the no-bubbles hypothesis.[12] Kearney and MacDonald (1990) apply a version of this methodology to the Australian–US dollar exchange rate and cannot reject the no-bubbles hypothesis.

An alternative way of testing for bubbles has been to adopt the variance bounds test methodology originally proposed by Shiller (1978) in the context of interest rates. This may be illustrated in the following way. If we define the *ex post* rational, or perfect foresight, exchange rate as:

$$e_t^* = \sum_{i=0}^{\infty} \beta^i x_{t+i} \tag{10.34}$$

which will differ from e_t by a rational forecast error, u_t (that is, $e_t^* = e_t + u_t$), and given that u_t is a rational forecast error e_t and u_t must be orthogonal so we have

$$\mathrm{var}(e_t^*) = \mathrm{var}(\hat{e}_t) + \mathrm{var}(u_t) \tag{10.35}$$

which implies

$$\text{var}(e_t^*) \geq \text{var}(\hat{e}_t) \tag{10.36}$$

In the absence of bubbles the inequality given by (10.36) should hold. However, in the presence of bubbles (10.36) is likely to be violated since on using (10.33) we have $e_t^* = e_t - b_t + u_t$ and the corresponding relationship to (10.36) is

$$\text{var}(e_t^*) = \text{var}(e_t) + \text{var}(b_t) + \text{var}(u_t) - 2\,\text{cov}(e_t, b_t) \tag{10.37}$$

Since, in the presence of bubbles, e_t and b_t are likely to be positively correlated, we cannot derive (10.36) from (10.37) and, if we find in an empirical study that (10.36) is violated (that is, excess volatility), this could be taken as evidence of bubbles. Huang (1981) tests versions of (10.36) for the dollar–DM, dollar–pound and pound–DM for the period March 1973 to March 1979. His results are supportive of excess volatility, and by inference he finds against the no-bubbles hypothesis. Kearney and MacDonald (1990) implement (10.36) for the Australian–US dollar over the period January 1984–December 1986 and generally find in favour of the no-bubbles hypothesis. There are, however, a number of problems with this kind of approach. First, they are conditional on an assumed model of the exchange rate: violation could be due to the inappropriate model. Second, and perhaps more importantly, there may be other possible explanations for the presence of bubbles, such as measurement error in computing the perfect foresight exchange rate, the stationary transformations may be inappropriate or there may be small sample bias.

10.8   Purchasing power parity: a review of the recent evidence

The concept of PPP has been mentioned on a number of occasions in this chapter and in previous chapters. More specifically, it features in some shape or form in nearly all of the asset market models. In the flexible price monetary model, PPP is assumed to hold continuously, whilst in the sticky price monetary model it holds only as a long-run phenomenon. In contrast, the existence of interest-bearing home and foreign bonds (which are imperfect substitutes) in the PBM means that even monetary impulses can change the real exchange rate. Hence the empirical evidence on PPP should help shed further light on what class of asset market model is the most appropriate, and indeed whether it is necessary to go much beyond relative prices when trying to explain exchange rate movements. The absolute version of PPP is written here as equation (10.38):

$$e_t = p_t - p_t^* \tag{10.38}$$

where p is the natural logarithm of the price level and other symbols have the same interpretation as before. Absolute PPP may be motivated in an equivalent way. Thus, if we define the log of the real exchange rate, c_t, as $e_t - p_t + p_t^*$, then for absolute PPP to continually hold, c_t should equal zero:

$$c_t = e_t - p_t + p_t^* = 0 \qquad (10.39)$$

However, few proponents of PPP (see, for example, Officer, 1976, for a useful discussion of the views of the traditional proponents of PPP) would argue for a strict adherence to PPP. Rather, PPP is usually seen as determining the exchange rate in the long run,[13] whilst a variety of other factors, such as trading restrictions, productivity and preference changes, may influence the exchange rate in conditions of disequilibrium. With this view, shocks to the exchange rate which cause non-zero values of c_t will be corrected in the long run; the real exchange is a mean-reverting process.

Much of the empirical evidence on PPP has utilised aggregate price indices to test absolute PPP.[14] One extremely popular way of testing PPP has involved the use of regression analysis. For example, Krugman (1978) and Frenkel (1981) present regression estimates of absolute PPP, based on a selection of aggregate price indices, for part of the recent experience with floating exchange rates . Frenkel and Krugman test absolute PPP using a regression equation of the following form:[15]

$$e_t = \alpha + \beta p_t + \beta^* p_t^* + u_t \qquad (10.40)$$

where u_t is a disturbance term. If PPP holds, it is expected that $\beta = -\beta^* = 1$ and that $\alpha = 0$ (if price indices are used instead of price levels, the intercept term need not be zero). Frenkel (1981) uses wholesale and cost of living indices from the recent floating exchange rate experience for the dollar–pound, dollar–French franc and dollar–DM exchange rates. It is demonstrated, *inter alia*, that absolute PPP is not supported by the data, since the a priori restrictions on β and β^* are not satisfied. Similar results are reported by Krugman (1978) using 1970s data.[16]

A further battery of tests of PPP relies on examining the time-series properties of the real exchange rate. Such tests may be viewed as tests of the efficient markets view of PPP (EMPPP), against a more traditional view of PPP. The EMPPP, which is derived using parity conditions from the capital account of the balance of payments, suggests that the real exchange rate should follow a random walk process. The EMPPP was originally proposed by Roll (1979) and may be motivated around the following first-order autoregressive process for the real exchange rate.

$$c_t = \alpha_0 + \alpha_1 c_{t-1} + u_t \qquad (10.41)$$

where u_t is a white noise process. In terms of (10.41), long-run PPP requires $\alpha_0 = \alpha_1 = u_t = 0$; that is c_t must be a zero-mean stationary process (again, if price indices are used instead of price levels, c_t may equal the constant, α_0). A less strict interpretation of PPP would, as we have indicated, additionally allow for short-run deviations from PPP which are eventually extinguished in the long run. In terms of equation (10.41) such behaviour may be accommodated by a value of α_1 which is less than unity in absolute value. Thus with α_1 less than 1, short-run deviations from PPP are allowed but such deviations are corrected at a rate equal to $(1 - \alpha_1)$: the real exchange rate is mean-reverting. Alternatively, a proponent of EMPPP would argue that $\alpha_1 = 1$, indicating that the real exchange rate follows a random walk with possible non-zero drift of α_0.

A number of researchers have tested whether the real exchange rate, for a number of currencies, follows a random walk by running regression equations of the form:

$$\Delta c_t = \gamma + \beta_1 \Delta c_{t-1} + \beta_2 \Delta c_{t-2} + \cdots \beta_k \Delta c_{t-k} + u_t$$

(10.42)

where Δ is the first difference operator and k is the lag length. The random-walk behaviour of the real exchange rate is usually assessed by testing the hypothesis that the β coefficients are zero. The majority of this evidence is unable to reject the random-walk hypothesis.[17] However, Abuaf and Jorion (1990) have argued that such tests, since they involve only the differences of the variables, are likely to have low power against the alternative of a near-random walk model. By estimating (10.41) directly for a number of bilateral US dollar exchange rates, and by additionally accounting for the potential cross-correlation of the error terms across the equations using a generalised least squares estimator, Abuaf and Jorion show that the value of α_1 lies in a range of 0.98 to 0.99 for monthly data. Although these point estimates are extremely close to one, they are not *exactly* one, indicating that there is some evidence of mean reversion.[18] Using annual data (which, in the context of a test of a long-run relationship like PPP, may be a more appropriate observational frequency) over the period 1901–72, Abuaf and Jorion report an average slope coefficient of around 0.78 this allows statistical rejection of the null of a random walk[19] and defines a half-life of 3.3 years, similar to that implied by the monthly data base.

The problematic nature of testing the stationarity of the real exchange rate using equations like (10.42) has been further emphasised by Huizinga (1987). Huizinga's (1987) insight follows on from the work of Cochrane (1988) and is that an equation like (10.42) is typically specified with only a relatively short lag length. However, the long-run behaviour of the real exchange rate may be affected by much longer lags than are usually modelled, and it is possible that the inclusion of such longer lags could force the real exchange rate back to its equilibrium level. In particular, if the changes in the real exchange rate are negatively serially correlated, the real exchange rate will be mean-reverting. One simple way of capturing the effects of such long lags is to take the ratio of the variance of a long difference of the real exchange rate to the variance of its first difference (scaled by the reciprocal of the long lag length). If the real exchange rate is truly a random walk then this ratio will equal unity. If, however, real exchange rates exhibit mean-reverting behaviour, the variance ratio will fall below unity. Applying this methodology to ten dollar bilateral rates, for the recent floating period, Huizinga finds evidence of mean reversion. This is indicated by the fact that after ten years the average variance ratio across the ten currencies is 0.65. Although this ratio seems to indicate substantial mean reversion, the deviation from one is not significant. To quote:

> While the magnitude of these deviations from random walk behaviour is obviously large in an economic sense, it is not significant in a statistical sense. Someone with strong *a priori* information that real exchange rates are random walks need not be persuaded otherwise by the data. Nonetheless, those who look to the data to obtain a reasonable 'best guess' are unlikely to select a random walk specification to describe the long-run behaviour of real exchange rates. (Huizinga, 1987)

An alternative way of testing whether real exchange rates obey a random walk process has involved exploiting the cointegration methodology proposed by Engle and Granger (1987). For example, if three variables – such as an exchange rate and the corresponding relative prices – are cointegrated then it means that in the long run they settle down together in a unique way. More specifically, this means that in terms of equation (10.40) the estimated residuals (that is, the $\hat{u}s$) should form a stationary series. If they do not, there will be no tendency for the exchange rate and relative prices to settle down; they will move apart without bound. The cointegration methodology is in some ways similar to tests discussed above of whether the real exchange rate is stationary. However, using (10.40) instead of (10.41) is slightly different since it does not restrict β to equal one and β^* to equal minus one. As Taylor (1988b) and Patel (1990) have pointed out, the corresponding results may differ because of measurement error that is, the observed price indices are not the 'true' indices; rather they are the observable indices related to the true series by measurement error and transportation costs.

For the recent experience with flexible exchange rates the cointegration methodology has been applied to aggregate price data by Taylor (1988b) and Enders (1988). Both these authors test for cointegration between bilateral dollar exchange rates and a relative price measure (thus the restriction $\beta = -\beta^*$ is imposed) using the Engle–Granger two-step methodology and monthly data. Both Enders and Taylor find that the null hypothesis of non-cointegration cannot be rejected: there is no long-run tendency for exchange rates and relative prices to settle down on an equilibrium track.[20] In contrast to these studies, Patel (1990) uses the two-step methodology to test for long-run PPP without imposing $\beta = -\beta^*$: however, little evidence of cointegration is reported and the use of the two-step methodology precludes testing for proportionality of the βs with respect to the exchange rate. Fraser, Taylor and Webster (1991) used the two-step cointegration methodology to test the law-of-one price for the sterling–US dollar exchange rate and a disaggregated industry price base over the period 1975–80; little evidence of cointegration was established.

Recently, however, a number of researchers have argued that the failure to find a cointegrating relationship between relative prices and exchange rates may be due to the econometric method used rather than the absence of a long-run relationship. For example, Cheung and Lai (1993), Kugler and Lenz (1993), MacDonald (1993) and MacDonald and Marsh (1994) all use the Johansen cointegration method to test for the number of cointegrating vectors amongst relative prices and exchange rates for bilateral US dollar exchange rates (Cheung and Lai, 1993; MacDonald, 1993; and MacDonald and Marsh, 1994) and DM bilateral dollar rates (Kugler, 1993; MacDonald, 1993; and MacDonald and Marsh, 1994). A considerable amount of evidence in these papers supports the contention that there *is* indeed a long-run PPP relationship for a variety of currencies and, further, that this relationship has sensible properties (in terms, for example, of displaying coefficients on domestic and foreign prices which are 'correctly' signed).

The above-noted evidence of cointegration has been exploited by MacDonald and Marsh (1994) in their estimation of dynamic error correction models (ECMs) for a number of US dollar and DM bilateral exchange rates. The estimated ECMs are used to conduct dynamic out-of-sample forecasting tests along the lines advocated by Meese and Rogoff (1983) (see Section 10.5) and it is demonstrated that for a number of currencies that these models can outperform a simple random walk. As MacDonald concludes in his 1993 paper, 'The tide would seem to be turning in favour of some form of purchasing power parity!'

10.9   Concluding remarks

In this chapter we have surveyed some of the empirical literature relating to the asset approach to the exchange rate. More specifically, we have focused our discussion around what this literature has to say about the validity of the monetary class of models relative to PBMs and, in the process, discussed the empirical evidence on a number of international parity conditions. As we noted at the outset, the key distinguishing feature of these two classes of model is the existence, or otherwise, of a foreign exchange risk premium: the monetary class of models assumes that the premium is zero, whilst proponents of the portfolio balance approach assert that it is a pivotal component of their models.

The main conclusion to emerge from our discussion of the UIP condition is that although there is a lot of evidence to suggest that UIP is not well supported by the empirical evidence, it is difficult, because of the jointness of the hypothesis being tested, to determine if this is due to the existence of a risk premium or some form of expectational failure; a similar picture emerges from the literature on the optimality of the forward rate as a predictor of the future exchange rate. There is, however, some evidence from researchers who use survey forecast data to suggest that risk premia may indeed be an important explanation for the rejections noted in both these literatures. On the basis of the evidence from these two literatures, it is therefore difficult to infer which of the two classes of exchange rate models is most valid.

Direct tests of portfolio and monetary models have largely concentrated on reduced form reductions of the corresponding structural models. Due to the difficulty in obtaining good reliable data on non-money assets, most of this work has concentrated on the monetary class of models. Empirical implementations of the models which rely on a static representation (that is, one which excludes data dynamics) have proved to be singularly unsuccessful. Some success for the monetary class of models has been noted by researchers who explicitly model dynamics; in particular, such models able to outperform a simple random walk, thus overturning a result which has become something of an industry paradigm. There has also been some success in modelling both monetary and portfolio balance models structurally, and in frameworks where proper account is taken of forward looking expectations. One interesting feature of the recent empirical exchange rate literature is the resurgence of interest shown in that old chestnut, PPP. Indeed, judged by the existence of a long-run relationship, and the provision of good out-of-sample forecasts, recent empirical work would seem to suggest that PPP performs about as well as the more sophisticated asset approach models.

Notes

1. We do not, for example, discuss the recent empirical literature on target zone models (see Hallwood and MacDonald, 1994).
2. That is, the (non-zero) probability of a regime change which does not actually occur in-sample, thereby biasing the results: see Krasker (1980) and MacDonald and Taylor (1989)
3. Froot and Ito (1988) test the 'consistency' of MMS (UK and US) expectional data. Such tests amount to testing whether the long-term forecast *implied* by a short-term forecast is consistent with the survey-based long-term forecast. Such a test is effectively an application of the cross equation restrictions tested in the context of a BVAR model of the forward and spot rates (see discussion above). Froot and Ito demonstrate that the different forecast horizons are inconsistent.
4. Canova and Ito use a Kalman filter technology to ensure that their k step ahead forecasts are only based on information available at period t.
5. It is further demonstrated the variance of the expected change in the exchange rate, and the covariance between the risk premium and the expected change in the exchange rate is larger than the covariance of the forward premium with the realised change in the spot rate.
6. The 'Driskell reduced form' differs somewhat from equation (26'); see Macdonald and Taylor (1993) for further details.
7. A slightly different reduced form version of the PBM has been estimated by Branson, Halttunen and Masson (1977, 1979), and Branson and Halttunen (1979) (this effectively amounts to a regression of the exchange rate on relative money supplies and relative bond supplies). However, the results from these estimates are not supportive of the portfolio balance approach : see Bisignano and Hoover (1982) for a critique of this approach and MacDonald (1988) for an extended discussion.
8. See for example Begg (1982), and Minford and Peel (1983).
9. The only restriction required on b_t is that $b_t = \beta E_t b_{t+1}$.
10. See Frankel (1985), and Dornbusch and Frankel (1988).
11. The version is simply one which incorporates an error term.
12. Meese uses monthly data over the period October 1973 to November 1982.
13. In an hyperinflation scenario, PPP is also expected to hold in the short run as well: see Frenkel (1980).

14. Isard (1977) and Kravis and Lipsey (1978) examine the law of one price relationship using disaggregated prices for the 1970s and find that the relationship is not upheld.
15. These authors also use a first differenced version of (10.4) to test *relative* PPP; similar results to those for absolute PPP are reported.
16. Interestingly, both Frenkel (1980) and Krugman (1978) find support for PPP using data from the 1920s experience with floating exchange rates.
17. See *inter alia* Roll (1979), Darby (1980), Frenkel (1981), Mishkin (1984) and MacDonald (1985) for papers which present evidence supportive of the random walk view.
18. With these numbers, it would take between 3 and 5 years for a 50 per cent over-valuation of a currency to be cut in half. The statistical significance of this result is, however, somewhat weak.
19. Interestingly, Adler and Lehmann (1983) used the same annual data set and could not reject the random walk model.
20. Taylor and McMahon (1988) apply this methodology to the early 1920s experience with floating exchange rates and find some limited evidence in favour of the hypothesis.

Mathematical Appendix

This very brief appendix is designed to bring together most of the mathematical tools necessary for a better understanding of the analysis in the main text. We have not presented any proofs as this would go well beyond the scope of this book. For a more detailed analysis, with proofs, the reader is advised to consult Dixit (1980), Glaister (1978), Hadley (1964) and Wilson (1979).

The main focus here is on presenting a very brief account of the tools necessary for appreciating the time path characteristics of the solution to systems of linear differential equations with constant coefficients and constant terms. In Section 1 a brief exposition of the notions of characteristic equations, eigenvalues and eigenvectors is followed by illustrative examples of computing eigenvalues and their associated eigenvectors. We then go on to illustrate the diagonalisation of a second-order matrix with distinct eigenvalues. Section 2 builds on Section 1 and goes on to illustrate the time path characteristics of systems of linear differential equations with constant coefficients and constant terms in the case where all state variables are predetermined. In Section 3 we modify the model offered in Section 2 to take account of state variables with no prescribed initial conditions with a view to deriving the unique stable path – the saddle path – which is intimately connected with the analysis of perfect foresight paths. Section 4 concludes this appendix with a brief account of the simplest way of linearising non-linear equations.

1. Characteristic equations, eigenvalues and eigenvectors

Given a square matrix $\mathbf{A}$ of order n, is there a scalar λ and a vector $\mathbf{x} \neq 0$ such that $\mathbf{Ax} = \lambda\mathbf{x}$? If so, then λ is an eigenvalue or a latent root of $\mathbf{A}$ and $\mathbf{x}$ is a corresponding eigenvector or characteristic vector. The case where $\mathbf{x} = 0$ is excluded because in that case any λ would satisfy $\mathbf{Ax} = \lambda\mathbf{x}$ and the problem is trivial.

The equation $\mathbf{Ax} = \lambda\mathbf{x}$ can be written as $\mathbf{Ax} - \lambda\mathbf{x} = 0$, or as $(\mathbf{A} - \lambda\mathbf{I})\mathbf{x} = 0$ where $\mathbf{I}$ is an nth-order identity matrix. If we choose a given λ, then any $\mathbf{x}$ which satisfies $\mathbf{Ax} = \lambda\mathbf{x}$ must also satisfy the set of n homogeneous linear equations in the n unknown elements of $\mathbf{x}$ defined by $(\mathbf{A} - \lambda\mathbf{I})\mathbf{x} = 0$. Thus a solution $\mathbf{x} \neq 0$ will exist if and only if $|\mathbf{A} - \lambda\mathbf{I}| = 0$, that is, if and only if

$$
\begin{vmatrix}
\alpha_{11} - \lambda & \alpha_{12} \cdots & \alpha_{1n} \\
\alpha_{21} & \alpha_{22} - \lambda \cdots & \alpha_{2n} \\
\vdots & & \vdots \\
\alpha_{n1} & \alpha_{n2} \cdots & \alpha_{mn} - \lambda
\end{vmatrix} = 0
$$

$$(A.1)$$

Expanding the determinant of (A.1) we arrive at an nth-degree polynomial in λ which can be expressed by

$$f(\lambda) = |A - \lambda I| = (-\lambda)^n + b_{n-1}(-\lambda)^{n-1} + \ldots\ldots + b_1(-\lambda) + b_0$$

(A.2)

This nth-degree polynomial is called the characteristic polynomial for **A** and $f(\lambda) = 0$ is called the characteristic equation for the matrix **A**. This characteristic equation has n roots. Not all these roots are necessarily distinct, but if a multiple root exists and if it is counted a number of times equal to its multiplicity, there are n roots, which may be either real or complex numbers. The eigenvector corresponding to some eigenvalue λ_i, to be identified with x_i is found by solving $(A - \lambda_i I)x_i = 0$.

As it turns out, the determinant of an nth-order matrix, such as **A**, is equal to the product of its eigenvalues and its trace is equal to the sum of its eigenvalues. As will become evident when we come to discuss the time path characteristics of the solution to a system of linear differential equations, this piece of information can provide valuable assistance in the conduct of stability analysis. At this stage we will merely illustrate, without providing a proof, the relationship described between the eigenvalues of an nth order matrix **A**, its determinant and its trace. To this effect consider writing the polynomial $f(\lambda)$ in factored form, using the roots of $f(\lambda) = 0$; that is

$$f(\lambda) = (\lambda_1 - \lambda)(\lambda_2 - \lambda)\ldots\ldots(\lambda_n - \lambda)$$

(A.3)

Comparison between (A.2) and (A.3) reveals that

$$b_{n-1} = \lambda_1 + \lambda_2 + \lambda_3 + \ldots\ldots + \lambda_n$$
$$b_0 = \lambda_1 \lambda_2 \lambda_3 \ldots\ldots \lambda_n$$

Setting $\lambda = 0$ in (A.2) we can see that $b_0 = |A|$. To establish that b_{n-1} equals the trace of **A** is more difficult. However inspection of (A.1) reveals that the terms $(-\lambda)^n + b_{n-1}(-\lambda)^{n-1}$ can only arise as a result of expanding the product of the terms along the main diagonal. That is, expanding $(\alpha_{11} - \lambda)(\alpha_{22} - \lambda)\ldots(\alpha_{nn} - \lambda)$ reveals that $b_{n-1} = \lambda_1 + \lambda_2 .. + \lambda_n$.

Example: calculating eigenvalues and eigenvectors for a 2×2 matrix

It would be useful at this stage to illustrate how to calculate the eigenvalues and the corresponding eigenvectors of a second-order matrix.

Letting $A = \begin{bmatrix} 0 & 3 \\ -1 & -4 \end{bmatrix}$ we will form

$$|A - \lambda I| = \begin{vmatrix} 0 - \lambda & 3 \\ -1 & -4 - \lambda \end{vmatrix} = f(\lambda)$$

where $f(\lambda) = (-\lambda)^2 - 4(-\lambda) + 3$.
Setting $f(\lambda) = 0$ yields the two roots: $\lambda_1 = -1$, $\lambda_2 = -3$. In order to determine the column eigenvector corresponding to λ_1, call it x_1, we must solve for $(A - \lambda_1 I)x_1 = 0$. Letting $x_1 = (x_{11}, x_{21})'$

we have $\begin{bmatrix} 1 & 3 \\ -1 & -3 \end{bmatrix} \begin{bmatrix} x_{11} \\ x_{21} \end{bmatrix} = \begin{bmatrix} 0 \\ 0 \end{bmatrix}$

which gives $x_{11} = -3x_{21}$. That the elements of $\mathbf{x}_1$ are not uniquely determined should not come as a surprise since if $\mathbf{x}_1$ is an eigenvector corresponding to λ_1 and $\mu \neq 0$ is some scalar, $\mu\mathbf{x}_1$ can also serve as a corresponding eigenvector which suggests the need for normalising eigenvectors. To this effect we can set $x_{11} = 1$, for instance, in which case $x_{21} = -1/3$. Similarly, to determine the column eigenvector corresponding to λ_2, call it $\mathbf{x}_2$, we must solve for $(A - \lambda_2 I)\mathbf{x}_2 = 0$. Letting $x_2 = (x_{12}, x_{22})'$

we have
$$\begin{bmatrix} 3 & 3 \\ -1 & -1 \end{bmatrix}\begin{bmatrix} x_{12} \\ x_{22} \end{bmatrix} = \begin{bmatrix} 0 \\ 0 \end{bmatrix}$$

which yields $x_{12} = -x_{22}$. Normalising by setting $x_{12} = 1$ gives $x_{22} = -1$. Letting $\mathbf{X}$ be the second-order matrix whose column vectors are formed by the normalised elements of the two eigenvectors, we have

$$X = \begin{bmatrix} 3 & 3 \\ -1/3 & -1 \end{bmatrix}$$

In general $\mathbf{X}$ will be an nth order matrix whose columns are the n eigenvectors $\mathbf{x}_1, \mathbf{x}_2, \ldots\mathbf{x}_n$.

Now suppose we want the left-hand side or row eigenvector of $\mathbf{A}$ associated with λ_i, call it $\mathbf{m}_i$. Then we simply solve for $\mathbf{m}_i(A - \lambda_i I) = 0'$, where $\mathbf{m}_i$ is the $1 \times n$ left-hand side or row eigenvector of $\mathbf{A}$ associated with λ_i and $0'$ is a $1 \times n$ vector of zeros. In turn, and since $[\ \mathbf{m}_i(A - \lambda_i I) = 0']' = (A' - \lambda_i I)\mathbf{m}_i' = 0$, the transpose of the row eigenvector of $\mathbf{A}$ associated with λ_i is the column eigenvector of $\mathbf{B} = A'$ associated with λ_i. Let us check.

$$(m_{11}\ m_{12})\begin{bmatrix} 1 & 3 \\ -1 & -3 \end{bmatrix} = \begin{bmatrix} 0 \\ 0 \end{bmatrix}$$

Hence $m_{11} = m_{12}$ and we can normalise by setting $m_{12} = m_{11} = 1$.

$$(m_{21}\ m_{22})\begin{bmatrix} 3 & 3 \\ -1 & -1 \end{bmatrix} = \begin{bmatrix} 0 \\ 0 \end{bmatrix}$$

Hence $3\ m_{21} = m_{22}$ and we can normalise by setting $m_{22} = 1$, and $m_{21} = 1/3$.

Now $A' = \begin{bmatrix} 0 & -1 \\ 3 & -4 \end{bmatrix}$, $(A' - \lambda I) = \begin{bmatrix} -\lambda & -1 \\ 3 & -4-\lambda \end{bmatrix}$

As before we let $\lambda_1 = -1$, and $\lambda_2 = -3$.

$$(A' - \lambda_1 I) = \begin{bmatrix} 1 & -1 \\ 3 & -3 \end{bmatrix}, \quad (A' - \lambda_2 I) = \begin{bmatrix} 3 & -1 \\ 3 & -1 \end{bmatrix}$$

Letting $(b_{11}\ b_{21})'$ be the column eigenvector of $\mathbf{A}'$ associated with λ_1 and $(b_{12}\ b_{22})'$ be the column eigenvector of $\mathbf{A}'$ associated with λ_2 we have

$$\begin{bmatrix} 1 & -1 \\ 3 & -3 \end{bmatrix}\begin{bmatrix} b_{11} \\ b_{21} \end{bmatrix} = \begin{bmatrix} 0 \\ 0 \end{bmatrix}, \quad \begin{bmatrix} 3 & -1 \\ 3 & -1 \end{bmatrix}\begin{bmatrix} b_{12} \\ b_{22} \end{bmatrix} = \begin{bmatrix} 0 \\ 0 \end{bmatrix}$$

so that $b_{11} = b_{21}$, $3b_{12} = b_{22}$ and so that $b_{11} = b_{21} = 1$ can represent the elements of the normalised column eigenvector of A' associated with λ_1 and $b_{12} = 1/3$ and $b_{22} = 1$ can represent the elements of the normalised column eigenvector of A' associated with λ_2 which is what we set out to show.

Diagonalising the matrix A

A remarkable and quite useful result for the purpose of dynamic analysis is the fact that under some conditions $X^{-1} A X$ is a diagonal matrix with the eigenvalues of A on its diagonal in an order which corresponds to the order in which we took the eigenvectors in the columns of X. This result presupposes that X^{-1} exists which requires the n eigenvectors to be linearly independent. A sufficient, but not necessary, condition to ensure that the n eigenvectors are linearly independent is that all the eigenvalues of A are distinct since, according to a theorem, eigenvectors corresponding to distinct eigenvalues are linearly independent.

Let us now confirm this result using the 2×2 A matrix and the associated X matrix considered in the example offered above. Inverting X we get

$$X^{-1} = \begin{bmatrix} 3/2 & 3/2 \\ -1/2 & -3/2 \end{bmatrix}$$

Hence

$$X^{-1}AX = \begin{bmatrix} 3/2 & 3/2 \\ -1/2 & -3/2 \end{bmatrix}\begin{bmatrix} 0 & 3 \\ -1 & -4 \end{bmatrix}\begin{bmatrix} 1 & 1 \\ -1/3 & -1 \end{bmatrix} = \begin{bmatrix} -1 & 0 \\ 0 & -3 \end{bmatrix}$$

which confirms that $X^{-1}AX = \begin{bmatrix} \lambda_1 & 0 \\ 0 & \lambda_2 \end{bmatrix}$

Now suppose we form a matrix M whose ith row m_i is the row eigenvector associated with the ith eigenvalue of A so that M' is a matrix whose ith column, $(m_i)'$, is the column eigenvector of $B = A'$ associated with the ith eigenvalue of A (or B). If the i row eigenvectors of M are independent the matrix M' will diagonalise A' so that $(M')^{-1} A' M'$ is of pure diagonal form with the eigenvalues of A appearing in an order which corresponds to the order in which we took the eigenvectors in the columns of M'. We leave it to the interested reader to confirm this.

2. Simultaneous differential equations systems, stability and time path analysis: the case where all state variables are predetermined

In what follows we will be considering systems of first-order linear differential equations with constant coefficients and constant terms with the view to establishing the requirements for stability and to describing the time path characteristics of the solution for the case where all state variables are predetermined. We will illustrate the general results obtained with the use of a specific example of a system of two linear differential equations.

Let y define an $n \times 1$ vector whose typical element is y_i ($i = 1, 2, ..n$) and let $\dot{y}_i \equiv \partial y_i / \partial t$ define the time derivative of y_i. Similarly let $\dot{y}$ define an $n \times 1$ vector whose typical element is $\dot{y}_i$. Finally let A define an nth order matrix whose typical element, α_{ij} ($j = 1, 2, ...n$), is a constant and let b describe an $n \times 1$ vector of constants. Then a system of n first-order linear differential equations with constant coefficients and constant terms can be described by

$$\dot{y} = Ay + b$$

Setting $\dot{y} = 0$ yields the steady state equilibrium defined by $\bar{y} = A^{-1}(-b)$. Using z to define a vector of deviations from the steady state so that $z \equiv y - \bar{y}$, we can write

$$z = y + (A^{-1})b$$

and hence

$$Az = Ay + b = \dot{y}$$

Since $\dot{z} = \dot{y}$, we have $\dot{z} = Az$, which suggests that for the purposes of stability analysis and the description of the time path characteristics we can focus our analysis on the dynamic behaviour of z, suppressing, for the moment, the influence of b. Let us now introduce an $n \times 1$ vector w defined by $w = X^{-1} z$ where, as before, X is the matrix of the eigenvectors of A. Hence

$$\dot{w} = X^{-1}\dot{z} = X^{-1}Az = X^{-1}AXw$$

Assuming that the eigenvalues of A are distinct, $X^{-1} A X$ will be of pure diagonal form and

$$\dot{w}_1 = \lambda_i w_i$$

where λ_i is the eigenvalue in the ith diagonal element. Hence the time path of w_i can be defined by

$$w_i = w_i(0)e^{\lambda_i t}$$

where e is the base of natural logarithms and $w_i(0)$ is the initial value of w_i. Since, by construction, $z = Xw$, the path of z is fully described by

$$\begin{bmatrix} z_1 \\ z_2 \\ \vdots \\ z_n \end{bmatrix} = \begin{bmatrix} x_{11} & x_{12} \cdots & x_{1n} \\ x_{21} & x_{22} \cdots & x_{2n} \\ \vdots & \vdots & \vdots \\ x_{n1} & x_{n2} & x_{nn} \end{bmatrix} \begin{bmatrix} w_1(0)e^{\lambda_1 t} \\ w_2(0)e^{\lambda_2 t} \\ w_n(0)e^{\lambda_n t} \end{bmatrix}$$

and the path of y_i is fully described by $y_i = z_i + \bar{y}_i$ or by $y_i - \bar{y}_i = z_i$. For instance,

$$y_1 - \bar{y}_1 = x_{11}w_1(0)e^{\lambda_1 t} + x_{12}w_2(0)e^{\lambda_2 t} \ldots\ldots + x_{1n}w_n(0)e^{\lambda_n t}$$

This system is stable if and only if each of the state variables is shown to approach its (long-run) equilibrium value after 'sufficient' time has lapsed since the (initial) equilibrium was disturbed. Given that all the $w_i(0)$ are predetermined, by assumption, the only way for each of the y_i to approach $\bar{y}_i$ as $t \to \infty$ is for each of the $e^{\lambda_i t}$ terms to approach zero as $t \to \infty$. In turn, this can happen if and only if the real part of every λ_i is negative. In the case where A is second-order stability translates to the requirement that the determinant of A is positive and its trace is negative since, as we have shown, the determinant of a matrix is equal to the product of its eigenvalues and the trace of a matrix is equal to the sum of its eigenvalues.

It will prove convenient and instructive, at this stage, to use the above analysis to illustrate the solution to a system of two first-order linear differential equations with constant coefficients and constant terms assigning specific numerical values to coefficients, to the constant terms and to the initial conditions. To this effect let

$$\dot{y}_1(t) + \; 2\dot{y}_2(t) + 2y_1(t) + 5y_2(t) \; = 77$$
$$\dot{y}_2(t) \; + y_1(t) \; + 4y_2(t) \; = 61$$

With initial conditions given by $y_1(0) = 6$, $y_2(0) = 12$. Dropping t and arranging the two equations in matrix form we get

$$\begin{bmatrix} 1 & 2 \\ 0 & 1 \end{bmatrix} \begin{bmatrix} \dot{y}_1 \\ \dot{y}_2 \end{bmatrix} = \begin{bmatrix} -2 & -5 \\ -1 & -4 \end{bmatrix} \begin{bmatrix} y_1 \\ y_2 \end{bmatrix} + \begin{bmatrix} 77 \\ 66 \end{bmatrix}$$

or

$$\begin{bmatrix} \dot{y}_1 \\ \dot{y}_2 \end{bmatrix} = \begin{bmatrix} 0 & 3 \\ -1 & -4 \end{bmatrix} \begin{bmatrix} y_1 \\ y_2 \end{bmatrix} + \begin{bmatrix} -45 \\ 61 \end{bmatrix}$$

which is of the form $\dot{y} = Ay + b$. Setting $\dot{y} = 0$ we obtain the steady-state equilibrium vector $\bar{y}$ given by $\bar{y} = A^{-1}(-b)$ where

$$\begin{bmatrix} \bar{y}_1 \\ \bar{y}_2 \end{bmatrix} = \begin{bmatrix} -4/3 & -1 \\ 1/3 & 0 \end{bmatrix} \begin{bmatrix} 45 \\ -61 \end{bmatrix} = \begin{bmatrix} 1 \\ 15 \end{bmatrix}$$

The reader will have noticed that the matrix A above is the exact same matrix we used in the example offered to calculate eigenvalues and eigenvectors. Hence the eigenvalues of A are given by $\lambda_1 = -1$, $\lambda_2 = -3$ and the matrix of the corresponding eigenvectors X and its inverse are given by

$$X = \begin{bmatrix} 1 & 1 \\ -1/3 & -1 \end{bmatrix}$$

and by

$$X^{-1} = \begin{bmatrix} 3/2 & 3/2 \\ -1/2 & -3/2 \end{bmatrix}$$

And since by construction $w = X^{-1}z$, the following must hold:

$$w_1(0) = (3/2)z_1(0) + (3/2)z_2(0) \quad \text{and}$$
$$w_2(0) = (-1/2)z_1(0) + (-3/2)z_2(0)$$

There remains to determine $z_1(0)$ and $z_2(0)$ to define the time paths of y_1 and y_2. But this is simple since $z_1(0) = y_1(0) - \bar{y}_1 = 5$, and $z_2(0) = y_2(0) - \bar{y}_2 = -3$. Hence $w_1(0) = 3$, $w_2(0) = 2$ and the paths of $y_1 - \bar{y}_1$ and $y_2 - \bar{y}_2$ are given by

$$y_1 - \bar{y}_1 = (1)(3)e^{-t} + (1)(2)e^{-3t} = y_1 - 1$$
$$y_2 - \bar{y}_2 = (-1/3)(3)e^{-t} + (-1)(2)e^{-3t} = y_2 - 15$$

Notice that at $t = 0$ the prescribed initial conditions obtain. To summarise: knowledge of the initial and the terminal conditions (or simply knowledge of the initial deviation from the steady state) together with the eigenvalues and the associated eigenvectors allows us to fully describe the time path of the variables. In what follows, and for obvious reasons, we will call the **A** matrix the matrix of coefficients.

3. Simultaneous differential equations systems, stability and time path analysis when not all state variables are predetermined

Typically, rational expectations models involve state variables which are free to 'jump' when the economy is subjected to a disturbance. This means that the initial condition for these variables is not prescribed by the model. Consequently, if all the roots of the relevant characteristic equation were to have real parts which are negative any initial condition for these jump variables would satisfy stability: the number of stable paths would be infinite. To guarantee the existence of a unique stable path – the saddle path – the number of stable roots must equal the number of predetermined state variables. Only then can we eliminate instability and non uniqueness because only then can we force the path of the economy to be fully defined by the initial condition of each predetermined variable and to be driven only by the stable roots.

The above procedure briefly describes the way economists have handled adjustments to purely unanticipated disturbances under rational expectations. Things are considerably more complicated when we allow for disturbances which are anticipated to occur at some future date. For the study of adjustments under rational expectations to previously anticipated disturbances the reader is directed to Wilson (1979).

To illustrate the characteristics of the time path of a system of differential equations involving state variables which are free to jump, let us consider, first, a system of two first-order linear differential equations where one of the state variables is predetermined and the other is a forward looking, free, or jump variable. We shall continue to use the notation previously used with one exception: to distinguish between the stable and the unstable root we shall denote the former by ρs and the latter by ρu. Thus, consider the path described by

$$z_1 = x_{11}w_1(0)e^{\rho st} + x_{12}w_2(0)e^{\rho ut}$$
$$z_2 = x_{21}w_1(0)e^{\rho st} + x_{22}w_2(0)e^{\rho ut}$$

where $z_1 \equiv y_1 - \bar{y}_1$ and $z_2 \equiv y_2 - \bar{y}_2$ and where, without loss of generality, we have taken x_{11}, x_{21} to be the elements of the eigenvector associated with the stable root and x_{12}, x_{22} to be the elements of the eigenvector associated with the unstable root. To fix ideas, let us assume that y_1 is a predetermined state variable and that y_2 is a jump variable. Let us also assume that we are interested in describing the path following a purely unanticipated disturbance occurring at $t = 0$. In that case the unique saddle path is found by setting

$w_2(0) = 0$. This eliminates the influence of the unstable root and, in turn, serves to define uniquely the path of the jump variable since $z_2 = (x_{21}/x_{11})z_1$ and the initial condition of z_2, $z_2(0)$ is fully defined by $z_1(0)$. Notice that x_{21}/x_{11} defines the slope of the saddle path drawn in (z_2, z_1) space. Notice also that $x_{21}/x_{11} = -(\alpha_{11} - \rho s)/(\alpha_{12}) = -\alpha_{21}/(\alpha_{22} - \rho s)$ where α_{11}, α_{12}, α_{21}, α_{22} are the elements of the coefficient matrix.

To better appreciate the analysis in Chapter 6, suppose that there are two pre-determined state variables and one jump variable. Let y_1, y_2 be the two predetermined state variables and let y_3 be the jump state variable and let us continue to use the vector $\mathbf{z}$ to denote deviations from steady states. Let ρ_1, ρ_2, denote the two stable roots and ρ_3 denote the unstable root. Finally let $\mathbf{x_1}$, $\mathbf{x_2}$ and $\mathbf{x_3}$ be the column eigenvectors associated with ρ_1, ρ_2 and ρ_3, respectively, not forgetting that each eigenvector contains three elements. Then we can write.

$$z_1 = x_{11}w_1(0)e^{\rho_1 t} + x_{12}w_2(0)e^{\rho_2 t} + x_{13}w_3(0)e^{\rho_3 t}$$

$$z_2 = x_{21}w_1(0)e^{\rho_1 t} + x_{22}w_2(0)e^{\rho_2 t} + x_{23}w_3(0)e^{\rho_3 t}$$

$$z_3 = x_{31}w_1(0)e^{\rho_1 t} + x_{32}w_2(0)e^{\rho_2 t} + x_{33}w_3(0)e^{\rho_3 t}$$

As before, we can set $w_3(0) = 0$ and proceed to obtain the saddle path from the model above.

This procedure, however, is not the most computationally efficient to employ. To make the connection of the analysis of Chapter 6 with the analysis offered in this appendix, consider the 3×3 system given by $\dot{\mathbf{z}} = \mathbf{A}\mathbf{z}$ with z_3 being the jump variable. Transposing, we get $\dot{\mathbf{z}}' = \mathbf{z}' \mathbf{A}'$. Letting $\mathbf{M}$ define a 3×3 matrix whose *i*th row is the row eigenvector of $\mathbf{A}$ associated with the *i*th root of the characteristic equation of $\mathbf{A}$, the *i*th column of $\mathbf{M}'$ will be the column eigenvector of $\mathbf{A}'$ associated with the same root. If $\mathbf{M}'$ is non-singular then $(\mathbf{M}')^{-1} \mathbf{A}' \mathbf{M}'$ will be of pure diagonal form with the roots of the characteristic equation of $\mathbf{A}$ appearing in the main diagonal. Let us also define a 3×1 vector $\mathbf{w}$ by $\mathbf{w} = \mathbf{M}\,\mathbf{z}$. Hence $\mathbf{z} = \mathbf{M}^{-1} \mathbf{w}$, and $\mathbf{z}' = \mathbf{w}' (\mathbf{M}^{-1})' = \mathbf{w}' (\mathbf{M}')^{-1}$. Taking time derivatives, $\dot{\mathbf{z}}' = \dot{\mathbf{w}}' (\mathbf{M}')^{-1} = \mathbf{z}' \mathbf{A}' = \mathbf{w}' (\mathbf{M}')^{-1} \mathbf{A}'$. Post multiplying by $\mathbf{M}'$ we arrive at $\dot{\mathbf{w}}' = \mathbf{w}' (\mathbf{M}')^{-1} \mathbf{A}' \mathbf{M}'$, which confirms that $\dot{\mathbf{w}}' = \rho_i \mathbf{w}'$, where ρ_i is the *i*th root of the characteristic equation with ρ_3 being the unstable root. So far it would seem that we have made little progress, until we realise the fundamental result that $m_{31} z_1 + m_{32} z_2 + m_{33} z_3 = w_3 = 0$. Normalising by setting m_{33} equal to -1 and using a tilde to denote the normalised values of the two other elements of the third row of $\mathbf{M}$, we have $z_3 = \tilde{m}_{31} z_1 + \tilde{m}_{32} z_2$ which can be used to fully define the initial value of z_3. The entire path of the model can then be derived by sub-stituting the initial value of z_3 into the model. The computational advantage of this pro-cedure is that we only need to compute one eigenvector, the eigenvector associated with the unstable root.

4. Linearising non-linear equations

More often than not economic relations are presented in non-linear form and this makes it very difficult to conduct dynamic analysis, in particular, and to obtain explicit solutions in general. In these circumstances economists resort to linearising non-linear equations using Taylor's expansion theorem. To illustrate, very briefly, consider an n component vector $\mathbf{x}$ and the relationship $f(\mathbf{x})$ evaluated at the equilibrium value of $\mathbf{x}$ given by $\bar{\mathbf{x}}$. Then, provided that $\mathbf{x}$ is close to $\bar{\mathbf{x}}$, we can evaluate $f(\mathbf{x})$, approximately, by

$$f(x) \approx f(\bar{x}) + f_1(\bar{x})(x_1 - \bar{x}_1) + f_2(\bar{x})(x_2 - \bar{x}_2) + \ldots\ldots f_n(\bar{x})(x_n - \bar{x}_n)$$

where $f_i(\overline{\mathbf{x}})$ is the derivative of $f(\mathbf{x})$ with respect to x_i evaluated at $\overline{\mathbf{x}}$ and where $x_i - \overline{x}_i$ is the deviation of x_i from its equilibrium value.

Consider, next, a very simple system of two non-linear dynamic equations given by

$$\dot{y}_1 = f(y_1, y_2)$$
$$\dot{y}_2 = g(y_1, y_2)$$

Letting $\overline{y}_1$ and $\overline{y}_2$ denote the steady-state values of y_1 and y_2, respectively, obtained by setting $\dot{y}_1 = \dot{y}_2 = 0$ and letting $\overline{\mathbf{y}}$ denote the equilibrium vector $(\overline{y}_1 \ \overline{y}_2)$ then, provided we are close to $\overline{\mathbf{y}}$, we can approximate $\dot{y}_1$ and $\dot{y}_2$ by

$$\dot{y}_1 \approx f_1(\overline{\mathbf{y}})(y_1 - \overline{y}_1) + f_2(\overline{\mathbf{y}})(y_2 - \overline{y}_2)$$
$$\dot{y}_2 \approx g_1(\overline{\mathbf{y}})(y_1 - \overline{y}_1) + g_2(\overline{\mathbf{y}})(y_2 - \overline{y}_2)$$

where $f_i(\overline{\mathbf{y}})$ is the derivative of $\dot{y}_1$ with respect to y_i $(i = 1, 2)$ evaluated at the steady state, $g_i(\overline{\mathbf{y}})$ is the derivate of $\dot{y}_2$ with respect to y_i evaluated at the steady state and where $y_i - \overline{y}_i$ is the deviation of y_i from its steady state. Letting, as before, z_i denote the deviation of y_i from its steady state and noting that $\dot{z}_i = \dot{y}_i$ we can write

$$\dot{z} = Az, \text{ where } A = \begin{bmatrix} f_1(\overline{\mathbf{y}}) & f_2(\overline{\mathbf{y}})_1 \\ g_1(\overline{\mathbf{y}}) & g_2(\overline{\mathbf{y}}) \end{bmatrix}$$

Bibliography

Abuaf, N. and P. Jorion (1990) 'Purchasing Power Parity in the Long Run', *The Journal of Finance*, vol. 45, pp. 157–74.

Adams, Charles and Daniel Gros (1986) 'The consequences of real exchange rate rules for inflation: Some illustrative examples', *IMF Staff Papers*, 33, pp. 439–76.

Adler, M. and B. Lehmann (1983) 'Deviations from Purchasing Power Parity in the Long Run', *The Journal of Finance*, vol. 38, pp. 1471–83.

Alexander, S.S. (1952) 'Effects of a Devaluation on a Trade Balance', *International Monetary Fund Staff Papers*, vol. 2, pp. 263–78

Alexander, S.S. (1959) 'Effects of a Devaluation: A Simplified Synthesis of Elasticities and Absorption Approaches', *American Economic Review*, vol. 49, pp. 22–42.

Ando, A. and F. Modigliani (1963) 'The 'Life Cycle Hypothesis of Saving: Aggregate Implications and Tests', *American Economic Review*, March.

Aoki, Masanao (1981) *Dynamic Analysis of Open Economies* (New York: Academic Press).

Backus, D. (1984) 'Empirical Models of the Exchange Rate: Separating the Wheat from the Chaff', *Canadian Journal of Economics*, vol. XVII, no. 4, pp. 824–46.

Baillie, R.T. and D.D. Selover (1987) 'Cointegration and Models of Exchange Rate Determination', *International Journal of Forecasting*, vol. 3, pp. 43–52.

Barr, D. (1989) 'Exchange Rate Dynamics: An Empirical Analysis', in R. MacDonald and M.P. Taylor (eds), *Exchange Rates and Open Economy Macroeconomics* (Oxford: Blackwell).

Barro, Robert, J. and David B. Gordon (1983) 'Rules, Discretion and Reputation in a Model of Monetary Policy', *Journal of Monetary Economics*, vol. 12, pp. 101–21.

Basevi, Giorgio and Francesco Giavazzi (1987) 'Conflicts and Coordination in the European Monetary System', in Alfred Steinherr and Daniel Weiserbs (eds), *Employment and Growth: Issues for the 1980's* (Dordrecht: Martinus Nijhoff).

Begg, D.K.H. (1982) *The Rational Expectations Revolution in Macroeconomics Theories and Evidence* (Oxford: Phillip Allan).

Bertola, Guiseppe (1989) 'Factor Mobility, Uncertainty and Exchange Rate Regimes', in Marcello de Cecco and Alberto Giovannini (eds), *A European Central Bank? Perspectives on Monetary Unification after Ten Years of the EMS* (Cambridge: Cambridge University Press).

Bhandari, J.S. (1982) *Exchange Rate Determination and Adjustment*, Praeger Studies in International Economics and Finance (New York: Praeger).

Bilson, J.F.O. (1978a) 'Rational Expectations and the Exchange Rate', in J.A. Frankel and H.G. Johnson (eds), *The Economics of Exchange Rates* (Reading, Mass.: Addison-Wesley).

Bilson, J.F.O. (1978b) 'The Monetary Approach to the Exchange Rate – Some Empirical Evidence', *IMF Staff Papers*, 25, pp. 48–75.

Bilson, J.F.O. (1981) 'The Speculative Efficiency Hypothesis', *Journal of Business*, vol. 54, pp. 435–51.

Bisignano, Joseph, and Kevin Hoover (1982), 'Some Suggested Improvements to a Simple Portfolio Balance Model of Exchange Rate Determination with Special Reference to the US Dollar/Canadian Dollar Rate', *Weltwirtschaftliches Archiv*, vol. 119, pp. 19–37.

Boothe, P. and D. Glassman (1987a) 'Off the Mark: Lessons for Exchange Rate Modelling', Oxford Economic Papers, vol. 39, pp. 443–57.

Boothe, P. and D. Glassman (1987b) 'The Statistical Distribution of Exchange Rates: Empirical Evidence and Economic Implications', *Journal of International Economics*, vol. 22, pp. 236–50.

Boughton, J.M. (1984) 'Exchange Rate Movements and Adjustment in Financial Markets: Quarterly Estimates for Major Currencies', IMF Staff Papers, 31, pp. 445–68.

Branson, W.H. (1977) 'Asset Markets and Relative Prices in Exchange Rate Determination', *Reprint Series No. 98*, Institute for International Economic Studies.

Branson, W.H. and H. Halttunen (1979) 'Asset-market Determination of Exchange Rates: Initial Empirical and Policy Results', in J.P. Martin and A. Smith, *Trade and Payments Adjustment under Flexible Exchange Rates* (London: Macmillan).

Branson, W.H., H. Halttunen and P. Masson (1977) 'Exchange Rates in the Short Run: The Dollar–Deutschemark Rate', *European Economic Review*, vol. 10, pp. 303–24.

Branson, W.H., H. Halttunen and P. Masson (1979) 'Exchange Rates in the Short Run', *European Economic Review*, vol. 10, pp. 395–402.

Buiter, W.H. (1987) 'Does an Improvement in the Current Account or the Trade Balance at Full Employment Require a Depreciation of the Real Exchange Rate?', Yale University and NBER, mimeo.

Buiter, W.H. and Richard C. Marston (eds) (1985) *International Economic Policy Coordination* (Cambridge: Cambridge University Press).

Buiter, W.H. and M.H. Miller (1981) 'Monetary Policy and International Competitiveness', *Oxford Economic Papers*, vol. 33 (supplement) pp. 143–75.

Buiter, W.H. and M.H. Miller (1981) 'Monetary Policy and International Competitiveness: The Problems of Adjustment', in W.A. Eltis and P.J.N. Sinclair (eds), *The Money Supply and the Exchange Rate* (Oxford: Clarendon Press).

Buiter, W.H. and M.H. Miller (1982) 'Real Exchange Rate Over-shooting and the Output Cost of Bringing Down Inflation', *European Economic Review*, vol. 18, (1/2), pp. 85–123.

Buiter, W.H. and M.H. Miller (1983) 'Real Exchange Rate Over-shooting and the Output Cost of Bringing Down Inflation: Some Further Results', in J.A. Frankel (ed.), *Exchange Rates and International Macroeconomics* (Chicago: University of Chicago Press).

Campbell, J.Y. and R.H. Clarida (1987) 'The Term Structure of Euromarket Interest Rates: An Empirical Investigation', *Journal of Monetary Economics*, vol. 19, pp. 25–44.

Canova, F. and T. Ito (1988) 'On Time Series Properties of Time-varying Risk Premium in the Yen/Dollar Exchange Market', *National Bureau of Economic Research*, Working Paper, no. 2678.

Canzoneri, Matthew B. and J.A. Gray (1985) 'Monetary Policy Games and the Consequences of Non-Cooperative Behaviour', *International Economic Review*, vol. 26, no. 3, pp. 547–64.

Canzoneri, Matthew B. and Dale W. Henderson (1991) *Monetary Policy in Interdependent Economies: A Game Theoretic Approach* (Cambridge, Mass.: MIT Press).

Canzoneri, Matthew B. and Carol A. Rogers (1990) 'Is the European Community an Optimal Currency Area? Tax Smoothing versus the Cost of Multiple Currencies', *American Economic Review*, vol. 80, no. 3, pp. 419–33.

Chen, C.N. (1975) 'Economic Growth, Portfolio Balance, and the Balance of Payments', *Canadian Journal of Economics*, February.

Cheung, Y-W and K.S. Lai (1993) 'Long-Run Purchasing Power Parity during the Recent Float', *Journal of International Economics*, vol. 34, pp. 181–93.

Chow, Gregory C. (1975) *Analysis and Control of Dynamic Economic Systems* (New York: John Wiley).

Cochrane, J.H. (1988) 'How Big is the Random Walk in GNP?', *Journal of Political Economy*, vol. 96, pp. 893–920.

Cohen, Daniel and Charles Wyplosz (1989) 'The European Monetary Union: An Agnostic Evaluation', discussion paper no. 306 (London: Centre for Economic Policy Research).

Cumby, R.E. and M. Obstfeld (1981) 'Exchange Rate Expectations and Nominal Interest Rates: A Test of the Fisher Hypothesis', *Journal of Finance*, vol. 36, pp. 697–703.

Cumby, R.E. and M. Obstfeld (1984) 'International Interest Rate and Price Level Linkages under Flexible Exchange Rates: A Review of the Recent Evidence', in *Exchange Rate Theory and Practice* (Chicago: Chicago University Press).

Darby, M. (1980) 'Does Purchasing Power Parity Work?', *National Bureau of Economic Research*, Working Paper, no. 607.

Davidson, J. (1985) 'Econometric Modelling of the Sterling Effective Exchange Rate', *Review of Economic Studies*, vol. 211, pp. 231–40.

De Long J.B., A. Schleifer, L.H. Summers and R.J. Waldman (1990) 'Noise Trader Risk in Financial Markets', *Journal of Political Economy*, vol. 98, pp. 703–38.

Delors Committee (1989) *Report on Economic and Monetary Union in the European Community*, Committee for the Study of Economic and Monetary Union.

Dixit, A.K. (1980) 'A Solution Technique for Rational Expectations Models with Applications to Exchange Rate and Interest Rate Determination', University of Warwick, mimeo.

Dominguez, K. (1986) 'Are Foreign Exchange Forecasts Rational? New Evidence from Survey Data', *Economics Letters*, vol. 21, pp. 277–81.

Domowitz, I. and C. Hakkio (1985) 'Conditional Variance and the Risk Premium in the Foreign Exchange Market', *Journal of International Economics*, vol. 19, pp. 47–66.

Dooley, M. and P. Isard (1982) 'A Portfolio Balance Rational Expectations Model of the Dollar–Mark Exchange Rate', *Journal of International Economics*, vol. 12, pp. 257–76.

Dornbusch, R. (1971) 'Notes on Growth and the Balance of Payments', *Canadian Journal of Economics*, August.

Dornbusch, R. (1975) 'A Portfolio Balance Model of the Open Economy', *Journal of Monetary Economics*, 1 January, vol. 1, pp. 3–20.

Dornbusch, R. (1976) 'Expectations and Exchange Rate Dynamics', *Journal of Political Economy*, vol. 84, pp. 1161–76.

Dornbusch, R. (1979) 'Monetary Policy under Exchange Rate Flexibility', in *Managed Exchange Rate Flexibility: The Recent Experience* (Boston: Federal Reserve Bank of Boston).

Dornbusch, R. (1980) 'Exchange Rate Economics: Where do we Stand?', *Brookings Papers on Economic Activity*, vol. 1. pp. 143–85.

Dornbusch, Rudiger (1988) 'The European Monetary System, the Dollar and the Yen', in Francesco Giavazzi, Stefano Micossi and Marcus Miller (eds), *The European Monetary System* (Cambridge: Cambridge University Press).

Dornbusch, R. and S. Fischer (1980) 'Exchange Rates and the Current Account', *American Economic Review*, vol. 70, pp. 1960–71.

Dornbusch, R. and J.A. Frankel (1988) 'The Flexible Exchange Rate System: Experience and Alternatives', *National Bureau of Economic Research*, Working Paper, no. 2464.

Driskell, R.A. (1981) 'Exchange Rate Dynamics: An Empirical Investigation', *Journal of Political Economy*, vol. 89, no. 2, pp. 357–71.

Driskell, R.A. and S.M. Sheffrin (1981) 'On the Mark: Comment', *American Economic Review*, vol. 71, no. 5, pp. 1068–74.

Edison, H.J. (1985) 'Purchasing Power Parity: A Quantitative Reassessment of the 1920's Experience', *Journal of International Money and Finance*, vol. 4, pp. 361–372.

Edison, H.J., Marcus H. Miller and John Williamson (1987) 'On evaluating and extending the target zone proposal', *Journal of Policy Modeling*, vol. 9, no. 1, pp. 199–227.

Enders, W. (1988) 'ARIMA and Cointegration Tests of PPP under Fixed and Flexible Exchange Rates', *Review of Economics and Statistics*, pp. 505–8.

Engle, R. and C.W.J. Granger (1987) 'Cointegration and Error Correction: Representation, Estimation and Testing', *Econometrica*, vol. 55, pp. 251–76.

Evans, G.W. (1986) 'A Test for Speculative Bubbles in the Sterling–Dollar Exchange Rate: 1981–84', *American Economic Review*, vol. 76, pp. 621–36.

Fama, E.F. (1984) 'Forward and Spot Exchange Rates', *Journal of Monetary Economics*, vol. 14, no. 3, pp. 319–38.

Finn, M.G. (1986) 'Forecasting the Exchange Rate: A Monetary or Random Walk Phenomenon?', *Journal of International Money and Finance*, vol. 5, pp. 181–220.

Fleming, J.M. (1962) 'Domestic Financial Policies Under Fixed and Floating Exchange Rates', *IMF Staff Papers*, 9, pp. 369–79.

Frankel, J.A. (1979) 'On the Mark – A Theory of Floating Exchange Rates Based on Real Interest Differentials', *American Economic Review*, 69, pp. 610–22.

Frankel, J.A. (1983) 'Monetary and Portfolio Balance Models of Exchange Rate Determination', in J.S. Bhandari and B.H. Putman (eds), *Economic Interdependence and Flexible Exchange Rates* (Cambridge, Mass.: MIT Press).

Frankel, J.A. (1982a) 'A Test of Perfect Substitutability in the Foreign Exchange Market', *Southern Economic Journal*, vol. 49, no. 2, pp. 406–16.

Frankel, J.A. (1982b) 'In Search of the Exchange Risk Premium: A Six-currency Test Assuming Mean Variance Optimization', *Journal of International Money and Finance*, vol. 1, pp. 255–74.

Frankel, J.A. (1984) 'Tests of Monetary and Portfolio Balance Models of Exchange Rate Determination', in J.F.O. Bilson and R.C. Marston (eds), *Exchange Rate Theory and Practice* (University of Chicago Press), pp. 84–97.

Frankel, J.A. (1985) 'The Dazzling Dollar', *Brookings Papers on Economic Activity*, vol. 1, pp. 199–217.

Frankel, J.A. and K. Froot (1989) 'Interpreting Tests of Forward Discount Bias using Survey Data on Exchange Rate Expectations', *Quarterly Journal of Economics*, vol. CIV, 1, pp. 139–61.

Fraser, P., M.P. Taylor and A. Webster (1991) 'An Empirical Analysis of Long-run Purchasing Power Parity as a Theory of International Commodity Arbitrage', *Applied Economics*, vol. 23, pp. 1749–60.

Frenkel, J.A. (1976) 'A Monetary Approach to the Exchange Rate: Doctrinal Aspects and Empirical Evidence', *Scandinavian Journal of Economics*, vol. 78, pp. 169–91.

Frenkel, J.A. (1980) 'Exchange Rates, Prices and Money, Lessons from the 1920's', *American Economic Association, Papers and Proceedings*, vol. 70, pp. 235–42.

Frenkel, J.A. (1981) 'Flexible Exchange Rates, Prices and the Role of 'News': Lessons from the 1970s', *Journal of Political Economy*, vol. 89, no. 4, pp. 665–705.

Frenkel, J.A., Morris Goldstein and Paul Masson (1989) 'Simulating the Effects of some simple Coordinated versus Uncoordinated Policy Rules', in Ralph Bryant *et al.* (eds), *Macroeconomic Policies in an Interdependent World* (Washington, DC: Brookings Institution).

Friedman, B.M. and V.V. Roley (1987) 'Aspects of Investor Behaviour under Risk', in G.R. Feiwel (ed.), *Arrow and the Ascent of Modern Economic Theory* (New York: New York University Press) pp. 626–53.

Froot, K.A. and T. Ito (1988) 'On the Consistency of Short-run and Long-run Exchange Rate Expectations', *National Bureau of Economic Research,* Working Paper, no. 2577.

Giavazzi, Francesco and Alberto Giovannini (1989a) *Limiting Exchange Rate Flexibility: The European Monetary System* (Cambridge: Cambridge University Press).

Giavazzi, Francesco and Alberto Giovannini (1989b) 'Monetary Policy Interactions under Managed Exchange Rates', *Economica*, vol. 56, no. 222, pp. 199–214.

Giovannini, A. and P. Jorion (1987) 'Interest rates and risk premia in the stock market and in the foreign exchange markets', *Journal of International Money and Finance*, 6.

Glaister, S. (1978) *Mathematical Methods For Economists* (Oxford: Basil Blackwell).

Gregory, A.W. and T.H. McCurdy (1984) 'Testing Unbiasedness in the Forward Foreign Exchange Market: A Specification Analysis', *Journal of International Money and Finance*, vol. 3, pp. 357–68.

Gros, Daniel (1988) 'Seigniorage versus EMS Discipline: Some Welfare Considerations', working document No. 38 (Brussels: CEPS).

Haberler, G. (1949) 'The Market for Foreign Exchange and the Stability of the Balance of Payments: a Theoretical Analysis', *Kyklos*, vol. 3, pp. 193–218.

Hacche, G. and J. Townend (1981) 'Exchange Rates and Monetary Policy: Modelling Sterling's Effective Exchange Rate, 1972–80', in W.A. Eltis and P.J.N. Sinclair, *The Money Supply and the Exchange Rate* (Oxford: Oxford University Press).

Hacche, G. and J. Townend (1983) 'Some Problems in Exchange Rate Modelling: The Case of Sterling', *Zeitschrift für Nationale Ökonomie*, vol. 3, pp. 127–62.

Hadley, G. (1964) *Linear Algebra*, (Reading, Mass: Addison-Wesley).

Hallwood, P. and R. MacDonald (1994) *International Money and Finance*, 2nd edn (Oxford: Blackwell).

Hamada, Koichi (1974) 'Alternative Exchange Rate Systems and the Interdependence of Monetary Policies', in R. Aliber (ed.), *National Monetary Policies and the International System* (Chicago: University of Chicago Press).

Hamada, Koichi (1985) *The Political Economy of International Monetary Interdependence* (Cambridge, Mass.: MIT Press).

Hansen, L.P. and R.J. Hodrick (1983) 'Risk Averse Speculation in the Forward Foreign Exchange Market: An Econometric Analysis of Linear Models', in J.A. Frenkel (ed.), *Exchange Rates and International Macroeconomics* (Chicago: University of Chicago Press for National Bureau of Economic Research).

Hausman, J.A. (1978) 'Specification Tests in Economics', *Econometrica*, vol. 46, pp. 1251–72.

Haynes, S.E. and J.A. Stone (1981) 'On the Mark: Comment', *American Economic Review*, vol. 71, no. 5, pp. 1060–7.

Hodrick, R.J. (1978) 'An Empirical Analysis of the Monetary Approach to the Determination of the Exchange Rate', in J.A. Frenkel and H.G. Johnson (eds), *The Economics of Exchange Rates* (Reading, Mass.: Addison-Wesley).

Hodrick, R.J. and S. Srivastava (1984) 'An Investigation of Risk and Return in Forward Foreign Exchange', *Journal of International Money and Finance*, vol. 3, pp. 1–29.

Hodrick, R.J. and S. Srivastava (1986) 'The Covariation of Risk Premiums and Expected Future Spot Exchange Rates', *Journal of International Money and Finance*, vol. 5, S5–S22.

Hoffman, D. and D. Schlagenhauf (1983) 'Rational Expectations and Monetary Models of Exchange Rate Determination: An Empirical Examination', *Journal of Monetary Economics*, vol. 11, pp. 247–60.

Hooper, P. and J. Morton (1982) 'Fluctuations in the dollar: A Model of Nominal and Real Exchange Rate Determination', *Journal of International Money and Finance*, vol. 1, no. 1, pp. 39–56.

Huang, R.D. (1981) 'The Monetary Approach to Exchange Rate in an Efficient Foreign Exchange Market: Tests based on Volatility', *The Journal of Finance*, vol. 36, no. 1, pp. 31–41.

Huang, R., (1984) 'Some Alternative Tests of Forward Exchange Rates as Predictors of Future Spot Rates', *Journal of International Money and Finance*, vol. 3, no. 2, pp. 157–67.

Huizinga, J. (1987) 'An Empirical Investigation of the Long-run Behaviour of Real Exchange Rates', in K. Brunner and A.H. Meltzer (eds), *Carnegie Rochester Conference Series on Public Policy* (Amsterdam: North-Holland).

Isard, P. (1977) 'How far can we push the Law of One Price?', *American Economic Review*, vol. 67, pp. 942–8.

Isard, P. (1980) 'Expected and Unexpected Changes in Exchange Rates: The Roles of Relative Price Levels, Balance of Payments Factors, Interest Rates and Risk', *International Finance Discussion Papers*, no. 156.

Ishiyama, Y. (1975) 'The Theory of Optimum Currency Areas: A Survey', *IMF Staff Papers*, pp. 344–83.

Ito, T. (1988) 'Foreign Exchange Rate Expectations: Micro Survey Data', *National Bureau of Economic Research*, Working Paper, no. 22679.

Jensen, Henrik (1991) 'Tax Distortions, Unemployment and International Policy Cooperation', *mimeo*, University of Aarhus.

Johansen, S. (1988) 'Statistical Analysis of Cointegrating Vectors', *Journal of Economic Dynamics and Control*, vol. 12, pp. 231–54.

Johnson, H.G. (1958) 'Towards a General Theory of the Balance of Payments', *International Trade and Economic Growth* (London: George Allen & Unwin) pp. 153–68.

Johnson, H.G. and J.A. Frenkel (1976) 'The Monetary Approach to the Balance of Payments. Essential Concepts and Historical Origins', in H.G. Johnson and J.A. Frenkel (eds), *The Monetary Approach to the Balance of Payments* (London: George Allen and Unwin).

Kaminsky, G.L. and R. Peruga (1988) 'Risk Premium and the Foreign Exchange Market', mimeo, University of California, San Diego.

Kearney, C.P. and R. MacDonald (1985) 'Asset Markets and the Exchange Rate: A Structural Model of the Sterling–Dollar Rate 1972–1982', *Journal of Economic Studies*, vol. 12, pp. 33–60.

Kearney, C. and R. MacDonald (1986a) 'A Structural Portfolio Balance Model of the Sterling–Dollar Exchange Rate', *Weltwirtschaftliches Archiv*, vol. 122, no. 3, pp. 478–96.

Kearney, C. and R. MacDonald (1986b) 'Intervention and Sterilisation under Floating Exchange Rates: The UK 1973–1983', *European Economic Review*, vol. 30, pp. 345–64.

Kearney, C. and R. MacDonald (1990) 'Rational Expectations, Bubbles and Monetary Models of the Exchange Rate: The Australian/US Dollar Rate during the Recent Float', *Australian Economic Papers*, June, pp. 1–20.

Kenen, Peter B. (1987) 'Global Policy Optimitization and the Exchange-rate Regime', *Journal of Policy Modeling*, vol. 9, no. 1, pp. 19–63.

Komiya, R. (1969) 'Economic Growth and the Balance of Payments: A Monetary Approach', *Journal of Political Economy*, January/February.

Kouri, P. (1976) 'The Exchange Rate and the Balance of Payments in the Short Run and the Long Run: A Monetary Approach', *Scandinavian Journal of Economics*, vol. 78 (2), pp. 280–304.

Krasker, W.S. (1980) 'The 'peso problem' in Testing the Efficiency of Forward Exchange Markets', *Journal of Monetary Economics*, vol. 6, pp. 276–96.

Kravis, I. and R. Lipsey (1978) 'Price Behaviour in the Light of Balance of Payments Theory', *Journal of International Economics*, vol. 8, pp. 193–246.

Krugman, P. (1978) 'Purchasing Power Parity and Exchange Rates: Another Look at the Evidence', *Journal of International Economics*, vol. 8, pp. 397–407.

Krugman, P. (1988) 'Target Zones and Exchange Rate Dynamics', *National Bureau of Economic Research Working Paper*, no. 2481.

Kugler, P. and C. Lenz (1993) 'Multivariate Cointegration Analysis as the Long-Run Validity of PPP, *Review of Economics as Statistics*, vol. 75, pp. 180–4.

Lee, D. (1983) 'Effects of Open Market Operations and Foreign Exchange Market Operations Under Flexible Exchange Rates', in M. Darby and J.R. Lothian (eds), *The International Transmission of Inflation* (Chicago: University of Chicago Press).

Lerner, A.P. (1944) *The Economics of Control* (New York: Macmillan).

Longworth, D. (1981) 'Testing the Efficiency of the Canadian–US Exchange Market under the Assumption of No Risk Premium', *Journal of Finance*, vol. 36, pp. 43–9.

Loopesko, B. (1984) 'Relationships among Exchange Rates, Intervention and Interest Rates: An Empirical Investigation', *Journal of International Money and Finance*, vol. 3, pp. 257–78.

MacDonald, R. (1983) 'Our Experience with Floating Exchange Rates: A Survey of the Empirical Evidence on Exchange Rate Models, News and Risk', Loughborough University Discussion Paper, no. 74.

MacDonald, R. (1985) 'Do Deviations of the Real Effective Exchange Rate Follow a Random Walk?', *Economic Notes*, vol. 14, pp. 63–9.

MacDonald, R. (1988) *Floating Exchange Rates: Theories and Evidence* (London: Unwin Hyman)

MacDonald, R. (1990a) 'Are Foreign Exchange Market Forecasters 'rational'? Some Survey Based Tests', *The Manchester School*, vol. LVIII, pp. 229–41.

MacDonald, R. (1990b) 'Exchange Rate Economics: An Empirical Perspective', in G. Bird (ed.), *The International Financial Regime* (Guildford: Surrey University Press).

MacDonald, R. (1993) 'Long-run Purchasing Power Parity: Is it for Real?', *Review of Economics and Statistics*, vol. 75, pp. 690–5.

MacDonald, R. and I.W. Marsh (1993) 'Foreign Exchange Forecasters are Heterogeneous: Confirmation and Consequences', International Centre for Macroeconomics, discussion paper, no. 15.

MacDonald, R. and I.W. Marsh (1994) 'Combining Exchange Rate Forecasters: What is the Optimal Consensus Measure?', *Journal of Forecasting*, vol. 13, pp. 313–32.

MacDonald, R. and M.P. Taylor (1989) 'The Economic Analysis of Foreign Exchange Markets: An Expository Survey', in R. MacDonald and M.P. Taylor (eds), *Exchange Rates and Open Economy Macroeconomics* (Oxford: Blackwell).

MacDonald, R. and M.P. Taylor (1990) 'International Parity Conditions', in A.S. Courakis and M.P. Taylor (eds), *Policy Issues for Interdependent Economies* (Oxford: Oxford University Press).

MacDonald, R. and M.P. Taylor (1991a) 'Testing Efficiency in the Interwar Foreign Exchange Market: A Multiple Time Series Approach', *Weltwirschaftliches Archiv*, vol. 127, pp. 500–23.

MacDonald, R. and M.P. Taylor (1991b) 'The Monetary Model of the Exchange Rate: Long Run Relationships and Coefficient Restrictions', *Economics Letters*, vol. 37, pp. 179–85.

MacDonald, R. and M.P. Taylor (1992) 'Exchange Rate Economics: A Survey', *IMF Staff Papers*, 39, pp. 1–57.

MacDonald, R. and M.P. Taylor (1993a) 'On the Foreign Exchange Risk Premium: Some New Survey-Based Results', mimeo.

MacDonald, R. and M.P. Taylor (1993b) 'The Monetary Approach to the Exchange Rate: Rational Expectations, Long-run Equilibrium and Forecasting', *IMP Staff Papers*, forthcoming.

MacDonald, R. and T.S. Torrance (1988a) 'On Risk, Rationality and Excessive Speculation in the Deutschemark–US Dollar Exchange Market: Some Evidence using Survey Data', *Oxford Bulletin of Economics and Statistics*, vol. 50, pp. 107–24.

MacDonald, R. and T.S. Torrance (1988b) 'Some Survey Based Tests of Uncovered Interest Parity', in R. MacDonald and M.P. Taylor (eds), *Exchange Rates and Open Economy Macroeconomics* (Oxford: Oxford University Press).

MacDonald, R. and T.S. Torrance (1990) 'Expectations and Risk in Four Foreign Exchange Markets', *Oxford Economic Papers*, vol. 42, pp. 544–61.

Machlup, F. (1949) 'The Theory of Foreign Exchanges', in H.S. Ellis and L.A. Metzler (eds), *Readings in the Theory of International Trade* (Philadelphia: Blakiston).

Machlup, F. (1955) 'Relative Prices and Aggregate Spending in the Analysis of Devaluation', *American Economic Review*, vol. 45, pp. 255–78.

Mark, N.C. (1985) 'Some Evidence on the International Inequality of Real Interest Rates', *Journal of International Money and Finance*, vol. 4, no. 2, 2 June, pp. 189–208.

McKibbin, Warwick (1988) 'The Economics of International Policy Coordination', *Economic Record*, pp. 241–53.

McKibbin, Warwick and Jeffrey Sachs (1988) 'Coordination of Monetary and Fiscal Policies in the OECD', in Jacob Frenkel (ed.), *International Aspects of Fiscal Policy* (Chicago: University of Chicago Press).

Meade, J.E. (1951) *The Theory of International Economic Policy, vol. 1: The Balance of Payments* (London: Oxford University Press).

Meese, R.A. (1986) 'Testing for Bubbles in Exchange Markets: A Case of Sparkling Bubbles', *Journal of Political Economy*, vol. 94, no. 2, pp. 345–73.

Meese, R.A. and K. Rogoff (1983) 'Empirical Exchange Rate Models of the Seventies: Do they Fit Out of Sample', *Journal of International Economics*, vol. 14, pp. 3–24.

Meese, R.A. and K. Rogoff (1984) 'The Out of Sample Failure of Empirical Exchange Rate Models: Sampling Error or Misspecification?', in J.A. Frenkel (ed.), *Exchange Rates and International Macroeconomics* (Chicago: National Bureau of Economic Research).

Miller, Marcus H. and Mark Salmon (1985) 'Policy Coordination and Dynamic Games', in Buiter and Marston (1985).

Miller, Marcus H. and John Williamson (1988) 'The international monetary system; an analysis of alternative regimes', *European Economic Review*, vol. 32, pp. 1031–54.

Minford, P. and D.A. Peel (1983) *Rational Expectations and the New Macroeconomics* (Oxford: Martin Robertson).

Mishkin, F. (1984) 'Are Real Interest Rates Equal across Countries? An Empirical Investigation of International Parity Conditions', *Journal of Finance*, vol. 39, pp. 1345–58.

Mundell, Robert A. (1961) 'The Theory of Optimum Currency Areas', *American Economic Review*, vol. 51, pp. 657–64.

Mundell, R.A. (1968) 'Growth and the Balance of Payments', *International Economics* (New York: Macmillan) ch. 9.

Mussa, M. (1979) 'Empirical Regularities in the Behaviour of Exchange Rates and Theories of the Foreign Exchange Market', in K. Brunner and A.H. Meltzer (eds), *Policies for Employment, Prices, and Exchange Rates*, vol. 11, Carnegie-Rochester Conference Series on Public Policy, supplement to the *Journal of Monetary Economics*, pp. 9–57.

Nerlove, M., F.X. Diebold, H. van Beeck and Y. Cheung (1988) 'A Multivariate ARCH Model of Foreign Exchange Rate Determination', mimeo.

Obstfeld, M. (1983) 'Exchange Rates, Inflation and the Sterilization Problem: Germany 1975–1981', *European Economic Review*, vol. 21, pp. 161–89.

Officer, C.H. (1976) 'The Purchasing Power Parity Theory of Exchange Rates: A Review Article', *IMF Staff Papers*, 23, pp. 1–60.

Oudiz, Gillez and Jeffrey Sachs (1984) 'Macroeconomic Policy Coordination among the Industrial Economies', *Brooking Papers on Economic Activity*, vol. 1, pp. 1–75.

Oudiz, Gillez and Jeffrey Sachs (1985) 'International Policy Coordination in Dynamic Macroeconomic Models', in Buiter and Marston (1985).

Papell, D.H. (1988) 'Expectations and Exchange Rate Dynamics after a Decade of Floating', *Journal of International Economics*, vol 25, pp. 303–17.

Papell, D.H. (1989) 'Monetary Policy in the United States under Flexible Exchange Rates', *American Economic Review*, vol. 79, no. 5, pp. 1106–16.

Patel, J. (1990) 'Purchasing Power Parity as a Long-run Relation', *Journal of Applied Econometrics*, vol. 5, pp. 367–79.

Penatti, Alessandro (1985) 'Monetary targets, real exchange rates and macroeconomic stability', *European Economic Review*, vol. 28, pp. 128–50.

Pikoulakis, E. (1981) 'Growth, Saving, the Balance of Payments and the Neo-Classical Growth Diagram', *Bulletin of Economic Research*, vol. 33, pp. 104–14.

Pikoulakis, E. (1985) 'Exchange Rates and the Current Account Re-Examined', *Greek Economic Review*, vol. 7, no. 2, pp. 89–107.

Pikoulakis, E. (1989) 'The Exchange Rate and the Current Account when Prices Evolve Sluggishly: A Simplification of the Dynamics and a Reconciliation with the Absorption Approach', in R. MacDonald and M.P. Taylor (eds), *Exchange Rates and Open Economy Macroeconomics* (Oxford: Basil Blackwell).

Pikoulakis, E. (1990) 'Efficient and Credible Exchange rate and Monetary Policies for Stabilising the Economy', in A.S. Courakis and M.P. Taylor (eds), *Private Behaviour and Government Policy in Interdependent Economies* (Oxford: Oxford University Press).

Pikoulakis, E. (1991) 'Relative Risk Aversion and the Demand for Assets in Continuous Time, when a Safe Asset is Present', *Hull Economic Research Papers*, no. 183.

Pikoulakis, Emmanuel (1992) 'The Relative Efficiency of Rules for Monitoring the Real Exchange Rate: Some Further Proposals', in Hans-Jurgen Vosgerau (ed.), *European Integration in the World Economy* (Heidelberg: Springer Verlag).

Pikoulakis, E. (with G.H. Makepeace) (1983) 'A Saving–Investment Approach to the Current Account of the Balance of Payments: Some Preliminary Empirical Estimates for the U.K. (1960–1980)', *Greek Economic Review*, vol. 5, pp. 223–47.

Ploeg, Frederick van der (1988) 'International Policy Coordination in Interdependent Monetary Economies', *Journal of International Economics*, vol. 25, pp. 1–23.

Ploeg, Frederick van der (1991a) 'Budgetary Aspects of Economic and Monetary Integration in Europe', Discussion paper No. *492* (London: Centre for Economic Policy Research).

Ploeg, Frederick van der (1991b) 'Macroeconomic Policy Coordination during the Various Phases of Economic and Monetary Integration in Europe', in M. Emerson (ed.), *The Economics of EMU*, Volume II, European Economy, vol. no. 1 (Brussels: Commission of the European Communities).

Ploeg, Frederick van der (1992) 'Fiscal Aspects of Monetary Integration in Europe', *De Economist*, vol. 140, no. 1, pp. 16–44.

Ploeg, Frederick van der (1993) 'Channels of International Policy Transmission', *Journal of International Economics*, vol. 34, nos. 3/4, pp. 245–67.

Ploeg, Frederick van der and Anton J. Markink (1991) 'Dynamic Policy Games in Linear Models with Rational Expectations of Future Events: A Computer Package', *Computer Science in Economics and Management Science*, vol. 4, no. 3, pp. 175–99.

Putnam, B.H. and J.R. Woodbury (1979) 'Exchange Rate Stability and Monetary Policy', *Review of Business and Economic Research*, vol. XV, no. 2, pp. 1–10.

Robinson, J. (1937) 'The Foreign Exchanges', *Essays in the Theory of Employment*, part 3, ch. 1 (New York: Macmillan).

Rodriguez, C.A. (1976) 'Money and Wealth in an Open Economy Income–Expenditure Model', in H.G. Johnson and J.A. Frenkel (eds), *The Monetary Approach to the Balance of Payments* (London: George Allen & Unwin).

Rogoff, K. (1984) 'On the Effects of Sterilised Intervention: An Analysis of Weekly Data', *Journal of Monetary Economics*, vol. 14, no. 2. pp. 133–50.

Rogoff, Kenneth (1985) 'Can International Monetary Policy Cooperation be Counterproductive?', *Journal of International Economics*, vol. 18, pp. 199–217.

Roll, R. (1979) 'Violations of Purchasing Power Parity and their Implications for Efficient International Commodity Markets', in M. Sarnat and G. Szego (eds), *International Finance and Trade*, vol. 1 (Cambridge, Mass.: Ballinger).

Sachs, Jeffrey D. and Xavier D. Sala-i-Martin (1989) 'Federal Fiscal Policy and Optimum Currency Areas', mimeo, Harvard University, Cambridge, Mass.

Salemi, M.K. (1984) 'Comment', in J.A. Frenkel (ed.), *Exchange Rates and International Macroeconomics* (Chicago: National Bureau of Economic Research).

Schinasi, G.J. and P.A.V.B. Swamy (1987) 'The Out-of-sample Forecasting Performance of Exchange Rate Models when Coefficients are Allowed to Change', *International Finance Discussion papers no. 301.*

Shiller, R.J. (1978) 'Rational Expectations and the Dynamic Structure of Macro-economic Models', *Journal of Monetary Economics*, vol. 4, pp. 1–44.

Smith, P. and M.R. Wickens (1988) 'A Stylised Econometric Model of an Open Economy: UK 1973–1981', mimeo.

Smith, P.N. and M.R. Wickens (1990) 'Assessing Monetary Shocks and Exchange Rate Variability with a Stylised Econometric Model of the UK', in A.S. Courakis and M.P. Taylor (eds), *Policy Issues for Interdependent Economies* (Oxford: Oxford University Press).

Svensson, L.E.O. (1991) 'The Simplest Test of Target Zone Credibility', *IMF Staff Papers*, 38, pp. 655–65.

Svensson, L.E.O. (1991) 'An Interpretation of Recent Research in Exchange Rate Target Zones', *Journal of Economic Perspectives*, vol. 6, pp. 119–44.

Taylor, John (1988) 'Should the International Monetary System be based on Fixed or Flexible Exchange Rates?', mimeo.

Taylor, M.P. (1987) 'Risk Premia and Foreign Exchange: A Multiple Time Series Approach to Testing Uncovered Interest Parity', *Weltwirtschaftliches Archiv*, vol. 123, pp. 579–91.

Taylor, M.P. (1988a) 'A DYMIMIC model of Forward Foreign Exchange Risk, with Estimates for Three Major Exchange Rates', *The Manchester School*, vol. 56, pp. 55–68.

Taylor, M.P. (1988b) 'An Empirical Examination of Long-run Purchasing Power Parity using Cointegration Techniques', *Applied Economics*, vol. 20, pp. 1369–82.

Taylor, M.P. (1989) 'Expectations, Risk and Uncertainty in the Foreign Exchange Market: Some Results based on Survey Data', *The Manchester School*, vol. LVII, no. 2, pp. 142–153.

Taylor, M.P. and P.C. McMahon (1988) 'Long-run Purchasing Power Parity in the 1920's', *European Economic Review*, vol. 32, pp. 179–97.

Tobin, J. (1969) 'A General Equilibrium Approach to Monetary Theory', *Journal of Money, Credit and Banking*, February.

Tobin, J. and W.H. Buiter (1976) 'Long-Run Effects of Fiscal and Monetary Policy on Aggregate Demand', in J. Stein (ed.), *Monetarism* (Amsterdam: North Holland).

Tsiang, S.C. (1961) 'The Role of Money in Trade–Balance Stability; Synthesis of the Elasticity and Absorption Approaches', *American Economic Review*, vol. 51, pp. 912–36.

West, K.D. (1986) 'A Specification Test for Speculative Bubbles', *National Bureau of Economics Research*, Working Paper, no. 2067.

Westerfield, J.M. (1977) 'An Examination of Foreign Exchange Risk under Fixed and Floating Regimes', *Journal of International Economics*, vol. 7, pp. 181–200.

Wilson, C. (1979) 'Anticipated Shocks and Exchange Rate Dynamics', *Journal of Political Economy*, vol. 87, pp. 639–47.

Wolff, C.P. (1987) 'Forward Foreign Exchange Rates, Expected Spot Rates, and Premia: A Signal-extraction Approach', *The Journal of Finance*, vol. XLII, pp. 395–406.

Woo, W.T. (1985) 'The Monetary Approach to Exchange Rate Determination under Rational Expectations', *Journal of International Economics*, vol. 18, pp. 1–16.

Zecher, J.R. (1976) 'Monetary Equilibrium and International Reserve Flows in Australia', in H.G. Johnson and J.A. Frenkel (eds), *The Monetary Approach to the Balance of Payments* (London: George Allen & Unwin).

Index

absorption approach   6, 13–24, 25
  balance of payments   13–20
  exchange rate   20–4
  expectations and current account   88–9
  sluggish evolution of prices   135–8
Abuaf, N.   240
Adler, M.   244
aggregate demand
  insulated from real exchange rate   162,
    173–5, 179–80
  international interdependence   189,
    189–90, 200–1
aggregate supply   188–9, 189–90, 201–2
Aoki, M.   161, 166
asset accumulation   13–14
asset market equilibrium   61–2
asset substitution/substitutability   33–4
  perfect   34, 165
  portfolio balance models   68, 81–3,
    84; comparison with monetary
    models   217–18; degree of asset
    substitution   71–3
  see also purchasing power parity;
    uncovered interest rate parity

Backus, D.   231
Baillie, R.T.   234
balance of payments   1–2, 5–6
  absorption approach   13–20
  accounting framework   6–9
  elasticities approach   9–13
  growth and   *see* growth
  monetary approach   24–9
  secular and cyclical movements   158
Barr, D.   235
Barro, R.J.   200, 203
Basevi, G.   200
Begg, D.K.H.   243
Bertola, G.   216

Bilson, J.F.O.   223, 230
Bisignano, J.   243
Boothe, P.   234
Branson, W.H.   221, 243
Bretton Woods   186, 195
bubbles   237–8
Buiter, W.H.   111, 193, 205
  full employment and depreciation   135
  wealth   147
  see also Buiter–Miller model
Buiter–Miller model   112–21, 130, 229,
  235
  conditions for stability and steady-state
    characteristics of disinflation
    115–16
  cumulative loss in output   120–1
  phase diagram and saddle path
    116–20
Bundesbank   186, 195

Campbell, J.Y.   225
Canova, F.   227, 243
Canzoneri, M.B.   192, 193, 214
capital, market price of   147–8, 148–9
capital immobility   1–2, 5–31
  absorption approach   13–24
  elasticities approach   9–13
  growth model with fixed exchange rates
    146–52
  monetary approach   24–31
capital intensity   147–8, 148–9, 149–50,
  151–2, 153–4
  wealth and   155
capital mobility
  European Community   186
  growth model: fixed exchange rates
    152–5; flexible exchange rates
    156–8
central banks' discipline   203–5, 206–7

characteristic equations 245–8
Cheung Y.W. 242
Chow, G.C. 168
Clarida, R.H. 225
Cobb–Douglas production function 151
Cochrane, J.H. 240
Cohen, D. 214–15
cointegration 233–4
  PPP 241–2
  competitiveness 200
  disinflation 111, 113–15, 116,
    117–19, 122
  economic stability 173, 178–9
  sluggish evolution of prices 131–3,
    133–5, 138, 139, 141–2
covered interest rate parity (CIP) 35,
  218
crawling peg 214
Cumby, R.E. 220
current account
  expectations and *see* expectations
  response to open-market operations
    76–83
  sluggish evolution of prices *see*
    sticky-price monetary models

Darby, M. 244
Davidson, J. 219
De Long, J.B. 228
debt
  foreign 155, 158
  public 214
Delors Committee 199, 209, 213, 214
demand
  aggregate *see* aggregate demand
  asset demands modelling 86, 92
  demand-determined outputs 49–58
  demand shocks
    economic stability 171–2, 173–5, 178,
      179–80
    global 193–4, 198, 213
  depreciation, expectation of 71, 72, 74–5
  devaluation
    adjustments to: absorption approach
      14–19; elasticities approach
      9–11; monetary approach 26–8
    European Monetary System 196
  diagonalising matrices 248
  differences, international 167–9
  discipline, central banks' 203–5, 206–7
  discretion, rules vs 203–5
  disinflation 3, 111–25
    basic Buiter–Miller model 112–21
    international interdependence 192–3

non-sterilised intervention 121–4, 125
Dixit, A.K. 138, 245
Domowitz, I. 225
domestic bonds
  market equilibrium 64
  open-market operations: foreign bonds
    63, 70–1, 71–3, 77, 81–3, 83–4;
    money 63, 69, 79–80
  portfolio balance responses to increase
    in 67–8
Dominguez, K. 227
Dooley, M. 221
Dornbusch, R. 73, 111, 193, 230, 234,
  243
Dornbusch–Fischer model 86, 92, 101
Driskell, R.A. 230

economic stability *see* stability
efficient markets view of PPP (EMPPP)
  239–40
eigenvalues 245–8
eigenvectors 245–8
elasticities approach 6, 9–13
  balance of payments 9–13
  exchange rate 13
employment
  full *see* full employment
  international interdependence 201–2
Enders, W. 241
Engle, R. 241
equity
  demand for 148–9, 151–2
  return on 147, 155
error correction models (ECMs) 242
error orthogonality 219
European Federal Monetary Authority
  213, 214
European Federal Transfer Scheme 209,
  213, 213–14
European Monetary System 185–6,
  195–8, 213, 233
  compared with European Monetary
    Union 198–200
  rational expectations and wage-price
    dynamics 205–8
  supply shocks 208–12
European Monetary Union 186, 198,
  213–14
  compared with European Monetary
    System 198–200
  rational expectations and wage-price
    dynamics 205–8
  supply shocks and case for 208–12

European System of Central Banks   199,
    213, 215
exchange rate policy/regime   19–20
    economic stability   172–82
    international interdependence   183–4
    seigniorage and   158–9
    see also under individual names
exogenous expectations   89–93
expectations
    and current account   2, 85–110;
        exogenous expectations and short-
        run equilibrium reponses   89–93;
        impact, dynamic and steady-state
        adjustments under static
        expectations   94–9; model
        87–9; perfect foresight and
        nominal exchange rate   100–9;
        portfolio balance models   73–6,
        88, 92
    rational   *see* rational expectations
    UIP   219–20
export demand   86, 88–9
    exogenous expectations   90, 91–3
    perfect foresight   104–5, 106, 106–7,
        108
    static expectations   96–7, 99
external balance   20–2

Fama, E.F.   223, 223–4, 224, 225, 227
Finn, M.G.   236–7
financial flow accounting   6
national accounts and balance of payments
    7–9
fiscal policy   131
    absorption approach   19–20, 21
    international interdependence   185,
        186, 189–90, 191, 214–15
    sluggish evolution of prices and fiscal
        expansion   131, 135, 139–42, 142
Fischer, S.   73
    Dornbusch–Fischer model   86, 92, 101
fixed exchange rates ch.1 *passim*
    growth model   159; capital immobility
        146–52; capital mobility   152–5
    policy coordination   184, 186, 213;
        see also European Monetary Union
    stability   162, 173, 177, 178–9, 181–2
flexible exchange rates
    growth model   156–8, 159
    stability   162, 172, 181–2
flexible prices   33–8
floating exchange rates
    absorption approach   20–2
    international interdependence   184,

198, 199, 213; monetary policy
    185, 187–91; policy coordination
    191–5; rational expectations and
    wage-price dynamics   205–8;
    supply shocks   208–12
managed   *see* managed floating
    exchange rates
stability   170–2, 177–9, 180
foreign bonds   74
    expectations and accumulation   74,
        75–6
    increase in number of holdings   65–6
    market equilibrium   64
    open-market operations: expectations
        and current account   63, 86,
        88–99 *passim*, 104–7 *passim*;
        portfolio balance models   63,
        70–1, 71–3, 77, 81–3, 83–4
foreign exchange market   11–13
foreign exchange regime   *see* exchange
    rate policy/regime
foreign income   129–30, 133–5, 136,
    137–8
foreign indebtedness   155, 158
foreign reserves   8–9, 26, 158–9
forward exchange market   222–8
forward looking models   235–8
Frankel, J.A.   243
    inflationary and liquidity effects   33
    reduced-form exchange rate modelling
        229, 230–1, 231
    risk premium   226, 227
    UIP and risk-adjusted UIP   220–1, 221
Fraser, P.   241
Frenkel, J.A.   215, 239, 243, 244
Friedman, B.M.   61
Froot, K.   226, 227, 243
full employment
    absorption approach   17–19
    policy coordination   191–2
    and sticky-price monetary models
        39–48

GDP deflator   169–70, 177–81 *passim*
Germany   199–200, 208, 211, 213
Giavazzi, F.   186, 195, 199–200
Giovannini, A.   186, 195, 199–200, 225
Glaister, S.   245
Glassman, D.   234
global economy   166–7
Gold Standard   186, 195
Goldstein, M.   215
goods market   127, 188–90
Gordon, D.B.   200, 203

government budget constraint 128, 130–1
Granger, C.W.J. 241
Gray, J.A. 192
Gregory, A.W. 223
growth 3, 144–59
  capital immobility and fixed exchange rates 146–52
  capital mobility and fixed exchange rates 152–5
  capital mobility and flexible exchange rates 156–8, 159
  secular and cyclical movements in balance of payments 158
  seigniorage and foreign exchange regime 158–9
  steady-state path 151–2

Hacche, G. 219, 231
Hadley, G. 245
Hakkio, C. 225
Hallwood, P. 243
Halttunen, H. 221, 243
Hamada, K. 184
Hansen, L.P. 225
Hausman, J.A. 237
Haynes, S.E. 231
Henderson, D.W. 193
high powered money 9, 88
  expectations and current account 88, 104, 105
  monetary approach to balance of payments 26–7, 28–9
Hodrick, R.J. 224–5, 225, 227, 230
Hoffman, D. 236
Hooper, P. 229, 231
Hoover, K. 243
Huang, R.D. 238
Huizinga, J. 240–1

income
  absorption approach 14, 15–16
  foreign 129–30, 133–5, 136, 137–8
  monetary approach 29
inflation
  Buiter–Miller model 114; superneutrality 130
  international interdependence 184, 192–3
  monetary models 33, 43–7, 48, 49–50, 50–2
  sluggish evolution of prices 129, 140, 141, 142
  see also disinflation

inflation tax 130, 158–9, 214
interdependence, international *see* floating exchange rates; managed floating exchange rates; policy coordination
interest rate(s)
  absorption approach 14, 15
  Buiter–Miller model 113–15
  differential 31; monetary models 39, 43–6, 49, 51–2, 53–4, 57–8
  economic stability 166–9, 171–2, 173–4
  international interdependence 189–90, 194, 200–1, 206, 207
  monetary approach 29, 31
  portfolio balance models 71
  real interest rate reduced-form models 229–31
  sluggish evolution of prices 131–3, 142
  see also covered interest rate parity; uncovered interest rate parity
internal balance 20–2
international differences 167–9
international interdependence *see* floating exchange rates; managed floating exchange rates; policy coordination
investment
  growth in small economy 147, 151
  national and balance of payments 8
  shift in propensity 138
  warranted rate 151
Isard, P. 221, 244
Ishiyama, 216
Ito, T. 227, 243

Jensen, H. 215
Johansen, S. 234
Jorion, P. 225, 240

Kaminsky, G.L. 225
Kearney, C. 223, 234, 235, 236, 238
Kenen, P.B. 200
Krasker, W.S. 243
Kravis, I. 244
Krugman, P. 233, 239, 244
Kugler, 242

labour mobility 209, 214, 216
Lai, K.S. 242
law of one price *see* purchasing power parity
Lehmann, B. 244

linearising non-linear equations   252–3
Lipsey, R.   244
liquidity
   disinflation   113, 116, 117–19
   sticky-price monetary models   33,
      131–3, 140; demand-determined
      outputs   50–2; full employment
      39, 43–7
Longworth, D.   223
Loopesko, B.   219

MacDonald, R.   218, 224, 243, 244
   cointegration   242
   forward looking models   236, 237, 238
   reduced-form exchange rate modelling
      230, 231, 234, 235
   risk premium   220, 223, 225, 226, 227,
      227–8
managed floating exchange rates
   economic stability   162, 173–6,
      179–81
   interdependence   185–6, 195–200,
      213; comparison with monetary
      union   198–200; rational
      expectations and wage-price
      dynamics   205–8; supply shocks
      and case for monetary union
      208–12
Mark, N.C.   225
market mechanism   183–4
Markink, A.J.   206
McCurdy, T.H.   223
McKibbin, W.   215
McMahon, P.C.   244
mean-variance analysis   61–3
Medium Term Financial Strategy   192
Meese, R.A.   232–3, 234, 236, 237, 242
Miller, M.H.   111, 161, 162, 181, 206
   see also Buiter–Miller model
Minford, P.   243
Mishkin, F.   244
market price of capital   147–8, 148–9
Marsh, I.W.   227–8, 242
Marshall–Lerner–Robinson condition
      9–13
Marston, R.C.   193, 205
Masson, P.   215, 221, 243
mobility   *see* capital mobility; labour
      mobility
monetary approach   6, 24–31
   balance of payments   24–9;
      verification   28–9
   exchange rate   29–31
   monetary growth
      disinflation   113, 115, 116, 117, 123,
124, 125; prices and output on
      reduction in rate   121
   sluggish evolution of prices   131,
      134–5
monetary models   2, 32–59
   evidence for   217–44; forecasting
      performance of reduced forms
      232–5; forward-looking models
      235–8; PPP   238–42;
      reduced-form exchange rate
      modelling   228–32; risk premium
      222–8; uncovered and
      risk-adjusted interest rate parity
      219–22
   flexible prices   33–8; adjustments to
      monetary disturbances   37–8
   as special case of portfolio balance
      models   71–3
   sticky prices   *see* sticky-price
      monetary models
monetary policy
   absorption approach   19–20, 21
   coordination   *see* policy coordination
   expansion as beggar-thy-neighbour
      policy   185, 190–1
   portfolio balance models   *see* portfolio
      balance models
   sticky prices and output   111
monetary union   *see* European Monetary
      Union
money
   high-powered   *see* high-powered
      money
   open-market operations: domestic bonds
      63, 69, 79–80; foreign bonds   63
   real money balances   151, 155
money market equilibrium   88
money markets
   absorption approach   14–15
   monetary approach   29–31
money supply
   economic stability   165, 171, 178
   international interdependence   207
   portfolio balance models   66–7
Morton, J.   229, 231
Mundell, R.A.   191, 195, 209
Mundell–Fleming model   128–35
   analysis of stability of equilibrium
      131–3
   government budget constraint   130–1
   inflation superneutrality   130
   interdependence under floating
      exchange rates   187–91
   steady-state characteristics   133–5
Mussa, M.   221

national accounts 6
  financial flows and balance of payments 7–9
national income 200–1
national investment 8
national saving 8, 156–7, 157–8
Nerlove, M. 225
net claims abroad 129–30, 133–5, 136, 137–8
nominal exchange rate
  absorption approach 22–4
  economic stability 172
  expectations and current account: perfect foresight 100–9; static expectations 97–9
non-sterilised intervention 111–12, 121–4, 125

Obstfeld, M. 220, 235
Officer, C.H. 239
open-market operations 63
  foreign bonds 63, 86, 88–99 *passim*, 104–7 *passim*
  portfolio balance models 61, 63, 76–83; between domestic and foreign bonds 63, 70–1, 71–3, 77, 81–3, 83–4; money for domestic bonds 63, 69, 79–80
optimum currency areas 209
Oudiz, G. 192, 206
output
  absorption approach 16–19, 22–4
  disinflation 112, 115, 117; cumulative loss in output 120, 123–4, 125; non-sterilised intervention 123–4, 125; reduced monetary growth rate 121, 122
  economic stability 166–9, 169–70, 173–4, 177–81 *passim*, 182
  international interdependence 203, 206, 207
  monetary approach 31
  sticky-price monetary models 2, 55–8, 140, 141; demand-determined outputs 49–58
overshooting 80
  monetary models 43–8, 55–8

Papell, D.H. 234–5
Patel, J. 241
Peel, D.A. 243
pegged exchange rates
  absorption approach 13–19
  elasticities approach 9–11

monetary approach 24–8
perfect foresight
  monetary models 39–42
  nominal exchange rate and current account 2, 100–9; algebraic derivation 107–9; impact and dynamic adjustments 105–7, 108; saddle path 100–3, 106, 109; steady-state adjustments 103–5, 106
Peruga, R. 225
phase diagrams
  disinflation 116–20
  sluggish evolution of prices 127, 128, 138–42
Phillips curve 22–4, 120
Pikoulakis, E. 61, 161, 162, 181
Ploeg, F. van der 204, 206, 209, 214, 215
policy coordination 3–4, 183–216
  as counterproductive 200–5
  floating exchange rates 191–5
  managed exchange rates 195–8; comparison with monetary union 198–200
  rational expectations and wage-price dynamics 205–8
  supply shocks and monetary union 208–12
portfolio balance models 2, 33, 60–84
  evidence for 217–44; forecasting performance of reduced forms 232–5; forward-looking models 235–8; PPP 238–42; reduced-form exchange rate modelling 228–32; risk premium 222–8; uncovered and risk-adjusted interest rate parity 219–22
  exchange rate, current account and expectations 73–6, 88, 92
  growth in small economy 148–9
  mean-variance analysis 61–3
  monetary policy: degree of asset substitution 71–3; expectations and exchange rate 63–71
  open-market operations *see* open-market operations
preferences
  portfolio 220–1
  shift in 137, 138
preferred habitat models 221
prices
  absorption approach 22–4

prices *cont.*
  cointegration and PPP   241–2
  differentials in monetary models   40, 42
  economic stability   169–70, 172, 182,
    209–11
  flexible   33–8
  international interdependence   188,
    190–1, 202–3; policy coordination
    and price stability   192–5;
    rational expectations and
    wage-price dynamics   205–8
  law of one price   *see* purchasing power
    parity
  monetary approach   29–30
  sluggish evolution   *see* sticky-price
    monetary models
  see also disinflation; inflation
private saving   73, 89, 94, 156–7, 157–8
production function   151
productivity   154–5, 201–2
public debt   214
public sector   134–5
purchasing power parity (PPP)   86
  evidence   238–42, 243
  monetary approach   29–31
  monetary models   32, 34, 34–5, 39
Putnam, B.H.   230

random walk model   232–3, 240–1
rational expectations   237
  current account and exchange rate
    100–9, 109; portfolio balance
    models   76, 77, 80, 82
  international interdependence   205–8
  monetary models   36–7
reaction functions   193–4, 196–7
real balance effect   18, 28, 54
real balances
  disinflation   117, 120
  monetary approach   27–8, 28
  sluggish evolution of prices   130, 131–3
real exchange rate
  absorption approach   22–4
  economic stability   169, 178;
    aggregate demand insulated from
    real exchange rate   162, 173–5,
    179–80; asymptotic variance
    169–70
real interest rate reduced form (RID)
  models   229–31
real money balances   151, 155
reduced-form exchange rate modelling
  218, 228–35
  forecasting performance   232–5

representative agent model   225
reserve currency systems   *see* European
  Monetary System
reserves, foreign   8–9, 26, 158–9
return on equity   147, 155
returns, asset   62
risk premium
  economic stability   163, 165, 167
  evidence   218, 219–28, 231–2, 242
  monetary models   36
Rogers, C.A.   214
Rogoff, K.   200, 204, 206, 221, 236, 242
  reduced-form exchange rate modelling
    232–3
Roley, V.V.   61
Roll, R.   239, 244
rules vs discretion   203–5

Sachs, J.   192, 206, 209, 215
saddle path   251–2
  disinflation   116, 116–20, 122–3
  exchange rate and current account
    under perfect foresight   100–3,
    106, 109
  monetary models   42, 51, 55
  portfolio balance models   76, 77
  prices evolving sluggishly   127;
    phase diagram analysis   138–42
Sala-i-Martin, X.D.   209
Salemi, M.K.   232
Salmon, M.   206
saving   138
  growth in small economy   149, 156–7,
    157–8
  national   8, 156–7, 157–8
  private   73, 89, 94, 156–7, 157–8
Schinasi, G.J.   234
Schlagenhauf, D.   236
seigniorage   158–9
Selover, D.D.   234
Shiller, R.J.   237
simulation exercises   127
simultaneous differential equations
  systems   248–52
single-bond world   72, 73
small economy   *see* growth
Smith, P.   235
Srivastava, S.   224–5, 225, 227
stability   3, 160–82
  Buiter–Miller model   115–16
  elasticities approach   11–13
  expectations and current account   96
  fixed exchange rates   162, 173, 177,
    178–9, 181–2

flexible exchange rates   162, 172, 181–2
floating exchange rates   170–2, 177–9, 180
international interdependence: consumer prices   192–5; monetary stability   191–2
managed floating exchange rates   162, 173–6, 179–81
simultaneous differential equations systems   248–52
symmetric two-country model   161–70
stagflation   185, 193
static expectations   94–9
sterilised intervention   2, 63, 70–1, 71–3, 77, 81–3, 83–4
sticky-price monetary models
current account and exchange rate   3, 126–43; extended Mundell–Fleming model 128–35; phase diagram of saddle path   138–42; reconciliation with absorption approach   135–8
demand-determined outputs   49–58; adjustments to monetary disturbances   50–2; responses to undershooting and overshooting 55–8
full employment   39–47; adjustments to monetary disturbances   43–7
Stone, J.A.   231
structural models, reduced-form   234–5
substitutability   *see* asset substitution/substitutability
superneutrality   128, 130, 135
supply, aggregate   188–9, 189–90, 201–2
supply shocks   198–9, 206–8, 213
idiosyncratic   208–12
survey data   225–8
Svensson, L.E.O.   233
Swamy, P.A.V.B.   234

tax, inflation   130, 158–9, 214
see also fiscal policy
Taylor, J.   215
Taylor, M.P.   218, 234, 237, 243, 244
PPP   241
risk premium   223, 224, 225, 227, 228
UIP   219
Taylor's expansion theorem   252–3
time-path analysis   248–52
time-varying model   234
Tobin, J.   147
Torrance, T.S.   220, 226

Townend, J.   219, 231
two-country model   161–70
asymptotic variance of output, prices and real exchange rate   169–70
foreign country   162–3
foreign economy   166
global economy   166–7
home country   162
home economy   166
international bond markets   163
international differences   167–9
monetary interdependence   187–91

uncovered interest rate parity (UIP)   218
disinflation   114, 120
evidence   219–22, 242
monetary models   34, 35–6, 39–40, 49
risk-neutral arbitrage   200, 215
underemployment   17
undershooting   52–4, 55–8
unemployment   184–5, 209–11
uniform preference   221
United States of America   209, 215
fiscal expansion   142

variance bounds test   237–8

wages
economic stability   164–5, 166–9, 169–70, 172, 173
international interdependence   188, 201–2, 205–8, 209–11
Walras's Law   24, 62
wealth
expectations and current account 87–8, 89, 91–2, 93, 94, 101
growth in small economy   147, 150–1, 153–4, 155
portfolio balance models   73–6, 77–9, 81
Webster, A.   241
welfare loss   199, 206, 207
floating exchange rates   191–2, 193
managed exchange rates   196, 198
rules vs discretion   203, 204
West, K.D.   237
Wickens, M.R.   235
Williamson, J.   161, 162, 181
Wolff, C.P.   225, 234
Woo, W.T.   236–7
Woodbury, J.R.   230
world return on equity   155
Wyplosz, C.   215